The Complete
IGGY POP

RICHARD ADAMS

The Complete
IGGY POP

RICHARD ADAMS

Reynolds & Hearn Ltd
London

Picture credits

Front cover: Ian Dickson/Redferns
Back cover: Rex Features

Picture section
Page 1: Michael Ochs Archives/Redferns
Page 2: Douglas R. Gilbert/Redferns
Page 3: Michael Ochs Archives/Redferns
Page 4: (top) Sipa Press/Rex Features (bottom) Sipa Press/Rex Features
Page 5: Rex Features
Page 6: Richard Young/Rex Features
Page 7: (top) Sipa Press/Rex Features (bottom) Action Press/Rex Features
Page 8: Richard Young/Rex Features

First published in 2006 by
Reynolds & Hearn Ltd
61a Priory Road
Kew Gardens
Richmond
Surrey TW9 3DH

© Richard Adams 2006

A CIP catalogue record for this book is available from the British Library.

ISBN 1 905287 02 X

Designed by Peri Godbold.

Printed and bound in Great Britain by Biddles Ltd, King's Lynn, Norfolk.

Contents

Acknowledgements

This book has been a long time coming. It's taken me a while, but I've had a lot of fun (and late nights) writing it. I hope you feel that it was worth it.

I'm bound to have forgotten lots of people so firstly a big thank you to all those who may not get a specific mention but whose assistance was very gratefully received. Any errors are, of course, my own, but I would appreciate help and information in making any further editions of this book even more accurate and informative. If you would like to contribute in any way please contact me either via Reynolds and Hearn or by email – richardadams66@hotmail.co.uk

Special thanks, in no particular order go out to:

Iggy Pop, Ron Asheton, Scott Asheton, Mike Watt and Steven Mackay – these guys **are** the Stooges and quite simply they put on the best rock show you'll ever see. Fact.

To Iggy and to all the musicians who have ever worked with Iggy, thank you so much for producing such inspiring music. Some of these songs have been a part of my life since I was 12, and I can't imagine being without them.

To Richard Reynolds and Marcus Hearn for being such understanding publishers and letting me get on with this book at my own speed, when I'm sure they wanted me to work much faster. Also thanks to Peri Godbold for a cool design.

To Nick Pegg for writing *The Complete David Bowie* (in my opinion, the very best book on Bowie) and therefore indirectly getting me started on this book.

To Martin Ralphs and Simon Bishop from the Side Effects for years of chat, insights, beer, curry, music and friendship.

Dan Lewsley, Chris Lawrence and Richard Wood for allowing me to talk about Iggy, and music in general, at great length at various times over the last 30 years.

To 'Blue' Gene Tyranny for answering my questions about the Stooges.

To Hugo Wilcken for allowing me access to some of his notes on *The Idiot* and *Low*. Hugo's excellent book about *Low* is definitive and highly recommended.

To Per Nilsen for clearing up the confusion over a few dates and his support and offers of help, which for various reasons didn't work out. Maybe next time Per?

No thanks whatsoever to Hotmail, for managing to lose various emails, especially those from Per.

To Simon Galloway for support and encouragement.

To Carlton Sandercock, of Easy Action Records, for useful information. Please support Easy Action as Carlton has more rare archive Iggy / Stooges material that he's hoping to release in the future...

To my brother Rob for encouragement, all the way from Moscow.

Thanks also to my Mum and Dad, who have worried about whether I'd ever get this project finished.

Big thanks also to David Bowie, Brian Eno, Robert Fripp, Mark Hollis and David Sylvian for musical inspiration.

Finally and most importantly, to my daughters Lucy and Charley, more appreciation than I can ever express for putting up with my hours hidden away in the study, and especially to my wonderful wife Nicky. This book was her idea. Tired of hearing me whitter on about music, and aware that my head was full of otherwise useless facts and figures that, wisely, she was not the slightest bit interested in, she encouraged me to write it all down. The result is the book you are holding.

For that simple fact alone I dedicate this book to Nicky and offer her my sincere and very heartfelt thanks for her love and patience.

Lastly, thanks to you for buying this book. Hope you liked it.

Cheers,
Richard Adams

Introduction

London, 30 August 2005

On the stage of the Apollo Theatre in Hammersmith, Iggy Pop screams out, 'We're thrilled and amazed to be here.' Then with a grin as wide as the stage he continues, 'We're amazed to be anywhere!'

This was a gig no one expected to see. Least of all the musicians on stage. Thirty-five years earlier, the Stooges had recorded their second album, *Fun House*. It's debatable whether anyone in 1970 would have expected the members of this drug-ridden band to be alive in the twenty-first century, let alone still be playing some of the most energetic, powerful, and downright thrilling rock shows that anyone has ever seen.

Ron Asheton must have boiled in his combat jacket, although he barely moved all night – hunched over his guitar blasting out monster riffs and squealing lead. His brother Scott Asheton, on the other hand, looked hot in his heavy shirt and baseball cap, and he whacked those drums like they'd really ticked him off. Replacement bassist Mike Watt jumped and twitched like his pants were on fire, all the time hitting some huge bass notes and locking tight with Scott's formidable primal beats. Steve Mackay turned up in a tour T-shirt, with his neat grey hair, looking rather like someone's dad trying to be cool, but he played some killer blows on his saxophone. Despite the mush of guitar and bass noise emanating from the stage, Mackay's sax flew out of the speakers clearly and he honked his way through the second half of the show.

Iggy Pop leapt around in his super low-waist jeans, and undid them towards the end – they gradually dropped lower, revealing plenty of backside, although for once we were spared the sight of little Iggy being waved around. His dancing was utterly mad, as if he was plugged into the mains, and he kept this up for the whole night. His vocals were harsh, raw and electric. The energy Iggy gave off was incredible. He could have powered the whole band. After his first bout of crowd surfing he appeared to be limping, but that didn't interfere with his lunatic dancing.

The Stooges were playing the whole *Fun House* album to a rabidly intense audience in 2005. Amongst the broiling crowd were kids young enough to be Iggy's grandchildren, Goths, nu-metal fiends, punks of all ages, even surprisingly smartly turned out men and women straight from work in the city – people from virtually every walk of life and fans of every type of music. What drew them to this wild, astonishing show?

Not only was it the chance to see a legendary band play some of their greatest songs, but it was also an opportunity to witness another life-affirming performance by Stooges frontman Iggy Pop.

He is a unique performer. He doesn't stop cavorting around the stage throughout the whole show. He leaps and dances and dives into the crowd, he crashes into both musicians and speakers, he destroys more microphone stands than anyone can count, he climbs the speaker stacks, he falls to the floor; he delivers, on every level, the most intense primal musical and visual experience. Everyone agrees it's an amazing experience, and everyone wonders – how much longer can Iggy carry on like this, putting so much effort and sweat and blood into his performances? It's a question that has been asked ever since Iggy first started performing back in the 1960s. Somehow he possesses superhuman strength and incredible reserves of raw power.

So who is Iggy Pop?

To some, he is inspirational, he's a legend, a survivor, often called the 'Godfather of Punk' (a moniker he despises), a truly great songwriter, one of the most energetic live performers ever, the leader of the infamous Stooges. To others, less familiar with his life and work, he's simply that old rock star with a faintly ridiculous name, who had a couple of songs in the film *Trainspotting*, and didn't he used to hang out with Bowie? To those who prefer Top Forty chart music he's pretty much unknown – but his influence over modern music is undeniable. Few musicians can genuinely claim to have changed the course of popular music. Elvis Presley, the Beatles, James Brown – their influence and importance is widely acknowledged. But Iggy Pop can claim to have had just as much influence – it's just that no one realised at the time. With the Stooges, Iggy laid the foundation and created the template for punk rock. But he was reviled and rejected in 1971 and it took at least five years before punk really got going. By then Iggy was unwittingly laying the groundwork for the new wave and synthesizer movement of the late 1970s and early 1980s. Since then, he's produced a catalogue of work of increasing maturity and resonance.

To those who know and appreciate his music, Iggy Pop is a true star, a gem, albeit sometimes flawed, and the creator of some of the most important and influential songs of the last thirty-five years or more. But Iggy Pop is also a fiction, the creation of a quiet and well-mannered guy from Ann Arbor, Michigan. And Iggy can be a monster, a shocking and frightening beast of a performer – his creator, James Osterberg, content to hide behind the façade, content to let Iggy make the headlines and take the flack. Sometimes, the stage persona has, like Frankenstein's monster, threatened to overwhelm his creator, the lines between Iggy and Jim becoming dangerously blurred. At times, Iggy Pop has nearly succeeded in utterly destroying Jim Osterberg.

The creation of Iggy Pop, the ups and downs of his life and career, and his ultimate survival is a tale that has been told before. But usually the story is riddled with inaccuracies and half-truths, with the lure of excess and debauchery getting the better of many a reporter. The truth is sometimes rather more prosaic, though sometimes the outlandish tales obscure a truth which is even more unbelievable.

The story of Iggy Pop is one of extremes – from the lows of severe drug addiction to Iggy's current high standing among, and influence over, much of the alternative music scene. In between were some fearsome troughs and some phenomenal successes, but all too often yet another defeat was snatched from the jaws of success...

A Brief Introduction

ggy first appeared on the US music scene in the late 1960s. Coming from the urban industrial sprawl surrounding Detroit, the sunny Californian hippy vibes meant nothing to Iggy and his contemporaries. They were bored, stoned and mightily pissed off. And they weren't afraid to say it. Iggy wrote songs about what he saw: simple, direct and angry explosions of noise and venom. Songs such as 'No Fun', 'Down On The Street' and 'Dirt' summed up the feelings of Iggy's friends, kids who had dropped out of society, those who felt alienated by the government, those who were furious about the Vietnam war, those who were just angry at life. Powered by the visceral overdriven guitar of Ron Asheton, backed by the primal force of Scott Asheton's drums and the rumbling bass of Dave Alexander, the Stooges were the ideal vehicle for Iggy's snotty snarl, the voice of the dispossessed. They soon built up a small but dedicated following, and gained a reputation for putting on an unpredictable and confrontational live show.

Stooges records however barely troubled the national charts. In its lifetime, the band's influence was felt only minimally in a few major American cities such as New York or Los Angeles. As cheap heroin began to flood the US underground music scene, the Stooges fell prey to the clutches of junk and disintegrated.

Salvation came from a very unlikely source. In the UK, a struggling singer songwriter called David Bowie had heard of the Stooges' extreme stage act, the bizarre antics of the outrageous singer, and the power of their music. Having hunted down their two records, Bowie was hugely impressed and vowed to make his next record harder and rockier in honour of the Stooges. Even the name 'Ziggy Stardust' was partially inspired by his new American idol. In late 1971, on a trip to New York to meet the art crowd that surrounded Andy Warhol, Bowie was introduced to Iggy Pop. Immediately a lifelong friendship was born and Bowie persuaded his manager to sign Iggy right there.

In the spring of 1972, Iggy and songwriting partner James Williamson flew to London to make a record. Unable to find English musicians in tune with their vision, Iggy called in the Asheton brothers and a new incarnation of the Stooges was born. Only one album resulted from this line-up, but its influence would be enormous. Five years before the punk explosion, *Raw Power* had created the template. James Williamson's scorching guitar sound continues to define punk and hard rock to this day. But once again commercial success eluded the Stooges and, amid deepening drug habits and personal animosity, the band broke up for a second time.

The mid 1970s passed with Iggy referred to only in the past tense. To anyone in the music business, Iggy Pop was now synonymous with unreliability, drug addiction and failure. A spell in a psychiatric hospital did further harm to his reputation, though he was finally able to kick his heroin addiction. In early 1976, David Bowie once again came to his rescue by inviting Iggy to join him on tour, not on stage, but as part of his entourage. It was a show of

personal support that Iggy never forgot. Later that year Bowie abandoned his own Los Angeles drug lifestyle and set up home in Berlin. Iggy went with him and rented a flat in the same block as David. They made a pact to sort themselves out and to recover their muses. Two highly influential collaborative albums resulted – *The Idiot* and *Lust For Life*. Both were released in 1977, just as the influence of *Raw Power* was finally being felt in the burgeoning punk movement. Iggy's new albums went far beyond punk and set the scene for much of the new wave movement of the *next* five years.

There are only so many influential albums a man can make. The late 1970s and early 1980s saw Iggy consolidate his position as the progenitor of punk by playing with the cream of the UK and US punk and new wave musicians. Sadly, decreasing album sales and dependency on drink and drugs for much of this period saw Iggy fall into a downward spiral again. Rescued by Bowie once more (indirectly this time, thanks to the huge sales of Bowie's cover of 'China Girl'), Iggy seemed to retire from the music business altogether in 1983. He took three years out, married Suchi, became solvent, dried out and detoxed, and when he returned in 1986 with *Blah-Blah-Blah* it was a new, positive Iggy Pop who faced the world.

The relative success of the new album increased Iggy's profile enormously. No longer the 'world's forgotten boy', Iggy was now fêted as the Godfather of Punk and acclaimed just as much for his formidable body of music as for the fact that he was still alive at all. Along with similar rock 'n' roll junkies such as Keith Richards, he was constantly referred to as a survivor. Aware that *Blah-Blah-Blah* was rather too polite, Iggy set about making a straight-ahead rock record for the 1980s. Hitching up with ex-Sex Pistol Steve Jones resulted in the riff-heavy thud of *Instinct*. This 1988 album was toured around the world, taking Iggy to South America for the first time. He followed this success with the radio-friendly, Don Was-produced *Brick By Brick*. On this album Iggy kept up with the new wave of rock stars by inviting members of the hugely successful Guns 'n' Roses to play on the record. A duet with Kate Pierson of the B-52s also saw considerable pop radio coverage.

His profile and influence remained high throughout the 1990s. His albums continued to sell respectably and Iggy became one of the most requested artists on the strong European summer festival circuit. His larger-than-life stage act translated well to the huge festival stages, and into any language. The hit film *Trainspotting* gave Iggy another boost by using a number of his songs in the soundtrack. Hollywood lined up to use Iggy songs after that.

The late 1990s was a period of transition for Iggy Pop. Jim and Suchi divorced in 1998 and he took the decision to leave New York for a new start in Miami. The divorce underpinned many of the songs on *Avenue B*, a downbeat, reflective and mature work released in 1999. It was assumed that Iggy had finally calmed down, grown up and was now, finally, acting his age. 2001's *Beat 'Em Up* proved those theories entirely wrong. It was a thrashy, trashy response to the nu-metal bands name-checking the Stooges as influences. Iggy proved that, once again, he could rock harder and faster than anyone, despite being more than twice the age of most of the competition. The touring continued with his most durable band, now dubbed the Trolls, most of whom had been playing with him for the best part of a decade.

Then in 2003 came the news that many had wished for, but none had ever truthfully expected. Iggy had been recording some new songs with Ron and Scott Asheton. Iggy had continued to record with the Trolls too, with modern day punks Green Day and Sum 41, and with industrial punk and all-round shocker Peaches. The resulting album, *Skull Ring*, was a surprisingly cohesive record, despite the disparate musicians involved. It was also one of Iggy's strongest sets of songs for some years, proving that he was not going to fade away gracefully.

The Stooges were booked for the Coachella Festival in April 2003, their first gig since February 1974. At this point it was just a one-off gig, but gradually more and more shows were added during 2003 and 2004. With ex fIREHOSE and Minutemen bassist Mike Watt filling Dave Alexander's shoes and Steven Mackay rejoining the band on sax, the Stooges careered through most of the first two albums, plus one or two new songs in an hour of brilliance. A series of summer festival shows in Europe in 2005 ended with the *Fun House* gig at Hammersmith. And that's where we came in.

The future looks bright – the Stooges are entering the studio to record their fourth album in early 2006. Producer Rick Rubin has expressed interest in the project.

The rest of this book seeks to tell the story of Iggy's life in rather more detail via thorough analysis of his primary work – his records, his songs, and his live performances. It's a remarkable story – full of drugs, depravity and death on the one hand, coupled with astonishing music, thrilling concerts and hugely influential songs on the other.

1947-1967

Long, Long Trailer

On 21 April 1947, Louella Osterberg gave birth to a son at Muskegon Osteopathic Hospital, Michigan. The boy was named James and was given the middle name Newell after his father.

Newell senior claimed to be of Irish and English descent, but had actually been adopted by the Osterbergs, a Swedish family. By 1947, Newell was a high school English teacher, but he had been a semi professional baseball player before the war and throughout his life championed his love of sports and fair play. Louella had worked as a controller for Bendix Aerospace but once James was born she stayed at home to raise him.

Home was a trailer, a mobile home situated in a park surrounded by other similar trailers. Whilst the term trailer trash is fairly common today, after the war there was not so much stigma attached to living in a trailer. For someone of Newell's education and profession living in a trailer was slightly unusual but not especially noteworthy. The Osterbergs kept themselves to themselves but got along fine with their neighbours, of whom many were poorly educated and from very low-class backgrounds. Many were migrants from the South in search of work in industrial Detroit. 'Our family was definitely the only literate occupant of the entire trailer park,' Iggy commented in 1981.

When Jim was nearly two, the family relocated to the Carpenter Trailer Park between Ypsilanti and Ann Arbor. They took plot 96 out of 99, surrounded by cornfields, and this would remain their home until the mid 1980s. Jim grew into a polite and caring boy. Though he suffered from bronchial asthma for many years, Jim was a happy and clever kid. He performed well at school, especially in English. His father had instilled in him a love of literature, although Jim seemed fascinated by just about everything. Louella once claimed that people would say to her, 'I wish my son was as well behaved and nice to talk to as your Jim.'

The young Jimmy's asthma was considered serious enough to warrant some restrictions being placed upon him. His parents didn't let him out of their sight at first for fear he would suffer an attack. By the time he was twelve, he was allowed further afield but still had to check in every twenty minutes. He was prescribed quadranol pills, which relieved the swelling in the bronchial tubes, thus allowing the sufferer to breathe more easily. Jim was supposed to take just half a pill at a time, but occasionally he would have a whole one. In his 1982 book of reminiscences *I Need More*, Iggy describes the scene one winter after taking a whole pill – he saw the snow shimmering with different colours and everything appeared bright and sparkling. This appears to have been the first, but by no means the last, time Iggy got stoned…

Despite his asthma, Jim was a keen sportsman. Encouraged by his dad, he became a strong baseball player, and would later take up golf, which he enjoyed primarily because of the solitude – 'There's so much room between you and the next guy.'

At the age of ten, Jimmy had begun to realise that most other people lived in houses and that they looked down on folks from trailer parks. This became more apparent when he went to high school and began mixing with more middle-class kids. He recalled times when his schoolfriends would come back to his home and make fun of the trailer, which succeeded only in making Jim hate their bourgeois middle-class attitudes. It also inspired in him a massive determination to succeed. A desire not just to better himself, but to better those who considered themselves superior to him, just by virtue of their upbringing. Throughout his career Iggy would always side with the underdog.

He didn't resent his upbringing at all, but began to think of ways to improve his lot. He would spend a lot of his spare time designing bigger and better trailers, with multi stories and swimming pools. Jim's outlook was always positive, his trailers had a lot of features that regular houses wouldn't have.

Iggy has painted a picture of a contented, if quiet childhood. His parents were both quite retiring, not outgoing gregarious people. Apparently the only time they visited the cinema was to see the Desi Arnaz–Lucille Ball movie *The Long Long Trailer*, because it featured exactly the same type of trailer – a 'New Moon' – that the Osterbergs lived in. 'My father loves trailers,' commented Iggy in *I Need More*. When he was thirteen, the Osterberg's traded up and moved into a larger Vagabond, in which they remained until they retired to South Carolina twenty-five years later.

As he grew older, Jim became interested in girls. One family, the Bishops, who lived in a nearby trailer, exerted a strong fascination for Jim. Their daughter Diane was apparently very voluptuous and would let the teenage Jim feel her breasts down by the railroad track – a place where Jim was banned from playing. This experience would later be recalled in the song 'Cold Metal'. Jim would also suffer nightmares about his father hunting him down by the railroad, armed with a two six guns and a cowboy hat, and these would also later manifest themselves in the song 'Sister Midnight'. Despite his early fumbling experiences of the opposite sex, it seems that nothing further occurred and Iggy would later claim that he remained a virgin until his late teens.

Sex would have to wait, primarily because Jim had discovered something that would take over his life. As early as fourth grade, Jim was becoming fascinated by music. He seemed able to discover music anywhere, in the unlikeliest places. A school trip to a Ford assembly plant opened his eyes, and ears, to the huge industrial sounds of the machinery. He adored the noise of the machine presses and the metal cutters. He found music in anything electrical – the heaters in the trailer, his dad's electric shaver, and in the noise of the busy road nearby. The Bishop's son David, with an Elvis-like appearance and a Duane Eddy guitar style, was apparently an early role model; Jim found him very cool.

Jim was desperate to play drums and badgered his parents until they finally relented and, once they realised how serious he was about music, they supported him wholeheartedly. At school Jim began kicking around with Jim

McLoughlin, who was learning to play the guitar. The two Jims formed the Iguanas, a neat beat combo comprising Nick Kolokithas on guitar and vocals, Jim McLoughlin on guitar and vocals, Jim Osterberg on drums and occasional vocals, Don Swickerath on bass and Sam Swisher on sax and backing vocals. By mid 1963, the Iguanas were gaining a small but devoted reputation based on their teen-pleasing repertoire of Beatles, Stones, standards such as 'Blue Moon' and garage favourites like 'Mona' and 'Louie Louie'. The Iguanas were guaranteed to get any teenage party swinging and dancing. Jim was the strongest character in the band, constantly trying to persuade the others to ditch the more MOR parts of their repertoire in favour of rougher tunes by the Kinks or Them. Sensibly worried about losing bookings if they dropped the tunes most folks wanted to hear, the Iguanas stuck firmly to their established set of crowd-pleasers.

By 1965, the band had moved on from playing teen parties at frat houses and local dances to a summer residency at the Ponytail Club in Harbor Springs. It was hard work – six nights a week, multiple sets each night, but each member of the band earned $55 per week, which was quite an achievement for a group that had left school only weeks before. They wore tidy matching suits and often Jim would play drums while perched on a very high drum riser, which looked very impressive. At the same time they began selling their home-made single at gigs. A cover of Bo Diddley's 'Mona' backed by Kolokithas' own Beatle-esque number 'I Don't Know Why', it sold well and gained the band support from further afield. Over the summer, they played gigs all over Michigan. But come the autumn most of the band members decided to call it a day and enrolled in further education.

Jim was accepted on an anthropology course at the University of Michigan. He only stayed for the first semester, becoming disenchanted primarily with the slow speed of the teaching. He had also grown his hair and was hanging around with guys who, like him, were more interested in music than anything else. During that term, Jim gradually dropped out. Though he was no longer attending classes, Jim still spent his spare time in the University of Michigan student union café. Called the Jug, it was where all the beatniks, dropouts, arty types and musicians sat around drinking coffee and making plans. Jim took a job at Discount Records, a record store in Ann Arbor where everybody seemed to hang out. He became good friends with another sales clerk there – Robert Scheff. Scheff had some fascinating, way-out ideas about music, and was determined to make it as a pianist. Their paths would cross for many years.

Every day, a group of bored youths would hang around in the street outside Discount Records. With little money to buy anything they just stood in front of the old drugstore, looking as mean as they could, smoking their cigarettes, attempting to be hoodlums – looking, as Iggy later said, 'as if they'd put the whole world down'. Ron and Scott Asheton and their friend Dave Alexander would spend their days standing around outside Discount Records, smoking and looking cool, but actually doing very little. Iggy would bump into them there and also in the Michigan Union café where they would be smoking and looking cool and still doing very little. Inevitably they became friends. Ron had actually met Jim at high school, but didn't hang out with him because the Jim at school was impossibly square, wearing neat sweaters and tasselled loafers. Ron was much cooler at school with his Brian Jones haircut and long sideburns and leather jackets.

Ron Asheton was a year younger than Iggy, his brother Scott another year younger still. They lived with their mother in Ann Arbor. Their father had died when Ron was fifteen and as he had been a Marine Corps pilot the family were relatively well provided for after he died. Iggy has often stated that the Asheton boys were incredibly lazy and lacked motivation, but this doesn't quite fit with Ron's determination to succeed in music. His love of English bands, especially the Beatles and the Rolling Stones, led Ron and his best friend from high school, Dave Alexander, to quit school in the spring of 1965 in order to travel to England. Their stated aim was to visit a relative of Dave's who had moved to England some years before, but in reality they just wanted to see the English bands for themselves. They financed their trip by selling their motorbikes and ended up in Liverpool where they immediately sought out the legendary Cavern Club. The Beatles no longer played there but Ron and Dave saw loads of up-and-coming bands including, crucially, the Who and the Yardbirds. When they returned to Ann Arbor neither had any intention of going back to school. The sight of Pete Townshend smashing his guitar and working the crowd to a frenzy was something that Ron would never forget. Ron even managed to get a splinter from Townsend's broken guitar as a souvenir. 'Never had I seen people driven so nuts... that's when I realised, "This is definitely what I want to do".'

Ron formed a band with Dave and another schoolfriend, Billy Cheatham. Scott was drafted in on drums. The Dirty Shames were the classic garage band, in fact they never played outside of their garage. But inside they played and played, desperately wanting to be like the Rolling Stones. They nearly got their break when a promoter asked at Discount Records if there were any local bands good enough to open for the Stones themselves. Although they came strongly recommended by the guys at Discount, the Dirty Shames chickened out because, despite their bravado, they really weren't anywhere near good enough to play in public, let alone open for the mighty Rolling Stones. Ron lied and told the promoter that they'd have to turn down the offer because they were auditioning in Los Angeles! The Dirty Shames struggled on, playing along with their Stones records for quite some time until Ron quit to play bass with Jim.

Since the break-up of the Iguanas, Jim had been playing drums with a blues band called the Prime Movers. They had been around on the local music circuit for a few years, playing heavy blues, influenced by the true originals such as Muddy Waters and Howlin' Wolf, rather than what they considered to be second-rate imitators such as the Stones or Them. Brothers Michael and Dan Erlewine had formed the Prime Movers after being hugely impressed with the original Paul Butterfield Blues Band. The Butterfield band was radical in that they played real blues and were a racially mixed group. They had also backed Bob Dylan at the legendary Newport Folk Festival gig when Dylan went electric for the first time. The Prime Movers, by sticking to traditional blues, were able to play in black clubs in the Midwest, places that few other white bands would play. Robert Scheff, who was already playing piano in the band, had introduced Jim to the Prime Movers. Jim would occasionally sing with the band, often straight blues songs such as Muddy

Waters' 'Mannish Boy'. When the bass player quit, Jim suggested Ron Asheton, but it soon became clear that Ron's primitive ability and lack of feeling for the blues was going to let him down. The Primer Movers was not the band for Ron who wanted to play more rock 'n' roll-based music – he left after a couple of months.

Throughout 1966, Jim's reputation as a solid and reliable drummer with the Prime Movers led to him playing drums for many bands that passed through the Detroit area. Around this time, Jim took a lengthy trip up to Chicago to see and hear the real bluesmen that he so idolised. This trip seems to have been blown out proportion by many biographers who have painted glamorous stories of Jim playing on records for some of the top Motown acts such as the Four Tops or the Marvelettes, backing the top blues bands and the like. These stories cannot now be verified, and the oft-repeated rumour that he played drums on the Shangri-Las classic 'Leader of the Pack' is, sadly, false. The truth is, as usual, more prosaic.

Jim simply went in search of his drumming hero, Sam Lay, the drummer with the Butterfield band. He had met Lay when the Butterfield band played in Detroit. Sam Lay had actually invited Jim to look him up if he was ever in Chicago but probably never expected the nineteen-year-old to actually do just that. Jim found Lay's house and knocked on the door. His wife kindly took Jim in and gave him some fried chicken, an act of kindness that Jim never forgot. Lay allowed Jim to watch him at work and would occasionally let him sit in on a couple of numbers. Being a skinny white kid in a black blues club never seemed to bother Jim – he simply loved the way the black guys had attitude and music just flowing out of them. They were also way better musicians than Jim ever thought he'd be. He remained in Chicago for some months, spending the winter cold and hungry, but happily surrounded by music. He played drums occasionally, filling in when other drummers dropped out. His experiences in Chicago changed his attitudes to music forever. He decided that his own music, whatever it was going to be, had to be real, had to describe his own experiences. The blues was right from the heart, from the soul, it was true, it was righteous. Jim's music would be different, but would have the same feeling.

One other crucial change for Jim was that the Prime Movers had referred to their drummer as Iguana, after his first band. This gradually got shortened to plain Iggy. He later claimed that 'for a person of my generation my name is really extreme. Just my name would get people violently angry.' Jim Osterberg began to realise that Iggy could be the way forward. Iggy needed to create his own music. He had spent his days in Chicago walking the streets singing quietly to himself and was sure that he could write his own songs. 'I wanted to make songs about how we were living in the Midwest. What was this life about? Basically it was no fun and nothing to do. So I wrote about that.'

In and Out
of the Funhouse

1967

Although he would later uncharitably dismiss the Prime Movers as 'bunch of effete beatniks', at the time the kudos of having played in such a highly regarded band stood him in good stead with the musicians of the Detroit area. Wayne Kramer, later the guitarist with the influential MC5, said that Iggy was widely respected for his no-nonsense style and rock-steady beat. When Iggy left, the Prime Movers continued with varying levels of success for many years. An ever-changing line-up kept the band fresh until the end of the decade when they finally folded. Michael Erlewine later got into computers in a big way and eventually founded the All Music Guide and its related film equivalent, the All Movie Guide, on the Internet.

Over the winter of 1966–1967, Iggy planned and plotted his next moves. He wanted to get together with Ron and Scott Asheton because he knew they all had similar ideas about how to make music. He called Ron Asheton from Chicago to ask if he and Scott wanted to form a band. And, by the way, could they come and collect him from Chicago? Since his abortive couple of months in the Prime Movers, Ron had been playing in a band called the Chosen Few. Alongside a charismatic singer called Scott Richardson, the band also featured an excellent young guitarist by the name of James Williamson.

Williamson clearly modelled himself on Keith Richards and Richardson obviously wanted to be Jagger, but the Chosen Few had ambitions beyond being just a Stones copy band. Sadly for the band, these ambitions were dashed when Williamson's strict father sent him away to a reform school. Apparently, James's attitude rubbed everybody up the wrong way. He was generally rude, never did what anyone told him and never cut his hair. To his father, this was the worst thing and, upon his arrival at the juvenile reform school, he was given a GI buzz cut. James would later return to play a crucial role in Iggy's life.

By spring 1967, the Chosen Few had split, with Scott Richardson forging a new career as the leader of a new band, the Scott Richardson Case. Richardson initially had the idea that Iggy and Scott Asheton would make an ideal double drum team for his new band, and that Ron would be great on bass. But neither Iggy nor the brothers were convinced that this was a viable way forward. Added to this, Iggy was now bursting with ideas and plans and would never have allowed himself to be subordinated into someone else's band.

Iggy first idea was that a trio of himself and the Ashetons could be a great band. Scott was initially suggested as the singer purely because of his smouldering Elvis pout and degenerate good looks. But Scott was unwilling

to sing and anyway they didn't have any songs. The music the trio began making was unlike anything any of them had played before. It wasn't the blues, it wasn't the Stones or the Beatles, it was... noise. A whole new sound, played on both traditional and home-made instruments. Ron was a huge fan of Harry Partch, the truly inventive American composer who wrote music that could only be played on made-up instruments. Add to that large doses of Ravi Shankar's sitar music, and the electronics and comedy of the early Mothers Of Invention and you have an eclectic mix of influences.

Iggy had also been hugely impressed with the first Velvet Underground album. Recorded during 1966, the album's release was delayed for various reasons until spring 1967. By then the Velvets were already a very different band, but their first album had an immediate impact on the few who heard it. Brian Eno has famously said that although very few people bought *The Velvet Underground & Nico*, everyone who heard it went out and formed a band. Iggy's ears were opened by the possibilities of pure noise showcased on the album, and by the unconventional mix of instrumentation. Above all he felt it gave him hope. Here was a record, played badly, recorded badly, yet it sounded amazing, totally unlike anything else. It also gave Iggy the feeling that there actually might be a market for what he wanted to do.

Meanwhile the band was taking shape. Iggy was back home with his parents and would have to trudge through the snow to the bus stop, before taking the forty-minute bus ride to the Asheton's house. Then he had the problem of waking the brothers up. Once awake, they'd rehearse until Mrs Asheton returned from work. Inspired by the musicality of the electrical equipment he'd loved as a boy, Iggy was incorporating vacuum cleaners and food blenders into the overall sound. Ron played bass and anchored the cacophony. Scott would have played drums, but they had no drums. Instead sets of oil cans and paint drums were pressed into service for Scott to flail about on. They dropped mikes into the oil drums, then thrashed them to create a thunderous din and Iggy invented what was known as a Jim-O-Phone. This consisted of a funnel which was raised and lowered around a microphone on a stand. This would create a whirring feedback, which would rise and fall in tone rather like a Theremin. Put through the amplifiers it created a truly unearthly whine. Iggy wanted a Farfisa organ on which they could set up some Indian-inspired drones. Louella struck a bargain with her son. She would buy him an organ if he cut his hair. Iggy readily agreed and got a crew cut. It soon grew again. Throughout the Summer of Love the band crashed and whirred and created some totally out-there music.

At the same time, they rented a house together at 1324 Forest Court, Ann Arbor. It was here that one day they watched a Three Stooges TV marathon. They loved the all for one–one for all mentality behind the comedy gang and adopted the name for their band. The Stooges was the perfect name. It seemed to sum up the members of the band exactly; it was partly insulting, partly self-mocking – Iggy later wondered, 'Is calling yourself a Stooge a self-insult?'

The summer of 1967 also resulted in Iggy finally losing his virginity and the band first experiencing the astonishing sounds of Jimi Hendrix. The power of the Experience spurred them on to create even more forceful music. The Ashetons encouraged Iggy to bring out his repressed anger and their music gradually became more and more intense and violent.

For a long time, it appeared that the Stooges would follow the Dirty Shames' example and never venture further than the garage. But on Halloween 1967 the trio performed in public for the first time. They had recently hooked up with Ron Richardson, a teacher who spent his spare time as a booking agent for local acts such as Bob Seger and the emerging MC5. He agreed to find work for the Stooges, but the only gig they played under his guidance was a Halloween party at Richardson's house. The Stooges took to the floor and totally baffled everybody. Ron Asheton attempted to hold the music together with his bass, Scott played his customised oilcans and other home-made percussion, and Iggy had a Hawaiian guitar. But instead of playing gentle Pacific lilts the guitar had been modified to produce a huge rumbling noise, described as akin to having an aircraft land in the room. The noise was apparently incredible; the music, if it could be called that, was freeform in the extreme. Iggy also played the vacuum cleaner to create a massive whooshing sound. Wayne Kramer of the MC5 said that the show 'was tremendously abstract and avant-garde. People didn't know what to make of it.' Even though no one knew whether to laugh or nod seriously along with the music, the show was judged a great success, though the fact that everybody was massively stoned probably helped.

Guests at Richardson's house that night included John Sinclair and members of the band he managed, the MC5. The MC5 had recently moved to Ann Arbor after the riots in Detroit during the summer. They set up home in a couple of large frat houses and proceeded to plan world domination via a series of political manifestos and some extremely raucous rock 'n' roll. Sinclair was a radical figure in the Midwest during the late 1960s – a dominant left-wing writer and musician, he founded the Rainbow People's Party which promoted the archetypal late-sixties ideals: free love, LSD and marijuana. The members of the MC5 were willing soldiers in his fight and their rabble-rousing concerts soon gained a strong following. Jimmy Silver was a friend of Sinclair's who had been impressed with the Stooges' performance, and fortunately saw the germs of something big in the ramshackle performance.

A little while later, Ron Richardson decided that he couldn't book the Stooges anywhere and bowed out. The pressure of holding down his teaching job and trying to organise the Stooges was simply too much. They were also rather too crazy for him. Jimmy Silver dropped out of his Ph.D. course (he had been studying Clinical Care) and eagerly took the reins. He would attempt to manage the Stooges for the next couple of years.

A 1967 concert by the Doors at the Yoest Field House at the University of Michigan turned the Stooges around. Iggy, who still had a student card, got in; Ron and Scott had to listen at the door. That year was a high point for the Doors. 'Light My Fire' was a number one hit and their first album was one of the biggest sellers of the year. It had been a dramatic rise for Jim Morrison, who responded to fame and adulation by hitting the bottle. The concert witnessed by Iggy was one of the first instances of Morrison performing heavily drunk or stoned. He seemed not to care about the audience, performed some tunes in a stupidly high Betty Boop voice and rolled around the stage imitating a gorilla. For many in the audience Morrison's behaviour was crass and obnoxious, and his disregard for his fans seemed callous and uncaring, but only a few walked out and most of the crowd still cheered for

him. Iggy was impressed, realising that once you were onstage you really could get away with anything. 'I loved the antagonism; I loved that he was pissing them off… but he was mesmerising them at the same time. That's when I thought, "Look how awful they are, and they've got the number one single in the country." If this guy can do it, I can do it.' Iggy also came to the conclusion you couldn't confront the crowd, and generate extreme reactions, by simply being a musician. Morrison was purely the singer, the frontman, with the freedom to do whatever he wanted, safe in the knowledge that the band would take care of the music. This is what Iggy required. After the show he announced his decision to Ron and Scott – he would stop playing the Hawaiian guitar and gadgets and concentrate solely on being the frontman and singer. To achieve this the band would need another musician.

Ron's old friend Dave Alexander was the perfect choice. Dave was a capable bass player, and this allowed Ron to switch to guitar, something he'd been keen to do for a while. Ron had grandiose plans to compose avant-garde rock operas, or to create one continuous piece that ebbed and flowed like classical music. None of these ideas would ever reach fruition but, with the addition of Dave, the band really knuckled down to working on a set of useable tunes. They rehearsed at Dave's house during the day while his mother was a work.

The Stooges were gradually becoming more like a regular band as Iggy began to sing. At first the 'songs' were primarily improvised jams or repetitive riffs over which Iggy would extemporise lyrics off the top of his head. But as they practised, genuine songs emerged. They may have been simple, basic tunes, but they were undeniably great songs.

The winter of 1967–1968 would see the Stooges gradually transform themselves from an aimless freeform experimental group into a 'proper' band. 1968 would be a crucial year.

1968

At the start of 1968, the Stooges moved to live with Jimmy Silver and his wife in a large farmhouse near Ann Arbor. The commune was a successful place for the band – they had space to practise, food to eat and TV to watch. Rarely venturing beyond the farm, Iggy was content in his simple life. The Stooges all loved TV. They watched it all day and all night, the weirder the better. As Silver later explained, Detroit area TV 'had a really bizarre selection of late-night movies in those days'. Iggy slept in the attic room. It was bare apart from the bed and a guitar. Ron brought his growing collection of military paraphernalia: he had an intellectual fascination for the Nazis, or rather the look of the Nazi uniforms and design, although he had no sympathies with their policies. He collected flags, coats, medals, weapons and liked to wear Nazi-style clothing. In the same way that the early punks would wear swastikas purely for the shock value, Ron would wear his Nazi clothes to goad people.

When not watching late-night movies, Iggy and Jimmy Silver would talk about how the Stooges would progress. Iggy had very firm ideas about how the band should be presented. He wanted to do something with the Stooges that no one had ever seen before. The rest of the band seemed less motivated. Happy with the TV and their regular supplies of hash, they have been called all sorts of names by Iggy over the years – usually referring to their laziness. In fairness, it appears that, for all his big ideas, Iggy was pretty lazy too. It took the band four months to progress from their first gig at Halloween to their next in early March 1968.

Between 1966 and 1968, all the members of the Stooges and many of their friends were called before the draft board. None wanted to be enlisted into the army, as they all knew of people who had been called to Vietnam, only to return in body bags. Homosexuals were exempt from the army, partly because the army considered that their sexual persuasion actually called their mental state into question. This then was a way of avoiding the draft – act gay. As the oldest, Iggy went first. He got high before the medical and attended wearing no underwear, then, 'I went and just beat my meat...' Sent straight to the army shrink, Iggy really played up, crying and shaking till they sent him away, 'unfit for military service'. The other Stooges 'fagged out' too and over the next few years they assisted John Sinclair in advising people how to beat the draft.

The first gig under Jimmy Silver's guidance was at the Grande Ballroom in Detroit, a venue that was hugely important to the music scene of the Midwest. It was run by Russ Gibb, who happily featured new and upcoming bands alongside established acts. The Stooges' debuted as support for Blood Sweat and Tears. They played a deafening, twenty-minute set comprising just two partially structured numbers that might have been called 'I'm Sick' and 'Asthma Attack' (as the lyrics were improvised any titles have to remain provisional). Iggy wore golf shoes, Dave played the blender and, for the finale, Jimmy Silver hammered an oil tank (the sort that people use to store oil in, not simply a drum), painted white and with a microphone dropped inside – Silver took a car repair mallet to it. This made, according to Silver, 'a noise like it was inside you, or you were locked inside the oil drum, because it was going through the PA system.' Amazingly, the band received a rapturous reception.

As with many of the 1968 shows, they were billed as the Psychedelic Stooges although privately the band never used the 'Psychedelic' tag. At this point, Iggy was just Iggy or, when two names were required, Iggy Osterberg.

These early shows would also sometimes feature the home-made instruments introduced at the Halloween 1967 gig but, as 1968 wore on, it became apparent that the Jim-O-Phone, the blenders, the oil drums and all the rest didn't really translate to proper concert stages. So by the autumn of 1968 the Stooges were only using conventional instruments. The music they performed was often nothing more than 'demented grooves' according to John Sinclair: 'They'd get a tremendous drone going... "trances" I called them. They were closer to North African music than they were to rock.' By the end of the year, the hollering and general unstructured noise making was gradually being honed into recognisably structured tunes. Early proper songs included 'The Dance Of Romance', a pounding, bruising monster of a riff over which Iggy would scream and Ron would play some wild lead guitar. 'I Wanna Be Your Dog' and 'No Fun' were also taking shape.

Iggy would frequently perform these shows with his face painted white, wearing a maternity dress and golf shoes. When the band appeared at new venues, his frankly bizarre appearance often shocked the audiences – and that was before the band even played. Michael Davis of the MC5 pointed out that, however strange the Stooges act seemed, it was never negative – 'Iggy usually made a crazy fool out himself to everyone's pleasure... they weren't turning people off. They were just weird and different and didn't play songs like everybody else.'

But whereas some shows would be supercharged and thrilling, others would fall appallingly flat. No one ever knew how a Stooges performance would go – not even the Stooges. They began to get reviews and the picture emerged of a highly original, but worryingly unpredictable band. Some reviewers praised the ambitious performance style adopted by Iggy; others preferred the powerful improvised music – few, however, could ignore the Stooges.

The Stooges soon earned a small but devoted following amongst the regular Detroit crowds at the Grande Ballroom, but they were not particularly ambitious to widen their appeal. They generally only played once a week, or at most on Friday and Saturday. Largely uninterested in broadening their horizons, the Stooges rarely played anywhere else, only venturing further afield in support of the MC5 as the more ambitious politico rockers started pushing for broader approval. Also, with only a small repertoire of tunes Jimmy Silver was reluctant to book them up for too many gigs. Even so the frequency of the weekend gigs elicited some complaints from the lazy band – even two gigs a week was deemed hard work.

On 21 April, the Stooges opened for the mighty Cream at the Grande Ballroom. It was one of their worst gigs – their amps didn't work properly and the audience only wanted the polished musicianship of Clapton, Bruce and Baker, screaming for Cream throughout the horrendous noise made by the Stooges. It was Iggy's twenty-first birthday and the disappointment directly contributed to the memorable couplet about not having enough fun in the song '1969'.

Now fascinated with Ancient Egypt, Iggy started performing topless; pictures of pharaohs always depicted the kings with no shirts. This was obviously because Egypt is a hot country and Iggy wanted to look as cool as the pharaohs, despite Detroit being decidedly chilly for much of the year. He also incorporated some of the striking stylised poses depicted in Egyptian paintings into his stage appearance, pulling his body into similar contorted two-dimensional poses. His dance moves were off-the-cuff responses to the rhythmic noise of the band, almost tribal in their intensity – over time, a series of stunning set pieces would develop. Iggy was very fit and lithe and was able to bend right over backwards so his head would touch the floor. He also began flinging himself at the microphone stand, falling forwards as if he would splat onto the floor, before saving himself at the last moment by grabbing the mike stand with his outstretched arms. All of which added up to a growing reputation for the Stooges as a must-see live act.

Iggy's on-stage actions were, however, often found to be shocking, especially outside of the band's regular Detroit haunts. After a show at Mother's in Romeo on 11 August, Iggy was arrested for indecent exposure. This was one of the first gigs the band had played outside of Detroit. Iggy claimed in 2001 that he wasn't getting enough reaction from the audience, so he stripped off, dived into the audience and rolled naked around the auditorium. It's a great story, and fully in keeping with the Iggy legend. The truth may be rather less dramatic. Ron Asheton remembered the incident this way:

'He had gotten a pair of brown vinyl pants and... the way he twists around and does his acrobatics, the crotch just split. So he probably was just hangin' out. And then he went backstage and came back with a towel wrapped around him...'

Unfortunately, there was a girl in the crowd whose Dad was a state policeman. As the gig ended, she went down the road to the police station and luridly reported that the gig she had just seen had featured a naked man. A whole bunch of local police turned up at the club. The owners tipped off the Stooges, suggesting they split before there was any trouble. Iggy decided to get away but, as the rest of the band hadn't done anything wrong, they remained in the dressing room. They cops announced they'd arrest the whole band unless they found Iggy, which worried Scott and Dave who each had a stash of marijuana, but the unfortunate Iggy was rounded up moments later trying to hide in the boot of a car. The naked hero of Iggy's story spent the night in jail and his parents had to drive down to Romeo the next day to bail him out. Iggy was fined $41 and $9 costs on a charge of being disorderly, a reduction from the indecent exposure charge, which turned out to be too hard to prove. Sadly, this brush with the law resulted in the landlords terminating the lease on Mother's club.

Amazingly, this turned out to be the only time Iggy was arrested during the early Stooges period. In 2001, Iggy seemed surprised too: 'Every year or so I do something that everybody murmurs about; "This is the end for him, he's gone too far this time." And usually I just get quiet for a while and see what happens. But, y'know, it's showbiz after all.'

A month later the Stooges got signed. This was something that no one had anticipated. Danny Fields was the young publicity director at Elektra Records. Elektra was home to the Doors and the label was keen to expand its roster of new rock acts. For some time, John Sinclair had been hassling Fields to come and experience the Ann Arbor scene – he badly wanted the get the MC5 a deal and had been sending him loads of MC5 propaganda. One such leaflet had said, 'If you like us, you'll like our baby brother band called the Psychedelic Stooges.' Fields eventually travelled from New York to Detroit to see the Union Ballroom show on 22 September. It was actually a benefit for the Children's Community School and the MC5 were supported by local bands the Up and the Stooges.

Fields loved what he saw. Iggy ended the Stooges set by walking around the stage as the amps fed back. He was wearing his maternity dress and, according to Iggy, he began spitting at people. Fields raced backstage to confront Iggy with the immortal line 'You're a Star'. At first Iggy didn't believe him, as Fields was dressed in a leather jacket and jeans – not what Iggy expected a record company executive to wear – but was eventually persuaded that Fields was the real deal. That night Danny Fields offered both the MC5 and the Stooges a contract with Elektra Records. Without prior approval from his office in New York, Fields didn't actually have the authority to do this. He phoned New York on Monday morning and somehow managed to sweet-talk label boss Jac Holzman into agreeing with what he'd done. Holzman told Danny to sign the MC5 for $20,000 and the

Stooges for $5,000. Fields did – the prices were incredibly cheap, but neither band had enough experience of the business to realise.

A few weeks later, Holzman and Elektra's vice president, Bill Harvey, flew to see their potential new acts at the Fifth Dimension in Ann Arbor. They brought with them the contracts that would be signed if the Elektra bosses were sufficiently impressed with Danny Fields' discoveries. Iggy had a fever and a very high temperature – he kept falling down and shivering – but this seemed to impress Jac Holzman, who assumed it was part of the act and that Iggy was totally into his art.

Both acts signed their contracts at the MC5's house straight after the show. This was a huge coup for the Stooges. Less than a year after their first tentative show, and only a matter of months since they'd begun regular performances, they'd secured a deal with one of the biggest records labels in America. The Stooges duly received their advance of $5,000 and later a further $20,000.

A month after signing with Elektra, Iggy surprised everybody by getting married. Wendy Weisberg was a girl he'd met at the Grande Ballroom. Her father owned a chain of stores in the Midwest and was very wealthy. Her parents were so shocked by her decision to marry a freakish singer that they refused to attend the wedding. The service was officiated by Jimmy Silver who, like Wendy, was Jewish. Ron Asheton was Iggy's best man and chose his smartest Nazi clothes to wear for the wedding – a Luftwaffe fighter pilot's jacket decorated with various medals, including a couple of Iron Crosses, plus jodhpurs and riding boots. After the service, the Stooges could be found outside the house taking bets on how long the marriage would last.

It lasted barely a month. Wendy lived with Iggy and the band at Silver's farm, recently christened Stooge Manor, and she made a real effort to be nice to the others. But the Stooges disliked her superior airs and graces and cruelly called her the Potato Girl because of her slightly lumpy complexion. They were also jealous of the fact that Iggy obviously spent more time with her than with them. After just four weeks, even Iggy had had enough. 'She liked to sleep at night, of all things, and I liked to sleep whenever I wanted to.' One night Iggy woke up with a tune buzzing around his head and, mindful of his sleeping wife, he hid in the closet while he worked on the song that became 'Down On The Street'. He tried to keep it quiet but suddenly flipped and took the amp out of the closet, blasting his wife with noise. 'It suddenly hit me, then and there. It was impossible. It had to be one or the other: her or a career.' Poor Wendy left soon after and sued for divorce on the grounds that the marriage hadn't been consummated, alleging that Iggy was homosexual.

Iggy was clearly nothing of the sort. The other Stooges were jealous of the ease with which he picked up girls without even trying. He quickly returned to his old ways and soon Stooge Manor was filled with Iggy's conquests again. As before, after Iggy had callously tired of his latest girl, Ron would be left to pick up the pieces, or give the hapless teenager the bus fare home.

The year ended on a high note with a New Year gig at the Grande Ballroom. They were now a formidable and thrilling live act. With a big record label deal under their belts, the Stooges were eager to get into the recording studios: 1969 would be a vital year.

1969

As 1969 opened, the Stooges began to work on the songs that would make up their album. Concerts in the early part of 1969 were scarce, so the band spent time honing the few songs that they had. The gigs picked up again in the spring, so the Stooges reputation as being one of the hottest live acts around grew rapidly. Elektra arranged for studio time at the Hit Factory in New York and the Stooges spent April and May gigging and improving their set, ready for the album.

THE STOOGES

Elektra EKS 74051. US release – August 1969. UK release – September 1969
Produced by **John Cale**

With growing opposition to the Vietnam war and the emerging drug scene throughout the US underground, the younger generation were pitching themselves in direct opposition to their parents. Iggy has referred to the late 1960s as a time of 'generational hatred'. This manifested itself in the flower power of the West Coast hippies and the arty nihilistic New York scene, with the far more militant political movement of the Midwest stuck in the middle. The MC5 were prime exponents of the sloganeering politicised rock of the Detroit area. Their 'baby brother' band, the Stooges, couldn't be bothered with all that rabble rousing. They were just seriously pissed off and that's all they wanted to say.

With only a tiny number of workable songs, the clothes that they were wearing and masses of attitude, the Stooges dutifully trooped off to New York to record their debut album at the Hit Factory. The Stooges first recordings began on 19 June 1969. Elektra had assigned John Cale to produce the record. He seemed ideal: classically trained, he also had a strong avant-garde background, from Terry Conrad's astonishing musical experiments of the early 1960s, via his groundbreaking and hugely influential work with Lou Reed and the Velvet Underground to his brilliant production of *The Marble Index* for Nico. Cale had seen the Stooges only once before, when Danny Fields had taken him to an MC5 gig at the Grande Ballroom. Cale saw in the Stooges the raw energy that the Velvets had originally exhibited, a strong sense of freedom of expression mixed with primitive and primal emotion. In Iggy, Cale saw a figurehead and a focal point, something the Velvets had consciously avoided. He also noted something that few people saw in the Stooges – namely an unselfconscious, bouncy sense of humour. He loved Iggy's impish quality – 'he'd be threatening you one minute and hugging you the next.' Cale wisely elected to record the band as straight as he could – there seemed no point in embellishing their sound with studio trickery as Stooges music only really worked on a very simple level. Cale was amused by the fact that Iggy in the studio was exactly the same as Iggy on stage. He would race about, 'climbing all over the amps and desks like a mad animal'.

As the band usually only played for a blisteringly intense twenty minutes, and often had to jam while Iggy crawled into the audiences, there had been no real need to work up many songs. 'I Wanna Be Your Dog', 'No Fun' and '1969' made up the bulk of their performances. They needed no more material for these shows. The band assumed that they would simply record their usual set – a handful of songs leading into improvisations they played onstage. Cale had other ideas and wanted the short songs but wasn't convinced that the sheer power of the instrumental sections would translate to record. More songs were needed. Iggy had told label boss Jac Holzman that that the Stooges had dozens of songs, but now his bluff had been called. After a couple of days recording their existing tunes, Iggy and Ron set about writing. They came up with the simplest of riffs which, married to some very basic lyrics, bulked out their meagre supply of songs. 'Not Right' and 'Real Cool Time' betray this desperate race against time, being basic in the extreme. With no more time to write, Ron dusted down the propulsive riff from an early song called 'Goodbye Bozos', which had basically the same tune as '1969' anyway, and Iggy rewrote the lyrics so it became 'Little Doll'. Even then, these seven songs amounted to only about twenty-five minutes of music – still too short for a long player. Cale came to the rescue by working on a lengthy mantra piece with Dave Alexander. The result was a ten-minute viola drone over which the Stooges would chant as Iggy sang some sort of incomprehensible Jim Morrison-esque lament. It did neither party any favours, but 'We Will Fall' did its job of filling the album's running time.

Another problem was that the Stooges only knew how to play with everything turned up to ten. Cale's studio experience led him to insist that the Stooges turn it down. After some initial opposition, with the band sulkily refusing to play, a compromise was reached – set everything at nine... After that, the sessions ran smoothly with the whole recording process taking only about six days. Oddly, despite Cale's intention to record the band as live, it's clear that the finished record bears only a fleeting resemblance to the Stooges actual animalistic live sound. The album sounds way too clean for a start. There's no distortion, little anger. Ron relies heavily on his wah-wah pedal to cover his lack of technique, though he does work this to his advantage in that many of the songs break down into some of the most brutal guitar ever heard on record. Ron used a Gibson Flying V on most of the album, though his more usual Stratocaster crops up on late arrivals 'Little Doll', 'Not Right' and 'Real Cool Time'. He favoured the Strat for the 'good clean sound it gets with the wah-wah, that biting hurts-your-ears sound.' To make the Stooges sound as big as he could, Ron also loved playing drones, a technique he lifted from sitar players such as Ravi Shankar.

In concert, Iggy's vocals were usually screamed out, violent and extreme. On record the vocals, while competently sung, often sound merely petulant, rather than mightily pissed off. Scott's drumming and Dave's bass playing rarely gel to form a convincing rhythm section, and both are alarmingly rudimentary in places. Whilst naive charm and ramshackle amateurish musicianship can be attractive at times, on occasion the playing on this record merely sounds poor.

Having said all of that however, *The Stooges* possesses a power and an influence which utterly transcends its obvious shortcomings. The key songs – 'I Wanna Be Your Dog', 'No Fun' and '1969' – unwittingly laid down the foundations for much of the punk movement. Many later New York new wave artists were to base their sounds entirely upon Ron's lacerating guitar work, while Iggy's obnoxious ranting, bored, angry, in-your-face singing would become the defining style of punk singers later in the decade, giving a voice to all those outsiders and alienated youths who so wanted to sing but who would previously have been barred from doing so. Here was Iggy: not a great singer in the obvious sense; he couldn't sing nice harmonies like the Beach Boys; he didn't write pleasant melodies like the Beatles. He simply wanted to express his anger and his annoyance in the only way he could – through his equally harsh music.

The album was mixed by John Cale as they went along, but the finished product was deemed 'too arty' by Iggy and he persuaded Elektra to allow him to remix a number of songs. Cale's original mixes, together with some extended takes and alternative vocal takes were added to the 2005 CD reissue.

The cover was something of minor masterpiece. At least Dave and Ron are half smiling, but Iggy and Scott look sulkily into the camera – neither looks like the sort of people you'd want next door. The back cover reveals Ron glaring meanly, Scott staring from under heavy lidded doped eyes and Iggy looking seriously pissed off. One reason might have been that he was credited as 'Iggy Stooge'. When preparing the cover, Danny Fields was asked about Iggy's moniker, as the Elektra art department weren't sure about just putting 'Iggy' on the cover. Fields suggested the surname Stooge, something Iggy wasn't consulted about and which really irritated him as the name stuck for many years. Fields eventually achieved his dream of naming the band members after the band, when he took over management of the Ramones in the mid 1970s.

1969

Opening with a lazy drumbeat and Ron's killer wah-wah before Iggy drawls 'Awright' and Scott kicks into the pseudo-jungle rhythm / Bo Diddley beat and Ron's see-sawing riff picks up. The lyrics are clear, up front and direct – 1969 is 'another year with nothin' to do'. Boredom and disenchantment are the overriding feelings on show. Iggy sings in a sort of sullen drawl, perfect for the emotions the lyrics convey.

The handclaps seem to have been added to compensate for the slight irregularities of Scott's jungle beat. But trying to even out the rhythm is unnecessary (even though Scott and Dave seem to be losing each other towards the fade out) and the overdubbed claps are merely an annoyance. Cale's original mix had pushed these still further to the forefront.

After the second verse, Ron's guitar overdubs crash in, submerging the rest of the music in distortion and noise. Ron has commented on how weak the guitars sound in comparison to the Stooges live sound, but it's still a shockingly powerful sound. Iggy gets to scream out the title at the 3.35 mark, which actually comes as a surprise after the rather stoned sounding slurring of the rest of the vocals. A longer version of the song, running to nearly five minutes, was released on the 2005 reissue. You get lots more of Ron's solo on this one.

I Wanna Be Your Dog

From the opening dirty downward slide of the guitar, you know this is gonna be good. Then, when Iggy enters with 'I'm so messed up', you know he's not mucking around. Here's a guy who means exactly what he says.

This is a feeling that pervades the whole album. Simple and short though the lyrics might be, every track is sung with total commitment. Iggy means every word. He'd worked hard to make every track as tight as he could.

'I Wanna Be Your Dog' is a love song, of sorts. Iggy pledges his commitment to... someone. He's ready to lose his heart, to 'be your dog'. The lyrics compliment the music perfectly – there's an exhilaratingly sleazy feel that undercuts the propulsive guitar work. However, the shortcomings of the Stooges compositional techniques are also laid bare on this, only the second track of the album. Once again we get a couple of minutes of traditional verse-chorus songwriting followed by a guitar freak-out. In concert, this would lead into anything up to ten minutes of chaos – and was the reason the Stooges had so few songs. In the studio, the lack of songs is cruelly highlighted and the very short length of the actual 'song' parts is made all the more obvious.

The guitar loses much of its dominance on Cale's original mix. The one-note piano and sleigh bells are highlighted at the expense of the rest of the instruments. Iggy's vocals also sound somewhat detached on this mix.

Another version of 'Dog' with a very flat unemotional vocal delivery makes for an interesting contrast on the 2005 reissue. Interestingly, the backing track is more dynamic as there is less separation of instruments so the band sounds more together.

Those ridiculous sleigh bells (what was Cale thinking?) are so omnipresent that they almost ruin the track – but not quite. Nothing could ever slay 'I Wanna Be Your Dog'. Its riff, relentless beat, simplicity, purity of conception and execution, and the superb delivery of the lyrics makes it hard to beat.

We Will Fall

Dave Alexander was heavily into meditation and the hippy way of life. The other Stooges hated the West Coast scene, as it was predominantly white and middle class. Bands such as Jefferson Airplane, Crosby, Stills and Nash and later *Rumours*-era Fleetwood Mac would all come in for some stick from Iggy. He hated the wishy-washiness of it all. Detroit music was hard, it had crawled out of the gutter and worked its way up. The Stooges were still in the gutter, but this was the way Iggy liked it. They all loved the Doors though – mainly because of Jim Morrison's clear sense of theatre and ability to project danger and unpredictability whilst onstage.

'We Will Fall' originated from one of Dave's meditation chants but, combined with Iggy's slow intonation, becomes almost Doors-like. They recorded it with candles and incense burning in the studio, together with a load of hash, and the whole band got happily high during the process. Sadly it doesn't progress much in all its ten-plus minutes, and the track conveys none of the intensity or vision of any of Morrison's laments. Instead it drones, assisted by Cale's viola (which is the most experimental thing on show here), for too long without building or changing. The song is simply not good enough to justify the length. But with every other track running short and Cale keeping the guitar berserk-outs to a minimum, the album was dangerously short as it was. So a long mantra-inspired drone filled up side one nicely.

No Fun

The riff was loosely based on the Johnny Cash classic 'I Walk The Line', with the middle eight intended to sound like the Rolling Stones. The full-length version gives a small indication of what the band must have sounded like in concert, with Ron's wailing soloing over the end section.

Iggy has since pointed out that he was trying hard to be economical with his lyrics, trying to get his point across in as few words as possible. In this he took a lead from TV comedian Soupy Sales who asked for letters that were twenty-five words or less. Iggy loved this idea of extreme economy. In a 1986 interview, he demonstrated how this worked by quoting from 'No Fun': 'No fun, my babe, no fun. No fun, my babe, no fun' – already halfway through the first verse and only four different words have been used. Iggy made it his mission to write songs with twenty-five words or less. That way his intentions were less likely to be misinterpreted. Most of the songs on the first album follow this pattern.

The handclaps are back – more so on the Cale mix, slightly reduced on the Iggy remix. But they are not as intrusive as on '1969'. Nothing could get in the way of 'No Fun'. The tune is wonderfully simple and extremely memorable. Iggy's lyrics are basic but direct, almost a hymn for the dispossessed. Iggy sounds by turns sullen and rabid.

Real Cool Time

One of the three songs written the night before recording, 'Real Cool Time' is closer to the Stooges live sound than the previous tracks. Having to record the song in a very short space of time didn't allow Cale to over-arrange things. So there's none of the handclaps or sleigh bells found elsewhere. The full-length recording on the 2005 reissue ends with Cale asking if he can cut the song at about 2.20. Cale got his way.

The song couldn't be simpler. Iggy described it as a one-sided phone conversation – 'can I come over, tonight?' – but its simplicity is its strength. The riff is wonderful, the song is short and doesn't overstay its welcome, and Iggy's vocal is satisfyingly sleazy.

Interestingly 'Real Cool Time' was used as the backing music for a TV ad for the Detroit raceway, which impressed the Stooges enormously. They were so naive in the ways of the music business that it never occurred to them that they should have been paid.

Ann

'Ann' is basically another short song married to a guitar freak-out. In this case, the second half is the 'Dance Of Romance', a bruising instrumental piece of riffing allowing Scott and Dave to thrash out a militaristic beat while Ron creates one of the most intensely horrible buzzing guitar parts on record. The guitar sounds like a particularly pissed off, but very loud, wasp caught in the speakers. On headphones it sounds as if the wasp is actually in your head. Not surprisingly this was another piece that Cale and Elektra kept to a minimum. The original record fades out at three minutes, but the full-length version released on the 2005 reissue pummels the listener with this repetitive power playing for another five minutes. It's quite breathtaking and is probably the only recording to fully convey the awesome sound that the Stooges made in concert.

The opening song part is played at a funereal pace. Scott's drums even sound dead. The song plods, but in an oddly ominous manner. There is a distinct

sense of suppressed power, which is realised as Iggy sings/screams 'I love you... Right Now!' and the song explodes into the 'Dance of Romance' section.

Not Right
Another of the three hastily written songs and this time it shows. A stop–start rhythm and some extremely basic lyrics characterise this rather enjoyable throwaway song. Iggy's vocals are great, achieving just the right level of dumbness – 'I'm... not right' – as the band run up and down their couple of chords with Ron sneaking in one of his best and probably most overlooked solos. It's not brilliant, but it'll more than do. An alternate take features a less committed vocal, though conversely the guitar attack sounds more full blooded.

Little Doll
Dave starts off the rumbling rhythm before Scott joins in with some superb tumbling drums. It's not far off the same tune as '1969' but so what? Once again Ron gets to play a scorching solo but, as with the other two late arrivals, he's not mixed too high and the guitar blends much better with the band. Cale's original mix emphasises Iggy's vocal more by setting it in some echo that makes it less whiney. The grind of Ron's guitar is also more prevalent. Iggy's remix, which ended up on the record, gives preference to the rhythm track.

*   *   *

Not altogether surprisingly the album bombed. It wasn't a complete disaster – with the power of Elektra behind it, the record was at least well promoted and it received more reviews that one might have expected. But most of the reviews were largely negative, and sales were poor considering the amount of publicity the record and the band generated. Lenny Kaye, writing in *Fusion*, saw the Stooges as a product very much of the times. As Jagger had summed up 1965 with 'I can't get no satisfaction', so Iggy was reflecting the boredom and frustration of 1969. But even Kaye's relatively positive review had to admit that 'neither the singing nor the musicianship attains any memorable level of competence.' Trade paper *Cash Box* was more encouraging, highlighting the 'intensity of the musicianship', and *Billboard* weirdly praised the 'sophisticated pop execution' (had they actually heard the record, one wonders?). The most perceptive comment came from local magazine *Creem*: singling out Ron Asheton's lacerating guitar work, the reviewer declared, 'This is probably the guitar style of the future...'

The general perception was that the Stooges were, as *Rolling Stone* put it, 'stoned sloths making boring repressed music, which I suspect appeal to boring repressed people'. In 1969, the underground press had a considerable influence amongst the underground communities, but in the music business itself it was the opinion of powerful magazines such as *Rolling Stone* that carried the most weight. Matters weren't helped by that fact that the Stooges were too lazy to mount a proper tour of the USA to promote their record, continuing to play mainly their regular slots at the Grande Ballroom and other local Michigan venues. They did, however, begin to venture further afield to areas where they already had a following. June 1969 saw a break-through for the Stooges as they played their first gig outside of Michigan.

They didn't venture far, only to Delta, Ohio, but it represented the first steps towards national exposure. Except for the trip to New York in August, the rest of the gigs from 1969 rarely strayed beyond Michigan with only a few in Ohio and one poorly received show in Boston.

Something that surprised music writers in the Detroit area was how 'professional' sounding the band had suddenly become. Used to the Stooges' short sets of unconventional noise with barely an identifiable tune, the new album, with eight proper songs, was a real shock.

'I Wanna Be Your Dog' was issued as a single. It sold next to nothing and picked up few reviews – *Variety* called it 'a mediocre rocker', though *Cash Box* was again more encouraging and referred to the song's 'sensational listener impact' and actually thought the song was Top Forty material, 'with the look of a winner'. Sadly, it wasn't.

One important result of the album was the brief but intense relationship that Iggy had with Nico. Since leaving the Velvet Underground in the summer of 1967, Nico had, as usual, drifted around. After playing sporadic gigs with a selection of devoted guitar players (often Lou Reed, Jackson Browne or Tim Hardin), she recorded her first solo album, *Chelsea Girl*. Musically this was chiefly the work of her guitarists and it wasn't until 1968 that Nico would create her first true solo album. *The Marble Index* was a series of songs created around her naive harmonium playing. The songs were then orchestrated and embellished by John Cale. Having found her ideal milieu, Nico doggedly stuck with this general sound for most of the rest of her career. Whenever she deviated from the harmonium the results were never fully satisfactory. During the sessions for the Stooges debut, Nico would sit in the control room with Cale. Despite the warm New York summer, Cale often wore a long Dracula cape, and Iggy claims that Nico spent her days knitting, an image which takes some getting used to. Occasionally she would offer doomy advice such as 'Your songs need more poison, Jim.'

When the band returned to Stooge Manor in July 1969, Nico went with them. She spent about a month living with Iggy, during which time he claims to have learnt about all sorts of European culture, fine red wines and, famously, was introduced to oral sex. Nico also gave Iggy his first dose of the clap. For someone so undomesticated, Nico oddly tried to look after the gang at Stooge Manor. But her idea of cooking generally involved huge pots of vegetables doused in gallons of Tabasco sauce, which no one could eat... An 'Art' film was made at this time, directed by Francois de Menil. Called *An Evening Of Light*, it consisted of little more than Nico and Iggy, plus John Adams ('because he looks like a Sphinx', said Ron) running about in a field dotted with bits of shop window dummies. Some of this frankly silly 16mm movie can be seen in the *Nico Icon* documentary. For a time the Stooges apparently closed their concerts with a track called 'Evening Of Light', but this was not the Nico song, purely a cheeky steal of the title. What they actually played to end a gig was far-out freak-out noise.

Down On The Street – 1969 Concerts

The Stooges became known as the band to out-shock any other. Alice Cooper tried similar tactics a few years later but his was obviously an act, a cheesy, though thoroughly entertaining horror film, compared to the scary realism of

a Stooges show. The MC5 were another band that the Stooges were frequently compared to – if anything their politics tended to detract from the fact that their music was pretty conventional compared with the stripped-down power of the Stooges. The MC5, for all their posturing, gave out none of the out-of-control, animalistic sense of danger that the Stooges did.

As the Stooges began to venture outside of Detroit in the second half of the year, after the release of *The Stooges*, their live set would begin with 'I Wanna Be Your Dog' followed by two or three other tunes from the album. The usual set closer was '1969'.

Elektra sent the Stooges to the East Coast. They played a number of shows in New York, kicking off with a double header with the MC5 at the New York State Pavilion in Queens on 29 August 1969. Legend has it that the wife of promoter Howard Stein suffered a miscarriage after seeing the Stooges. Stein never promoted the Stooges again. The two shows at the Pavilion were crucial in gaining the band some much-needed national press. Many members of the New York arts scene attended and the Stooges responded with a spectacular performance. They played a short four-song set and at the end Iggy returned to the stage, picked up Scott's discarded drumsticks, and slowly cut welts into his chest with them. New York had never seen anything like this before. *Rolling Stone*'s Chris Hodenfield once again trashed the performance, though *Rock* magazine loved it. Backstage, *Rock*'s Karin Berg managed to ask Iggy a few questions and received one of the earliest recorded explanations of his remarkable stage act. 'I get this feeling, this area of concentration here, the genital area. It starts out that way, I can feel it, I just let it go, and then it moves up my body through here to the back of my neck, and it just kind of explodes. That's similar to what happens to people in religious dancing or rituals, the trance like thing.' Elsewhere Iggy commented, 'I'm just feeling the music... nobody ever knows how it's going to end up.'

Throughout the autumn of 1969, the Stooges played more and more shows and gradually ventured further and further from home. Not everyone was impressed with their short but intense gigs. A set supporting heavy rockers Ten Years After resulted in total silence from the Boston audience. Iggy responded with further self mutilation, just to get a reaction. This began a slightly worrying trend – if the gig wasn't going too well, Iggy would draw blood and start taunting the audience, just to get the crowd going. *Rolling Stone*, who despite their alleged hatred of the Stooges certainly gave the band considerable press, reviewed the Boston Tea Party gig and after cataloguing Iggy's increasingly dangerous stage moves concluded with a comment from a member of the audience – 'I'm surprised they didn't need a stretcher to carry him off... How long can a guy like that last?' It wouldn't be the last time that question was asked.

Towards the end of the year, 'Loose' was introduced as the new opener, 'Dog Food' would fall somewhere in the middle and an early version of 'Fun House' was closing the set, dissolving into the Energy Freak Out Freeform – as much noise and feedback as the Stooges could muster.

The Stooges last gig of 1969 took place at the Aragon Ballroom in Chicago as part of the Chicago Pop Festival. But the Stooges were already way beyond pop music. Most of the tunes that would end up on *Fun House* were in the set and large steps had already been taken to move the Stooges towards funk and jazz.

1970

The Stooges' first album had not impressed Elektra much, but they decided to pick up the option on a second album anyway. There was some initial haggling over who would produce the record. The Stooges initially favoured Jim Peterman from the Steve Miller Band; Danny Fields suggested the well-regarded Eddie Kramer after his work with Led Zeppelin; and Elektra, watching the pennies, suggested staff producer Frazier Mohawk. After some argument Don Gallucci's name came up. Initially the band was resistant as Gallucci had been well known as Little Donnie in Don And The Good Times, the house band on Dick Clark's show *Where The Action Is*. But they changed their minds when they realised that Gallucci had also produced and played keyboards on the Kingsmen's glorious garage classic 'Louie Louie'.

'Louie Louie', released in 1963, predates the Stooges sound almost exactly. From the drawled vocals via the scratchy and nasty guitar to the almost tribal rhythm, it could easily have fitted on the Stooges first album. Iggy acknowledged the debt he owed to 'Louie Louie' by playing the song on almost every tour and immortalising it on record on a number of occasions. Frank Zappa also loved the song and would return to it throughout his career, using it at the basis of a number of other tunes. Both men loved 'Louie Louie' and both understood that great music is, at its heart, simple and pure. Whereas Zappa celebrated the dumb ass nature of 'Louie Louie' by using it as a sort of shorthand to suggest a certain type of sound within his own horrendously complex music, Iggy simply loved the song. There was no cleverness about Iggy's renditions. It was a just a great tune and Iggy still loves performing it. A number of his own songs use the three-chord thrash of 'Louie Louie' as a starting point, notably 'I'm A Conservative' from 1979, which is more or less the same tune.

Don Gallucci accompanied Danny Fields to see a number of Stooges concerts before recording commenced. These gigs coincided with the addition of saxophonist Steve Mackay to the band. Mackay had previously played with Carnal Kitchen, Commander Cody And His Lost Planet Airmen and the wonderfully named Charging Rhinoceros Of Soul. (On one occasion he played with all three bands in one night.) Influenced by John Coltrane, he was an intriguing addition to the Stooges. The band had been developing a number of new songs that went far beyond the straight-ahead riffing on the first album. The new songs, especially the funky 'Fun House' were more like some form of mutant jazz-rock, for which Iggy envisaged the Stooges changing into a sort of rock version of James Brown's band. During the winter, the band had relocated to a new home on Packard Avenue in Ann Arbor. They christened their new headquarters Fun House and set about writing a song to immortalise their home, and it and other songs had been in the band's live set since the end of 1969.

The addition of some out-there sax playing took the simple James Brown-ish groove into another dimension entirely. Iggy described the band's new sound as being a 'sweeping sound, like Mongolian horsemen charging in.' One of Mackay's strengths in the Stooges was that he knew when he was needed and more importantly when not to play. He wouldn't join in until about halfway through the set and the sudden arrival of the saxophone during '1970' would come as something of surprise to the audience. But it was precisely what was needed and pushed the Stooges live shows up a gear. But Steve, assuming that he would only sit in occasionally, didn't consider that he was proper member of the band, until they told him to pack his bags for Los Angeles.

In April 1970, the Stooges, plus Jimmy Silver and roadie Bill Cheatham, took their first trip to Los Angeles, where they booked into the Tropicana Hotel, on Santa Monica Boulevard. The Elektra studios were a couple of blocks away, as was the Doors' office, which impressed the Stooges. (According to Ron there was a two-way mirror in the Elektra studios and he claims that Jim Morrison and Ray Manzarek secretly came to check out the Stooges.)

The Stooges immediately played a gig at the Whisky A Go Go. The show began at midnight and was notable because Iggy wandered into the crowd and picked up a candle off one of the dining tables. He then poured the hot wax over his chest. Interviewed the next day by John Mendelsohn for *Entertainment World*, Iggy calmly stated, 'I don't expect anyone to like our music.' Mendelsohn perceptively noted that Iggy was using 'a madman's persona to achieve notoriety'.

In Los Angeles, Iggy got himself a haircut. Not something that is usually noteworthy but his surprisingly short 'schoolboy' cut went right against the prevailing trends. More in keeping with the Stooges ethos, he also bought a red dog collar and silver evening gloves to augment his stage clothes. At the same time he adopted a new surname. Adapted from a drug dealer acquaintance, Jim Popp, the transformation from gentle Jim Osterberg to Iggy Pop, wild rock star, was now complete.

After a couple of days rehearsal at SIR Studios, the band entered the Elektra studios on 11 May 1970. Every day they would walk the two blocks from the Tropicana, carrying their equipment and instruments. Their daily walk, all in a row, reminded Iggy of the Beatles crossing Abbey Road.

FUN HOUSE

Elektra EKS 74071. US release – August 1970. UK release – December 1970
Produced by **Don Gallucci**

Don Gallucci was assisted on the board by an English engineer, the flamboyantly named Brian Ross-Myring, more used to working with the likes of Barbra Streisand, and they spent the first two days getting the studio set up correctly. As they did so, the Stooges ran through a selection of their songs. Rykodisc issued *1970 – The Fun House Sessions* in 1999. Seven full CDs containing all the existing material taped at the *Fun House* sessions. It's a marvellous record of these two weeks containing umpteen takes of all the *Fun House* songs plus a couple of unfinished tracks that never made it past these sessions. Gallucci had been blown away by the energy of the Stooges shows he'd attended and he was keen to capture the scope and style of a typical Stooges gig, He opted to record the band as 'live' as possible. A PA was installed in the studio and instead of laying down individual tracks the whole band played at once, each instrument miked in the most natural way. This suited the Stooges perfectly as their lack of studio technique would have hampered any attempts to record the various instruments separately. The songs only really worked when played at full tilt. Gallucci also insisted that the order of the album should follow the order of the live set, as he rightly felt that each song built upon the previous one until the final climax of the big freak-out ending. This plan also pleased the band. Despite the age difference and Gallucci's 'square' appearance (his smart shiny suits had caused some consternation amongst the band when they first met him) the Stooges actually had a producer whose ideas matched their own.

Legend has it that *Fun House* was recorded entirely live in the studio, with no overdubs. The box set almost backs up this claim – it's clear that all the basic tracks were recorded live, but even Ron couldn't play two guitars at once and the finished album contains a number of guitar and vocal overdubs, notably on 'Loose'. Unusually, all the lead guitar work was recorded first with the bulk of the songs, and the rhythm guitar was filled in later with some judicious lead overdubs. This method of working suited Iggy too, as he preferred to sing live with the band.

Possibly the most astonishing revelation of the whole box set is that the Stooges reveal unerring consistency. For a band often written off as stoned morons the fact that they can fire off twenty-eight takes of 'Loose' one after another, nearly all of them good enough to make it to the album, says a lot for their professionalism and musicianship. The sessions demonstrate above all that the Stooges had made huge advances in the ten months since their previous studio work.

The listener cannot fail to be impressed by the consistency of the Stooges' playing. Time after time they run through their limited repertoire with surprisingly few mistakes. They are so good that almost every completed take could have been used on the final record. It's also intriguing to hear Iggy's ever-changing lyrics. He's honing the words as he goes along. Early versions of 'Loose' contain lyrics about Iggy's 'big hot weenie', which leaves little to the imagination, and '1970' initially runs with 'all night in a world that's lame' before later settling with the more familiar lyrics.

Space doesn't allow for a full run through of the *Fun House* sessions. Suffice to say that if you're a fan of *Fun House* it's well worth hearing these sessions at least once. If you're a diehard Stooges fan then you'll want to track down the box set but, as a limited run of only 3,000 copies, it's becoming rare.

For the more money-conscious Stooges fan, the recent 2005 reissue of *Fun House* contains twelve of the best performances from the box set, plus the single versions of 'Down On The Street' and '1970' on a bonus disc. Back in 2000, a one-disc limited-edition promo album called *Declaration Of War* also collated a selection of tracks from the sessions. Both discs contain different tracks.

For now, I'll restrict the commentary to the original *Fun House* record with some reference to the 2005 reissue bonus tracks.

Down On The Street

The album kicks off magnificently with this mid-tempo track. Propelled by Ron's chugging, snarling riff and Scott's perfectly captured drumming, this song powers along like a locomotive. The beat echoes the feeling of stomping along the street. Iggy claims he wrote the song hiding in a closet so as not to disturb his sleeping wife, though it's unlikely that the lines

about being 'lost in love' refer to Wendy. There are references to the 'Real O Mind' – a drugged out state of blissful nirvana that was the aim of many drug users at the time. The mantra-like lyrics, repeated over and over hint at this, as Iggy stakes his claim to be one of those down on the street 'where the faces shine'. Early takes reveal a different, less impressive set of lyrics. As Iggy would generally still improvise many of his lyrics on stage it's noticeable that most of the *Fun House* songs would have their lyrics honed and pruned to arrive at their final form during the sessions.

In fact, as in the Stooges live set, 'Down On The Street' was originally intended to be the second song on the album, but was switched at a late stage when Elektra decided that it would be better to lead the album with the track they had chosen as the single. The single itself, backed by an edited version of '1970' re-titled 'I Feel Alright', was issued without the Stooges' knowledge. In an effort to make it more commercial, a Doors-like organ had been overdubbed onto the edited song. Rumour has it that Don Gallucci was the organist and it's actually quite effective. As with the Stooges' previous single 'Dog', 'Down On The Street' did not unduly bother the charts.

Loose

Simply one of the most exciting Stooges tracks ever recorded, it is infectiously catchy and thrillingly electric. The energy injected into this song is all the more remarkable considering how many times they had played it. The album track is take number 28. After two days of recording almost nothing but 'Loose', they finally nailed the definitive version on 18 May, although for my money take 13 pretty much has it all too. Take 28 explodes out the speakers, as Iggy calls 'Now look out!' – Scott tumbles all over the drums and Iggy roars his approval. 'Loose' ended up with lyrics that were less explicit than the ones Iggy had originally sung, but were nevertheless still blatantly obvious – 'stick it deep inside' doesn't require much thinking to work out the meaning – but it's the cocksure exuberance and sheer energy that takes your breath away. Ron's gets to play a shattering solo and adds some carefully constructed overdubs as the songs pounds to a close. As with 'Down On The Street', and in fact all the songs on *Fun House*, many of the lyrics are repeated over and over achieving a tribal primitive quality. This also echoes the call and response effects generated by James Brown's singers.

Interestingly the main riff of Deep Purple's 'Smoke On The Water' recorded some eighteen months later, is not a million miles away from 'Loose'.

TV Eye

Initially known as 'See That Cat', the more familiar title apparently comes from a phrase used by Ron and Scott's sister Kathy. She had developed a code when out with her girlfriends to indicate when guys were checking them out. The phrase they used was Twat Vibe Eye – as in 'See that guy over there – he's got a TV Eye on me.' Iggy has also indicated a different – and probably more likely – point of origin. CBS television used to have a large eye logo that seemed to stare out of the TV at Iggy. He thought that was way cool – 'I could do something with that!'

Opening with another huge roar of 'Lord' from Iggy, this song pounds solidly for the next four minutes. Scott's drumming is astonishingly powerful and Ron has come up with yet another superbly circular riff that nags constantly in the left speaker. Dave's wandering bass is fascinating, seemingly playing his own song at times but always coming back. Iggy's vocals are sung in a throaty scream, which he somehow managed to keep up throughout all the takes. Some slight echo has been added. The lyrics are basic but effective, with every line repeated for maximum impact. Following the lascivious lead of 'Loose', the lyrics to 'TV Eye' are once again to the point and emphasise the callous disregard Iggy had towards groupies particularly and women in general at this time.

One of the most impressive parts of 'TV Eye' is the sudden breakdown after two and a half minutes. Both Ron and Dave pound just one note, in the background you can hear Iggy clearing his throat and screaming some more then, as Ron turns up the heat, Iggy returns with 'Ram It', repeated several times as the band does just that before slamming to a halt. Then Ron cranks up the riff again to lead the song to its conclusion. In concert this section would be thrilling, and on record it's just as breathtaking.

Early versions began with an amusing mock wrestling announcer called Red Rudy (played by Bill Cheatham, who sometimes performed the same role on stage) introducing 'Da Stooches'. Take 14 was the one used for the album, and was actually captured on the same day as the final and fifteenth take of 'Down On The Street', and the twenty-eighth attempt at 'Loose'. This hugely successful day, 18 May, occurred after a two-day jaunt to San Francisco to play at Bill Graham's Fillmore West. They headlined over Alice Cooper and the Flamin' Groovies and the show was attended by a group of drag queens, the Cockettes, who quite fascinated Iggy as he'd never met people like this before.

Dirt

This track originated with Dave Alexander and is Ron Asheton's favourite Stooges song. Take 12 made the album and was taped on 25 May. Dominated by Dave's strong but simple bass lines and Scott's rock-solid percussion, 'Dirt' allows Ron plenty of space to wail and prove how much he'd improved as a soloist since the first album. The imagery of burning and fire is echoed in Ron's smouldering playing, as Iggy once again states his defiant case against those who slate the Stooges. Iggy's burning inside so what does he care what you think? Iggy cleverly keeps the vocals to a minimum allowing the band to build the mood.

The song also gives the listener a breather after three pummelling songs. The downbeat mood is perfect for the end of the side. Oddly the big climax that you might expect doesn't ever happen. The song seems to meander slightly towards the end and then it just finishes. But this was quite intentional as all the other takes preserved in the box set do exactly the same. This lack of bombast sets the song apart, and arguably contributes to its longevity.

1970

In total contrast to the underplayed 'Dirt', '1970' roars out of the starting gate at full pelt. The album uses take 8, recorded on 20 May, to kick off side two with the jubilant cry of 'Outta my mind on Saturday night'. Whereas '1969' had reflected the bored and pissed off state of Iggy's mind the previous year, '1970' deserves its subtitle 'I Feel Alright', as it's a far more upbeat and positive track. Ron's riff rides upwards the whole time, Dave's bass does the same over Scott's identical drum pattern. They're all playing the same groove and will do so 'all night till I blow away!' Iggy shouts over and over, 'I feel alright' in a challenging guttural scream. Just when you think you've got the measure of '1970', Steve Mackay makes his killer entrance at the three-and-a-half-minute mark. With the tenor sax blasting out of the right speaker, the song is thrust into another dimension altogether. The band repeats the main riff for the rest of the song allowing Mackay space to do his thing and Iggy to ad-lib 'Feel alright', daring you to disagree. This was a new kind of music – neither rock, nor free jazz, nor funk, but a bizarre and frightening mixture of them all. With the addition of Steve Mackay, the Stooges had somehow stumbled across something quite unique. That Mackay, a far more accomplished musician than any of the Stooges, was happy to play this hybridised music says a lot for his generosity of spirit and desire to push boundaries. Although Iggy had intended the band to move into a freer style he cannot have been aware quite how much energy Mackay would bring. The fact that the reformed Stooges have recalled Mackay to perform with them from 2003 onwards speaks volumes about how much they value his contributions.

Fun House

Take 5, recorded on 22 May, was the one used on the album. It's the shortest take from the sessions – some of the earlier ones lasted well over ten minutes (take 3 featured Mackay cheekily quoting 'A Love Supreme'), and its compactness probably accounts for the decision to use this track. Nevertheless, there's more madness and thrills and sheer excitement in this one song than in whole albums by most other artists. The song kicks off at full pelt, with Steve blowing like a man possessed and Iggy whooping and hollering and exhorting the band to play harder and faster, ('blow Steve!!') eventually demanding to be allowed into the song. Scott hammers the loping funky beat and Dave somehow managing to anchor the song to Scott. Then there's Ron – his astonishing guitar squeals and screams and wriggles everywhere. You can't keep up as the guitar melds with the freeform sax. Certainly one of the most amazing song intros ever. The rest of the tune just doesn't let up. The energy is maintained at full tilt for the next mind-blowing 7.45 minutes of rock/funk/jazz fury.

The initial inspiration came from Dave Alexander, whose funky bass jamming was immediately latched onto by Scott. The guitar seems to be in solo mode for the whole song playing in and out of the rhythm and the icing on the cake is Mackay's amazingly cool sax. Again he's restrained into the right speaker as Ron's guitar strains to burst out of the left – bass and drums are dead centre and Iggy flies in over the top. For what was clearly a tremendously loud song, the instruments are beautifully recorded. Elektra's studio was state of the art for 1970 and Gallucci and Ross-Myring were expert at achieving a crystal clear sound. If listening to this song doesn't make you want to get up and shake and dance like a fool then you've got to be dead.

LA Blues

Most Stooges shows at this point ended with a freak-out – a deafening totally out-there climax to 'Fun House' as the whole band thrashed and screamed with all the energy they could muster. Trying to capture that power and sheer visceral excitement in the studio proved somewhat elusive. The problem was exacerbated by Gallucci's insistence on separating it from 'Fun House'. Creating the freak-out stone cold was pretty much impossible. Scott in particular couldn't get into it all and later overdubbed some extra drums to try to push the track further. None of the band was happy with the result. The full seventeen-minute freak-out jam that ended up on tape makes for sadly dull listening. After a few minutes, the limited fun to be had from listening to five guys thrashing and squealing and screaming and making as much 'free-form' noise as possible, palls. Steve Mackay's mad saxophone work is the most interesting part, Iggy's screams and whoops unfortunately become rather wearing. The edited five-minute version is slightly more palatable. The jam was retitled 'LA Blues' to reflect the fact that the band were getting homesick. Despite the band's misgivings, this is five minutes of noise, which has to be heard to be believed. It's way out there. Astonishingly the recorded version of the freak-out pales in comparison with what the band was doing onstage. They found it very hard to whip up the necessary level of energy to record the piece.

Iggy hoped that the piece would be used as the b-side of the single – he had visions of some poor soul seeing it on a jukebox and choosing 'some cool blues'. Then, of course, they'd get us!' Great idea – sadly 'LA Blues' remained as the final astonishing track on *Fun House*.

*   *   *

The album cover consisted of pictures of the band members taken by Ed Caraeff, merged and melded into one homogenous mass. Steve Mackay had his photo taken for the cover but it was decided that he was not yet a true Stooge and so his likeness wasn't used. Bathed in eerie red and orange light the pictures used by art director Robert L Heimall created an unforgettable image of a bare-chested Iggy, resplendent in his silver gloves, writhing around the rest of the band.

As the Stooges returned to Ungano's for a week of shows, *Fun House* was released on 18 August 1970, into a market dominated by the Doors' *Morrison Hotel* (also on Elektra) and softer hippy albums such as Neil Young's *After The Goldrush*. It sold respectably and only just missed the US Top 100. The American press generally loved it – foremost among the reviews was an astonishing 10,000-word essay by Lester Bangs published in *Creem*. Other reviewers were less wordy but no less enthusiastic. Ben Edmonds considered that the record went 'a long way toward capturing the emotional, if not the visual, content of a Stooges performance, and is also able to stand on its own as a recorded statement'.

Many reviews commented favourably on how far the Stooges had progressed since their debut and *Circus* even went as far as calling it 'the cosmic answer to *Let It Bleed*'. Across the Atlantic, the UK press hated it. *NME* referred to 'a tortured non-voice over repetitive riffs' but this was praise indeed compared with *Melody Maker's* 'muddy load of sluggish, unimaginative rubbish'.

The recent CD reissue features a selection of out-takes from the *Complete Fun House* sessions box. Two songs were recorded at these sessions that do not appear anywhere else – 'Slidin' The Blues' is a dirgy tune, thin on ideas, which appears to have cropped up when the band were idling. More

impressive, but sounding rather unfinished, is 'Lost In The Future'. Its similarity to the far better 'Dirt' accounts for the dropping of the song. Steve Mackay, as always, shines on this one.

Down On The Street – 1970 Concerts

The early part of 1970 saw the Stooges sharpening the *Fun House* songs before largely baffled audiences. They rarely played anything from the first album. In January, they played a couple of benefit shows on behalf of the Free John Sinclair campaign. Sinclair had been jailed for a massive ten years for possession of just two joints in what was clearly overkill by the authorities attempting to stifle his political and social ambitions.

In February, the Stooges returned to New York. A four-night engagement at the small but influential Ungano's club between 21 and 24 February attracted bags of publicity, but marked the very public beginning of the Stooges' drug problems. In an astonishingly cocky display, Iggy demanded $400 for cocaine, otherwise, he claimed, he'd be unable to perform. Even more astonishingly, Elektra's Bill Harvey gave him the money. The shows were a success, the band played hard and fast and the demonic energy, no doubt magnified by the sheer amount of cocaine ingested, emanated in waves from Iggy. During the freak-out conclusion Iggy exposed himself, intentionally, for the first time. Ron thought that he'd be arrested for sure. Amongst the audiences were Patti Smith and Lenny Kaye plus some of the guys who would later form the Ramones, Blondie and Suicide. The *New York Times* described the Stooges' music as 'one big noise that throbs… The audiences love it. They don't understand it. Neither does he [Iggy], most likely.'

After New York, the Stooges played some shows with Chubby Checker. This unlikely pairing had important consequences as Checker warned the band not to use producer John Madera. At one point Madera was a strong contender for the *Fun House* producer's chair, but Checker had fallen out with him badly and considered Madera to be a control freak.

Steve Mackay joined the band just before the Los Angeles sessions and his position in the Stooges strengthened when they returned to Detroit in June as they incorporated his sax playing more fully into the set. Unfortunately in just a few weeks, Detroit had changed. Cheap imported heroin had flooded the market and all the Stooges fell prey to it. Only Ron Asheton steered clear of junk and was therefore well placed to watch the sorry decline of the band – a decline that the others couldn't see.

At first, the Stooges were on a high – buoyed with the success of the sessions they played at the Crosley Field festival in Cincinnati. This huge event was televised by NBC, and the national broadcast allowed the Stooges into living rooms across America. Two songs were partly shown, '1970' and 'TV Eye', but the biggest talking point was the sight of Iggy walking across the outstretched hands of the crowd. Classic photos of the festival show Iggy held high above the audience, his arm pointing dramatically forward. Then Iggy turned the beautifully framed drama into farce as he was given jar of peanut butter which he proceeded to smear all over his chest, before flinging gobbets of peanut butter into the crowd. 'I guess I thought I was Jesus Christ, I just knew that if I walked out there I was just gonna walk across that crowd – it was a wonderful feeling.' To this day he has no idea where the peanut butter came from…

To emphasise the feelings of having 'made it' this was also the first night he stayed in a Holiday Inn and paid for it with earnings from his records. In 1998, he ruefully reflected his life hadn't changed that much since, except that the quality of the hotels had improved.

Further successes occurred at larger and larger festivals through the summer culminating with the huge audience of 100,000 people at the Goose Lake Festival at Jackson, Michigan on 8 August. After the show, Dave Alexander was told to leave the band. He had been getting more and more nervous and on the massive festival stage he simply froze and forgot all the songs. Somehow the show wasn't that bad – Iggy was exhorting the crowds to break down the fences between the audience and the stage. To stop Iggy causing utter chaos, the organisers tried to spin the revolving stage they had installed, but the Stooges' roadies fought back and the Stooges revolved back onto the stage where they finished their set. Iggy was however furious with the hapless Alexander and fired him as soon the band left the stage. Ron tried to defend his friend but Iggy was adamant that he didn't want to play with Dave any more. Dave's heavy drinking and drug intake had left him lethargic and uninterested and the other Stooges had been gradually sidelining him. Dejected, Dave Alexander returned home.

A few years later, his folks inherited a substantial sum of money, which Dave invested wisely on the stock market. In turn this generated even more money. Dave spent much of it on booze. He died on 10 February 1975 from a combination of malnutrition and septic ulcers, both exacerbated by too much alcohol. Dave met Ron only weeks before he died and seemed aware that he didn't have long to live.

With another set of dates lined up at Ungano's in August, roadie Tommy 'Zeke' Zettner was installed as a temporary bassist. Although Zeke, a six foot four giant, was well liked by all the band, his bass playing was rudimentary. Ron argued that a more accomplished bass player was really required, but as the heroin was taking hold of the others they couldn't really be bothered. They liked Zeke, he would do just fine. To allow Ron to concentrate on his increasingly complex solos, Bill Cheatham was also promoted from being a roadie to rhythm guitar player.

During the summer, Jimmy Silver gradually lost interest in the Stooges. He had become interested in natural food and went into business with friends in California. He had tired of trying to nursemaid the Stooges and felt that their worsening addictions were the last straw. Without his soothing influence the Stooges began to fall apart.

The Ungano's shows were notable more for what occurred offstage than on. Meeting and snorting cocaine with Miles Davis seems to be Ron's favourite memory. Davis attended a number of Stooges gigs ('They've got spirit' he was heard to say) and was hugely impressed with their electric mix of jazz and rock, a direction he too had been taking with albums such as *Bitches Brew*. The Stooges played the whole *Fun House* album, Iggy often singing from amongst the small crowd. The six-piece line-up expanded the sound impressively despite both Zeke and Bill's inexperience.

As the year wore on, Ron and Iggy stopped talking. Ron couldn't seem to shake Iggy or his brother out of their habits, and found that he had nothing to say to a junkie. Their behaviour grew more erratic, small fires would start as people nodded off whilst smoking. It fell to Ron, as the only relatively sober one, to be a fire marshall – 'I had to be on alert twenty-four hours and I'd make periodical sweeps of the house just to make sure it wasn't on fire.' The squalor was getting to Ron – he described how Scott's room at Fun House was the shooting gallery, dirty tiles spattered with blood from syringes; 'Such degradation… I was so disgusted.'

As a result of deepening addiction, the new songs started to dry up. Iggy began composing on his own, but in his junkie world the results were startlingly weird. The Stooges played a number of Iggy's bizarre tunes, closer to free jazz than anything else, during the autumn. None have ever surfaced although various titles have been bandied around for years – 'Big Time Bum', 'Way Down In Egypt' and 'I Got A Right' all debuted in late 1970. During soundchecks, Scott and various roadies would play their own songs – usually disgusting little ragged tunes that they found funny. One crossed over from this band within a band called Rock Action, to the main Stooges set – 'Searching For Head'.

By October 1970, Steve Mackay had had enough. He had come to the conclusion that leaving the band would be the only way to get off heroin. And he seriously thought that if he left it any longer he might never escape. Once out of the band he lost his connection and had to endure cold turkey which left him with terrible pains in his arms. Mackay would later form the Mojo Boogie Band. In 2003 he was invited to rejoin the Stooges where his incendiary playing is one the undoubted highlights of each gig.

Around the same time, Bill Cheatham backed out. Uncomfortable on stage and unsure of his ability, he preferred the life of a roadie. Ron had become used to a second guitar player though and began looking around for a replacement. He didn't look far before James Williamson cropped up again. He had been following the Stooges' progress and had attended many of the Detroit area gigs during the autumn. What he saw and heard of the Stooges unique style impressed him. James had of course played with Ron in the Chosen Few years before and was actually living with the Rock Action guys not far from Fun House. Ron was delighted, especially as James picked up the Stooges' style of playing very quickly. As James later noted, 'Things were pretty screwed up by then. The drug scene had started taking its toll and the band was disintegrat-ing… then one day Iggy asked me to join the band and take Bill's place. So, I began playing with the Stooges. Danny Fields was managing the band and he liked the way I looked and played, or so he said. So I was now a Stooge.'

It was immediately apparent that not only was James way better than Bill, but he could play killer lead as well as Ron. As James loved writing songs, he also quickly teamed up with Iggy, effectively sidelining Ron. Tired of attempting to compose alone, Iggy was enthused by James' arrival and set about writing a new set of tunes which dispensed with the loose jazz/funk vibe in favour of a tighter more straight-ahead rock feel. 'I knew from the first rehearsal with James that I had here something I could really use stylistically,' said Iggy. But James had joined at a bad time. After a set of gigs with James in November and December the Stooges decided to take a break in order to escape from their drug problems.

But, as with most great ideas that the Stooges had, it didn't go as planned.

1971

In early 1971, the Stooges began preparing for their third Elektra album. Sadly, most of the band members were in bad shape due to their deepening dependency on heroin. Iggy, James and Scott Asheton were now heavily mixed up in a dark crowd of dealers and low-lifes, which also included the MC5's Wayne Kramer. Soon after Christmas, James, Iggy and Scott moved into a high-rise apartment in University Towers, a block in downtown Ann Arbor. The reason was to be closer to their junk connection, right across the street at Biff's all-night diner, a popular haunt for dealers. There were even rumours that various Stooges had held up a gas station. The band did virtually nothing for four months except score drugs and sink further into heavy addiction.

Despite the drugs, the band, minus Zeke, regrouped in March to plan some live work. Possibly there was an ulterior motive – heroin addiction was expensive and none of the Stooges were wealthy. A new tour, and the possibility of a new record would generate funds. A proper booking company, the Diversified Management Agency lined up a series of gigs throughout the Midwest. The Stooges found that many venues were refusing to book them thanks to their reputation as wild and dangerous junkies.

The Stooges recruited Jimmy Recca to fill in for the departed Zeke on bass. Recca was an old friend of James and, as he too stayed out of the heavy drug scene, so James gradually withdrew from constant heroin use. Jimmy was far more competent than Zeke, and the new tunes that Iggy and James had been working on were sounding good; the twin-guitar attack of both Ron and James was especially effective. Danny Fields, now working at Atlantic, but also the de facto manager of the Stooges after Jimmy Silver's departure, persuaded Elektra executive Bill Harvey to see the band run through their new material. Fields was relieved that the band played well at their audition, but was crushed when Harvey declined to pick up the option of a third album. Harvey couldn't hear anything that would make an album worthwhile. With years of hindsight, Danny Fields agreed that the Stooges just weren't commercial enough. It was hard for Fields to manage the band from a distance – he was in New York, they were in Detroit. And it seemed as though the Stooges were content to stay in the gutter. Fields described the scene backstage at the Chicago Opera House. At this show, the Stooges supported Alice Cooper – just a year before the billing was the other way round, a measure of how far Cooper had come, or how little progress the Stooges had made. Danny Fields recalls: 'Come showtime and there would be the guys in Alice's band... being real professional – and then we'd have to go look for Iggy. And I'd find him lying there, down around the toilet bowl with a spike in his arm...'

The new songs took the jam aspect of the *Fun House* songs then pushed further into hard rock territory. The songs tend to hit a relentless groove then allow space for both Ron and James to solo. Iggy's lyrics were still tentative and improvised at this point. As with *Fun House*, they would probably only have been fixed as and when the band recorded them. Sadly a poor quality bootleg is the only record of tracks such as 'Fresh Rag' and 'You Don't Want My Name'.

The beginning of the end was the gigs at the Electric Circus in New York in May 1971. Iggy and Scott sold Ron's vintage Stratocaster for just forty dollars, which they spent straight away on smack. They told a heartbroken Ron it had been stolen, something he believed for a long time. 'Years later, my brother Scotty told me what really happened. Yeah, by the time of the Electric Circus gig I'd given up...'

At least the first night was a good solid gig, although by playing a whole set of unfamiliar material the Stooges were in danger of alienating the usually partisan New York crowd. The second night was a complete contrast. The gig was very late starting because Iggy's arms were so damaged that he couldn't find a vein. When he did arrive on stage, wearing only hot pants and smeared all over in silver glitter paint, Iggy knew he was going to throw up. According to Dee Dee Ramone he declared 'You people make me sick!' before vomiting. Later Iggy said, 'It was very professional. I don't think I hit anyone.'

The feeling of finality was strengthened by the fact that their home at the Fun House was about to be torn down to make way for a new road. Then Scotty drove a twelve foot six truck under a ten foot six bridge. At first Scott didn't know what had happened. He'd been thrown from the cab and when he looked back he saw that the truck clearly didn't fit under the bridge. Ron describes what happened at the Washington Street Bridge – 'Scotty was driving. He was doing like thirty-five miles per hour and BAM! It took the top right off – peeled back the top of the truck.' Scott and two roadies, Larry and Jimmy, were fortunately not seriously hurt. Larry had most of his teeth knocked out when he hit the dashboard and Scott had to have stitches in his chin and his tongue, which he describes as the worst pain ever. However, the truck and the instruments on board were wrecked, and both were rented. The bridge wasn't in good shape either. Danny Fields claims that the owners of the truck, the owners of the instruments and the city of Ann Arbor itself attempted to sue the Stooges. Many years later Scott said, 'You can look at the bridge even now and you can tell. That bridge is still fucked up.'

The first of the two shows at the Eastown Theatre had to be cancelled because of the accident. Instruments were borrowed for the next gig but Scotty was still unable to play. Ex-Stooge Steve Mackay gallantly stepped in to play drums. Although he was actually a reasonably good drummer, Iggy spent the whole show unfairly berating Mackay, who just stiffened up and got worse and worse until Iggy had to start telling him the beat. Poor Steve was so embarrassed that he refused his pay.

The final straw came in St Louis. After missing the gig at the Music Palace because their equipment truck arrived too late, the Stooges hastily agreed to a rescheduled show the next day. This was cut short after Ron was accidentally hit on the head by Iggy's mike, which caused the promoter to withhold payment due to the short set. Then they discovered that their rental car had been stolen during the show. They were stuck, penniless and without any transport in St Louis. Danny Fields did his best to wire them some money but it was too little too late and the band had to miss the next three gigs they had lined up.

With hardly any instruments and, after the bridge accident, no one willing to lend them any, the Stooges just fell apart. Knowing that Fun

House was about to be demolished, the band began to destroy their home by shooting the place up, until it was finally torn down. The *Ann Arbor Sun* reported that Iggy split the band on 1 August 1971. He disappeared to New York for a while. Ron and Scott went back to their mother's place where Scott attempted to clean up his habit. The year had begun quite promisingly but by August the Stooges had simply disintegrated.

*   *   *

The story of how Iggy Pop's career was restarted by David Bowie is one that's been told many times. After the Stooges fell apart in the summer of 1971, Iggy was taken under the wing of Steve Paul. He was a friend of Danny Fields and the manager of, amongst others, bluesman Johnny Winter and rocker Rick Derringer. Steve Paul had the idea that Iggy's stage presence would mesh well with the heavy musicianship of Derringer, and so paid for Iggy to come to New York. Iggy was happy to be paid to travel, and although he had no intention of working with Derringer, went along with the plan just to please his new sponsor. Out of politeness and respect for Derringer, Iggy did attempt a few rehearsals, but it was clear to both artists that there was no chemistry and no chance of this liaison working.

Whilst in New York, Iggy was bedding down on Danny Fields' sofa. Fields had a regular table at Max's Kansas City, a club frequented by the Warhol crowd. This was the main reason that Velvet Underground fan David Bowie visited Max's one night in August 1971.

David Bowie had been a cult artist in the UK for some years. He had begun his recording career in 1964, but had floundered during the 1960s, attempting a variety of musical styles, straight blues, mod, music-hall whimsy, and folk rock. Years of perseverance paid off in 1969 with a top ten hit for 'Space Oddity', a wonderfully ambitious single partially inspired by Kubrick's *2001: A Space Odyssey*. With typical and perverse wilfulness, Bowie switched styles again, embracing the emerging heavy metal movement on his brilliant album *The Man Who Sold The World*. The power trio that created this music was Mick Ronson on lead guitar, Woody Woodmansey on drums and producer Tony Visconti on bass. Bowie called them the Hype. As it turned out this would be a prophetic name. At the same time, Bowie acquired a dynamic new manager. Tony Defries was a London lawyer who helped Bowie get out of a previous management deal. The two hit it off straight away, Bowie realising that ambitious Defries had the potential to be Colonel Tom Parker to Bowie's Elvis. Defries set about building up a management team. With little previous experience of the music business, Defries took the unusual, but surprisingly successful, step of recruiting some of the Warhol crowd to his team, dubbed MainMan during the summer of 1971. He wisely realised that Bowie wanted to encourage outrageousness, and so the best way to promote this would be to employoutrageous people. Who was more flamboyant than a Warhol Superstar? Despite having no business experience, actor Tony Zanetta was appointed President of the MainMan organisation. Defries' strategy was that to become a star, you should act like a star, and then convince everyone that you were already a star.

Bowie had been singing the praises of the Velvet Underground since 1967. He had incorporated two of their songs into his live act and would later produce Lou Reed's second solo album, *Transformer*, in the summer of 1972. Although he didn't play their songs in his live sets, Bowie was just as big a fan of the Stooges two records. During the summer of 1971, Bowie and Defries planned their next moves. Bowie had already recorded most of his next album, the beautiful *Hunky Dory*, and he was eagerly planning the one after that. It would involve a fictional rock star called Ziggy Stardust. Ziggy's name was in part a direct reference to Iggy, at that time virtually unknown outside of America. Although he had never seen the Stooges in concert (apart from the film of the Cincinnatti Festival from 1970), David was eagerly talking to journalists of how his new stage act would be more outrageous than Iggy and the Stooges. Most of the British journalists probably didn't have a clue who he was talking about.

In August 1971, Bowie and Defries travelled to New York. There they took in an Ali fight, and spent some time at Max's Kansas City, as David wanted to meet the arty crowd. In turn, the New York glitterati wanted to meet David – he acted like a star, so he must already be a star...

Inevitably, Danny Fields met up with the Bowie crowd and, hearing David talk so enthusiastically about the Stooges, Fields immediately got on the phone to Iggy. Back in Fields' apartment Iggy was happily watching Jimmy Stewart in *Mr Smith Goes To Washington*. He was so into the film, 'practically in tears over Jimmy Stewart fighting these corrupt bastards and all that, so I didn't go down. So Fields called me about half an hour later, "Get down here, goddamn it!" I said, "When the movie's over..."'

Eventually, once the film had finished, Iggy wandered into Max's. Fortunately, Bowie and Defries were still there and warmed to Iggy straight away. Iggy quickly saw that Defries was something of a shark, and loved the fact that with his big cigars, Afro hair and fur coats he looked exactly like the American caricature of a top manager. He had the right image to get things done in the USA. Bowie was the new circus in town and Iggy wanted in. In return, Bowie wanted Iggy on side as he felt that the association with the ex-Stooge would give his fey English image a shot of genuine gritty American theatre.

The next morning, Iggy was invited up to Bowie's suite at the Warwick Hotel for a working breakfast. He was hungry and, after eating six breakfasts, he was signed to MainMan. At this point, it was just Iggy who was signed, although he still had dreams of reforming the Stooges. Defries suggested that Iggy could front Edgar Broughton's band World War 3, but thankfully this idea never went any further.

However, if Iggy thought his career would be kick-started straight away he was in for a shock. When Defries and Bowie returned to the UK, Iggy was forgotten for months. Too busy concentrating on the build-up to Ziggy Stardust, Bowie had no time for his new friend. Iggy spent a cold and penniless winter commuting between friends' couches and floors in both New York and Michigan. The other Stooges were similarly destitute. Ron and Scott Asheton were back home at their mother's place doing precisely nothing, and James Williamson had been laid low for months after a serious bout of hepatitis.

It was only after the *Ziggy* album was in the can and the resulting tour was well on the way to making Bowie a huge star, for real this time, that the MainMan organisation finally had time for Iggy Pop. He was asked to come to London to make a new record. It was March 1972.

1972

In March 1972, Iggy called up James Williamson and said he was off to London to make a record, and would James like to come too, as Iggy's songwriting partner? MainMan got a bit of a shock, as they thought Iggy would be on his own, but nevertheless decided to put Pop and Williamson up in the Royal Gardens Hotel. James and Iggy found themselves in the bridal suite. Unaware that a second bed could be folded down out of the wall James and Iggy had to share the pink bridal bed for a week or so. After nearly a month, to keep costs down, MainMan moved them to a rented house in leafy St John's Wood. Iggy remembers walking around the prosperous suburb in his leather jacket adorned with a cheetah's head – the one that can be seen on the back of the *Raw Power* album. This directly inspired the opening line of 'Search And Destroy', with its wonderful reference to being a 'streetwalking cheetah'.

During the spring of 1972, Iggy and James wrote new songs and auditioned musicians. Various members of the Pink Fairies or Mott the Hoople were suggested or tried out, but none proved suitable. They weren't aggressive enough for Iggy. It was James who suggested getting Scott Asheton over, as he was the most powerful drummer he could think of. And Iggy replied, 'If we're gonna get Scotty, might as well just get his bloody brother Ron and bring the whole can of worms over here and open it up.'

Ron and Scott had been mightily pissed off when they found that Iggy and James had gone to London. Back home with their mother, neither had done much since the break-up of the Stooges. Although they felt rejected by Iggy and James, and resentful that they hadn't been invited to London in the first place, the brothers nevertheless jumped at the chance to make music again. On 6 June 1972, nearly a year after the disintegration of the Stooges, the Ashetons arrived at Heathrow. Ron was slightly disappointed to be playing bass, but was kept happy by constant promises that it would only be temporary, until a suitable bass player could be found, when he would move to second guitar. Williamson, however, had no intention of relinquishing his position. The Ashetons were quickly added to the MainMan payroll. All four Stooges lived in the St John's Wood house, had access to unlimited taxis and rental cars and could charge drinks and meals to MainMan at various swanky establishments across London. It is unclear what Iggy was earning, but James, Ron and Scott were more than happy that they'd asked for and were receiving $150 per week, much of which was spent on hash. (Incidentally, Ron was astonished to find out that the Stooges were receiving at least twice as much as the boys in David Bowie's band, who in the summer of 1972, were probably the hottest musicians in the UK.)

Rehearsal time was immediately booked at RG Jones Studios in Wimbledon. There the band worked on the new songs Iggy and James had been writing. Faster and harder than anything the Stooges had done before, these new songs were impressively violent and nasty. Ron and Scott were as good as Iggy had known they would be and rose to the challenge of the material admirably. The band rehearsed constantly. With nothing stronger than hash to distract them, the Stooges were focused and intent on creating their best music. After a few weeks intensive practising the band moved to Olympic Studios. They were delighted to find themselves in the same studios that had given rise to major Rolling Stones' albums such as *Beggar's Banquet* and *Let It Bleed*. Iggy later said, 'The engineer was shit-hot at the time... Keith [Harwood] was a slammin' dashing young dude-about-town, making Stones records, in his Ferrari... It was good working with him.'

I Got A Right

The first results of the Olympic sessions were quickly apparent. This wonderful song, written entirely by Iggy, had first appeared in late 1970. The St Louis gig from May 1971, available on a number of semi-legal releases, opens with 'I Got A Right', powered by the twin guitar attack of Ron and James. Sadly this line-up of the Stooges never made it to the studio and most of the songs they performed at that point exist only on the terrible-sounding tapes of this show.

'I Got A Right' was one of the only tunes from the previous year that the Stooges attempted to record. At RG Jones, the song had been improved dramatically and transformed into a fast and fearsome slab of noise. Iggy would later claim that it presaged thrash metal, and he's not far wrong. 'I don't think anybody was doing anything like that before. I just remember that I wanted it really fast, dude.' Iggy had a certain sound in his head and was determined that the band should make the songs sound as insane as possible. Scott sounds like he's destroying his drums and Iggy simply screams the vocals. 'I Got A Right' is a very simple song. Basically a powerful and very straightforward statement of intent. There's a large Rolling Stones influence – on their 1969 tour of the USA the Stones reintroduced 'I'm Free' into their set and, as huge Stones fans, all the Stooges attended their Detroit gig on 24 November 1969. As 'I'm Free' begins with the gentle rallying cry of 'I'm free, to do what I want, any old time,' it's easy to see the starting point for Iggy's lyrics. Whereas Jagger's vocals are casually sung in his trademark mid-Atlantic stoned drawl, Iggy's delivery is so fierce, so angrily mad that it becomes a huge 'Fuck You' to just about anyone who would dare to listen.

For a long time it appeared that there were two basic studio versions of this track, one fast and the other even faster. However, the 1997 Bomp! CD single 'I Got A Right' appeared to collect six versions recorded on 19 and 20 July, although it's clear that the single contains just two main takes with various stages of vocal and guitar overdubs. The faster attempt has a lot of echo added to it, which somehow increases the manic energy, especially at the beginning as Iggy's thrilling 'Yeeooow' gets the song off to a flying start. Williamson's distorted yet powerfully controlled guitar work keeps the song rooted to the basic riff until a furiously harsh solo crashes in. It's short, but not especially sweet. *Heavy Liquid* contains the entire tape recorded on 21 July – fourteen attempts at 'I Got A Right' all of which are as dangerous as each other. This tape was a lucky find – Olympic was being refitted in the late 1980s and tapes were being junked. Fortunately somebody recognised one tape containing Stooges songs and took it to fan and record company owner Carlton Sandercock. As with the *Fun House* sessions, it is a fascinating insight into the workings of the band. Once again, we can hear how consistent and professional they were. Almost every attempt is good enough for release. Iggy, as with *Fun House*, recorded his vocals live, with the band playing hard alongside him. 'This sort of material could stand up and walk around the house before the overdubs,' said Iggy. The only overdubs, in fact, were James's scorching solos, over what must be one of the most energetic songs ever recorded.

After the recording, the Stooges surprisingly played 'I Got A Right' only once – at their sole UK show at the Kings Cross Cinema in July 1972. It was around this time that the band signed to CBS under the terms of the deal arranged by David Bowie's manager, Tony Defries. Unfortunately this was one of the many songs that Defries utterly hated. He persuaded the band that CBS would never release such violent tracks and so the Olympic recordings were abandoned. Whether the replacement songs that made up the eventual *Raw Power* album are any less violent is open to debate, but the tapes containing 'I Got A Right' and other songs were consigned to a storeroom. In 1977, the tapes ended up at Bomp! Records and 'I Got A Right' received its first release as a single, backed with the equally vicious 'Gimme Some Skin' from the same session. These two songs perfectly fit Iggy's description that this new music 'really grabs you and punches you around a little bit'. Coming at the height of punk, this five-year-old song, arguably more than anything else, contributed to Iggy being dubbed the Godfather Of Punk.

It was probably the release of the single that prompted Iggy to add 'I Got A Right' to the set list of the autumn 1977 *Lust For Life* tour. On stage, it would often follow a surprisingly coherent rant by Iggy about the dangers of drugs. A wonderful version from the tour appears on *TV Eye 1977 Live*; slightly slower and more majestic than the original, and featuring some brilliantly jagged guitar from Stacey Heydon. After 1977, tour the song was rarely performed and all but forgotten, until it was reworked as the opening number of the 1986 *Blah-Blah-Blah* concerts.

Since then 'I Got A Right' has become a staple part of almost every Iggy Pop gig. Now often played at an insanely fast pace, more than thirty years after its first performance this song is still as exciting a piece of rock as you'll ever hear. If you need a basic guide as to what Iggy is all about just listen to 'I Got A Right'.

Gimme Some Skin

Just as fast as 'I Got A Right' and even nastier. The barely comprehensible lyrics are screamed out in a feverish rush of expletives and deeply unpleasant imagery. Probably something of a blessing that the words are so hard to hear… Scott's rock solid beat and some surefooted bass from Ron, back Williamson's stuttering yet complex guitar.

Scene Of The Crime

A bit slower this time, this song's funky rhythm and stabs of harsh guitar mirror one of Iggy's roughest vocals to date. If he didn't have a sore throat at the end of this recording it was a miracle. 'Scene Of The Crime' is one of the more underrated songs from the 1972 sessions – the fact that it's not so rabidly insane allows the more musical side of the Stooges to become apparent.

I'm Sick Of You

One of the most impressive Pop/Williamson songs, and one of the best
Stooges tracks ever recorded. As this track shows an expert understanding of
composition and structure that goes way beyond that demonstrated on riff
rockers such as 'Gimme Some Skin', it's quite baffling that 'I'm Sick Of You'
was rejected by Tony Defries along with all the other Olympic recordings. Of
course, the fact that the second half is actionably identical to the Yardbirds'
'Happening Ten Years Time Ago' may also have contributed to it being
dropped. Such a shame, though, as it was undoubtedly the most mature piece
of music then recorded by the Stooges. Ron's bass ebbs and flows like a boat
in a storm during the gentle and delicately played guitar intro. Iggy croons
his paean to Betsy, a girlfriend he'd known in Ann Arbor in 1970. She was
apparently only thirteen at the time – a fact recorded in the song 'Dog Food',
allegedly written in 1970 but not recorded until 1980's *Soldier*. Betsy inspired
another song, nearly twenty years later, 'Candy' on *Brick By Brick*.

Iggy has rarely shied from the truth, and rarely changes the names to
protect the innocent. Whether he obtains permission to write about these
people is unclear – but it's unlikely. So Betsy is named in 'I'm Sick Of You' –
Iggy's going away, partly because he's sick of Betsy, her mum and her dad.
Sad but true.

Halfway through, and without warning, the Stooges throw caution to the
wind, crank everything up, Spinal Tap-style, to eleven and rock like hell with
the Yardbirds' tune. It's quite relentless – Ron plays some blinding bass runs,
Scott clatters and crashes like a man possessed, James gets to do a Jeff Beck
screamer of a solo and Iggy just screams. It's a truly exhilarating ride. The
gentling of the intro returns for the moody coda.

Tight Pants

A great piece of studio chat introduces this short and snappy, even
commercial-sounding song. With its grinding guitar and chirpy handclaps
it's surprisingly catchy and is far more upbeat in tone and mood than any of
the other new songs. Defries suggested that the lyrics could do with being
changed, and with minor alterations 'Tight Pants' became 'Shake Appeal'.

Down On The Street – 1972 Concerts

The 1972 tour consisted of just one show at the Kings Cross Cinema,
renamed the King's Sound for live music, in London on 15 July. Mick Rock,
fast becoming one of London's top music photographers had been asked to
shoot the gig by MainMan. In the week before the show, he met with the
band in their rented house and at the rehearsal rooms. He took hundreds of
photos, many of which were published many years later in the marvellous
book *Raw Power*. Bare-chested, covered in glitter, his nails painted black,
skintight silver lamé trousers and streaks of silver in his hair – this was Iggy
at his most visually aware. To complete the look, a beauty spot was added to
his cheek. The rest of the band doesn't get a look in. The camera dwells
almost exclusively on Iggy. One of the shots was chosen many months later
to be the cover photo of *Raw Power*. Although Rock wasn't snapping with an
album cover in mind, it became one of the most individual and strikingly
recognisable cover photos ever.

The gig itself consisted of one short hard set – forty minutes of new material, nothing from *Fun House* or the first album, nothing in fact, that anyone in the audience had ever heard. During an electrical fault, Iggy sang Sinatra's 'The Shadow Of Your Smile' unaccompanied. At other times he would crash into the audience, assaulting the crowd. London had never experienced a show like this before. It represented the only time the Stooges ever played the Olympic songs in concert. None of them would be played when the Stooges returned to active service the following year.

After the gig, the band were told that the new songs were unacceptable for release and that further studio time had been booked so they could come up with more palatable material. They spent August working on new songs ready for the next set of sessions scheduled to begin on 10 September.

RAW POWER

Columbia KC32111. US release – May 1973. CBS 65586. UK release – June 1973.
Produced by **Iggy Pop**

'I knew it was gonna finish my career commercially,' Iggy commented, but it was an album he had to make. Once under way, the sessions progressed quickly. The eight songs that made up *Raw Power* were captured on tape within a couple of weeks in late September 1972 at the CBS London studios. A number of rough mixes have made their way out on bootlegs and semi-legitimate albums. Mostly these are just alternate mixes of the same tracks but there are a number of songs which contain different vocals and early lead guitar overdubs. The backing tracks, however, all seem to be the same as the finished album. Legend has it that the *Raw Power* tapes were virtually unsalvageable, as Iggy, unused to the finer techniques of the recording studio had used only three tracks – one for the vocals, one for James' lead guitar, and one for the rest of the music. Bowie later confirmed this and pointed out how hard it was to mix the album. Although it's well known that 'Tight Pants' was rewritten as 'Shake Appeal', it's worth pointing out that the earlier track contains the exact same backing track as that on 'Shake Appeal', even down to the guitar overdubs. Which implies that at least some of the *Raw Power* songs originated from the Olympic sessions. It also points to the fact that the tapes were in nowhere near as bad a state as history would have us believe.

When the sessions ended, each band member was given a set of rough mixes. By the autumn, the Stooges were all back in the States, waiting to hear when the record would be released and when they could tour the new songs. Ron soon tired of waiting, and wanted people to hear the new material. As CBS hadn't even set a release date, Ron took his tapes to WABX radio in Detroit. This station had always been supportive of the Stooges and in late 1972 happily played the rough mixes which promised an album of real fire.

Iggy mixed the album as soon as the recording was finished, but he was frazzled from the recording process and desperate to make the record sound as extreme as possible. With hindsight, he wished he had taken a break, then returned to the tapes refreshed but, in his quest for the ultimate rock album, the most extreme sound, the craziest record ever, Iggy at first refused to let anyone near the tapes. He claims he even slept with the tapes. The result was a mess, which Tony Defries and CBS thought was unsuitable for release. As it had been David Bowie who had insisted that Iggy be signed to CBS, so it was to Bowie that CBS turned when confronted with the first draft of *Raw Power*. The record company insisted that something be done to remix or rerecord the songs to bring them up to what they considered a releasable standard. In between dates on his first US tour, Bowie booked two days at Western Sound Studios in Hollywood. Iggy reluctantly agreed because he realised that otherwise his album would never come out. David and Iggy's 'mixing' on 24 and 25 October 1972 mainly seemed to consist of pushing the lead vocals up a bit, cutting some of the backing vocals altogether, and oddly suppressing the bass and drums, which at times almost lost Scott's impressive rhythms altogether. The lead guitar was emphasized too, sometimes so much that it shrieked louder than the vocals, louder than everything. James's guitar sharply attacks everything, cutting loose from the speakers. Some intriguing echo effects were added using a gizmo called a Time Cube. The main beneficiary was 'Penetration' which now seemed to have a second drum track, slightly out of phase with everything else. Some effective reverb was added to Iggy's voice on a couple of other songs. Bowie has since joked about how little he actually did but his changes, whilst not to everyone's taste, certainly altered the overall sound of *Raw Power* quite dramatically.

The net result was an album that was extremely heavy on the treble, shrill, scratchy and harsh. Whether it sounded any better than Iggy's original version is a moot point. At the time, Iggy loyally praised his friend's efforts, but the rest of the Stooges hated it. Ron stated in 1973 – 'That fucking carrot-top ruined that record. I know what it could have been,' and later made further disparaging remarks about the 'cocaine artsy-fartsy mix'. James was more philosophical – 'We tried to mix it ourselves, but I didn't know about it [mixing] at that time and Jim didn't either... so we ended up with a just a big bunch of crap. I don't think Bowie did justice to it either, but it was too late.' Certainly the Bowie mix had a detrimental effect on the rhythm section, which comes out sounding very weak. The early mixes broadcast by WABX have been bootlegged numerous times and reveal a mix much closer to Iggy's 1996 reworking. The bottom end is much more dense, there are more backing vocals and the whole album is more listenable. Although Bowie's mix was the definitive one for 23 years it has become apparent since Iggy's 1996 remix that the version released in 1973 was severely hampered by the mixing technology of the time and that Ron Asheton's assessment has proved to be correct.

However, even the neutered Bowie mix makes for an extreme album. Upon its release in May 1973, nine months after recording, *Raw Power* garnered some impressive reviews and was generally praised as being a worthy successor to the first two Stooges albums. *Creem*'s Dave Marsh loved it: 'The band accelerates beyond anything that's been recorded, or played live or even dreamed of, in years...' *Let It Rock* bizarrely let *Raw Power* share a review with Mike Oldfield's beautiful hippie dreamwork *Tubular Bells*, but praised the album as the 'best high energy record since *Kick Out The Jams*'. Lenny Kaye, writing in *Rolling Stone* and obviously unaware of the problems incurred in mixing the record, especially liked the 'ongoing swirl of sound... guitars rising and falling, drums edging forward and then toppling back into the morass'. Even *Billboard* pointed out that, although the Stooges were a visual act, 'they manage to push their brand of deviant rock well on disk.' In the UK, Bowie's mix often came in for praise; in retrospect this seems surprising, but it must be remembered that in 1973 Bowie could do no wrong. The *NME* somewhat sycophantically referred to his 'expertise as master of sound'.

The cover also contributed to the album's legendary status. At the time, the band hated the cover, which was put together without their input. *Raw Power* was credited to *Iggy and* the Stooges, which relegated the others to just a backing band, and all the cover pictures reinforced this idea by not portraying the rest of the band. The monster-movie-style dripping letters were the last straw. In retrospect the glorious cover shot by Mick Rock has come to be seen as one of the most iconic album covers of all time. Partly due to the cover picture of Iggy in his mascara, silver hair and silver lamé pants, and partly because of the Bowie connection, *Raw Power* was seen as another glam rock album, in the same vein as Lou Reed's *Transformer*, or Mott's *All the Young Dudes*, or Bowie's *Aladdin Sane*. Never mind that all of these albums contained relatively commercial songs, some of which had been big hit singles. *Raw Power* had nothing remotely close to a Top Twenty hit, was resolutely not commercial and what's more, it really didn't care. Listening to *Raw Power* was hard work. *Creem* featured a great cartoon showing a shell-shocked audient rooted to his chair. His friend asks 'So what did you think of *Raw Power* then?' This was the public perception of the album, that it was so shocking and so extreme. Four years later, the Sex Pistols' album *Never Mind The Bollocks...* would garner the same reactions. More talked about than bought, *Raw Power* became one of the albums you had to own to make a statement.

During the 1990s, Sony set the Columbia/Legacy arm of their huge organisation the task of reissuing classic albums in the best possible version. Tapes would be cleaned up, bonus tracks added, new sleeve notes written and photos found – producer Bruce Dickinson would oversee many of these releases. One such project was to be *Raw Power* but, wary of the criticisms levelled at the existing mix, Sony sought to go one further than just a straight reissue, they intended to remix the tapes.

Iggy had been asked to remix *Raw Power* many times before, and he had complained himself about how bad the original CD transfer sounded, compared to the original vinyl. But he had always resisted changing the album, claiming that he didn't like the idea of altering history, or exhuming his old work. After hearing some of the rough mixes from 1972, Henry Rollins declared that he would like a chance to remix *Raw Power* too. But it was only after Sony decided to remix and reissue the album, with or without his input, that Iggy decided he would have to get involved. Being told that he'd be able to get the record to sound the way he'd always wanted proved irresistible and so Iggy, together with mix engineer Danny Kadar and supervising producer Bruce Dickinson, finally got to rework *Raw Power*.

Iggy's new mix produced what is surely one of the most consistently loud records ever. According to Iggy's enthusiastic sleeve notes, the rationale was very Spinal Tap: 'Why isn't that meter in the red...with the rest of those meters!' Sony were a bit freaked by the first attempts – 'It sounded like the speakers were gonna explode, bleeding and melting and distortion' – so they tried what Iggy called a 'nice' mix which clearly didn't work. 'They were

embarrassed,' laughed Iggy. So Iggy's all-the-way-up, everything-in-the-red mix was brought down just half a decibel, which suited everyone. Iggy's intention was to create a record that could stand up against 1990s music and win. In that, he certainly succeeded but, as a lasting legacy, I'm not sure the 1996 Iggy mix is entirely successful.

For a start, the new mix creates a horrendously violent-sounding album, lacking the little subtlety that the Bowie mix had. Whereas the original version had shades of dark and light, strange fluctuations in both the mix and the volume of some instruments, this new mix is completely in your face the whole time. The new version screams non-stop the whole time. Even 'Gimme Danger' seems to have lost its air of restrained menace; in its place is more totally upfront confrontation. That's not to say I don't like it, because I do, but listening to the whole of the new *Raw Power* is now an utterly exhausting process. It's one which, although exhilarating and thrilling for the duration of the album, doesn't make me want to play it all that often, as it's just too draining. The original version, however, doesn't have that effect on me. Ron Asheton agreed, finally admitting in 1998 that after all this time he really did prefer the old Bowie mix.

Search And Destroy

With a terrific blast of guitar, 'Search And Destroy' kicks off the album in stunning style and almost immediately wrong-foots the listener when the original rhythm track is suddenly overtaken by seriously overdriven guitars playing what at first seems to be a totally different song. As the track progresses you realise that it does actually all fit together but after just six seconds it's clear that you won't be able to take anything for granted. James Williamson's sound is not far from Keith Richards' coruscating, raw guitar on 'Sympathy For The Devil' but it's taken to another level entirely. It seems to be one fiery solo after another, or rather on top of each other.

The basic tune was written at the Wimbledon rehearsal studio and for a while existed as 'RG Jones', named after the studio. Along with the basic riff from 'Penetration' and 'Tight Pants', these were the only tunes that Defries allowed them to bring from the summer rehearsals. Various early mixes emphasise the shouted 'Hey!' backing vocals and there appears to be a weird little effect after the line 'using technology'. Iggy claimed he wanted a more militaristic boot camp style and, in an attempt to achieve this, had arranged to record the sounds of a swordfight! The early mix also carries a lot more echo and reverb compared with the released version. Scott is playing some fantastic drums but Bowie's mix makes it sound as if he's playing across town somewhere, and Ron is almost nowhere to be seen. It's a shame, as they played together extremely well, locking tight into the groove, as Iggy pointed out, as only brothers can.

After the second lead guitar has trashed the original, the song simply powers along, Iggy singing at the top of his range, the vocals nailed in one take. The title came from a *Time* magazine article about the Vietnam war, but the song is not about Vietnam despite its throwaway references to firefights and napalm. It's about Iggy, the American lost in London, the world's forgotten boy in a leather jacket with a cheetah emblazoned on the back. Iggy loved the Yardbirds' song 'Heart Full Of Soul' and wondered what his heart was full of. Napalm was the answer he came up with. So he wrote about that. The imagery suited the killer guitar sound and the intense power of the band. 'Somebody gotta save my soul,' he shrieks at one point, but he doesn't sound like he means it. He doesn't want to be saved. Iggy sounds happy in this violence, proud of who he is and what he's doing. 'Search And Destroy' opens the album with this 'Here I am, back again' attitude – defiant against those who had written Iggy off.

Gimme Danger

The original Bowie mix virtually knocks out the drums altogether, although it does contain a lot more light and shade. The quieter intro with the guitar on the left and everything on the right is effective and, as when Iggy starts singing and then the electric guitar begins on the second verse, they are both mixed right down the middle. The gentle intro contrasts strongly with the electric second half, whereas the remix is simply loud (possibly too loud) the whole way through. There's a piano in there somewhere too and a number of different interlocking leads over the end section, both elements that are lost in the 1996 remix. Written about the girls he was meeting who seemed to bring trouble with them, Iggy found he had a love/hate relationship with the girls he met in London. The worse they were the more he was attracted to them. So he wrote about that.

Iggy's vocals are often compared to Jim Morrison's, and nowhere is the comparison more appropriate that on 'Gimme Danger'. That dangerous croon owes quite a debt to the Lizard King. A reference to the 'ocean breeze' is the signal for James to let loose the guitars he's been holding back. The second half has Iggy seemingly improvising lyrics. The first couple of verses sound like a sort of slightly twisted love song but the second half turns into something darker, hinting at unappetising misogynistic violence.

Your Pretty Face Is Going To Hell [originally titled 'Hard To Beat']

Apparently about a girl named Johanna with whom Iggy had a brief but intense relationship soon after he arrived in London. According to legend, she would tease Iggy whilst having sex by running off at the crucial moment – 'She wasn't a nice girl.' She was later to inspire the 1973 song 'Johanna'. Obviously, even years later, the relationship still resonated as Iggy would often introduce both songs with comments about her, along the lines of 'She spent all my money on heroin, but I still loved her,' or 'This is called "Your Pretty Face Is Going To Hell" – she deserved it, she was a real piece of shit.' He has also commented on how it was directed at Johanna along the lines of 'You're pretty now, but just wait, you're not gonna have that weapon all the time.'

At some point in the remixing 'Hard To Beat', was renamed, though the album always carried the original title in brackets. Bowie's mix takes out a layer of guitar overdubs which were present on the rough mixes. Interestingly it seems that a slightly different set of guitar overdubs were used on the 1996 remix, especially towards the conclusion. At least you can hear the Ashetons on Bowie's mix, and on the remix Iggy boosted the brothers' excellent rhythm section even further. Their solid and unchanging groove is as powerful and unstoppable as a locomotive and is crucial to the song's success. James seems to be playing one big solo throughout, his guitar

squealing and crunching everywhere, never repeating himself. The song is one of the key tracks on *Raw Power* in that the furious power of the Stooges at this time is finally captured on tape. None of the other album tracks quite match 'Your Pretty Face…' in terms of naked primal force.

Penetration

The Bowie mix is probably the one to beat, with its very successful echo effect on the drums almost creating a second beat fractionally behind the first. Another disconcerting quirk of 'Penetration' is that Iggy's vocals are really high in the mix which has the effect on headphones of sounding as if Iggy is right beside you. The early mixes benefit from some extra shakers and more obvious 'whoo whoo' backing vocals, which owe their origin to those on 'Sympathy For The Devil'. The 1996 mix sadly loses the drum echo but surprisingly boosts the celeste, which plays that incessant rising motif throughout the song. It's a weird little touch, unusual for the Stooges, and was simply incorporated after James found the instrument in the studio one day.

The chugging riff that starts the song continues throughout. Although the song isn't obviously about sex – the title refers to penetrating people, breaking down barriers – Iggy's breathless vocals are nonetheless marvellously sleazy. The song originated the previous autumn after Iggy had been offered the MainMan deal. Visiting the sick James one day, the pair came up with the basis of this song which proved to Iggy that working with James would be the way forward. All the songs on *Raw Power* were credited solely to Pop and Williamson – this left them open to accusations, mainly from the Ashetons, that the duo were on some sort of Jagger and Richards trip. Despite helping to shape the tunes the brothers received no credit whatsoever.

Raw Power

The rhythm guitar holds the song together as James rides that stuttering riff constantly – 'the beat of the living dead'. What is surprising listening to the original after years of live performances, is quite how restrained and tight-assed the studio track is. The raw power is oddly rather repressed on this track, unlike the wild abandon and insane screaming of 'Your Pretty Face…' or 'Search And Destroy'. It always seems to be on the verge of breaking into something else, which makes it all the better when, at the three-minute mark, James stops holding back and lets out a solo which screams and distorts and threatens, once again, to consume everything in its path. The other notable feature is the nagging one-fingered piano part, which is partly recycled from 'I Wanna Be Your Dog' and which Bowie would steal for 'The Hearts Filthy Lesson' in 1995.

The lyrics are some of Iggy's best up to this point. Lengthy and direct, they indicate what pushes Iggy onwards: Raw Power. It's the basis of everything Iggy does, the unseen force that inspires and frightens him. There are echoes of 'I Got A Right' as Iggy declares his right to do whatever he wants. The original mixes contains long 'ooohs' under the guitars and Iggy's vocal is treated with more echo, which Bowie erased. Other than that the Bowie mix, the 1996 remix and the WABX rough mixes all seem much the same.

When the Stooges returned to the concert stage, the song would open every show, its repetitive riff played for as long as it took Iggy to decide to start singing. Iggy would open many of his later shows with 'Raw Power' too, and with few exceptions it's been played on almost every tour since. No matter which musicians Iggy shares the stage with, 'Raw Power' almost always sounds the same. Nothing defeats the song, nothing can harm its inner spirit. It's always the same powerful declaration – Raw Power. Can't be beat.

I Need Somebody

As the second track on the second side, 'I Need Somebody' repeats the 'Gimme Danger' trick of starting slow and gentle with the acoustic–electric mix. As a mutant blues, it owes a fair bit to classic tune 'St James Infirmary'. It had originated the previous summer in the final days of the Stooges, but it appears that the song had never been properly finished. The music is slow and mournful, and the vocals carry an air of resigned hopelessness. The song would be played at nearly all the 1973 concerts in a vastly extended and even more relentless form. Scott would anchor the band to his dead beat and James would be able to play his twisted version of the blues. An impressive, though oddly unlikeable, song.

All the various versions are much the same, except that, as with all the songs, the 1996 remix turns everything up to the max.

Shake Appeal

Recycled from 'Tight Pants', and almost certainly the same recording as the earlier tune, 'Shake Appeal' is, alarmingly for CBS, the most commercial song on the album. The rising jumpy guitar pattern and the cheesy handclaps propel the song in a wonderfully upbeat manner which is a relief after the depression of 'I Need Somebody'. The title refers to Iggy's love for rough and ready early rock 'n' roll – Link Wray, Little Richard, Jerry Lee Lewis – 'stuff that ROARS' as Iggy notes.

The rough mixes allow the song to reach its natural conclusion, whereas the official versions fade just before the three-minute mark. The Bowie mix adds a bit of echo on Iggy's super-loud vocals, which dominate the song totally. The super-heavy solo is also astonishingly loud and utterly drowns out everything else. Thankfully, it's a brilliant monster of a solo that leaves the listener utterly breathless when it suddenly cuts out.

Death Trip

The song's title came from Iggy's awareness that the album was doomed from the start. Although he totally believed in the record and was totally convinced that this was the best he could do, he knew many people wouldn't like it and that it wouldn't be promoted, so it wouldn't sell. He was quite right. It's as unstoppable as 'Your Pretty Face...' and to end the album with such a song was simply a gesture of defiance. It's an awesome song, in the most literal sense. There's an all-pervading feeling of malevolence, a feeling that the song itself means you harm, wants to inflict pain and suffering.

Bowie tried to make the song more interesting by playing around with the lead overdubs, turning the guitar up to a painful level, then making the killer guitar flip from speaker to speaker. This makes the stupendously shrill and nasty guitar sound like a dentist's drill attacking the listener from all sides. It's quite fitting, however, for a song called 'Death Trip'. The drums and bass are,

sadly, very quiet, as if the multiple layers of guitars have literally buried poor Ron and Scott. The song also fades out surprisingly quickly which makes for a very unsatisfactory conclusion to the album. Rapid fades like this would strangely dog Iggy albums in the future (the sudden demise of 'Fall In Love With Me' creates the same sense of anticlimax on *Lust For Life*). Iggy's remix at least restores the ending, properly played out as the intro riff returns to drive the song home. The remix also thankfully reduces the pain level from James' guitar overdubs, integrating them more into the body of the song.

*   *   *

On a personal note, I remember buying *Raw Power* in 1981. As a Bowie fan, I'd got both *The Idiot* and *Lust For Life* and was ready for some more Iggy. So I chose *Raw Power* as it still had a (vague) Bowie connection. But it was only stocked in the dingiest record shop in town – Parrot Records. It was dark, there were large, tattooed, hairy, leather-jacketed men sitting on the floor smoking intriguing-smelling cigarettes and the whole shop was hugely intimidating to this skinny fourteen-year-old schoolboy.

One lunchtime, I plucked up the courage to venture in. Feeling very out of place in my school uniform, I sifted through the albums in the big wooden racks and finally found *Raw Power*. As I took it to the counter, I felt the gaze of the various heavy dudes hanging around the shop. 'He's buying *Raw Power*' was the general buzz. The long-haired biker type behind the counter looked approvingly at my choice '*Raw Power* eh?' I'd already worked out my next move and as casually as I could said 'Yeah, and I'm going to get *Metallic KO* next,' a statement which was met with another rumble of approval from the guys on the floor. I was 'in'. For quite a while after that, whenever I shopped in Parrot, someone would mutter, 'That's the kid who bought *Raw Power* and *Metallic KO*.'

1973

The year began on a high note for the Stooges. They had a powerful album awaiting release, they had a dynamic management team who had promised that when the time was right the Stooges would be catapulted to stardom, and they were living on Torrenson Drive in the Hollywood Hills. Paid for from MainMan's seemingly bottomless coffers, the luxurious house was a typical Hollywood retreat. Ron Asheton's description is like something out of rock star heaven: 'Naked girls in the pool, Cadillac in the driveway, maids, plenty of pot...'

Leee Black Childers, as MainMan's representative, was instructed to stay with the Stooges as a minder/chauffeur/gofer. Living in a separate apartment over the garage for several months, Childers' main job soon became 'trying to keep him [Iggy] straight, but he was too quick for me. With all the roadies, groupies and band members hanging around, I could never cut off his supply.' Despite being friends with the band for some time Childers was unaware of the extent that a junkie will lie and steal to get his next fix. Childers also had to learn to swim pretty fast as Iggy would regularly fall into the pool while stoned. The rest of the Stooges, already tired of his destructive behaviour, would just ignore Iggy floating face down and it was down to Leee, a non-swimmer, to rescue his star attraction. There were other ugly scenes. Sable Starr, the famous LA groupie, lived at the house for some weeks, dividing her attention between Iggy and Ron. On one occasion, she ended up in the pool after cutting her wrists and Leee had to rescue her too. Another time she attempted to slash her wrists again – a somewhat fruitless attempt as she had tried to use Ron's safety razor.

Despite the lifestyle, the future was looking bright for the Stooges as they waited for Tony Defries to say the word. And they waited. And waited some more. CBS was still delaying the release of *Raw Power*, unsure of how to market it. During the early part of 1973, the band spent some time dutifully rehearsing and working on new songs, but with no gigs lined up there was the sense that they were practising for nothing.

Defries had told them to wait until interest had built up, but how could that happen when the album wasn't being released? The band soon became despondent. And when that happened they turned, once again, to drugs. Ron had been happy with his regular supply of pot but the other Stooges gradually returned to harder drugs. Usually this meant that band were dragged down into the mire of dealers and hangers-on. Occasionally though, the funny side showed through. Iggy related a marvellous story to Alvin Gibbs about the day he nearly gassed himself. After being up all night on a frightening combination of pills Iggy had decided he was hungry. He turned on the gas oven, grabbed a couple of burgers and knelt to put them in. At this point he realised he need a match to light the gas, but experienced some kind of muscular seizure. Unable to move a muscle, kneeling in front of the gas oven with a burger in each hand, Iggy was sure that before long the gas would render him unconscious and, as his head was bound to fall into the oven, when he was found it would look like suicide. Fortunately, before this could happen, someone smelt gas and rescued him. But if they hadn't, mused Iggy, 'What the fuck would they have made of the burgers?'

Defries' avowed strategy was to talk up the Stooges' reputation in order to drum up demand for the band. It was a strategy that had worked in the USA for David Bowie. Back in September 1972, Bowie had been virtually unknown in the States. Yet Defries boldly booked an extensive tour, at relatively large venues. Somehow RCA were persuaded to fund a massive entourage and to pay for the best hotels. So Bowie's first American tour looked like a huge success and he appeared to be a huge star, when in fact neither were actually true. Inspired by Warhol, the MainMan team believed that if they *acted* like stars then they would *become* stars. And to an extent this strategy actually worked. By the end of 1972, Bowie was at least well known in all the right circles and was treated with the respect accorded to a successful star, even though his record sales did not reflect his status.

Iggy claims that they kept asking Defries when they were going to be allowed to perform, but every time the MainMan president would fob them off with platitudes. Iggy has said that he never really understood Defries' strategy pointing out that he had been to shows by Bowie or Mott the

Hoople that had been sparsely attended – where was the demand for them? Yet Defries had still pushed Bowie out on tour. Defries clearly thought less of the Stooges. He was very aware that they had only got their record deal because of Bowie's influence, and the fact that CBS had refused to release *Raw Power* until it had been remixed, by Bowie, implied that they too thought little of the band. Defries' energy and drive were primarily devoted to building and maintaining Bowie's success. David was a far more marketable and mainstream artist. This was where the money was. A scruffy, drugged-out band from Detroit did not seem a very bankable option. So it was clear that, having signed the Stooges, Defries really had no idea what to do with them. There was also little inclination to try, as the band themselves appeared to have little ambition and were not really hassling for attention.

In March 1973, Defries relented slightly and arranged a homecoming gig at the prestigious Henry Ford Auditorium in Detroit. The Stooges were thrilled and booked some time at Morgan Sound Studios in Ypsilanti for final rehearsals. It was at this point that they also decided to augment their sound. James apparently vetoed the use of another guitarist arguing that a pianist would be a valuable addition, broadening the overall sound of the band. With little time before the gig, Iggy called up Bob Scheff. Iggy had known Scheff in the Prime Movers and, since then, Scheff had been a regular on the Detroit scene, often using the name 'Blue' Gene Tyranny – indeed as 'Blue' Gene he continues to play his own brand of avant-garde jazz piano to this day. Scheff had little to do on some numbers, but the bar-room piano he added to tracks such as 'Raw Power' and 'Head On' and his pounding counterpoint to James's guitar on others more than justified his presence. As the Stooges were such a guitar based band, there was little room for Scheff to really stretch.

It had been decided that nothing prior to *Raw Power* was to be performed, and as a number of new tunes had been written the band considered that they now had plenty of songs from which to select their repertoire. In retrospect, it seems surprising that they didn't play more songs from *Raw Power*. As far as can be ascertained, 'Penetration', 'Shake Appeal' and 'Death Trip' were never played live by the Stooges; and while 'Your Pretty Face…' was at least rehearsed, the ramshackle nature of the desultory attempt heard on the Morgan Studios session on the *Heavy Liquid* box set (the snippet is oddly titled 'Can't Turn You Loose'), explains why the song was never taken any further. The other four *Raw Power* songs were played consistently at virtually every concert for the rest of the year. The best of the new songs, 'Head On', was a great live track, showcasing some gloriously exciting piano from Scheff and some sterling bass work from Ron. The guitar solo was no slouch either. This song made its concert debut at the Ford Auditorium and would remain as the second number in the live set until the band fell apart the following year.

The show itself seems to have gone off well. The Stooges played to a packed house in what was promoted as a sort of homecoming. In true MainMan style, the gig had become a lavish affair, not quite what Iggy had envisaged. Lots of important guests were invited to the after-show party and it was decided that the Stooges shouldn't attend for fear of lowering the tone. They rather sadly hung around in the kitchens scrounging food. It was arguably this rejection, not being allowed to attend their own party, which marked the beginning of the end for the Stooges and MainMan.

Despite this encouraging return to the stage (Iggy: 'the people loved it') it was clear that relations between band and management were at rock bottom. Defries began to see James Williamson as a threat. Quite why is not immediately apparent, but Defries came to hate Williamson and James hated Tony in return. In frustration, James quit the band. Defries retaliated by immediately booking a gig in Chicago in a somewhat childish effort to prove how disposable Williamson actually was. Iggy had to quickly recruit a new guitarist. It's odd that Ron wasn't promoted back to the guitarist's position; he remained on bass and Detroit guitarist Sky Warnklein was drafted in to replace James. Warnklein went by the fabulous stage name Tornado Turner, but after just one gig it was decided that his style did not fit with that of the Stooges at all. His flashy solos and guitar hero posturing irritated Iggy enormously. Turner/Warnklein later played on the *Visions of the Future* album for Kim Fowley, who had recommended him to the Stooges.

To promote the Warnklein show in Chicago, Iggy went on local radio. Unfortunately he was too loaded to make any sense and for no readily apparent reason took off his clothes. Live on air he graphically described how he was playing with himself. This 'interview' had serious consequences – firstly the radio station nearly lost its FCC license, and secondly the Stooges were dropped by MainMan. It seems as if Defries had been waiting for an opportunity to drop the band, and this very public display of apparent depravity was the final straw. Leee Black Childers describes how Defries also instructed him to gather evidence of the extent of the band's drug use.

Defries terminated the Stooges contract, but he made Leee break the news. Iggy and the Stooges had been MainMan employees for less than a year. As Ron describes it, 'We were sitting by the pool... Leee came over and he was very upset. He gave us our paychecks and said, "I have some very bad news for you. MainMan just fired you."' Lee handed them tickets back to Detroit and told them to leave the Hollywood house. The Stooges just packed and left, no fuss, no tantrums. Looking back, Iggy understood why. 'They [MainMan] must have thought these guys are maniacs, the singer attacks the audience, they're all loaded, they don't communicate... their songs won't go on the radio, the drummer won't even talk to us... so I could see their point. But hey, I thought we were the best band in the world.'

As ever, Ron Asheton, the only non-junkie in the band, had saved some money and paid for himself, Iggy and Scott to move into the Riviera Hotel where James was already staying. Then he put the band on a wage of ten bucks a day. With no pressure from MainMan, James was swiftly reinstated and the band began working urgently on a new live set. As the band rehearsed and built up their repertoire they also sought out a new manager. Being dropped by MainMan meant the loss of their substantial weekly wages. As record sales of the recently released *Raw Power* had been minimal, and royalties from the other albums almost non-existent, it left regular gigging as their only option. Without management it would have been almost impossible to secure gigs, and without work Ron's money would soon run out, so this was an urgent search.

Jeff Wald, husband of wholesome sixties star Helen Reddy, was the unlikely saviour of the Stooges. It was Williamson's couple of months out of the band that provided the link. Wald managed some of the musicians Williamson had been playing with and so it was to Wald that James and Iggy turned.

The recent addition of a keyboard player had assisted enormously in the shaping of the new songs and the emphasis of the Stooges' music shifted from straight-ahead hard rock to a more bluesy sound. Indicative of this new approach is 'Head On', which loosely takes its starting point from the 'Mr. Mojo rising' section of the Doors' 'L.A. Woman'. With Ron's bass to the fore it becomes a powerful throbbing mantra, allowing James to crash in occasionally with a riff that seems all back to front. Another new song was the rock 'n' roll style 'Cock In My Pocket', which features some splendid bar-room piano, a touch that lifts an otherwise basic tune. Over the years, there have been a huge number of official and semi official releases containing rehearsal material from this period.

The origin of these rehearsal tapes is very unclear. The first semi-official release of this material came when *Rubber Legs* was issued in June 1988. The sound is good for a bootleg, but somewhat rough for an official album. However *Rubber Legs* was seized upon by the music press as something approaching the Holy Grail for Stooges followers. It sold remarkably well too. Iggy had made a lot of new fans with *Blah-Blah-Blah* who were eager to find out what the Stooges were really like. The French label Revenge capitalised on this during the late 1980s and early 1990s by issuing a series of records and cds containing many of the rehearsals from 1973 – the sonic quality was variable, but the songs were almost all of very strong archival interest. Later Bomp! records issued much of the same material, plus various bootleg quality live recordings in North America. In recent years there have been dozens of other releases containing a variety of these 1973 rehearsal tracks. In almost every case the quality is the same, or worse, than the first Revenge releases and the songs have been duplicated over and over. It appears that no one seems to own the copyright in these rehearsal tapes, and, more worryingly, the actual tapes themselves seem to have been lost. Recent releases are clearly created from previous cds. Whether Iggy or any of the Stooges receive royalties on these songs is unclear. What would be of interest to all Stooges fans is a proper reissue of this material, remastered if at all possible from the original tapes, with clear notes as to where and when these songs were actually recorded. However, without the masters, which were not the highest fidelity tapes anyway, to attempt such a project would be almost impossible. The recent *Heavy Liquid* box goes some way to redressing this, in that virtually everything worth hearing from this era has been thoughtfully compiled in one place, but even so the same sound quality as before has been maintained, as the actual master tapes, if they still exist, were not used.

However, even the existing rough quality recordings reveal some of the Stooges working processes. On the whole these tapes contain complete songs, which have clearly been worked up to a (nearly) finished state. And most of the new songs are gratifyingly strong. By being the first release, *Rubber Legs* got arguably the lion's share of the most interesting songs, and the best sound of all the rehearsal tapes, with none of the sounds of barrels being scraped that can be heard on nearly every subsequent release. Reviews were exceptionally good, with many comparisons being made with the recent sanitised Iggy of *Blah-Blah-Blah*. The legacy of the Stooges was gradually being reassessed.

The version of 'Open Up And Bleed' is amazingly powerful, with Iggy's delivery as strong as if he was on stage. In fact all the performances on this album are as good as any live show, the passion and fire in the playing are matched by Iggy's vocals. 'Johanna' also has some fine singing, with Iggy straining at the leash before going wild at the conclusion. Many releases of this material, including the recent *Heavy Liquid*, imply that this seven song set was recorded in New York in July with Scott Thurston on piano, prior to the week of shows at Max's. But there's a problem in that that clearly Bob Scheff plays piano on most, if not all, of the *Rubber Legs* songs - Iggy actually calls his name a number of times. Thurston plays harmonica, most dramatically, on 'Open Up And Bleed' at the Max's shows. But this version of 'Open Up...' has no harmonica, which points to Scott's absence. Bob Scheff had left the band before they decamped to New York, so the only explanation is that most of the songs that claim to be from the CBS Studios rehearsal in New York are actually from an earlier set. The very same version of 'Open Up And Bleed' also crops up amongst another batch of rehearsal songs which claim to be from Detroit earlier in the spring (where sonically it fits more precisely). This then implies that the *Rubber Legs* / 'CBS New York' set is probably not from New York in July, and maybe not actually one set at all. Confused yet? Until the genuine master tapes are rediscovered it's unlikely that the true story will ever come to light.

Revenge Records continued to issue the rehearsal tapes into the early 1990s. *Until The End Of The Night* contains some longer songs. Apart from an excellent version of 'Johanna', the other tracks on this disc seem to be largely improvised around simple riffs. 'Born In A Trailer' and 'Until The End Of The Night' prominently feature Bob Scheff's keyboards and although both are way too long and rambling, with some judicious pruning and general tightening up both could have been good additions to the Stooges growing repertoire. A pity then that neither was ever properly finished. *My Girl Hates My Heroin* contains the best of the rest. Some rather desultory run-throughs of 'Search And Destroy', 'Raw Power' and 'Gimme Danger' do not exactly inspire the listener, but a fiery 'Cock In My Pocket' and the title song, also known as 'Wild Love', rescue this collection. Sadly the overall sound quality is generally lower on this album.

Most of these tracks are neatly compiled on the recent box set *Heavy Liquid*. There are also a huge number of other compilations which tend to mix the rehearsal material with occasional *Kill City* songs, 1972 songs such as 'Gimme Some Skin', a version of 'Death Trip' which is simply the *Raw Power* recording in a very poor mix, and sometimes a badly copied version of 'Not Right' from the first album. The fact that these erroneous tracks keep cropping up suggest that most reisssues have simply copied songs from previous issues, with little thought as to the relevance of the songs and with no recourse to master tapes.

So when were the bulk of the 1973 rehearsals recorded? Virtually every release contains information that contradicts previous releases (if they contain any information at all). According to various albums and reissues the songs were recorded in February, or March, or Spring, or any time up to July, in maybe Detroit, or New York, or Los Angeles. Some bootlegs claim actual recording dates throughout February and March. This is apparently based on scribbled notes on the tapes themselves. But it is clear that the original tapes were not used in the preparation of bootlegs and there is no evidence to prove these dates conclusively.

Clearly some intensive rehearsals took place prior to the March show in Detroit, and one such session has now been issued on *Heavy Liquid*. At this point 'Head On' is the only new song, and is somewhat embryonic. It would therefore be surprising if the rest of the 1973 rehearsal tapes (which contain a wealth of new material, including versions of 'Head On' which sound much more finished) dated from before then. Soon after the Ford Auditorium gig, James Williamson dropped out of the band. The Sky Warnklein gig followed in April and then MainMan dropped them. Some time was spent scratching around. Gigs began again when Jeff Wald took over as the band's manager and James returned. The most likely scenario is that most of these tapes date from rehearsals when James rejoined the band, and were therefore probably taped in Los Angeles (or possibly Detroit) in late May/early June. What follows is a list of the songs usually found on the variety of reissues with commentary on the most important.

The so-called CBS Studio rehearsal, July 1973, New York

This set, which may not be one set of songs at all, judging from the variable sound quality and differing levels of instrumentation was first issued as *Rubber Legs*.

Rubber Legs

A storming song that surprisingly never made it any further than the rehearsal room. With a little more work this could have been a wonderful live track. It's basically just another of Williamson's classic stuttering riffs, though the guitar is often overtaken by Bob Scheff's piano. Scheff is pushed to the fore, taking James's riffs as a starting point for some thrilling bar room keyboard work. Iggy takes control of the structure of the song with asides to the keyboard player 'Come on, Bob' and to Williamson.

A slightly longer (5.41) version of 'Rubber Legs' from the same session has been issued on various releases.

Open Up And Bleed

This slow-burning song is one of the best the Stooges ever wrote. Beginning with another stunning circular guitar motif from James, vaguely reminiscent of 'Gimme Danger' or 'I'm Sick Of You' in both sound and intensity, it slowly builds in volume and power throughout the song. Unfortunately this recording then criminally fades out just before the five-minute mark. In concert, the song would generally be used as the set closer, and the track would speed up into a shattering vortex of noise and feedback, recalling the 'LA Blues'/'Freak' set closers of 1970. Despite the fade, this version is still one of the best recordings from 1973. Iggy's vocals are ferociously strong and the imagery in the lyrics is graphic and disturbing. This same track crops up twice in the *Heavy Liquid* box, once as part of the CBS New York session and again as part of the general set of rehearsals (where it fades very slightly later). It's not altogether clear where it genuinely belongs.

A second version of 'Open Up And Bleed' was made available on *Till The End Of The Night* and consists of just the second half of the song, cutting in just as the tempo quickens.

Johanna

Another cracking tune, with some stunning Williamson guitar – the siren like squeals and ferocious downward slides are superb. Iggy was inspired by his old London girlfriend – the same Johanna who was behind 'Your Pretty Face Is Going To Hell' – and contributes a truly original lyric summing up the love/hate relationship he had with women. 'I hate ya baby, 'cause you're the one I love' is delivered with real venom. Yet at other points he seems to be pleading for forgiveness. This recording is tight and controlled from the Stooges, yet wild and insane from Iggy.

By contrast a second, much longer, attempt (8.42), first issued on *Till The End Of The Night*, ambles rather aimlessly and drags on far too long. Bob Scheff is name-checked on the longer take and his keyboards are one the most interesting features of this take.

Cock In My Pocket

A storming rock 'n' roll song. James came up with this Chuck-Berry-on-speed number, Scheff's honky-tonk piano taking centre stage for much of the action until Iggy calls 'anytime James, anytime' and Williamson crashes back in with a red hot solo. Iggy once claimed the song was co-written with his mother. But the lyrics actually came about when Iggy sat down one day wondering what he carried around to get himself through the day. The answer was simple – his cock. So he wrote about that. Never has the basic sex life of a singer on the road been so graphically recalled – it is as direct and to the point as it gets. The song was rapidly installed in the Stooges live set, and remained a highlight of the concerts for the rest of 1973.

A second version, rougher in sound and heavier on the bass, was first issued on *My Girl Hates My Heroin*. It was also surprisingly reworked as a slow burning blues number by the Side Effects on their 1993 album *St George's Road*, a collection of garage band classics.

Head On

One of the first songs to be worked on in 1973, and still one of the best. The opening is terrific – Ron's rumbling one-note bass, then Iggy mutters, 'I think I hear it coming' and Scott smashes in as Ron descends the bass to meet James's wide open splintered riffs. Live versions would sometimes keep the bass intro running for ages and could end up sounding sloppy, but this studio take is incredibly tight. Iggy's lyrics are surprisingly autobiographical – lots of stuff about the trailer camp – although many lines wouldn't be finalised until the Stooges hit the road.

The earliest known recording comes from the Morgan Studio rehearsal in March 1973, available on *Heavy Liquid*. These attempts are clearly more embryonic than the more familiar *Rubber Legs* version. Another take, slightly shorter (5.01) and rougher sounding, but clearly recorded around the same time as the usual 5.41 version, was first issued on Revenge's *Death Trip* EP in 1988.

Cry For Me [aka 'Pin Point Eyes']

As this was a one-time-only jam, the title has never been quite decided by the bootleggers over the years. Iggy spends the beginning of this swinging bluesy number exhorting the band to join in. 'Scotty, get on those drums!' And he's enjoying the song so much that he jokingly threatens to kill someone if it's not being recorded. Bob Scheff plays some excellent piano, with Ron contributing some lead work on the bass. Iggy's lyric about an overdose ('she looked into my pin point eyes and cried') is dramatically effective, especially as it seems to have made up on the spot.

*   *   *

The rest of the 1973 rehearsals include a number of attempts at already recorded songs – 'Raw Power', 'Gimme Danger', 'Search And Destroy' were all made available on *My Girl Hates My Heroin*. But the majority of the other common tunes are all new.

Wild Love [aka 'My Girl Hates My Heroin']

There are three versions kicking around – the 5.04 take of 'Wild Love' is probably the best, coming on with loads of menace and appropriately manic screams from Iggy. This track and the short 3.03 version were both available on Bomp!'s *Wild Love*.

An earlier attempt, with very loose lyrics, is titled 'My Girl Hates My Heroin' and first appeared on the album of the same name.

How It Hurts

An inferior, earlier attempt at 'Rubber Legs'. Musically, the band are still feeling their way into this one allowing Bob Scheff considerable scope on the electric piano, and Iggy's lyrics are barely half formed. Oddly there's no sign of Scott Asheton until about thirty seconds from the end.

Born In A Trailer

Sometimes known as 'I Come From Nowhere' or just 'Nowhere', this is a simple, repetitive jam, which gives Bob room to stretch out while Iggy seems to spout lyrics off the top of his head. There's a selection of autobiographical lines, but most are just nonsensical rhymes. The band seems to be making it up as they go along though Iggy appears to have an idea where the song is heading. There's only one main recording of this song although many reissues have differing running times as, for some unaccountable reason, some versions have been faded in or out at different points.

Till The End Of The Night

This can be something of a trial to listen to all the way through. At least it is a properly written song, not just a jam, but it meanders dreadfully. This is shame as there is the germ of a potentially great song. It aims for the attitude of 'Open Up And Bleed', but sadly ends up too slow and dragging. Halfway through, James scythes in with a ragged solo. Then, at six minutes, the song steps up a gear in an attempt to recreate the excitement of 'Open Up...' but this quicker section is somewhat leaden and fails to convince. With work, however, this could have been a contender. As with Born In A Trailer', careless bootleggers and compilers have chopped and faded this song into a few slightly different lengths. But it's always the same recording.

She Creatures Of The Hollywood Hills

Often credited solely to Ron Asheton, this is a gem of a tune. Set around a driving jumpy bass riff which punches its way out of the speakers, punctuated with harsh electric keyboard stabs and some gloriously metallic rasps from Williamson, this is the only known studio recording. Iggy's lyrics are indistinct and are probably improvised. It's short and direct and does its job well. When the Stooges introduced it into the live set in the autumn of 1973 the song gradually extended to a numbing ten minutes plus.

Hey Baby

Little more than a half-formed jam along the lines of 'Born In A Trailer' with minimal unintelligible lyrics. Scott Asheton again seems to be absent. But at least it's more fun than the next batch of songs.

*   *   *

Included on many of the 1973 rehearsal tapes are tracks credited solely to Iggy with James on guitar. The quality is usually dreadful and the playing isn't too hot either. No one seems to have any idea when these recordings were made. They are unlikely to have been taped during spring 1973 with all the other tracks – for a start the quality is much poorer, and where are the rest of the Stooges? On some tracks a primitive drum machine is even utilised. One suggestion is that they predate the *Kill City* sessions in 1975 with James and Iggy warming up on a series of covers. Another likely alternative is that they are preparatory recordings made in London in spring 1972, before Ron and Scott flew in. Whatever the truth, these songs are often reissued, and are nearly always rather unwelcome additions to the Iggy catalogue.

There are allegedly hours of this material but the few songs that have been released give a good idea of what's going on. Iggy sounds pretty stoned, James prods and harasses his guitar during a bunch of covers. 'I'm a Man', 'Waiting for the Man', and 'Purple Haze' are just about bearable, but a lengthy attempt at Dylan's 'Ballad of Hollis Brown' is simply monotonous and dull. The simple drum machine doesn't help matters either.

Worse still are the muffled tracks that appeared on the final Bomp! Release, *Wild Love*. Amongst the usual suspects ('Hollis Brown' and 'Born In Trailer' again) there are terrible-quality and poorly played covers of songs by the Butterfield Blues Band ('Mellow Down Easy'), Cream ('I'm So Glad') and so on.

Probably the most unusual tune from any of these rehearsal tapes is 'Jesus Loves The Stooges', a piano-led dirge that first appeared on *I'm Sick Of You* along-side the pre-*Raw Power* recordings. It was clearly out of place there, and the exis-tence of another version of this tune amongst the main batch of 1973 rehearsals indicates it may have come from there. Certainly the piano sounds like Bob Scheff attempting a twisted bluesy torch song. Iggy moans and grunts his way through a largely unintelligible lyric (about Jesus saving him, it seems) and Scott Asheton is on hand to thud the drums out of time with the piano and at other inopportune moments (plus he demonstrates a total inability to play a shuffle when the song unexpectedly speeds up). But it's a strangely addictive mess and a real oddity amongst the rest of the cacophony the Stooges usually made.

After all the rehearsing the Stooges were ready to hit America.

Down On The Street – 1973 Concerts

June – August. Usual set list:

'Raw Power', 'Head On', 'Gimme Danger', 'Cock In My Pocket',
'Search And Destroy', 'I Need Somebody', 'New Orleans'/'Heavy Liquid',
'Open Up And Bleed'

The first gigs to be arranged by Jeff Wald were a set of shows at the Whisky A Go Go (20–24 June). With James back in the band and a whole bunch of new songs rehearsed, the Stooges were in better shape than ever before. Today Scheff's main memory of the few gigs he played with Stooges is of the bizarre outfit he wore: 'The rest of the band were dressed in some punkier form of glitter rock while I wore torn military outfits and garbage and (new at the time) small battery-powered LEDs in my hair (people kept rushing up to me batting at my hair because they thought it was on fire from cigarettes; the batteries began shocking me as I sweated while playing) ... these clothes were part of a conceptual piece.'

Sadly the rejuvenated band would suffer another blow – straight after the Whisky gigs, Bob Scheff decided that being a Stooge was not for him. The insane lifestyle led by Iggy, James and Scott was simply too much to take. Of course the new tracks the band had been working on (including 'Rubber Legs', 'Open Up And Bleed' and 'Heavy Liquid') featured strong piano, so a replacement keyboard player was needed urgently.

Jeff Wald had been busy and had secured the Stooges a week's residency at Max's Kansas City in July. However, the tight schedule meant finding and breaking in a new pianist in just a couple of weeks. Fortunately James knew just the man – Scott Thurston. James and Scott had played together during James's couple of months out of the Stooges. As well being a versatile keyboard player, Thurston was also an excellent guitarist, although it appears that he was never allowed to play guitar in the Stooges. His subsequent career has proved what a superb musician he is and he has been a mainstay of Jackson Browne's bands and has also played alongside Tom Petty and Bonnie Raitt amongst many others.

With Scott Thurston on board, James now led the band through an intensive set of rehearsals. According to Ron, the first rehearsal began without Iggy who showed up late, having missed his flight. Eventually, Iggy 'just came running right in... up to a microphone and started to do his thing like nothing had happened'. Courtesy of Bill Whitten, a top LA designer who had created stage clothes for Neil Diamond amongst others, came a new stage outfit for Iggy – his bizarre human fly outfit ('It was kind of cool in a way, but I don't know what I was thinking'). The Stooges were ready for New York, but New York wasn't quite ready for the Stooges. Iggy was mildly disappointed in the upstairs room at Max's because all the folding chairs were laid out in neat rows, 'like a Pentecostal church or something'.

Max's was though the perfect place for the Stooges. This New York club was still the main hangout of the Warhol crowd, had a debauched and depraved vibe, and was one of the best places to be seen in the city. The band was guaranteed a sympathetic audience every night. The Stooges themselves were well known at Max's and would hang out in the exclusive back room whenever they were in New York.

Opening on 30 July, Iggy and the Stooges were an immediate hit. The audience was packed with rock critics, ready to experience some sort of happening. The mostly enthusiastic reports established the Stooges as a desirable act in 1973, and assisted Jeff Wald enormously in booking further gigs. A number of *Raw Power* songs were mixed with the new tunes 'Cock In My Pocket', 'Head On', 'Heavy Liquid' and the astonishing set-closer 'Open Up And Bleed'. The band were really on form; powerful, dark and brooding on 'Gimme Danger' and 'Open Up and Bleed'; wild and savage on 'Search and Destroy' and 'Heavy Liquid'.

What was shaping up to be a good week sadly took a turn for the worse on the second night. Various versions of what happened have circulated for years. The most lurid stories claim that Iggy intentionally slashed at his chest with a broken bottle after complaining of a broken heart. The more realistic refer to Iggy doing another of his admittedly dangerous falls to the floor where he accidentally landed on a bottle which cut his chest. The actual result was a series of deep gashes to his chest which bled profusely. Stooges soundman Nitebob remembers trying to persuade Iggy to stop the show: 'He was pumping out some blood. It wasn't the kinda thing you could solve with a Band-aid.' The rest of the band were concerned too but Iggy, as ever, was too wrapped up in the intensity of the concert to be concerned, and finished the gig. Backstage, the blood wouldn't stop flowing and it was clear that the wounds were rather deeper than first thought. It was the remarkably sensible Alice Cooper who insisted that Iggy go to hospital where he was stitched and bandaged and was told to cancel the next few shows in order to allow the wounds to heal. For once, Iggy heeded medical advice and the next two shows (scheduled for 1 and 2 August) were postponed. During his few days off, however Iggy managed to end up back in the emergency room after walking into a door backstage at a New York Dolls concert at the Felt Forum. He cracked his head so badly that he virtually knocked himself out cold. When he returned to the Max's stage on 6 August, not only was Iggy still sporting a bandaged chest, but also a huge egg on his forehead. The shows were a triumph however. Lenny Kaye wrote a very favourable review in *Rock Scene*, in which he quotes Iggy defiantly stating, 'You can't slander the Stooges.'

What is somewhat surprising is that with the comparatively large number of new songs worked up in rehearsals, only a few actually made it into the set lists. The performances from summer–autumn 1973 contain nearly the same songs every show, which is a little disappointing when the band had songs as strong as 'Rubber Legs' and 'Johanna' ready to go. Even when the band played two shows in one night they would usually just play the same set a second time.

Usually the gigs would open with 'Raw Power' and the band often had to pound out the riff for as long as it took Iggy to get himself together. 'Head On' kept the energy levels high before 'Gimme Danger' allowed both band and audience to take it down a level. 'Cock In My Pocket' and Search And Destroy' followed and the show would end with either 'Heavy Liquid' or 'Open Up and Bleed', sometimes both. Iggy would frequently berate the audiences or get heckled and this could lengthen the shows from around the usual forty minutes to anything up to an hour. It was rare, however for a Stooges gig to last much more than that. By the time of the Whisky A Go Go shows in September the lengthy jam number 'She Creatures Of The Hollywood Hills' had been added as an occasional encore, and 'Johanna' was played a couple of times. Most of the Whisky concerts were recorded. The best of these audience recordings was issued by Revenge as *Live At The Whisky A Go Go*. An accompanying twelve-inch single contained 'She Creatures...' which was too long to fit on the album.

Whilst in LA, the Stooges apparently attempted to record a number of new songs with Todd Rundgren producing. 'Johanna' was rumoured to be one of the songs attempted, but no other details of this abortive session have emerged.

As the autumn wore on, the Stooges' hand-to-mouth existence relied solely on their concerts. Although Wald was still booking engagements whenever he could, the Stooges schedule became more and more erratic as they were forced to take every gig they could get. Zigzagging around the States with no fixed itinerary began to takes its toll. Alcohol, amphetamines and cocaine crept back in. Iggy in particular would ingest, snort or smoke virtually anything. At one memorable engagement at Poor Richard's club in Atlanta, Elton John came to see the band. Elton had been playing across town and arrived just as the Stooges were starting their set. He expressed a desire to play with the band. Road manager Chris Ehring was unsure, especially when, for reasons that no one can adequately explain, Elton thought it would be cool to dress up as a gorilla. Quite where the gorilla suit came from is another mystery but halfway through the set the audience were confronted by the bizarre sight of a tubby English singer in a moth-eaten gorilla suit chasing Iggy Pop around the stage. What nobody realised was that Iggy, having taken way too much PCP, thought that Elton was a *genuine* gorilla. He was terrified, and his running away and freaking out was not an act.

Another show at the J F Kennedy Centre in Washington DC folded after just three songs when Iggy simply collapsed, virtually paralysed after too much crystal THC. Chris Ehring thought that Iggy had been stabbed at this show, only to find that 'it was a jelly sandwich smeared all over him...'

The band was exhausted from too much travelling, too little sleep and too many drugs. But they soldiered on. Most concerts were promoted as Iggy and the Stooges or, sometimes, just as Iggy Pop, which began to drive a wedge between Iggy and the others.

By November 1973, further new songs including 'Wet My Bed' (something of an amalgamation of 'Wild Love' and 'Rubber Legs') and the flagrantly abusive 'Rich Bitch' (which developed from improvised parts of 'Head On' into its own song) were added and the standard set list was amended slightly to include these. November's gig at the Latin Casino in Baltimore has been issued on *Double Danger* and the rough-sounding bootleg tape reveals the Stooges unusually playing for more than an hour, running through most of their repertoire:

'Raw Power', 'Head On', 'Gimme Danger', 'Rich Bitch', 'Wet My Bed',
'I Got Nothing', 'Search And Destroy', 'Cock In My Pocket',
'I Need Somebody', 'Heavy Liquid', 'Open Up And Bleed'

The year ended with a gig with Kiss and Blue Oyster Cult at the Academy of Music in New York on 31 December. Rumours circulated in the hip New York circles that this concert would be the band's last. By the time the rumours reached Andy Warhol, they were luridly suggesting that Iggy would commit suicide on stage. This at least had the effect of ghoulishly securing a full house. Iggy was thinking about giving up – worsening drug dependency and utter lack of success had plunged the whole band into despair. Journalist Anne Werher, who later compiled Iggy's marvellous book *I Need More* in 1981, was sent to cover the show by *After Dark* magazine. She describes a sad and depressing scene backstage after a less than stellar performance. 'Iggy sang with demonic energy, in his hot pink pants and high top black boots. But his body control was off, backbends collapsed... Backstage he was flat out on the red concrete floor, rolling in spilled beer, dead cigarettes and broken dreams.'

Columbia reportedly recorded the show for a possible live album but on reviewing the tapes decided that the performances just weren't good enough. An audience recording of the Academy Of Music show has since been released on *Double Danger*. As with most of the Stooges' live albums, the quality is sadly atrocious, worse than the tapes of the September Whisky A Go Go shows, but marginally better than the Max's recordings from July. The tapes reveal a pretty standard Stooges set from this period. The murky recording doesn't really allow the listener to judge the quality of the performance, but it does show yet again that, despite the drugs and the exhaustion, the band were remarkably consistent players. The material is solidly played, no messing around, nothing sloppy.

In early 1974, Columbia chose not to take up the option of a second album. Things began to look bleak for the Stooges.

1974

By early 1974, Iggy had begun baiting the crowds even more than usual, just to get some sort of reaction, just to liven the shows up. The gigs were getting more violent as the crowds began to lob more and more debris onto the stage. With his love of military regalia, Ron seriously considered wearing a flak jacket or even a riot helmet on stage. Coins were being thrown: 'A well-thrown coin, when it hits you, it feels like you've been shot. I always had to keep my eyes open and my head down,' commented Ron.

Amongst the violence was some humour however. Iggy describes how he went home with a girl after a gig. The next morning, the girl's parents invited Iggy to join the family for breakfast, which he did, even though he was still wearing his stage clothes from the night before – black tights and a pseudo ballerina outfit...

Famously, what became the final Iggy and the Stooges concert descended into farce and violence as 9 February 1974 saw another homecoming concert at the Michigan Palace. As with the previous October's show at the same venue, Ron's friend Michael Tipton was asked to tape the gig on his portable four-track recorder. Although the existing recording of this show is incomplete (only the second half of the show appears to have survived) it has become half of one of the most famous albums ever – *Metallic KO*. It wasn't released until 1976, but *Metallic KO* documents the beginning of the 10 October 1973 concert and the end of the 9 February show, the all-too-audible end of the Stooges.

The story of the final gig begins a few days before at the Rock 'n' Roll Farm in Wayne, Michigan. The legendary writer Lester Bangs attended this show on 7 February, where the audience was exceptionally hostile. Sick of all the bottles and missiles, Iggy stopped the show. 'All right,' he said, 'you assholes wanta hear "Louie Louie", we'll give you "Louie Louie".' According to Bangs, who was prone to exaggeration, the Stooges proceeded to play 'Louie Louie' for the next forty-five minutes! Iggy improvised some new words along the lines of 'biker faggot sissies' etc. Which, of course, only served to enrage the crowd even more. What Iggy wasn't aware of was that a local biker gang called the Scorpions had sent a contingent down to the Rock 'n' Roll Farm specifically to taunt the Stooges as part of a stupid initiation rite. Iggy finally flipped and leapt off stage to kick the ass of the worst heckler. Sadly for Iggy, the guy was massive and proceeded to punch Iggy with his huge fist covered in a studded knuckle-duster. Iggy went down with the first punch...

He wasn't badly hurt, but he was extremely pissed off. He talked about the incident on WABX-FM the next day. Then the Scorpions phoned the radio station and threatened to kill Iggy at the Michigan Palace gig on 9 February. Iggy responded bullishly, if rather unwisely, by daring them to do their worst. As the gigs had been getting gradually more violent anyway, this was perhaps not the most sensible thing to do. Nevertheless it was a pumped-up Iggy, ready to take on the world, who bounded onto the stage that night. Predictably the Scorpions arrived and kept up a relentless barrage throughout the show. Thankfully, no one was killed, but Iggy continued to bait the crowd, and especially the gang, in front of their dates ('Ya girlfriends'll still love me, ya jealous cocksuckers'). And, confident as ever, he acted like he was fronting the world's greatest band, despite the constant hail of missiles. But Iggy's bullish mood gradually evaporated. He managed to spit out a few choice insults – one of the best being 'You're paying five bucks and I'm making ten thousand, baby... So screw ya!'

By the end of the show, weariness had taken hold and he sounded hugely fed up as he moaned, 'What do you wanna hear?' before launching into the last refuge of a desperate band – 'Louie Louie'. James and Ron were as much in the firing line as Iggy – the two Scotts were slightly protected behind their instruments as the barrage of debris got stronger – bottles and coins plus paper cups, light bulbs, eggs amongst other things. Iggy weathered this attack for just a short while; despite his parting crack of 'You nearly killed me, but ya missed again' he sounds tired and lifeless and with the alarming sounds of debris hitting microphones the career of the Stooges was over.

Two days after this show, Iggy phoned Ron. He was quitting. Sickened by years of struggling, weakened by deepening drug usage, and exhausted by touring, Iggy announced that he'd simply had enough. Ron wasn't at all surprised.

At the time, barely anyone noticed. Ron and Scott Asheton went back home to their mother's house and hung around in Detroit. James Williamson and Scott Thurston hung around in Los Angeles and tried to form new bands. Iggy just hung around, sleeping on friends' floors, scrounging money and drugs and generally doing nothing constructive.

METALLIC KO

Skydog SGIS 008. French release – 1976.
Skydog SKI 622321. Double album reissue with extra tracks. French release – March 1988.

The album *Metallic KO* documents some of the final gig and it remains one of the most frightening records ever released. Lester Bangs famously wrote '*Metallic KO* is the only rock album I know where you can actually hear hurled beer bottles breaking against guitar strings.'

There has long been confusion over the source of the tapes. According to Ron Asheton, his friend Michael Tipton had recorded a number of Stooges gigs in the Detroit area on his four-track machine. Tipton had given copies of the Michigan Palace tapes to each member of the Stooges. It seems that, two years later, James Williamson gave his copy to journalist Nick Kent, who in turn passed it to Mark Zermati, founder of Skydog Records. This French label had issued a number of semi-bootlegs, including a well distributed Velvet Underground record called *Evil Mothers*. Zermati was delighted with the tapes of the final Stooges concert and took them to a London studio to clean them up as best he could. Zermati claims that the studio engineer thought he was crazy to want to release such a bad-sounding recording. He also claims that he sent money to both James and Iggy as payment for the recordings. Ron and Scott, as always, never received a dime.

Raw Power

The original vinyl opened with three songs from the 10 October 1973 concert. 'Raw Power' is a hard-hitting version, honed by playing months of concerts with much the same set list. Whilst the repetitive riff seems far more obvious and less interesting in concert it is still a wonderful way to begin a show. There's also the added bonus of Scott Thurston's superb piano work.

Head On

Until the release of the many rehearsal tapes in the late 1980s, this was the only place to find 'Head On' and it's a brilliantly driving version too. Ron's bass powers the tune neatly accompanied by Scott's drums.

Gimme Danger

A strong version of the *Raw Power* tune. In concert, 'Gimme Danger' was played with none of the subtlety of the studio original, but with an increased sense of desperation and futility. Iggy's vocals are surprisingly good.

Search And Destroy

This was added to the various reissues of *Metallic KO*, first appearing on the double vinyl *Metallic 2xKO* in 1988. It's a solid take, but contains no surprises – James is clearly the star of this recording.

Heavy Liquid

A track redolent of the Gary 'US' Bonds number 'New Orleans'. Having said that, the Stooges rip through 'Heavy Liquid' like a band possessed. They seem to have enjoyed playing this one, as I've never heard a bad version, and there's always bags of energy on display, plus some raucous backing vocals from Ron and Scott Thurston which push Iggy further. James rides the riff until the whole thing seems to turn inside out after about three minutes and there's an insanely fast section for a minute before the band twist back into 'New Orleans' again. The Stooges never worked out a decent ending though – it just sort of stops in a muddle.

This recording ends with Iggy reciting a verse from 'I Wanna Be Your Dog' which was the closest a 1973 audience got to a pre-*Raw Power* song.

Open Up And Bleed

Scott Thurston's penetrating harmonica dominates this take, virtually drowning out everything else. 'Who hates the Stooges? We don't hate you and we don't care...' calls Iggy before starting the vocal. Iggy sings with real passion. You can also hear Ron's backing vocals clearly on this recording. It's a good version of the song, which makes it something of a pity that it fades out just before the four-minute mark.

Heavy Liquid

The first of the tracks from the final Stooges show, this version of 'Heavy Liquid' cuts in a minute or so into the song and cuts out again way before the end making it a frustrating excerpt from one of the better new Stooges songs.

I Got Nothin'

Subtitled 'I Got Shit' on some releases, this is an interesting, but not terribly successful attempt at a song that would later be recorded on *Kill City*. The Stooges never quite got the measure of 'I Got Nothin''. Scott Asheton especially seems to be having problems with the beat at the start. Iggy however appropriately sings like a man at the end of his tether and James' solo is good, if somewhat badly recorded.

Rich Bitch

One of the meanest, most derogatory songs ever recorded. Once again, Iggy doesn't shirk from telling it like it is, but it's deeply unpleasant and offensive. It says much for Iggy's general state of mind in the winter of 1973–1974 that he could come up with a song such as this. It speaks volumes about the whole band's attitude towards women in general and groupies in particular that they'd consent to play a song such as 'Rich Bitch'. 'Keep your hands off me,' they chant repeatedly. Musically, it's fairly standard Stooges bar-room rock 'n' roll in the same vein as 'Rubber Legs' or 'Wet My Bed' but, given room to stretch out, 'Rich Bitch' becomes more like an extended jam, with plenty of space for Scott Thurston to pound the piano as Williamson contributes some scorching guitar flourishes. It's an undeniably exciting recording, primarily due to the obvious tension captured on tape, but as a piece of songwriting 'Rich Bitch' fails to convince in the same way as many other Stooges songs.

Gimme Danger

A fine version, oddly inserted into the running order after 'Rich Bitch' on the current two-disc version of *Metallic KO*. As with all the songs from the final Stooges gig, Iggy is too loud compared with the muted recording of the rest of the band. Some stunning drumming keeps this one going; by contrast, the rest of the Stooges sound like they are struggling at times to keep up. Scott Thurston contributes some surprisingly melodic piano and, with James playing the gentle guitar parts, it's left to Ron to add what becomes almost lead bass. Along with the edited 'Heavy Liquid' and 'I Got Nothin'' this was originally released on a 1978 EP.

Cock In My Pocket

Metallic KO saw the first appearance of this incendiary rocker 'co-written by my mother', as Iggy states. It's a hysterically funny statement of intent – furiously rude but with humour rather than the venomous spite of 'Rich Bitch'. James gets to fire off another burning solo, although he's mixed way too low on the version here. A seriously harsh edit ends the song as the record jumps to the final part of the gig.

Louie Louie

There's about three and a half minutes of Iggy talking to the crowd before we get to the final Stooges song. Iggy is trying to be positive, trying to keep control. But when he introduces the band, his comment of 'let's hear it for the singer... I am the greatest' is followed by a bunch of eggs chucked at the stage. This clearly bothers Iggy, and the light bulbs that follow cause Ron and James to leave. Back after a tape break, Iggy sounds totally fed up and, as 'Louie Louie' cranks up, Iggy shouts, with real feeling, 'I never thought it'd come to this, baby!' It's a solid version of 'Louie Louie', complete with Iggy's favourite obscene lyrics. With the sounds of bottles hitting microphones the tape runs out. 'Keep trying next week' mutters Iggy, but it wasn't to be. A few days later Iggy quit.

*   *   *

Upon its release in 1976, *Metallic KO* immediately entered the realms of legend. As punk was breaking on both sides of the Atlantic reviewers fought to praise this live record as an unsurpassable example of the Stooges as punk pioneers. Nick Kent called it 'the most vicious, malicious slice of rock ephemera ever made available'.

In reality, once the hype had died down, it was clear that although it's a vital document of a significant event, as an album of live music it leaves a lot to be desired. In the first place although the four-track recordings aren't bad, they are still muddy and distorted and don't do the band any favours. The sound wobbles across the stereo spectrum, James's guitar is almost inaudible at times and the audience, always a vital part of any Stooges concert, is virtually missing altogether. It is still the best-recorded Stooges live album, and for years was the only place to find the scorchingly powerful although sometimes obscene songs from the final Stooges show.

The Aftermath

After dropping out of his own band, Iggy's intention was to straighten himself out and start writing new songs. As was so often the case with Iggy, these plans fell by the wayside and he ended up drifting around Los Angeles for the rest of the year, sleeping on friends' floors, and getting beaten up by dealers. His behaviour became more and more erratic and bizarre.

Danny Sugerman took Iggy under his wing. He was also managing the remaining members of the Doors and suggested to keyboard player Ray Manzarek that Iggy might make a good frontman for the songs Ray was writing. They attempted some work together, which culminated in a tribute to Jim Morrison gig at the Whisky A Go Go on 3 July 1974, the third anniversary of Jim's death. James Williamson helped out on guitar and Iggy performed a series of Doors songs. He improvised many of the words. Ray mentioned on a few occasions that he would produce a solo album for Iggy but, because of Iggy's worsening behaviour, this project was quietly dropped. Iggy seemed at the mercy of anyone he talked to – a bunch of gay fans dressed him up as woman and the police picked him up on Sunset Boulevard. Manzarek and Sugerman bailed him out. Another time Sugerman had to stop Iggy from destroying, with an axe, a car belonging to the rich father of a girlfriend. The final straw for Manzarek came when Iggy showed up late for the first full band rehearsal, seemingly unaware that he was totally naked.

There were further occasional forays onto the concert stage – the most notorious being a truly bizarre improvised performance on 11 August called 'The Murder Of The Virgin'. This weird show at Rodney Bingenheimer's English Disco ended when, horrifically, he cut his chest with a carving knife. Even for Iggy this was extreme behaviour. Astonishingly, Danny Sugerman tried to pass this off as Iggy's 'most committed statement ever', but it was clear, even to his most ardent supporters, that Iggy was not a well man, physically or mentally. The rest of 1974 was a waste. Iggy cannot remember much of the year, but it seems as if there was nothing worth remembering anyway.

Passenger from Kill City

1975

Towards the end of 1974, Iggy suggested to James Williamson that they form a new band. James had already been working with Scott Thurston and the Sales brothers. Drummer Hunt Sales and his bassist older brother Tony were well-known faces on the LA music scene and were renowned for their uncompromising attitude. They had worked for some years with Todd Rundgren, starting with the groundbreaking *Runt* album in 1970 when Hunt Sales was only sixteen. In fact, the brothers had formed their first band in 1966 – Tony and The Tigers had appeared on an edition of the TV show *Hullaballoo* hosted by their father, the well-known comedian Soupy Sales.

This could have been a powerful band but, after only a few abortive rehearsals, it was clear that Iggy could not cope. Disillusioned with the whole scene, musically and chemically, Iggy took the long-overdue decision to clean up his act. In typical Pop fashion, his method was far from orthodox. He decided on the extraordinary step of voluntarily checking himself into the UCLA Hospital, figuring that hospital would the best place to detox, undergo cold turkey and get some much-needed rest. As his behaviour had been so erratic, he was committed to the Neuropsychiatric Ward but Iggy was not unduly worried and apparently thought that a short stay would be enough to sort him out. After a week, however, Iggy decided he'd had enough and tried to leave but found that the doctors intended to keep him in. The medical staff declared that he was not safe to release onto the streets of LA. He had no actual home to go to and none of his 'friends' were considered responsible enough to look after him. With no one willing or able to vouchsafe for his wellbeing, Iggy was forced to remain in the Neuropsychiatric Ward for some weeks.

Interestingly, an interview in *The Face* in 1986 implies that committal to the UCLA was actually in lieu of a jail sentence for string of petty crimes, something which is rarely mentioned. He was put into the care of Dr Murray Zucker, a psychiatrist who gained Iggy's trust by virtue of the fact that they were almost the same age. Gradually, Iggy recovered from being a slobbering pill popping idiot into a more socially acceptable human being.

Nobody visited at first; possibly his few friends were unaware of where Iggy actually was. Gradually word got around that he was in an asylum but, considering his reputation and behaviour over the previous year, no one

seemed that surprised. The Sales brothers eventually visited, as did Scott Thurston (Iggy recalls this visit during a vitriolic outburst at the Paris Hippodrome show in September 1977).

Encouraging and supportive though this was however, the most important of his visitors was undoubtedly David Bowie. Iggy had not seen David since the *Raw Power* mixing sessions, as MainMan supremo Tony Defries had deliberately kept them apart, fearing that David would somehow be tainted by Iggy's dangerous reputation. By early 1975, Bowie's rocky relationship with Defries was hitting an all-time low and, after taking advice from John Lennon, David fired his manager and embarked upon legal action against him.

According to Iggy, when David visited he apparently smuggled in some cocaine for them to share. Suitably refreshed, he then proposed yet another revival of Iggy's career. Bowie initially suggested renting some studio time together and, as he had plenty of half written songs, Iggy could help him finish them. Iggy was delighted. Finally someone was showing faith in him. But, sadly for the beleaguered Pop, Bowie was busy dealing with his own demons and addictions, and the proposed studio time ended up being some months away.

The meeting with Bowie was enough to galvanise Iggy back into action. The newly inspired Pop contacted James Williamson, who had been continuing to work on songs with Scott Thurston. During the spring of 1975, Williamson and Thurston, together with Brian Glascock on drums and Steve Tranio on bass, recorded most of the backing tracks that became *Kill City* at Jimmy Webb's home studio. Mostly based around Rolling Stones-type riffs, Williamson's tunes were direct, hard and very catchy. There were some excellent ballads too, and this project was shaping up to be some of the most commercial material that he'd recorded. Released into the dubious care of James, on carefully sanctioned weekend leave from UCLA, Iggy would pitch up at the studio and record his vocals in short sharp bursts.

A few weeks later, things were really looking up – Iggy was finally released from hospital and he and James had a powerful album in the can. But while Iggy clearly thought the recordings were of sufficient quality to release, James began having second thoughts. Always a perfectionist, he seemed to consider that the sessions had yet not resulted in finished songs, simply quality demos, but with no record deal, and no more money for studio time James just put the tapes away. To his dismay, Iggy began hawking the unfinished tapes around record companies – not only did Iggy need the artistic boost a new album would give him, but he also badly needed the money. There were no takers. Summer 1975 saw LA music coasting with the likes of the Eagles and Steely Dan. Armed only with a reputation as an unreliable junkie and an album of punky snapshots of LA life, it's no surprise that Iggy couldn't find a record label willing to take a chance on him. Iggy: 'I had a bad reputation in LA, which is a bad place to have a bad reputation.'

The tapes would remain locked away for two years. Ironically it was James Williamson who, having virtually retired from the music business, decided to make some cash from his time with Iggy. After Iggy's resurrection in 1977, James dug out the 1975 tapes and decided to finish them off. He called in John Harden to overdub some saxophone during the summer of 1977 and, after some more tinkering, James decided that the record was good enough to release. James signed a deal with Greg Shaw at Bomp! records. In 1977, the ferocious roar of the Stooges finally began to make some sense amongst the thousands of snotty punk bands that were starting up. To Shaw, an album's worth of unreleased Iggy songs was a godsend. James was quoted as saying it was the best work he and Iggy had ever done. Now it was Iggy's turn to disagree – he called the album half finished, but significantly he immediately added a number of *Kill City* tracks to the 1978 live set and a good many of the album's songs have been performed over the years.

KILL CITY

BOMP! BLP 4001 (US). Released – November 1977.
Radar RAD 2 (UK). Released – February 1978.
Produced by **James Williamson**

Issued in late 1977, the album garnered excellent reviews from the punk press. Although Iggy was now frequently hailed as the Godfather of Punk, his most recent album, *The Idiot*, was far removed from the prevailing musical climate and so when *Kill City* came out the punks could really see what all the fuss was about. Never mind that the songs had been recorded in Los Angeles two years previously – here was a collection of hard rock songs, perfectly in tune with the punk ethos.

Kill City

Opening the album is a tight and vicious song about LA; the 'Kill City' of the title. James Williamson rides his Stones-inspired riff throughout the track as Iggy spits out his diatribe against the town he'd called home for too long. His bitterness was also fuelled by his enforced stay in the UCLA Neuropsychiatric wing and, with his treatment drugs clearly not mixing well with any other substances he could score, Iggy slurs his words occasionally, yet manages to pour more bile into two and a half minutes than most songwriters could achieve in a lifetime.

'Kill City' was regularly played on many of the tours from 1978 to 1981 and, along with other *Kill City* songs, was dusted down for the *Instinct* world tour in 1988.

Sell Your Love

'Sell Your Love' is a surprisingly tender ballad, boosted by some soulful multi-tracked saxophone and some Bowie-esque backing vocals from Thurston and drummer Brian Glascock. Iggy's delivers his lines in a tired, wasted voice. The backing track is somewhat muffled compared to the clarity of the title song, or the solid rock of the following track.

Beyond The Law

The urgent 'Beyond The Law' kicks off with another inspired Williamson riff, not a million miles from Keith Richards' 'Happy'. (It has a sleazy debauched air, similar to that on the Stones' *Exile On Main Street*.) This excellent yet often overlooked track has some of the best hooks on the album and the killer saxophone, doubling the guitar, is very effective. Coupled with Iggy's raucous, almost shouted lyrics, the energy level remains right at the top. The lines about being 'negative' were appropriated for 'Dum Dum Boys' on *The Idiot* – when that album was released no one had heard *Kill City*. The song received its first live airing on the 1978 tour, and was a semi-regular fixture ten years later on the *Instinct* world tour.

I Got Nothing

The Stooges originally performed 'I Got Nothing' during the winter of 1973–1974. Existing live recordings demonstrate that the Stooges never really got to grips with this song, seemingly stumped by the changes in tempo. But on *Kill City* this Dylanesque tune (check out the 'Knockin' On Heaven's Door' vibe of Thurston's organ playing) is performed immaculately. Iggy's vocals are among his best so far recorded and the stop–start chorus is nailed perfectly. The lyrics are more appropriate than ever before – Iggy genuinely had nothing at all at the time the song was recorded. Living either in hospital or borrowing friends' couches, he had no money, no possessions, no home.

Johanna

Another old Stooges song written in the spring of 1973, 'Johanna' was one of the songs attempted at the abortive session with Todd Rundgren in August 1973 but, until *Kill City*, a proper studio recording had never been completed. With layers of guitars, Williamson builds the song up from the basic thrash of the Stooges rehearsals. A finished take with masses of guitar overdubs but prior to the addition of the omnipresent saxophone circulates amongst collectors. For my money though, the *Kill City* version is the one to beat. The sax pushes the song up a notch, adding a desperate accompaniment to the already desperate lyrics. The piano breakdown at the end echoes the breakdown of the relationship. As noted before, the song refers to a girlfriend Iggy had in London in 1972 – the same Johanna who inspired 'Your Pretty Face Is Going To Hell'. Apart from a couple of performances in late 1973 the song wouldn't be played regularly on stage until the 1988 tour. It was dug up again for the 1993 concerts.

Night Theme/Night Theme (reprise)

Closing side one and opening side two with a reprise of the same little tune gives the vinyl a touch of continuity, although it now merely sounds odd on CD. Nevertheless it's a neat but inconsequential instrumental with suitably nocturnal wailing from Gayna, marvellously on loan from the Count Dracula Society, and Iggy darkly muttering something incomprehensible about living in the night.

Consolation Prizes

The reprise of the 'Night Theme' segues directly into 'Consolation Prizes' by way of a backwards tape. The song itself is a cool *Exile On Main Street*-style rocker with James's guitar layers and some added synth effects from Scott. Iggy's vocals seem rather murky, as if from a poorer quality recording, though oddly an earlier mix that circulates amongst collectors has a clearer vocal but is missing the synthesizer. Drummer Brian Glascock keeps the song racing along.

No Sense Of Crime

Opening with some unusually delicate acoustic guitar makes for a great setting for Iggy's plaintive vocals. The song builds with electric overdubs, some splashy drumming, faint synths and delicate piano – and that's before the congas join in. One of the undoubted highlights of *Kill City*.

Lucky Monkeys

This song was actually taped at Maconnel Studios in Los Angeles, and sounds surprisingly different from the other *Kill City* tunes. The quality of the recording is somewhat poorer and more distorted, but as the song is another *Exile On Main Street*-alike the harmonica/guitar/vocal muddiness only adds to the overall mood. The 'born dead crazy' lines at the conclusion are especially effective as the mantra is repeated over and over.

Master Charge

A stately tune from James and Scott Thurston. It was originally intended that Iggy should add some vocals, but somehow this never happened, so we are left with a sombre and rather downbeat instrumental to end the album. Despite the attempts by John Harden to liven up the proceedings it's ultimately something of an anticlimax.

*   *   *

Back to 1975 and, undeterred by the lack of takers for *Kill City*, Iggy then took up Bowie's offer of studio time. A couple of studio sessions were witnessed by *Rolling Stone*'s Cameron Crowe, who admiringly wrote of Iggy's ability to improvise at the mike, and of David's coke-induced paranoia and weariness of the whole music scene – 'another song, that's all I need!' he was heard to exclaim at one point. The sessions were also attended by Warren Peace, sometime backing singer in Bowie's band – as Geoff MacCormack he'd been at school with Bowie and remains one of his closest friends to this day.

Peace brought a soulful piano melody to the sessions, over which Iggy improvised a semi-spoken, semi-sung reflection on heavy drug use. The resulting piece, the stunning 'Turn Blue', was sadly left unfinished at these sessions. But thankfully, two years later, Iggy returned to the song for the *Idiot* tour where it became a regular highlight; and it was finally committed to tape during the recording of *Lust For Life* in May 1977. 'Drink To Me' was a new tune which Iggy improvised over a dirge-like Bowie instrumental. Bowie called Iggy's ability to improvise at the mike 'verbal jazz'. Another track, 'Moving On', was abandoned and left unfinished while a further song, 'Sell Your Love', was a failed attempt to remake the already Bowie-esque *Kill City* track.

But the sessions ground to a halt when Iggy failed to show up on the third day. He was still missing the day after and Bowie was concerned. But not enough to do much about it. 'I hope he's not dead,' David told *Rolling Stone*, 'he's got a good act.' Bowie had other priorities. He had to travel to New Mexico at the end of May to begin work on his first major film. *The Man Who*

Fell To Earth, directed by Nic Roeg, was to occupy Bowie for the rest of the summer and all thoughts of a collaboration with Iggy were forgotten.

By the time Bowie returned to LA in late autumn, his mental state was extremely fragile. In the grip of extreme cocaine addiction and possibly suffering a drug-induced breakdown, this was his lowest period. He first attempted to record a soundtrack for the Roeg film, but these sessions were abandoned, probably due to Bowie's worsening state. He then embarked on the recording of *Station To Station*, a series of sessions that years later he claimed he could not remember at all. 'I know I recorded [the album] in LA, because people have told me I did,' he recently stated. As the sessions ended, Bowie seems to have been perilously close to madness. According to legend, a good friend (possibly the loyal MacCormack) apparently picked David up one morning and stood him in front of a full-length mirror to show him what he had become. David was seemingly so shocked by this confrontation with his emaciated shaking reflection that he vowed to leave LA, and kick his cocaine dependency once and for all.

Over Christmas, he rehearsed for his forthcoming tour at Keith Richards' place in Jamaica (which frankly doesn't seem the most sensible place to go to kick a drug habit, but anyway…). David began to eat more healthily, work out and get some much-needed rest.

A few weeks later and the *Station To Station* tour touched down in LA. This was the first time Bowie had been back for some months. Amongst the many backstage visitors was Iggy Pop. The two immediately renewed their friendship and Iggy was invited to join the tour entourage. Depressed by his bare existence in LA and his utter lack of success during the latter part of 1975, Iggy was delighted to accept the offer to travel the world.

1976

The seeds of *The Idiot* were sown in a funky guitar piece that guitarist Carlos Alomar brought to the rehearsals for David Bowie's 1976 *Station To Station* tour. Bowie quickly recognised the tune's potential and added some sketchy lyrics, which seemed to refer to his recent film role in *The Man Who Fell To Earth*. This work in progress was performed a handful of times on the *Station To Station* tour, a bass heavy, slow funk track that seemed to baffle most of the audiences. Once Iggy Pop had joined the entourage mid-tour in Los Angeles, talk turned to a collaboration between the two, and the new song, often referred to as 'Calling Sister Midnight' at this point, was suggested as a possible single – to be performed by Pop and produced by Bowie. As the song began to be thought of more as a potential Iggy Pop track it was dropped from Bowie's set. The tour was an enjoyable experience for Iggy, apart from one incident. After a show in Rochester on 20 March, Bowie's suite was raided. Four people, including David and Iggy were arrested, but the case was later dropped. Considering the scope of the pair's drug usage over the years this was, amazingly, the only time that they came close to being busted.

The proposed single was often mentioned as the tour weaved its way across the USA and Europe, but nothing concrete happened until David and Iggy booked studio time at the Chateau d'Herouville after the tour concluded in June. The sixteenth-century Chateau was set in a glorious estate about an hour from Paris and was the first residential studio suite when it opened in 1969. As soon as they entered the studio, it became apparent that David and Iggy had enough song ideas between them to fill an album and the plan to record just a single fell by the wayside. David used his influence with his record company RCA to secure a three-album deal for Iggy. It is a measure of the high regard with which Bowie was held in mid 1976 that RCA were willing to bankroll three albums by someone who had spent some months on the UCLA Neuropsychiatric Ward only a year earlier and whose previous albums had shown little discernible commercial appeal. It is unclear exactly how much RCA put up front to pay for *The Idiot* but it is unlikely to have been very much – the album seems to have been recorded on a shoestring budget compared with Bowie's own records. Much of the music was played by David and Iggy themselves, and the production and much of the engineering was mostly carried out by the duo. Post-production and mixing took place during the sessions for Bowie's *Low* and was partially overseen by an uncredited Tony Visconti in his spare time, whilst he should have been working on the Bowie project.

While the budget may have been small, the sounds created by Bowie and Pop were nothing short of miraculous. Iggy described how Bowie suggested the collaboration should progress – 'He pushed forward the proposition that my bass registers were more impressive and interesting than my rock registers… I worked to make it as dark and kinky as possible.'

Work began at the Chateau in July 1976 but, since other artists had booked studio time, Iggy and David shifted the sessions to Munich's Musicland Studios for a couple of weeks in August. Donna Summer's producer Giorgio Moroder worked there and Bowie was delighted to meet the synth disco supremo. During their time in Munich, Bowie and Pop travelled to Düsseldorf to meet Kraftwerk. Bowie had asked the German group to be the support act for his 1976 tour. When Kraftwerk turned down his request, Bowie simply played their whole *Radioactivity* album instead. Iggy too had enjoyed Krafterk's music and was thrilled when he found that Ralf Hutter had, surprisingly, been a huge fan of the Stooges. Their meeting was later immortalised in Kraftwerk's song 'Trans-Europe Express' – 'from station to station, to Düsseldorf City, meet Iggy Pop and David Bowie'.

In September, Bowie returned to the Chateau to commence work on the album that would become *Low*. When the facilities at the French studio proved to be lacking (Visconti and Bowie both suffered from food poisoning due to the inadequate catering), they decided to move again, this time to the Hansa Studios in West Berlin. Here *Low* would be finished, and *The Idiot* would be finally mixed. It was only at this point that Bowie decided to rent an apartment in the city, not as is often reported, straight after his spring tour. Iggy decided to go with him.

As Bowie has often commented, since West Berlin offered twenty-four-hour bars, clubs, more drugs and more drink than Los Angeles, it seemed an odd place to settle to try to flee the craziness of their lives. But crucially the city, remote in its isolation in East Germany, offered anonymity. It was somewhere that both men could escape to, seeking refuge in the faded glamour of the nightlife. David described Berlin as a 'therapeutic' place and certainly both men benefited enormously from their sojourn there. While Bowie only really resided in the city for just over a year, from October 1976 to Christmas 1977, Iggy's love of Berlin went deeper and he maintained an apartment there, in the Schoneberg district, in the same block as Bowie's apartment, until at least 1979, sharing his life for much of the time with Esther Friedmann, the daughter of a diplomat. Esther was a photographer and had not heard of Iggy before she met him in a bar in late 1976. The couple were largely unheralded in the press and Esther has remained silent ever since. The eventual souring of their relationship manifests itself in some oblique lyrics on Iggy's Arista albums at the end of the decade.

Iggy loved Berlin. He would later comment, 'I always wanted to come to Germany, even when I was a kid. I read everything about it. I always knew I wanted to come here, just like some guys always knew they wanted to wear a dress.' A pleasant surprise was the city's feeling of spaciousness: 'It's a big thing, the Berlin *luft*... the air sweeps in off the Ukraine plains. I like to walk around. When I first got here, I just walked and walked. Not thinking about anything. Just talking to myself.' Iggy would take himself off on lengthy runs around the many parks of Berlin, gradually becoming fitter and stronger in the process.

His new home was as extravagant and exuberant as Iggy had imagined – the cabaret scene was flourishing and there was a big drag queen crowd that intrigued Bowie and Iggy. The characters that inhabited the divided city also fascinated the pair, especially the old Nazis, and mysterious spy types.

Typically all sorts of stuff would 'just happen' to Iggy. 'One night I got locked in a phone booth. God, I was drunk as hell. It was outside of a pretty tough place called the Jungle. Well, a guy's been doing this. He sneaks up on people when they're inside a phone booth and locks them in, and watches the police come and get them out. But I didn't know that. I was just trying to make this phone call, and I was saying, "Oh, this is me, I can't get out." Somebody saw me in there and they were slipping me cigarettes under the door. I was in there for a half hour until the police came. I was waiting for some strong words, but they just dismissed it. It's happened to about ten people lately.'

Another big fallacy that is frequently repeated is that Bowie and Pop made a pact to get off drugs when they moved to Berlin. While both men acted as mutual supports to each other and certainly inspired each other creatively, there is only a little evidence that their drug habits were decreasing. Iggy has described a typical week in Berlin during the winter of 1976: 'There's seven days in a week. Two days for bingeing for old time's sake. Two more days for recovery, and that left three days to do any other activity.' Music was created in those three remaining days. David, whose physique was not as strong as Iggy's, would suffer more from the effects of narcotics and booze. One story reports Bowie seemingly very drunk in a café, with his head in his bowl of soup. Any attempts to help him were met with the response, 'Please leave me alone.'

Nevertheless despite relatively heavy reliance on stimulants both men were generally in a more positive frame of mind than at any time in the previous couple of years. Both seemed to have rediscovered their enthusiasm for music, and sessions for *The Idiot* would find them pushing each other to new heights. Bowie played much of the guitar, despite only limited ability. Iggy recalls David struggling with the continual riff on 'Dum Dum Boys', determined to get it right. 'David plays better Angry Young Guitar than any Angry Young Guitar Player I've ever heard, apart from James Williamson.' And Bowie's new tunes in turn inspired some of Iggy's most impressive lyrics and vocals to date.

THE IDIOT

RCA PL 12275. (UK) Released – March 1977.
RCA APL1-2275. (US) Released – March 1977.
Produced by **David Bowie**

The title of the album came from Bowie, intended as both an affectionate jibe at Iggy's seemingly inept social graces, and as a reference to Dostoevsky's novel about a Russian prince who returns home from an asylum, and who's honest soul and big-hearted kindness is often taken for simple mindedness. The parallels with Iggy's previous few years are fairly apparent.

Not surprisingly, thanks to the Bowie connection, *The Idiot* had enormous expectations to deliver on. *Billboard* said the same as virtually all the other reviews when it somewhat surprisingly praised Bowie for making Iggy more commercial. Whether this was actually true is a moot point, but the Bowie touch was assumed to have softened Iggy's nihilistic vision. Certainly *The Idiot* was nothing like as commercial as any of Bowie's records. It's swampy, muddy sound wasn't radio friendly and, despite RCA's efforts, there were no obvious singles to be found. But the critics were impressed and *The Idiot* had some high-profile fans. Brian Eno loved the heavy industrial sound of the album, and he described listening to *The Idiot* as like having your head encased in concrete. Eno was delighted when he first met David and Iggy – they could both hum, apparently note for note, the *(No Pussyfooting)* album of guitar abstractions and tape loops that he'd done with Robert Fripp in 1973.

The grey cover photo of Iggy in the rain, standing awkwardly and looking slightly fearfully into the camera, was taken by Andrew Kent, not Bowie as is often claimed. Kent often photographed Bowie and Iggy during the Berlin period and even took some photos of the pair at Hitler's bunker – photos which have never been released. However it was Bowie that arranged the photo shoot and suggested that Iggy adopt the weirdly twisted, stiff armed pose. It was directly copied from *Roquairol* by Erich Heckel, a painting that hung in the Brucke Museum in West Berlin. Bowie would later copy a similar pose from another Brucke painting (Walter Gramatte's self portrait) for the cover of his 1977 album *"Heroes"*. The pose invoked feelings of madness and insanity, ideas that are reinforced by the stark title of the album. The grey back cover contained all the lyrics but very little else – no list of musicians for example. Apart from Bowie and Pop it has always been assumed that members of Bowie's regular band helped out, but drummer

Dennis Davis and bass player George Murray only play on a couple of songs taped at Hansa.

In fact the initial Chateau sessions utilised a couple of French session drummers, Michel Marie and Michel Santageli. Most of the bass was played by Laurent Thibault, formerly bassist in experimental French band Magma, and now the manager of the Chateau. Thibault also engineered and co-produced the Chateau sessions and was subsequently disappointed to find no credit for this when the album was released. Bowie himself played keyboards, sax and much of the guitar. The exceptions being the work that session guitarist Phil Palmer (and nephew of Ray Davies) contributed to 'Nightclubbing', 'Dum Dum Boys' and principally the stirring conclusion to 'China Girl'. Ricky Gardiner was scheduled to play on *The Idiot* but was told he wasn't needed at the last minute, and only flew to Berlin later to join the sessions for Bowie's *Low*. It seems that Bowie would construct loops of music from jams with the musicians. They were unsure of what they were playing and the song structures only became apparent later. Iggy would write lyrics on scraps of paper strewn about the studio. One song that wasn't finished during *The Idiot* sessions was 'What In The World'. With new lyrics and an urgent guitar line the song ended up on *Low* – with Iggy on backing vocals.

Sister Midnight

Based on Carlos Alomar's tune from the Bowie tour rehearsals, the recording of 'Sister Midnight' for *The Idiot* loses some of the overtly funky aspects as played on the tour, becoming instead darker and denser. Apparently the song's backing track was begun in London, with Alomar contributing guitar. As good as finished at the Chateau in August, an uncredited Brian Eno remixed the song during a break in the *Low* sessions. The bass and drums just thud remorselessly along and the guitars build a soupy wall of distortion. There's an air of worrying menace and foreboding which pervades the whole song. Iggy added new lyrics and rewrote some of the existing ones. He incorporated elements of a disquieting Oedipal dream, which concluded with his father hunting him down 'with his six gun'.

'Sister Midnight' was played on the 1977 *Idiot* tour, at some of the spring 1979 shows and on most of the 1980 gigs. Resurrected as regular for the *Blah-Blah-Blah* tours the last time 'Sister Midnight' was played at an Iggy show was during some of the 1996 gigs.

Bowie later used the Carlos Alomar tune as the basis for a new song, 'Red Money', on his 1979 album *Lodger*. He resurrected 'Sister Midnight' as a regular fixture on the 2003/2004 *Reality* tour and a wonderful version from Dublin in November 2003 can be found on the *Reality* tour DVD.

Nightclubbing

More than any other track on *The Idiot*, this song lives up to Iggy's claim that the album was a sort of cross between James Brown and Kraftwerk. With its mechanised drums and blanked-out beats, 'Nightclubbing' is a fearsome slice of European music. Note the 'we' in the lyrics – as they describe quite accurately the lifestyle Iggy and David were living.

It became a favourite of the UK new wave bands – the machine-like feeling evoked by the song was slavishly copied by artists such as Gary

Numan and Human League, (who incorporated it into a wonky medley with Gary Glitter's 'Rock and Roll Part Two'). Grace Jones used it as the moody title track of her 1980 album.

The song was first performed live during the Autumn 1977 tour and here it took on an extremely menacing air – the swirling synth noises and the heavy thud of Hunt Sales' drums is topped off by Iggy's decision to sing the first part in German, the guttural nuances of the language entirely suiting the song. After this tour it wasn't performed again until, appropriately, the short *Nightclubbing* tour of 1980. It would occasionally be played during the late 1981 shows and on the 1982–1983 tour. As with many Bowie tunes, it was aired again on the *Blah-Blah-Blah* concerts, though, like 'Sister Midnight', it's not been performed since.

Funtime

As with 'Nightclubbing', this song reflects Iggy and David's life at the time – going to bars, being sociable in a way neither had thought possible a year previously. Originally called 'Fun, Fun, Fun', the title was amended late in the day. To avoid the overtly 'rock' vibe of early attempts David apparently instructed Iggy to sing the song in the style of Mae West... Again the plural throughout the lyric emphasises that this song is about the duo, rather than just Iggy. There's a cheerful carefree air about the song and it succeeds in roping the listener in – 'all aboard for funtime'.

'Funtime' was a regular fixture on the *Idiot* tour, and at most concerts between 1979 and 1981. The late 1979 tour found the song drenched in whirling synth effects – this rather tiresome version can be found on the very loosely official *Heroin Hates You* release from 1998.

Baby

With the ominous downward stabs of synth punctuated by shards of guitar doing the job of the rhythm track, 'Baby' is an oddity on *The Idiot*. The only track never to be performed live, its lyrics seem to show Iggy pleading for another chance after doing something wrong. It's sung in a numb Sinatra-style croon, which only adds to the disorientating mood. He's constantly walking down 'the street of chance', but there's nothing to see. Ultimately 'Baby' is the slightest song on the album and ends up more as filler between the two hugely influential tracks on either side.

China Girl

One of the stand-out tracks on *The Idiot* and, in fact, one of the most impressive songs of Iggy's career. Originally titled 'Borderline', 'China Girl' is probably Iggy's best-known song, primarily because of David Bowie's international hit single of 1983. Another in the series of classic Bowie melodies married with Iggy's lyrics and imagery, the song includes elements of imperialism, and the corrupting influence of the West. Iggy would later describe 'China Girl' as being about falling in love with someone from another culture. There's a lovely self-referential moment towards the end of the lyric as the little china girl asks a certain Jimmy to shut his mouth. The use of Iggy's real name contributes to this delightful moment of real emotion on an album packed with detached and blanked-out feelings.

Oddly 'China Girl' is not the clearest of recordings, suffering from a rather muffled and muddy mix in which the clarity of the instrumentation is somewhat lost in the general swirl of music. Fighting to be heard are some lovely synthetic strings and rinky-dink snatches of oriental sounding percussion. The piano was actually a toy found in the kitchen at the Chateau. There have been claims that Neil Young's 'Like A Hurricane' influenced the sound of this song and while there are undoubted similarities between the two, especially in the way the string sounds are mixed with Phil Palmer's guitar lines during the lengthy fade-out, it seems unlikely that 'Hurricane' can have actually been an inspiration for 'China Girl'. Although Young was performing 'Like A Hurricane' as early as autumn 1975 the song was not released until late 1977 on the triple album *Decade*, well after *The Idiot* was completed.

As one of Iggy's best-known songs it has featured on most tours since 1977.

Dum Dum Boys

Side two of *The Idiot* opens with Iggy asking himself questions about the whereabouts of the Stooges, while a mournful piano plays below. It's a depressing litany of failure and death taking in the fates of Zander (died in 1975 from alcohol related illness), Zeke (died of an overdose in 1975 after joining the army to get cheap heroin from Vietnam), Scott (living with his mother, but still playing drums) and James ('he's going straight' working as a studio engineer). Oddly, there's no mention of Ron who was beginning a solid if unspectacular career as a guitarist in New Order (not the UK band formed from the remains of Joy Division) with ex-Stooges Jimmy Recca and Scott Thurston. He would later move into film, producing a series of low-budget horror movies. There's a slight ambiguity over which 'James' is being referred to – it could be Iggy himself, though the surely intentional use of 'Straight' (James Williamson's nickname) points the finger more directly at the guitarist.

Anyway, once the roll call is done, the drums clatter in and Bowie's 'angry young man' guitar blasts out. In fact, although Iggy has often referred to Bowie trying to play the twisted guitar lines on this song, Phil Palmer, a more accomplished player than Bowie, overdubbed much of the guitar, based on Bowie's original attempts.

The song itself is a surprisingly straightforward and accurate recollection of the early Stooges. The last verse offers a sort of olive branch to those Stooges that remained alive – 'Where are you now, when I need your noise?' All the time the nagging rise and fall of the guitar squeals evokes the feeling, if not the actual sound, of the Stooges while Iggy really lets rip for the only time on this album.

'Dum Dum Boys' was rarely played live, only appearing at some 1981 concerts and occasionally on the final 1983 Australian shows.

Tiny Girls

The most tender song Iggy had written up to that point, this beautiful ballad is frequently overlooked in appraisals of *The Idiot*. Opening with a gentle Bowie saxophone melody, the song drifts peacefully along for nearly a minute before Iggy's vocals appear. Delivered midway between a croon and a snarl, the lyric reflects upon the demands of the young groupies who pursued Iggy. Their age, their ambitions to be stars, their inexperience – all these perceived shortcomings are documented over the stately pseudo-waltz backing. And then a sarcastically weary 'Ah, what did ya think?' reintroduces Bowie's asthmatic sax which returns to play the tune out for a final minute. Bathed in echo and reverb, with even the drum machine sounding warm and welcoming, this is a gorgeous interlude between two of the more intense tracks on the album. Although the credits are not specific, the music must have been Bowie's – it is so unlike any other Iggy tune. Lyrically the song represents a departure for Iggy. A truly adult, poetic quality, which had not previously been apparent in his writing, reveals itself.

Mass Production

From the factory sounds of the long fade-in via the wonky synthesized middle section to the foghorn like blasts at the song's end, this track is unlike any other Iggy song. Modern factory mass production is often said to have begun at the huge Ford plants in Michigan. Iggy visited one such plant on a school trip and was very impressed with the massive sound of the machinery. The song, which was the last to be finished, arose from a dinner conversation during which Iggy recalled that parts of Berlin reminded him of the bleak and nightmarish industrial nature of his home state. The music seeks to conjure up *Metropolis* like visions of men and machines – not in harmony as with Kraftwerk's pristine, ultra-precise Man Machine, but more in conflict. The destructive side is emphasised, smokestacks belch – it's a depressing scene. The lyrics reflect the despairing music, with the suicidal line 'though I try to die, you put me back on the line' being one of the more disturbing. There are also references to the miserable nature of groupies, the sad production-line feeling of girls lining up for Iggy. This massive slice of Germanic rock is simply one of the best and most underrated tracks that both Bowie and Pop have ever been involved in. This track, more than any other on *The Idiot*, points the way forward to Joy Division, Gary Numan and the doomy side of the European new wave. *The Idiot* and *Low* especially influenced Joy Division. They were originally called Warsaw, taking their name from the track 'Warszawa' on *Low*. And when lead singer Ian Curtis was found hanging, the record still spinning on his turntable was *The Idiot*.

* * *

The album was released to great acclaim in March 1977. Most reviewers commented on how strong the Bowie influence was, leading to accusations throughout the year that Iggy was now somehow Bowie's puppet. David went to considerable effort to redress this viewpoint, even writing to the British music papers to deny that he was any kind of Svengali figure. *The Idiot* was not a big success in 1977, but it has sold steadily over the years, and remains one of Iggy's best-selling records. The Bowie connection has meant that many people have discovered Iggy Pop this way, myself included. The album received a considerable promotional boost when David agreed to tour with Iggy in March 1977. The duo conducted a number of interviews together, which also significantly raised Iggy's profile. This had the result that *Raw Power* was reissued and actually hit the UK charts during 1977. James Williamson dug out the *Kill City* tapes and was able to finish the songs off because Iggy was suddenly a bankable proposition.

This was all some way off. The remainder of 1976 was spent enjoying Berlin. Both David and Iggy loved the anonymity – Bowie got a crew cut and grew a moustache and Iggy let the blond grow out of his hair then had it cut short, even sporting a Mohican for a while. The winter of 1976–1977 was spent recovering from the strains of the previous few years and the next year was to see a newly energised Iggy Pop, ready to take on the world.

1977

Down On The Street – 1977 *Idiot* Tour

Iggy Pop – vocals
David Bowie – keyboards
Ricky Gardiner – guitar
Hunt Sales – drums
Tony Sales – bass

Iggy's first solo tour would be crucial in establishing him as a marketable durable proposition. RCA were happy to finance the tour in order to promote *The Idiot*. In order to reintroduce Iggy to the public, it was decided that the tour would have to include older Stooges songs alongside tracks from *The Idiot*. As *The Idiot* had been created primarily by David Bowie and Iggy, there was a need to form a new band.

Although Bowie's regular musicians were suggested, Iggy knew whom he wanted right away. Good though Dennis Davis and George Murray were, they didn't have the street attitude and punk muscle of the Sales brothers. Hunt and Tony Sales had worked on some of the *Kill City* songs and had remained friends with Iggy ever since. As the sons of Iggy's favourite comedian, Soupy Sales, they also had their father's offbeat sense of humour – something that was essential when cooped up on the road.

On guitar, there was the urgent need for someone who could emulate Ron Asheton and James Williamson and still do justice to the newer material. Iggy looked no further than Ricky Gardiner. He was a friend of Tony Visconti's, who had formed the progressive Scottish band Beggar's Opera in the late 1960s with Virginia Scott, later his wife. In the mid 1970s, Scott worked on songs with Visconti, and Gardiner played on Visconti's record. When Bowie required a new lead guitarist, Visconti suggested Ricky Gardiner. Bowie initially invited him to the Chateau to work on *The Idiot*, but used Phil Palmer instead. Gardiner eventually came to France to work on *Low*. His versatility, ability to rock and experiment, and his amenable nature made him the natural choice for Iggy's tour. Ricky's wife, Virginia Scott, came along for the ride as the tour's astrologer. Recently, *Uncut* magazine asked Tony Visconti about Ricky Gardiner. Visconti replied 'He was totally left-field and completely savvy with special effects. I was in awe of him.'

Finally on keyboards, was David Bowie. This was a remarkable gesture from David. At his own request, he wouldn't be spotlit on stage – he didn't want to take away any of the limelight from Iggy. At the same time, David was aware that his presence in the band would generate much more publicity for his friend's tour than if Iggy had simply gone on the road on his own.

Rehearsals took place in the huge UFA Studios in Berlin during February. The tour was selling well, although the band members hadn't been announced at this stage. There were rumours as soon as the dates were announced but it appears that no one genuinely thought that Bowie would be simply the piano player. Fans first noticed Bowie at the soundcheck during the afternoon of the first date. Clearly the band was relaxed as Iggy and David spent some time drinking in the bar of the Bell Hotel in Aylesbury after the soundcheck.

The opening night was well received. Iggy's performance was somewhat restrained compared with his stage manner with the Stooges, but still wild compared with just about any other performer. Interestingly, David had never seen Iggy perform to a crowd until the Friars show. Bowie himself was not lit, and was placed to the side of the stage where he added some electric piano and backing vocals whilst chain-smoking Gitanes. The rest of the band contributed much more than their famous keyboard player. Ricky Gardiner had the unenviable task of recreating all the Stooges guitar sounds, a task for which he seemed more than capable. In the Sales brothers, Iggy had a rhythm section he could rely upon to lay down a solid base for his songs.

The set list hardly varied for the whole tour, and, as the 1973–1974 Stooges gigs had done, the gigs began with a pounding 'Raw Power'.

'Raw Power', 'TV Eye', 'Dirt', '1969', 'Turn Blue', 'Funtime',
'Gimme Danger', 'No Fun', 'Sister Midnight', 'I Need Somebody',
'Search And Destroy', 'I Wanna Be Your Dog', 'Tonight',
'Some Weird Sin', 'China Girl'

There is a sense that by closing the show with 'Dog' and then encoring with three brand new songs Iggy was attempting to draw a line under the Stooges and present his new material as the future of Iggy. 'China Girl' made for a suitably anthemic final song as Ricky Gardiner surpassed himself with some sterling guitar.

The tour is well represented by the numerous issues of the 21 March show in Cleveland. Originally an excellent quality bootleg called *Suck On This!*, this gig was later issued as a semi-official album under a number of titles (*Wild Animal*, *Sister Midnight* et al). For no readily apparent reason, most releases have the songs in the wrong order and none contain the encores. Two tracks from this gig ended up on *TV Eye 1977 Live*.

After six UK concerts, the tour continued in the USA. The short gap between gigs meant flying across the Atlantic – something Bowie hadn't done in years. To remain as Iggy's keyboard player, David had to overcome his fear of flying.

The support act on the US dates was the rapidly rising Blondie, darlings of the New York scene. Iggy became firm friends with Debbie Harry and Chris Stein, both of whom would work with Iggy in various capacities through the years. Some of the later US concerts saw 'No Fun' moved to after '1969' and ? and the Mysterions' '96 Tears'. Occasional April concerts would also see Van Morrison's classic 'Gloria' added as a final encore number.

The Detroit concert on 25 March was significant in many ways. Not only was it Iggy's first hometown concert as a solo artist, but also it was the first time he'd seen his son for seven years. Eric Benson was born in 1970. His mother, Paulette Benson, had simply been another of Iggy's conquests after a Stooges show at the Grande Ballroom. Although Iggy had remained in contact with Paulette since the birth and had contributed financially to Eric's upbringing, he'd not seen his son since 1970. Over the next few years, Paulette seemed to struggle to control Eric. It has been hinted that she suffered some sort of breakdown. By the end of the 1970s, Iggy had taken over full responsibility for his son but, as he was constantly on the road, elected to send Eric to a private school near New York.

Back in 1977, Iggy was adopted by the emerging punk movement, though he wasn't pleased to be labelled as such. In an interview with Peter Gzowski on Canadian TV station CBC on 11 March, Iggy fiercely derided the naming of this movement ('punk' was a term 'used by dilettantes and heartless manipulators' based on 'contempt and elitism'). To Gzowski's amazement, he also maintained that Johnny Rotten put as much effort into his work as Sigmund Freud had done in his. When asked if he somehow channelled the energy and anger of his audiences, Iggy disarmingly stated that what he did on stage had absolutely no purpose. He also spoke very candidly about the end of the Stooges – 'I became very nasty and paranoid and vicious. I became a guy I didn't like. So I stopped.' Sadly musicians' union regulations prevented Iggy and his band performing on this show.

At the end of the tour, Iggy made another high-profile nationwide TV appearance, with David Bowie on the US housewives' favourite *The Dinah Shore Show*. This time, they performed 'Funtime' and 'Sister Midnight'. To avoid causing major offence to middle America, Iggy changed the most contentious line in 'Sister Midnight' to the nonsensical, but utterly clean,'Potatoes were in my bed, and I made love to them'. Dinah then interviewed Iggy and David, with Bowie again denying any accusations that Iggy was somehow his protégé. Iggy came across as charming, funny and open and this show did much to dispel some of the myths that portrayed him as some sort of degenerate lunatic.

LUST FOR LIFE

RCA PL 12488. (UK) Released – September 1977.
RCA APL1-2488. (US) Released – September 1977.
Produced by **Bewlay Bros**

The *Idiot* tour finished in San Diego 16 April 1977. Iggy wanted to record his next album straight away, so as not to lose the momentum gained on the road. There were already three songs ready to go. 'Tonight', 'Turn Blue' and 'Some Weird Sin' had gone down well in concert so they needed little further work. Iggy and David flew back to Berlin where, in just a few weeks, they wrote most of the rest of the album. For this record, Iggy wanted a more energetic sound, one which would reflect the live show rather more than the introspective doom found on *The Idiot*. Buoyed by the ecstatic reception he had received on his comeback tour, Iggy was determined to build on this with a killer rock album. To that end the tour band arrived at the Hansa Studios in Berlin in May to spend just three weeks recording one of Iggy Pop's most enduring albums.

While many of the tunes were still Bowie's, Iggy spent longer in the studio than anyone else, shaping the sound, directing the band, honing his lyrics. The sessions for *Lust For Life* saw a new Iggy, sharper, focused, happy and completely in charge. 'During that album, the band and Bowie'd leave the studio to go to sleep, but not me.' Iggy would take the tapes home to continue working solidly. As Bowie was a quick worker, Iggy would have to be even quicker to stay one step ahead. The general line has usually been that after cleaning themselves up in Berlin in 1976, both Pop and Bowie were off drugs by this point. Interestingly both David and Iggy have, in recent years, alluded to the amount of drug usage on the tour. And Iggy has admitted that once the money started coming in the cocaine use went up again, which allowed him to work flat out on the new record and explains the edgier voice and faster tempos on *Lust For Life*.

Carlos Alomar, who had been Bowie's regular guitarist since 1974, joined the Sales brothers and Ricky Gardiner. With David on keyboards, most of the tracks were cut live. A week was spent rehearsing the songs before recording began. During the warm-up period, Ricky Gardiner could be heard playing an insistent chugging circular riff. Iggy loved it and encouraged the guitarist to work on the tune while Iggy composed a stream of consciousness lyric, which vaguely describes his trips around East and West Berlin. Catchy yet moody, with a cheerful yet slightly eerie singalong chorus, 'The Passenger' rightly became one of Iggy's most famous songs. Another sign of Iggy's new-found confidence was 'Sixteen', the first song to be officially credited solely to Iggy Pop. (Although Iggy claimed to have written much of *Fun House* on his own, the songs were always credited to all four Stooges.) Along with 'The Passenger' and the album's title track, 'Sixteen' has remained a regular fixture in most Iggy concerts to this day.

What is interesting is how little *Lust for Life* resembles any of the punk records released around the same time. Both Iggy and Bowie have commented on how remote West Berlin actually was in relation to prevailing trends and fashions in the rest of Europe. This was, after all, one of the reasons they liked the place, but it also had the fortunate effect of setting them both apart from the UK's musical climate. Bowie especially benefited from his German exile. Other early 1970s stars were slated by the punks – superstars such as Rod Stewart, Elton John, most of the progressive bands, even the Stones, came in for abuse and disparaging remarks from the punks and the punk-aligned music press. Bowie seemed immune from this, partly through his physical distance from it all. The 1978 Rolling Stones album *Some Girls* was perceived as their riposte to punk but, by not attempting to jump on the bandwagon in that way, Bowie avoided the ridicule and the contempt from the press. Iggy, on the other hand, had been almost entirely unknown in the UK prior to *The Idiot*, and European audiences were now discovering the Stooges records for the first time. Iggy was touted as the originator of punk, and was immediately garlanded with all the accolades that befitted a pioneer. What was entirely overlooked was the fact the *The Idiot* was nothing remotely like the cheap and cheerful, gobbing, safety-pin-wearing punk sound that was being pushed in late 1976.

The music press simply mentioned Iggy Pop and Godfather Of Punk in the same sentence and immediately Iggy was credible and revered. In 1977, two main trends were dominant in pop music – punk and disco – and, although totally different from *The Idiot*, *Lust for Life* was just as out step as its predecessor with the prevailing sounds of the day.

For a start, *Lust For Life* sounds huge. Many UK and European punk albums sound terrifically cheap. This is not to demean them in any way, as cheap, home-made, scratchy, thin, trebly, nasty sounds were the order of the day. But *Lust For Life* begins with some of the biggest drums you've ever heard. Recorded in a room that had previously been a dance hall used by the Gestapo, with all the ambient echo of the room preserved on the excellent recording, the track 'Lust For Life' just bursts out of the speakers with its boomy panoramic sound. Other tracks like 'Turn Blue' and 'Neighborhood Threat' have a similar expansive feel achieved by recording the band live. Microphones were flown over the musicians who were positioned around the room. Old microphones were used on some songs, which give a slightly distorted electrical effect. The crackling voice on 'The Passenger' or 'Fall In Love With Me' sounds as if it's coming from a long way off, down some sort of tube, yet it's clearly a deliberate effect as it's so clearly recorded. And, best of all, the stunning vocal chorus that opens 'Tonight' is an almost Spectorish wall of sound.

Behind the controls were Iggy and David again, assisted by Hansa engineer Eduard Meyer and a young British engineer learning his craft. Colin Thurston would later go on to produce a number of new wave bands including the Human League, Talk Talk and, most successfully, Duran Duran's first few albums. The album's production was credited to the Bewlay Brothers. This was the name of the closing song on Bowie's *Hunky Dory* album of 1971, which is widely thought to refer to David and his schizophrenic step-brother Terry. By appropriating the name for *Lust For Life*, Bowie was implying a brotherly bond between Iggy and himself, as well a taking a sly dig at Mick and Keith's nom-de-production, the Glimmer Twins.

The cover presented another contrast to the doomy and disturbing cover for *The Idiot*. A cheerful Iggy grinned infectiously, almost manically – staring directly out of the record sleeve. The inference was that here was a man with a real lust for life – just look at how happy he seems.

Lust For Life

Rather wonderfully, the album's title song allows all the instruments time to gradually build up, beginning with Hunt Sales' Motown style, 'You Can't Hurry Love' influenced drum pattern. Brother Tony soon joins in with his simple yet perfect bass, pumping along with the drums before the little descending pattern appears. Ricky Gardiner plugs in and starts up the jumpy riff, Bowie adds some piano flourishes and the song is already more than a minute old before Iggy makes his entrance. The gradual layering of instruments and vocals continues throughout as the relatively simple song is expertly stretched over five minutes. By the end there are multi-tracked vocals from Hunt and Bowie, the drums are swamped with Hunt's slightly overbearing crashing on the cymbals, there's masses of other percussion in the background too and Iggy is repeating and repeating the title like a mantra. It's an astonishingly powerful and above all positive song.

Iggy's lyrics on the title song betray his new-found enthusiasm, his positive attitude and his determination to get things done. 'I'm through with sleeping on the sidewalk, no more beating my brains, with the liquor and drugs'. Iggy's nihilistic, couldn't-care-less attitude of just a couple years previously has been comprehensively banished. There's a neat element of knowing self-deprecation in the lines about Johnny Yen and his striptease – clearly referring to Iggy's own public persona and on stage antics. His defiant and celebratory cries of 'I got a lust for life' set the tone for the whole album (although there are darker moments to follow, the sheer exuberance of the opening song is what carries the listener through). The doom and introspection of *The Idiot* has been turned completely around, replaced by a kind of idiot glee, bolstered with a steely determination and an incredibly strong sense of self-belief that borders on arrogance. It's an infectious track, and its sheer energy and bouncy charm can't fail to capture the listener.

One of the most likeable aspects of the song is the fact that it's surprisingly laid back. Although the thumping rhythm seems fast it's clear that no one is really hurrying. The tempo is only mid-paced, allowing a warm and cheerful air to permeate the track. Later live renditions would often be played at almost twice this speed and, with the consequent lack of subtlety, most live versions suffer in comparison. Having said that, it's still an inspiring concert favourite, and rightly so, but the careful layering of music and vocals on the original simply cannot be beaten. Incidentally, the main riff was composed by David Bowie after watching the US services news. The faux Morse code theme tune that accompanied the broadcasts inspired David and grabbing the first instrument he could find, he started bashing out the tune. Rather surreally, the first instrument he could find was a ukulele.

Not surprisingly 'Lust For Life' is one of Iggy's most enduring live tracks, featuring on almost every tour since 1977. The original took on a new lease of life in 1996 thanks to the surprising success of *Trainspotting*, an uncompromising British film based on Irvine Welsh's book about heroin addicts in Scotland. Featured heavily on the soundtrack were a number of Iggy Pop tunes and 'Lust For Life' was issued as a single to promote the film.

Sixteen

Short and sweet, and introduced by Hunt's insistent cowbell. Here, Iggy's vocals sound like they've been beamed down from the moon via a valve radio – there's a very old fashioned distorted compressed quality to the vocal, which is at once endearing and irritating. There's an air of desperation in the vocals, and Iggy sings with a slightly weary, downhearted quality. Lyrically it's another song about a teenage girl (Iggy himself was nearing thirty), although he does declare towards the end that he loves her, and genuinely sounds like he means it. Live performances would emphasise the lascivious aspects of the lyrics as Iggy would ham up the 'leather boots' lines for all they're worth. Iggy put in a marvellously sleazy rendition on *The Tube* (Channel 4) in 1982, changing the next line to 'I know *I'm* not normal' as he leered at the girls on the catwalk above the stage. Understandably, and probably very sensibly, they backed away as much as they could...

Interestingly, for what is actually one of the slightest songs on *Lust For Life*, 'Sixteen' has proved to be one of Iggy's most-played live songs. It was the opening number of the autumn 1977 tour, featured in the set in 1979, 1982–1983 and on almost every solo tour since 1996.

Some Weird Sin

Debuted on the *Idiot* tour as an encore song, 'Some Weird Sin' is one of the more obvious Bowie tunes. Although it boasts a suitably obscure Iggy lyric, which originated simply as an angry poem written in Berlin, musically it's all Bowie; from its solid pumping rhythm reminiscent of songs like 'John, I'm Only Dancing' to the squealing guitar licks that introduce the verses. David is also loud and clear as the second singer doubling Iggy's lead vocal. It's a great song, the title implying some sort of weirdness that the lyrics don't exactly supply.

It seems to be about the desire to be accepted, both as a person and probably as a musician too. As with 'Sixteen', there's an air of desperation, and also of weariness in Iggy's singing. The dichotomy of wanting to be both out on the edge, and to break in is neatly expressed by the next line 'things get too straight, I can't bear it' and he somewhat sadly accepts that it's not for him, and that's when he wants some weird sin. Iggy is implying that he'll never be accepted, allowed into the mainstream, probably because he always wants to be that little bit fucked up.

After the *Idiot* tour this song was rarely performed until the Bowie-heavy set list of the *Blah-Blah-Blah* shows of 1986–1987. It's not been played live since.

The Passenger

Ricky Gardiner's unforgettable tune and Iggy's evocative words add up to one of the classic rock songs of all time. Gardiner came up with the riff almost by accident. In his garden in April 1977, with the apple trees in bloom, Ricky found himself absentmindedly strumming his guitar, but not really paying it any attention. It was only after some time that he realised quite how good the riff was. Opening with Gardiner's clanging guitar, the main riff see-saws its way through the song as Iggy's vocals veer from eerie and scary (the first la la las are quite creepy) to the almost soothing crooning over the fade out. With some clever additional vocals from Hunt and David double-tracking the main lyric at significant points, the song traces a journey through the 'backsides' of West Berlin. Iggy sees the lights and the stars and everything looks good. From being simply an observer, a passenger, an outsider watching from 'under glass', by the end of the song the protagonist has become part of the city. The 'la la la' choruses also undergo a subtle transformation. The first is harsh and stridently Germanic, with Iggy's rasp dominating the vocals. The second chorus is softer, with more emphasis on the harmonics and the third is a lovely piece of harmony singing from Bowie, Pop and Hunt Sales, with David's croon well to the fore and Iggy's most gentle vocals yet. A sense of resolution pervades the fade out. For once, this is song where a fade works perfectly; the listener is given the impression that the song is simply spinning off into the distance happily la la la-ing to itself. The sense of movement implicit in the song is given added emphasis by Tony Sales's bass, which rumbles like a tube train as the song busily lurches along.

Like 'Lust For Life', this is a song that has become an integral part of the Iggy live set in recent years. It was first played live on the autumn 1977 tour where, with Scott Thurston's swirling keyboards, it took on a very harsh edge. 'The Passenger' was missing from the set list for a few years, but was picked up again in 1981, then again in 1986. Since then there haven't been many shows which haven't featured this song, often as an opportunity for audience participation both as a singalong and as a chance to get up onstage with Iggy (bouncers permitting). The cleverness of the original is generally lost in these performances, replaced by something almost primal, as thousands of people sing the simple la la la chorus. What could be easier – a chorus with no words and only a handful of notes! After 'Lust For Life' and 'China Girl', this is probably Iggy's most well-known song amongst the general public, cropping up on numerous compilation albums of punk-era classics, and classic songs in general. For a track that was never a hit, nor even a single, to be classed in this way is somewhat surprising. Nevertheless its longevity and enduring appeal has allowed Iggy the freedom to create far less commercially successful music. Along with Bowie's cover of 'China Girl', 'The Passenger' has almost certainly contributed the most to Iggy's pension fund. Siouxsie and the Banshees released a great cover in 1987, in a neatly updated version that virtually matched the sound on the contemporaneous *Blah-Blah-Blah*.

As a postscript, you may be interested to know that Ricky Gardiner has released an album recently featuring a laid-back version of 'The Passenger'. You can download a snippet of this song, sung by his wife Virginia Scott, from his website:

freespace.virgin.net/ricky.gardiner/index1.htm.

Tonight

The dramatic opening of this song finds Iggy histrionically crying about his girlfriend's overdose – 'she was turning blue' – backed by the massed choir of Bowie and the Sales' brothers. It's rather arch, taking its cue from those sixties songs with spoken interludes such as 'Leader Of The Pack' but setting it firmly in the squalor of junkiedom. Then, somewhat at odds with the intro, the main part of the song is one of Bowie's most obvious and straightforward romantic melodies.

Without the OD intro, 'Tonight' can be seen as a gorgeous love song, which was how Bowie interpreted it on his 1984 cover version. Restructuring the song as a duet with Tina Turner was not a bad idea in itself, but the backing track was also reworked into a soft reggae lilt. In the process it became one of the worst Iggy cover versions ever.

The original boasts a classy arrangement with Bowie's swirling synths to the fore and some excellent guitar from Ricky Gardiner. But it's Iggy's assured vocal delivery, a passable impression of Bowie's rich 'Wild Is The Wind' croon, which really carries the song. There's also David and Hunt's wailing backing vocals and the result is one of the most un-Iggy like tracks recorded so far in his career. But, by going against expectation, and also by going totally straight after the overblown intro, it works beautifully.

Success

A catchy, warm, cheerful song with a simple call-and-response vocal and some genuinely funny lyrics, bolstered by some muscular guitar work and a clapalong beat. This gives the impression of being a one-take vocal, although it's much more complicated than it first appears and a fair amount of rehearsal was required to achieve this level of relaxed fun.

Ignoring the warnings of 'Some Weird Sin', Iggy seems to be embracing the idea of success rather more positively. Singing in a slightly gormless but innocently happy manner, Iggy professes bemusement at the thought of success coming his way – 'It's plain bizarre.' The line about his Chinese rugs has a basis in reality. Iggy would be an avid collector of rare and unusual Chinese rugs in the years to come. He explained why in a 1980 interview: 'I'd advise anybody to put their money in rugs... they can take you anywhere. You can sit on 'em; best of all you can pawn 'em.' He actually used some funds generated in this way to finance some of the *New Values* sessions. The best bit of the song is of course the ending, where the band frantically attempt to copy Iggy's increasingly nonsensical lyrics. One crazy line too many for the band causes the response vocals to dissolve into laughter. Iggy chuckles 'Oh shit', which is then enthusiastically copied by the band as the track chunters away.

Turn Blue

From the chirpiest Iggy song ever to one of the darkest, 'Turn Blue' is more a piece of musical theatre than a song. Originally written in 1975, when Warren Peace (Bowie's childhood friend Geoff MacCormack) was noodling around on the piano and Iggy began improvising some words. Bowie and Peace developed the piece into a soulful torch song, and Iggy added some more words with Walter Lacey, which turned the track into a dramatic piece of self-examination. Finished off during the *Idiot* tour rehearsals, this was not a song for the fainthearted. With drug references aplenty, Iggy's half-sung, half-spoken vocals add an enormous amount of tension, and his sudden explosions into rage push the song forward in unexpected ways. You never know what will happen next. The song thrashes around – from the soul ballad beginning via the stop-start shouts in the middle and cries from the heart to pleas for understanding and forgiveness. The final part, backed by more excellent choral work from Bowie and the Sales' brothers, contains some of the most heartrending singing we've ever heard from Iggy. The devastatingly honest and open delivery of the line 'I didn't know what I was doing' is almost tossed out as an aside yet it remains one of the most important lines in the song. It's not an apology, just an explanation.

'Turn Blue' was one of the new songs featured on the *Idiot* tour and must have confounded audiences expecting simply Stooges retreads. It shows a massive amount of maturity in both its construction and execution. Iggy rose magnificently to the challenge of writing and performing lyrics to accompany the twists and turns of this complex tune. The studio recording is almost identical to the live performance save for one detail. The slightly drawn-out ending of the live version, which features a final unaccompanied and rather subdued confessional 'I shot myself up', is abruptly curtailed in the studio as the song crashes suddenly and shockingly to a dead stop.

'Turn Blue' was only ever performed on the *Idiot* tour.

Neighborhood Threat

After the sudden conclusion of 'Turn Blue', it seems like an age before Carlos Alomar's winding guitar introduces 'Neighborhood Threat'. It's another dramatic song, full of rolling timpani, and an ever-increasing sense of urgency. It's also yet another testament to Hunt's ability to hit everything in sight – in this case the cymbals are thrashed throughout most of the song. As with the title song, there's a build-up of instruments, though the layering is not so leisurely, and by only a minute into the track there is a dense forest of sounds underpinning Iggy's desperate-sounding vocals. Ricky Gardiner is the man of the match here. His squally guitar dominates the latter part of the song, even topping Bowie's marvellously forceful keyboards. Gardiner's very individual sound was much imitated by new wave acts.

Oddly for an Iggy Pop song, it's one that works far better in the studio than in concert. Live performances have been rare – it was played on the autumn 1977 tour but, apart from some 1982 concerts, subsequent tours have ignored this song.

Fall In Love With Me

According to Ricky Gardiner, this song evolved from a jam session where he played drums, Hunt was on bass and Tony on keyboards. It's not clear whether the final version on the album retains this line-up of musicians but the simplistic drumming and bass-like runs on the keyboard would seem to imply that it is.

The lyrics are a muddle of fleeting impressions of seeing a girl in the snow, or in an old saloon. Many lines are repeated over and over throughout the song giving it a dreamlike quality, as if time is somehow out of joint. There's a pleading quality in his voice, and a feeling of hopelessness. The relentless tune emphasizes this, as if it doesn't matter how much Iggy wishes it, she just won't fall in love with him. Just as you think the tune is running out of steam, it seems to pick up again, only then to fade out ridiculously quickly. This makes for a sadly unsatisfactory conclusion to an otherwise faultless album.

*   *   *

Lust For Life has become one of Iggy's best-selling albums over the years. Upon its release in September 1977, it received good reviews with much emphasis once again focusing on David Bowie's involvement. The consensus however seemed to be that Iggy's influence on this album was stronger than before and represented a huge leap forward.

Down On The Street – 1977 *Lust For Life* Tour

Iggy Pop – vocals
Stacey Heydon – guitar
Hunt Sales – drums, vocals
Tony Sales – bass, vocals
Scott Thurston – keyboards, guitar, harmonica

To promote the album, Iggy undertook an extensive autumn tour, beginning with his first concerts in mainland Europe. The tour opened in Rotterdam on 14 September and took in major European cities before trekking round the UK for a week of gigs culminating at the Rainbow in London on 1 October. After just a couple of days off, the tour resumed in the States and continued until the Santa Monica show on 18 November.

With both Bowie (busy promoting *"Heroes"*) and Ricky Gardiner (unwilling to commit to another rigorous tour) out of the picture, Iggy needed a new piano player and a new guitarist. David suggested Stacey Heydon – the Canadian had been the excellent lead guitarist on Bowie's 1976 tour, and had become friends with Iggy on the tour. On keyboards and occasional guitar, Iggy called up his old accomplice Scott Thurston. With the Sales brothers still holding down the rhythm this was 'the best fuckin' band in the world right now' according to Iggy. A couple of weeks of rehearsals in Berlin saw most of *Lust For Life* included in the set list, plus a few select oldies. Due to its new-found status as an original punk single, 'I Got A Right' was played live for the first time, and 'Shake Appeal' also received its live debut. The tour started off with a fairly fixed repertoire, but somewhere along the way the whole set list was reworked. The early part of the tour is well represented on the Revenge *Paris Hippodrome* release:

'Sixteen', 'Lust For Life', 'The Passenger', 'I Got A Right', 'Neighborhood Threat', 'Fall In Love With Me', 'Nightclubbing', 'Raw Power', 'Jenny Take A Ride'/'CC Rider', 'Success', 'That's How Strong My Love Is' (sometimes segued into a cover of Bowie's 'Fame'), 'I Wanna Be Your Dog'

The sometime medley of 'That's How Strong My Love Is' and 'Fame' has given rise to the enduring but entirely false story that Bowie himself performed this medley with Iggy on the *Idiot* tour. Neither of these tunes were played on the early 1977 tour, and Bowie never guested on the autumn tour.

The version of 'Fall In Love With Me' played in Paris featured a long drawn-out descending 'oooohhhhhh' repeated a couple of times – interestingly these were exactly the same as the long drawn-out descending 'oh's on Roxy Music's 'The Thrill Of It All' from 1974.

'Shake Appeal', 'Tonight' and 'Some Weird Sin' were often, but not always, included in the early part of the tour, but 'Shake Appeal' was played more regularly on the American leg. Thick, exaggerated lipstick, pale face paint and jet-black, greased-down hair gave Iggy an almost expressionistic appearance – at some venues he sported a flowing horses tail out of the back of his shiny plastic trousers. It was a striking image.

In Berlin, Iggy wasn't able to hook up before the gig with David Bowie, who had been working on a film, *Just A Gigolo*. So Iggy was surprised and delighted to see David in the front row cheering his friend on. During a French television interview on 22 September, he was asked who were the most important people in his life. Touchingly he named his son Eric and his mother and father.

After the European leg, Iggy substantially revised the song list to a more fluid set of songs. Two brand new songs were added – 'Modern Guy', a fun but rather lightweight song about a guy who eats a Naked Lunch (of course he does...) and the slow burning 'Rock Action' which deserves to be much better known as it's one of Iggy's best songs from the late 1970s. A worthy successor to songs such as 'Dirt', 'Gimme Danger', or 'Open Up And Bleed' and ideally suited to Stacey Heydon's grinding guitar style, it's a great shame this song was never performed after this tour, and never recorded in the studio. The oft-bootlegged San Diego show on 16 November runs as follows:

'One, Two, Brown Eyes', 'I Wanna Be Your Dog', 'Modern Guy',
'Lust For Life', 'Rock Action', 'Fall In Love With Me', 'Shake Appeal', 'Gloria'
(with Iggy spelling his own name out instead of G L O R I A), 'TV Eye',
'Nightclubbing', 'I Got A Right', 'Raw Power'

The tour received more excellent reviews. Free from the overwhelming interest in Bowie, Iggy was once again the centre of attention. He gave a number of TV interviews around Europe, boosting his appeal, especially in France. And the concerts were uniformly well received, with much praise being given to the excellent band, and Iggy's theatrical appearance.

After the tour, the Sales brothers played with Ray Manzarek but further session work stopped when Tony Sales suffered a serious car accident in early 1979. Tony explained, 'They found me basically dead, not breathing, with the gearshift through my chest.' He spent a frightening eight months in a coma and it would be some years before he was strong enough to play again. After an album with the band Chequered Past (which included ex-Pistol Steve Jones) sank without trace, Tony took up carpentry and only returned to the music scene when he bumped into David Bowie at an after-show party during the *Glass Spider* tour of 1987. Bowie recruited Tony and Hunt into a new band project he was starting with guitarist Reeves Gabrels. Called Tin Machine, the group divided Bowie's fans and the critics like never before. Sadly, received wisdom these days is that Tin Machine was a laughable folly on Bowie's part, but in reality Tin Machine was actually a commercially successful and surprisingly influential hard rock band. Since the demise of Tin Machine in 1992 both brothers have kept a relatively low profile, playing intermittent session work.

Stacey Heydon returned to the lucrative world of sessions and production and has maintained his position as a successful producer and guitarist ever since.

Scott Thurston remained with Iggy for the time being and worked on a number of songs with him during the winter. He would accompany Iggy on his next tour and the following album project – *New Values*.

1978

TV EYE 1977 LIVE
RCA PL 12796 (UK). Released – May 1978.
RCA APL1-2796 (US). Released – May 1978.
Produced by **David Bowie** and **Iggy Pop**

Iggy's live act was legendary so it made sound business sense for RCA to request a live album as the third and final instalment of their deal. Iggy was paid a sizeable advance (possibly as much as $90,000) and then spent just a few dollars and a few days at Hansa Studios throwing together a motley collection of live recordings. Both Pop and Bowie are credited with mixing the live tapes, but clearly hardly any work was carried out. No attempt was made to equalise the differences in the recordings, the sequencing of the album is quite bizarre, and some of the tracks included are questionable choices. By mixing up tracks from the spring and autumn tours there is no sense of progression. It would have surely been more sensible to sequence the March songs on side one and the October songs on side two – the jarring difference in recording quality would also not have been so obvious had this been done.

Yet *TV Eye* retains a quirky charm and contains a number of bullish performances, some of which have arguably never been bettered. 'TV Eye' and 'Funtime' are taken from the Agora Ballroom concert on 21 March. Much of this concert was broadcast on US radio during the summer of 1977, leading to one of the most common Iggy bootlegs, *Suck On This!* In recent years this show has been repackaged numerous times as a variety of semi legal releases. Some have inexplicably reordered the set list; some retain the original song order. 'Dirt' is from the next night at the same venue and 'Dog' from the Aragon Ballroom in Detroit on 28 March. This concert was played in an empty theatre for a WKQX radio broadcast, and has often been bootlegged as the 'Midnight Mantra'. The original broadcast is interesting as it highlights the excellent backing vocals from the band. These vocals are often mixed down on *TV Eye* and the various versions of *Suck On This!* The *TV Eye* version of 'Dog' has also been judiciously remixed to eliminate most of Bowie's annoying keyboard sounds. It's still a killer version. The rest of the songs come from the Uptown Theatre in Kansas City on 26 October and despite the lesser sound quality contain some fiery performances. In particular the version of 'I Got A Right' is splendidly fearsome. It's a pity that the rest of this concert, presumably held in its entirety by RCA, has never come to light.

The bright red cover of the album shows an odd photo of an almost unrecognisable Iggy wrapped in a towel. The surround is supposed to represent a TV, but it's a cheap concept and is poorly executed.

TV Eye

...opens the album with a bang. Iggy's huge roar shoots out of the speakers as the band blast into a song that hadn't been performed since 1970. It's almost the equal of the *Fun House* version, powered by the Sales brothers' rhythm section and Gardiner's scorching guitar. The breakdown mid-section is enlivened by Iggy's now-famous comments on the ubiquity of televisions.

Funtime

Looser and more, er, fun than *The Idiot* original, with some swirling keyboards and obvious backing vocals from Bowie. The performance lurches from side to side as if drunk.

Sixteen

The first of the four cuts from the Uptown Theatre; there is a marked drop in fidelity as for some reason the October 1977 show sounds little better than a bootleg. It's far more trebly than a professional live recording ought to sound, and incongruously retains the announcer's intro from the start of the show at the beginning of this song. This sounds decidedly odd halfway through side one. However it's a pounding, bruising version of 'Sixteen', slightly slower than the original, yet sounding more desperate than ever.

I Got A Right

Almost certainly added to the tour due to the release of the 'Bomp!' single during the summer of 1977, this is a monster of a tune. Again, it's slower than the original, which lends it an air of majesty and grandeur that the fast and dirty 1972 versions lack. Stacey Heydon's superb guitar work, especially his brilliant solo, is worthy of mention. Once again, Iggy's vocals are great; his shrill shriek at the beginning is thrilling. Note also Hunt's over-reliance on the cowbells, an element of his drumming that quickly becomes tiresome.

Lust For Life

Shorn of its spoken introduction – usually a rant about the evils of drugs – 'Lust For Life' kicks off side two at a ferocious pace. Despite some of the other songs on this tour being slowed down slightly on stage, 'Lust For Life' is sped up, though somewhat unsuccessfully. The whole band seems to be rushing, losing the thread, and the result is a very unsatisfactory performance. Scott Thurston's harmonica becomes wearing very quickly and the poor recording doesn't help either.

Dirt

A quite brilliant re-arrangement of the *Fun House* original – in many ways this equals the power of that track. The keyboards are to the fore, Tony Sales's bass takes the basic Alexander template and extemporises, and Iggy has rejigged the lyrics to great effect. The climax with the 'sky is black' section contains some of his most accomplished singing to date. One of the undoubted highlights of the album.

Nightclubbing

Appropriately, for such a Germanic song, half the track is sung in German, despite the fact that this recording comes from an American gig. Iggy's voice suits the guttural nuances of the German language remarkably well and despite the poor-quality recording this is a successful reworking of one of the most synthesized tracks on *The Idiot*. It sounds more malevolent, more sinister and, despite Hunt Sales's extra-loud backing vocals, it's another of the best tracks on the album.

I Wanna Be Your Dog

Gardiner has totally nailed Ron Asheton's heartless guitar work and Iggy rises to deliver one of his best-ever vocals on this song. It's just a pity that the song inexplicably fades right at the end. Quite why this was considered a sensible idea is baffling.

*   *   *

TV Eye 1977 Live was released in May 1978 and picked up few reviews. Those who did review it spotted straight away that it was a contractual obligation album, and that it represented little more than a marking-time episode. RCA were less than impressed, and although *The Idiot* and *Lust For Life* have always remained constant sellers, *TV Eye* was allowed to drop out of the catalogue for many years. Nevertheless, Iggy decided to promote the record with another European tour.

Down On The Street – 1978 *TV Eye* Tour

Iggy Pop – vocals
Scott Asheton – drums
Gary Rasmussen – bass
Fred 'Sonic' Smith – guitar
Scott Thurston – keyboards, guitar

The *TV Eye* tour kicked off in Marseille on 10 May and wound its way across mainland Europe spending a week in Scandinavia, before concluding with two nights at the Music Machine in London on 12 and 13 June. The set list remained pretty static for the whole month long tour. A standard night would run roughly as follows:

'Penetration', 'TV Eye', 'Kill City', 'The Endless Sea', 'Lust For Life', 'Five Foot One', 'Curiosity', 'Girls', 'Beyond The Law', 'Gimme Danger', 'I Got A Right', 'Dirt', 'I Wanna Be Your Dog', 'One For My Baby', 'Cock In My Pocket'

Using Fred Smith's Sonic Rendezvous band was a sound move. Iggy had known the ex-MC5 guitarist for ten years and Fred relished the chance to play with Iggy. Gary Rasmussen was another old friend – his band the Up had played on the same bill as the Stooges on many occasions, and of course Scott Asheton and Iggy went right back. Scott Thurston joined this existing band with Iggy and the pair spent some time prior to the tour working on new material. Thurston's 'Curiosity' was one of four brand new tracks showcased (which wouldn't appear on record until the release of *New Values*, more than a year later) but this tour also saw live premieres for a couple of tracks from the just released *Kill City*. 'Penetration' made its live debut, as did the Frank Sinatra classic 'One For My Baby', which would become a live staple in Iggy's shows over the next four years. 'Little Doll' and 'Funtime' were also sometimes played. The soundcheck from Brunnsparken has been bootlegged many times and the poor quality tape reveals a couple of little gems – 'There Is A Place' and a creepy take on 'Crawling King Snake', neither of which were played in concert.

The new songs are especially interesting as they reveal works in progress. Both 'The Endless Sea' and 'Five Foot One' differ from the final studio recordings, with neither sounding entirely finished. This was a solid professional tour, the like of which Iggy had rarely experienced. Fred Smith had fallen in love with Patti Smith just prior to leaving for Europe and apparently spent as much time as he could on the phone to her. Rock 'n' roll excess it wasn't.

After the tour, Iggy spent a couple of weeks travelling the UK with the Bowie tour entourage, before returning to Esther in Berlin where he spent the rest of the year working on new songs.

1979

NEW VALUES

Arista SPART 1092 (UK). Released – April 1979.
Arista 4237 (US) Released – October 1979.
Produced by **James Williamson**

Encouraged by Fred 'Sonic' Smith during the *TV Eye* tour to develop his guitar playing, Iggy spent the second half of 1978 working on a new set of songs. He was determined that his next album wouldn't rely so heavily on others writing the tunes. Self-composed on electric guitar, these songs would enable Iggy to land a new record deal in late 1978. Surprisingly, considering how Clive Davis had lost so much money signing the Stooges to CBS in 1972, Davis' Arista Records would have been the last label you would have expected Iggy to sign with. In truth, Davis was pretty much left out of the deal, as it was London Managing Director Charles Levinson, encouraged by Head of A&R and long-time Iggy supporter Ben Edmonds, who sealed the contract. The redoubtable Clive Davis reserved judgement, and would allow a US release of the forthcoming album only when he saw how it had performed in Europe. Whilst this may seem harsh it was by no means a solitary opinion. The prevailing feeling was that Iggy's previous two studio albums had been a success predominantly due to the Bowie connection and the clout that David had at RCA. This time Iggy was on his own, with a new label and his own songs. Arista was actually a good place for Iggy – New York mavericks Lou Reed and Patti Smith were also on the label. Once the quality of the new material was apparent, Arista put a lot of effort into promoting the record.

Without a band, Iggy first contacted the James Williamson to play guitar and produce the new record. Although Williamson had all but retired from the music business, (by 1978 he was a studio engineer at Paramount Recording Studios in Hollywood, and would shortly give all this up in favour of an extremely successful executive career at Sony), this was still a smart move on Iggy's part. Reuniting with James would give him some of the Stooges recent punk credibility, plus James understood how to get a song out of Iggy. Iggy stated that James had a lot to do with the final form of the lyrics – 'We started with my usual "blurting". Once a song was created, we stopped there. I took a long vacation in Mexico, came back to LA, and James and I sat down with paper and pencil together and tried to refine the content of what I'd said so that people would understand it.'

Initially, the album was to be called *Don't Look Down* after one of the first songs the two wrote together. As James no longer played guitar, Iggy suggested allowing keyboardist Scott Thurston to take on the guitar duties as well. Scott was a sharp guitar player, but had never been allowed to demonstrate this talent in the Stooges. Despite spending a long time working on new material, many of Iggy's tunes were still fragmentary or only contained the skeletons of fully-realised songs. They were full of great

ideas, but unfinished and only rough sketches. Thurston's skill at arranging the material would prove invaluable. Scott also revived a couple of tunes he'd begun in 1974, which had been intended for the Stooges. 'Curiosity' had already been played on the 1978 tour, but Thurston was delighted to be able to finally record this and 'Angel'.

With Scott's assistance, the songs were quickly finished off and studio time was booked at Paramount in January 1979. Iggy called up Klaus Kruger, a drummer friend from Berlin. Kruger had spent the previous year or so playing with avant-garde synth band Tangerine Dream (his drumming, on his innovative polyester kit, appears on 1978's *Cyclone* and 1979's *Force Majeure*) and he was apparently delighted to be summoned to Los Angeles to play some straightforward rock 'n' roll. The band was completed with the arrival of Jackie Clark, a bassist with many years experience and an alumnus of Ike and Tina Turner's band. Despite their disparate backgrounds, the musicians worked well together, creating some confident tracks in a very short time. According to *Record Collector* magazine, fifteen tracks were taped, twelve of them making the final album. The ones that were left on the shelf were 'Pretty Flamingo' used later as a b-side, 'Contribution', about which nothing more is known, and 'Lucky Guy'. As this was the original title for 'Tell Me Story' it's possible that this isn't a different song at all. The other alternative is that in fact it was 1977's 'Modern Guy' that was attempted but the names became confused.

Well aware that his reputation as a solo performer would rest on this album, Iggy worked hard to make sure that the new songs were just perfect. Williamson claims that despite the work he and Thurston put in before they entered the studio, Iggy still demanded multiple takes before he was satisfied. 'He wanted every word, even the simple dumb ones, to say something about him,' said Williamson. James's experience of the studio and easy understanding of what Iggy wanted led to touches not previously found on an Iggy Pop record – a neat horn section, strings, female backing vocals, professionally sung backing vocals, expert use of synths, and a really great mix. Which makes it all the more surprising that *New Values* wasn't more of a hit album. Released in the UK in April 1979 it did relatively well in the charts, though as Ben Edmonds states in the sleeve notes to the CD reissue of the album in 2000, it may have done better had the more commercial 'Five Foot One' been released as the first single instead of the equally excellent but less obvious 'I'm Bored'. After its good performance in the UK and mainland Europe, Clive Davis consented to a US release – in October. By then however, so many copies had been imported that virtually anyone who wanted it already owned a copy of *New Values*, and consequently official US sales were very poor indeed.

Tell Me A Story

The album kicks off in fine style with this commercial and catchy mid-tempo rocker. Iggy's in a declamatory mood, demanding to be told a story, and claiming he's 'too tough to cry'. It's clear from the outset that this is a very different album to previous Iggy Pop records. The production is crisp, there are little elements of synthesised percussion and the song is awash with excellent backing vocals. Originally entitled 'Lucky Guy', this makes for a strong start to his first proper solo album. The short, snappy guitar solo (a world away from his scorching Stooges style) marks James Williamson's only recorded musical contribution to this record.

New Values

In a deep resonant voice, Iggy lays down the new rules of engagement. He's got a hard-assed pair of shoulders and he's keeping out of trouble. He's backed by busily swirling synths and some striking guitar from Scott Thurston. The song itself is basically just the same riff over and over, reminiscent of 'Shake Appeal' with the handclaps and the churning guitar, but without the manic hysteria of the 1972 song. Here Iggy is totally in control, and as the song draws to a close there's a spoken passage, heavily overlaid with effects, about living in the twentieth century. It's a great track, rarely performed live.

Girls

One of the most genuinely amusing tracks in Iggy's canon. From its opening deep throaty 'I love girls' it's clear that this song has its tongue very firmly in its cheek. Iggy's lyrics are fantastic – who else would have the nerve to rhyme 'beautiful shapes' with 'ninety eight!' The guitar riff switches neatly from speaker to speaker, and Scott contributes yet another superb solo just before Iggy tries out his own version of 'Summertime', his voice wonderfully rich and full, close-miked and beautifully recorded. It's quite clear that Iggy had a ball recording this song. Interestingly the structure of the verses is almost identical to those of 'Born In A Trailer', the unreleased Stooges track from 1973.

I'm Bored

From the opening cymbals to the introduction of the up and down riff to Iggy's great opening line, 'I'm bored, I'm the chairman of the board', takes just twenty seconds. It's one of the best beginnings in Iggy's catalogue. This is pure classic Iggy all the way. A supremely confident delivery of a smart lyric, over a cleverly constructed backing track that also includes delicately applied synths and occasional horns for emphasis. Lyrically this song doesn't really celebrate boredom in the way that the first Stooges record did, it's more a cry of defiance, of frustration at being bored. Iggy's sick of all the dips, all the stiffs, even of the girls he happily celebrated in the previous song. 'I'm Bored' was the first single taken from *New Values*, and was backed with the delightfully loopy 'African Man.'

Don't Look Down

Originally this was to be the album's title track, and was the only tune co-written with James Williamson. With Scott's keyboards, especially the swirling Hammond, to the fore, and an angelic choir of female backing singers it's an unusual song for an Iggy Pop album. Mary and Anna Alfono were hired by Williamson, along with Alex 'Earl' Shackleford – all three were members of a band called the Strutters, who James had heard playing Motown covers. Shackleford helped James arrange harmony vocals for most of the songs on *New Values*, but only a few were used in the end. As well as this song, 'Angel' and 'The Endless Sea' benefited the most from these late additions.

Klaus Kruger keeps the song moving at quite a pace and with the introduction of a great sax solo the song seems to move up a gear, Iggy singing his socks off against the masses of backing singers. Rudi Valentino was the professional name of Freddy Burretti, a London Italian clothes designer involved in the early look of Ziggy Stardust. Freddy was a great friend of David Bowie and Iggy undoubtedly met him during the summer of 1972. Although the song refers to Rudi's burial, Freddy/Rudi didn't actually die until 11 May 2001, in Paris. However the song isn't specifically about him (or the great silent film actor of the same name), more a rumination about not looking back, looking down, having no regrets – though there is an element of sadness in the vocals about the passing of a friend. That crazy sound spurs Iggy on; he has no time for looking down.

The Endless Sea

One of the most unusual Iggy Pop songs, it opens with a metronomic drumbeat before being joined by a mournful bass and a swirling synthesiser. Only after a minute and a half does Iggy make his entrance. Gentle but spooky backing vocals chorusing 'Endless...' add to the eerie atmosphere and the masterfully played synth that crashes in after the first chorus is a marvellous touch. Iggy's vocals are excellent, strong and dominant and sung in that deep authoritative croon that was fast becoming Iggy's preferred method of singing. By the second chorus, a faint, melancholy violin doubles the tune and a sax pops up from nowhere, plus backing vocals that create a stirring conclusion. You think it's all over, then Iggy croons the title one more time before the synth makes its winding down farewell. It's a stunning production that owes a lot to Williamson's mastery of the studio, and echoes much of the new wave sound that was becoming predominant in the UK.

Interestingly however, this song had started life on the 1978 tour, where it was played in a rougher arrangement, without so much reliance on the synths.

Five Foot One

He's not of course, despite what many writers have said. Iggy, though not the tallest of rock singers, measures up at about five foot eight. But somehow that doesn't sound as good in a song title.

This is a marvellous tune, punchy and aggressive, with a hysterical lyric about how the singer has been continually dumped on and how he wishes that life could be more like Swedish magazines. Somehow the lyrics work better because of the mildness of the tone at the start. 'What the heck' seems to be a very tame expression of anger.

Musically this has a brilliant opening rumbling bass line and Klaus Kruger plays some especially crisp drumming, before the sharp stabs of guitar get the song underway. An understated horn section completes the backing track before Iggy gets going. Describing the working life of an amusement park attendant and his aspirations to go home, this is one of Iggy's best and earliest attempts at writing obviously in the third person, rather than the more abstract or personal lyrics he had written previously. The allusion to 'Swedish magazines' is an evocative image of envy and the desire for advancement. But the character won't grow any more in status amongst his peers; he's stuck down there. The line about aspirin and jokes is of course stolen from 'Sell Your Love' on *Kill City*, which had only received limited release when Iggy was writing 'Five Foot One'.

'Five Foot One' is one the few songs from this era still performed by Iggy after 1982. It crops up on virtually every tour from 1986 onwards, but was never played with such lightness as on *New Values*.

How Do Ya Fix A Broken Part

One of the slightest songs on *New Values*, dominated by Thurston's piano and characterised by some odd time signatures and some very Bowie-esque doo-doo-ing in the background. Once again Kruger's drumming excels and Thurston's layers of guitars create another wall of sound, which make the song seem more impressive than the fragment that it really is.

Angel

A ballad apparently begun in 1974 by Scott Thurston, though it's hard to see how this would have fitted in with the Stooges. Iggy sings a simple though clearly heartfelt lyric in a half-whispered, understated performance. Female backing vocals and that uncredited violinist add to the slightly sugary production. Little touches of strings and electric piano create a romantic air. With the straightforward piano and guitar this song could easily have fitted onto any MOR album of the 1970s. What makes it successful here is both the surprise of finding a love song on an Iggy album, and the obviously sincere love being expressed towards Esther. The lyrics relate very much to the salvation that she gave him in Berlin.

Curiosity

Another Thurston track intended for the Stooges five years earlier. It's easy to imagine that band playing this song, as its bar-room piano and Stonesy riffing invite comparisons with 'I Got Nothin'', or 'Wet My Bed'. Again it's the little touches that impress, especially the layers of guitar. It's infectiously catchy too and the instrumental break contains some delightful piano work. For a song that's pretty much a throwaway it's such a lot of fun.

African Man

An absurd, yet oddly likeable little song, Iggy sounds like he's having a whale of a time with the vocals, which only increase the enjoyment of the song. It's stupid, for sure. Iggy's lyrics are in turns bizarre and poignant, and contain some odd resonances, considering Iggy had never been to Africa. This also represents the first time on record that Iggy appropriates that sort of tribalism that would reach a peak on *Zombie Birdhouse* a few years later. Although he had often invoked African stomping rhythms with the Stooges, this was the first explicit reference to Africa.

Billy Is A Runaway

A straightforward rock song, undercut with spiky synths. The jumpy tune perfectly encapsulates the sentiment of the song, about the crime-ridden family of Billy and his dope-dealing sister. Some cool echoes on the vocals towards the end, as the synths create a siren effect and odd bubbling noises.

Chains
Even the credits on the sleeve of the reissue weren't aware of the origins of this song. Clearly from the *New Values* sessions – the backing vocals and Thurston's piano give that away – but it doesn't sound quite finished. There's an odd hollow quality to the track as it stands.

Pretty Flamingo
Originally used on the b-side of 'I'm Bored' this is a welcome addition to the reissue of *New Values*. Its loping drum beat and judicious use of horns create another memorable love song. Thurston contributes a brilliant guitar solo, and vibes, occasional sax, and a barely audible heavenly choir all add to a masterful production. The pretty flamingo of the title is almost certainly Esther – 'built like a willow' describes her perfectly. Interestingly, the line 'I, I will protect you...' echoes almost exactly the crucial lines in Bowie's 'Heroes'. It's simply a lovely song.

*   *   *

Down On The Street – 1979 *New Values* European Tour

Iggy Pop – vocals
Jackie Clark – guitar
Klaus Kruger – drums
Glen Matlock – bass
Scott Thurston – keyboards, guitar

To promote *New Values* Iggy set off on an extensive UK and European tour in April and May 1979. Retaining Kruger and Thurston from the sessions, Iggy moved Jackie Clark to rhythm guitar in favour of ex Sex Pistol Glen Matlock on bass. Widely regarded as the most accomplished musician in the Pistols, Matlock had been shunted out of the band due primarily to his not so punk appearance. Spiky-haired sneering junkie Sid Vicious fitted Malcolm Maclaren's preferred image far better and the fact that Vicious could barely play bass only added to the punkness of the band. Since the Pistols, Matlock had formed the new wave band the Rich Kids, fronted rather improbably by Midge Ure, previously in Scottish teen band Slik. The Rich Kids achieved headlines but very little success and before long Ure had departed for the more lucrative pastures of the synth new wave, (via a surprising stint in Thin Lizzy) ending up in 1980 as the new front man for Ultravox. Matlock preferred his music basic and raw and a place in Iggy's band was a dream come true. He also gave Iggy some UK punk kudos.

Jackie Clark's flashy stage outfits amused Iggy: 'a very beautiful, fine wide-brimmed Stetson hat, tan, in good taste, and those toreador-type pants – very overdone cowboy'. Clark's intention was to look his best for the gig, which is what he'd have done for an Ike 'n' Tina show, and so he was not amused when all the audiences did was spit at him. After the first night, he complained to Iggy, 'I don't care what they do to me, but when they gob on my hat, I get mad.'

A strange choice of support act for the European tour was the Human League. At this point, the Sheffield-based band were still playing in their original line-up, with tape machines and electronics dominating their cold sterile sound. Despite professing an admiration for Iggy (indeed they had recently recorded an awkwardly brilliant version of Gary Glitter's glam stomp 'Rock and Roll' which segued with Iggy's 'Nightclubbing') the Human League's actual sound was as far removed from that of Iggy's as could be imagined. Interestingly, the Human League's singer Phil Oakey has commented on how low Iggy seemed on this tour. Off stage, Iggy appeared quiet and withdrawn, with little of his usual fighting spirit. Oakey recounts an astonishing story about how Iggy taunted some Hell's Angels at one show. After the gig some of the Angels forced their way backstage and threatened to kill Iggy if he didn't apologise. Oakey claims that Iggy then went back onstage, in his bathrobe, to apologise to the angry gang. If this had happened a few years before, Iggy would probably have unwisely squared up to the threats. Now he was getting too tired to argue.

The tour kicked off at the Factory in Manchester on 20 April and spent the next couple of weeks travelling the length and breadth of the UK. A memorable appearance on the BBC's classic rock show *The Old Grey Whistle Test* was taped on 24 April, the day before a sell-out show at the Music Machine. On 15 May, the band crossed the Channel to begin two weeks of touring around mainland Europe. Parts of the first show at the Palace in Paris ended up on one of the best Iggy bootlegs from this period. The gigging concluded with two hastily arranged dates back in England. To satisfy demand, the large Hammersmith Odeon was the setting for the final gig. Not surprisingly, this tour contained many *New Values* tunes amongst a few classic oldies and real surprises.

> 'Kill City', 'Fortune Teller', 'New Values', 'Billy Is A Runaway',
> 'The Endless Sea', 'Cock In My Pocket', '1970', 'Sister Midnight',
> 'Down On The Street', 'Girls', 'Loose', 'Dirt', 'Batman Theme',
> 'Louie Louie', 'I Wanna Be Your Dog', 'Five Foot One', 'Shake Appeal',
> 'I'm Bored'

'Little Doll' was also played at some of the early shows. The theme from the 1960s TV series *Batman* was one of the more surprising songs – performed as a sort of dialogue between Jackie Clark as Robin and Iggy as Batman, with lots of swearing and band in-jokes, and leading directly into Iggy's usual filthy version of 'Louie Louie'.

It was a successful tour, re-establishing Iggy as a bona fide solo artist, free from Bowie's shadow. The band was strong and muscular and the choice of songs suited both the old Stooges fans and the new admirers of the Berlin albums. Europe was fast becoming a staunch supporter of Iggy and this tour helped to cement his growing reputation. To build upon this wave of support Iggy elected to record his next album in the UK.

SOLDIER
Arista SPART 1117 (UK). Released – February 1980.
Arista 4259 (US). Released – February 1980.
Produced by **Pat Moran**

As soon as the European tour was over, Iggy was eager to get back into the studio. Although *New Values* hadn't yet been released in the USA, Iggy had a lot of new songs he was keen to record. The original intention was to use the tour band on the new record, but Scott Thurston had a prior appointment with US new wave act the Motels, and Jackie Clark had quickly tired of being spat on by British punks and returned to the USA. Glen Matlock recommended his former Rich Kid partner Steve New to replace Thurston on guitar. Barry Andrews, formerly of XTC, came in on keyboards and Ivan Kral of the recently defunct Patti Smith Group arrived to play rhythm guitar. This new wave heavy line-up travelled to Rockfield Studios in North Wales in the late summer of 1979. Iggy had a selection of tunes ready but not enough for an album, and the band spent some time jamming. One session has made its way out onto the bootleg circuit and reveals a lot of almost funky tracks being worked on. Steve New's choppy guitar sounds oddly similar to that of Nile Rogers, the leader of New York disco kings Chic. The really weird thing is that some of the tracks actually sound rather good in this mutant disco-rock-new wave conglomeration and its something of a pity that this direction was dropped.

James Williamson was again asked to produce the album, although he expressed misgivings about working away from Los Angeles. His hunch turned out to be right. James did not get along with the staff at Rockfield, nor did he get along with Iggy's band. He came to the studio each day with a gun sticking out of his pocket, something which unnerved the British musicians. James had grandiose ideas of a forty-eight-track production, and ran two twenty-four-track machines together. Even Iggy wasn't sure about the lavishness of James' ideas, accusing him of trying to be like Phil Spector. The final straw, according to Matlock, came when David Bowie showed up at the studios one day. Bowie and Williamson argued over the production, and James just quit. He'd had enough problems getting the sound he wanted and to have someone like Bowie (who James says he has no respect for) swanning in and criticising was just too much. Matlock also claims that Steve New argued with Bowie and threw a punch at him. This was to have big implications later.

With James gone, it fell to studio engineer Pat Moran to complete the record, which he did with the minimum of fuss. *Soldier* wasn't finished yet however. Iggy had a US tour booked to promote *New Values*, which had just been issued in the States, but days before the tour started Steve New pulled out. Fortunately Iggy was able to replace him with Brian James, who had recently left the Damned – after the Pistols, they were arguably Britain's best punk band. However, Iggy began the tour in a foul mood.

After the tour, Iggy took the *Soldier* tapes to the Record Plant in New York for remixing and, still pissed off at New's defection, and possibly his punching of Bowie too, proceeded to erase much of New's guitar work. Ivan

Kral's rhythm guitar remained, and Kral added some necessary overdubs, but one of *Soldier*'s most defining features is the almost total absence of scorching lead guitar, making it a real oddity in Iggy's catalogue. Yet it's precisely this absence that strangely makes *Soldier* such a success. The eleven songs are a collection of the most varied styles yet attempted on an Iggy Pop album. The lack of strong guitar forces the listeners' attention onto the other instruments – sax, organ, piano – and forces the songs to stand on their own, which on the whole, they do rather successfully. Far from being one of the weakest albums of Iggy's career, as is often reported, *Soldier* holds up today as a quietly inventive, melodically catchy and, despite the problems along the way, well-produced album. Of course it doesn't contain a slew of bona fide Iggy classics, and it was one of his poorest-selling albums too, but it's an unassuming collection of clever pop/rock songs with some excellent lyrical and musical twists, ripe for rediscovery. Iggy himself obviously feels that way too. In 2002, two of *Soldier*'s songs were reintroduced into Iggy's live set for the first time since 1983. And 'Knocking 'Em Down' and 'I Snub You' stand up very well against the harsh nu-metal of the *Beat 'Em Up* tracks they were sandwiched between.

Sadly *Soldier* has one of the least attractive album covers in history. Iggy, with his scary red painted eyelids, looking strung out and plain unappealing. The picture is surrounded by some cheap and vaguely militaristic stencilling and graphics. Mind you, compared with the following year's *Party*, it's a masterpiece...

Loco Mosquito

From Iggy's opening cry – ('My mama told me...' lifted from an old nursery rhyme) – backed by Andrews' pumping Wurlitzer sounding organ, it's clear that this is a very different album to *New Values*. 'Loco Mosquito' is an absurd song featuring daft rhymes ('mosquito'/'Hirohito') and manic, though seemingly impassioned, vocals about very little in particular. The backing vocals have a cheery amateurishness about them, a far cry from the polished singing on *New Values*. And 'Loco Mosquito' immediately shows up the lack of lead guitar. There's some good acoustic rhythm work, and the occasional electric flourish, but otherwise the song is led by the organ.

Ambition

Similarly the organ dominates 'Ambition', one of Glen Matlock's tunes. It's a much more serious song than 'Loco Mosquito', a rueful reflection on the pitfalls of ambition, friends letting one down, being spun a line and stood up on dates. It ends with the resonant line 'Don't lose ambition', words that Iggy never lost sight of. Oddly, the song appears to be sung from the female perspective – 'I'm the kind of girl, I want that whole wide world'. It's a much more mature piece of songwriting than some of Iggy's own songs of the time. The acoustic guitar and carefully built-up organ and electric guitar climax is excellent and it's a shame that the songs fades so rapidly at this point.

Take Care Of Me

Another of Matlock's songs, with additional lyrics from Iggy. A strong showing from Klaus Kruger powers the song as, for the first time, on *Soldier*

we hear some grinding electric guitar. Iggy's lyrics have a strong autobiographical note to them. Whereas some of *Soldier*'s songs continue the
third-person writing of *New Values*, there are a number of seemingly very
personal tracks – this is one such tune. 'Take care of me, somebody should...'
is sung by someone who quite clearly means what he's singing. Strangely,
the backing vocals threaten to drown Iggy out at times, but on the whole it's
a very successful song. Reminiscent at times of other UK punk tracks of that
era, the whole boys-in-the-band shouty vocals and simple riffs could have
come from bands such as Sham 69.

Get Up And Get Out

With a breathy saxophone playing the melody in place of the missing guitar,
and Barry Andrews' upbeat organ underpinning this intriguing tune about
how you shouldn't abuse women, it constitutes a rare instance of Iggy
putting an overtly moral stance into a song. Coming from Iggy, who didn't
exactly have an unblemished record when it came to the treatment of
groupies and girls on the road, makes this song all the more surprising. It's a
welcome and mature lyric, not preachy or pushy, but cleverly listing a
couple of strong 'chicks' – Bette Davis and Little Eva – as examples of those
'who got up and got out'. Although there's no credit for the saxophonist,
the asthmatic style here bears a strong resemblance to Bowie's sax playing.

Play It Safe

This was the song being worked on when David Bowie visited the studios,
and David's contributions to the song earned him a co-writing credit.
Indirectly, he was also responsible for getting members of Simple Minds
involved in the *Soldier* sessions. Simple Minds were recording their *Real To
Real Cacophony* album in Rockfield's number two studio. Aware that two of
their heroes were next door they plucked up enough courage to ask if Bowie
would like to contribute a bit of saxophone to their record. Bowie declined
but roped in as many of Simple Minds as he could to join the leery raucous
chorus on 'Play It Safe'. They were rewarded with Iggy including their name
in the song: 'you're too simple minded...' Simple Minds would play 'Sister
Midnight' at some of their 1980 concerts.

Yet again, the keyboards dominate, this time though it's via a doomy
drone that continues throughout the song, building gradually in intensity.
Kruger keeps a martial drumbeat pounding constantly, and Iggy's vocals are
sung with a real passion. Lyrically, it's another Iggy song that throws images
at the listener without any real sense. Quite what Eisenhower saw that was
so sickening is unclear, though to this audient there's an apocalyptic feeling
conjured up by the song. This feeling carries on through a number of songs
on *Soldier* ('Mr Dynamite' especially) and partially via the title of the album
itself. There's a sense that Iggy is fighting, for a better world, for his own
sense of self worth, or possibly simply for more pickle and relish.

I'm A Conservative

Iggy's love of 'Louie Louie' manifests itself in this great track, the main riff of
which is loosely based on Richard Berry's classic. Early versions make the
connection more explicit by clearly pumping out 'Louie Louie' throughout

the song. Even on the album you can still hear traces of Berry's tune towards the end.

'I'm A Conservative' is one of the best-constructed tracks on the album, building from a gentle opening with Iggy intoning the frankly unbelievable declaration of his former 'quiet' life over a delicate piano and guitar backing, to a full band thrash fest at the end. The changeover occurs at the wonderful cry of 'Is everybody happy?' It's an inclusive remark, which has the effect of bringing the audience into Iggy's inner circle. The loopy la-la-la-ing that crashes in only serves to remind the listener that in no way is this song to be taken too seriously. Having said that, there's a load of lyrics that seem autobiographical, referring directly to all the usual rock star excesses for which Iggy had become known. Iggy seems, however, to feel the need to veil such personal comments in a really great, rocking, and overtly humorous track, as if this will detract from the personal nature of the words. Musically the band are on top form – there's some lovely piano, especially the rollicking playing in the middle of the song, the guitars growl in a very satisfactory manner (though still mixed way down).

Dog Food

For years, it's been assumed that 'Dog Food' was first attempted during the *Funhouse* sessions. This was due to remarks made by Iggy that it was part of the 1970 live set. Since the release of the *Complete Fun House* sessions it's clear that 'Dog Food' was never even attempted in the studio in May 1970. Iggy was actually talking about the jazzier performances given by the Stooges in the latter half of 1970. There's a large element of autobiography in this short snappy tune. Iggy's then girlfriend Betsy was indeed fourteen. The line about having nothing better to do also points to the song's origination with the Stooges – it's very reminiscent of those in '1969'. Glen Matlock shed a little more light on the background in the sleeve notes to *Soldier*'s 2000 reissue saying that the song 'was about big housing projects... where the shops sell lots of dog food – and nobody there is allowed to own a pet!' The song's opening 'hurrrgghhh' from Iggy sounds like a stoned version of the opening roar on 'TV Eye', the rest of the song bounces along on a bed of handclaps and martial drumming, assisted by some cheerful piano and some equally happy-go-lucky backing vocals. It's stupid, it's dumb, there's no message, no underlying metaphors and, at one minute and forty eight seconds, it doesn't outstay its welcome at all.

I Need More

Probably the strongest track on *Soldier*, 'I Need More' is a powerful litany of what Iggy requires to keep himself going, but all he has is the 'ordinary grind'. He needs a lot of stuff. From the intellectual – culture, truth, intelligence, to the material – cars, money, champagne, to the mundanely absurd – mustard, pickle and relish...

There's a strange little middle eight where Iggy exhorts everyone to love their jobs and be happy with their situation, but in the context of this song it's fairly clear that this is meant sarcastically. In any case this sort of life is no good for Iggy. His life's been going all right up till now, but there's still something missing. He needs to play scratchy records and enjoy his decline.

Iggy's personal life at this time was something of a non-starter. His relationship with Esther had fizzled out, and with that came the end of a period of stability, both domestically and emotionally. Throwing himself totally into his work, as shown by the speed with which he embarked on recording *Soldier*, Iggy would spend the next few years touring virtually non-stop, only pausing to record more records. It was a nomadic life of cheap hotels, cheap girls, expensive drugs, and booze. Throughout this period, Iggy was to see his commercial stock sink lower and, in his own mind, see his live performances become more erratic. He would suffer extreme exhaustion from too much alcohol and too little sleep, and by mid 1983 would have to bow out of live performance altogether. 'I Need More' was therefore a rather prophetic song. It just took Iggy another six years to finally shake the 'ordinary grind' and actually gain the more laughs and more freedom that he really wanted.

Knocking 'Em Down (In The City)
Back to basics seems to be the point of this song. Sung with the strong band-gang mentality which would reach a peak with the following year's *Party*, 'Knocking 'Em Down' presents Iggy as the leader of the pack, ready to take on the world with his band. The lyrics constantly refer to 'we', Iggy's vocals are double-tracked to give the impression of more singers and the title of the song is chanted by the band throughout. At the end Iggy calls 'Are you ready?' to which he receives the response 'We're ready' which sounds like it's sung by a football crowd. The 'we don't care' attitude is straight from the UK punk movement that had embraced Iggy so strongly. It's one of the few songs on *Soldier* that couldn't survive without a scorching electric guitar. It's an infectious, rough and raucous song, and one of only two from this period that was resurrected in recent years.

Mr Dynamite
There's some stunning saxophone on display towards the end of this track – such a shame then that the sax player is uncredited. The song opens with co-writer Glen Matlock's throbbing bass, atmospheric piano, cool chords from Kral and more of Kruger's militaristic drumming. Then Iggy comes in with another variation on his 'Looooorrrddd' from 'TV Eye' and introduces himself as 'Mr Dynamite'. The song is a sort of new wave, smaller-scale version of 'Sympathy For The Devil'. Mr Dynamite seems to be a kind of low-rent terrorist, someone from down the block who everyone knows, but with disturbing habits, who is finally turned in by his neighbours. Iggy, typically, identifies with the outsider who lives among us, and towards the end speculates about where Mr Dynamite may finish up. Interestingly, the long fade-out beginning with 'Poor Mr Dynamite' contains strong hints of the similar long fade on Roxy Music's 'For Your Pleasure' with the echoed piano and sustained chords. One of the more successful of Iggy's experimental songs.

I Snub You
Probably the most overtly UK punk-style track that Iggy has ever recorded. The sneery vocal affected by Iggy is very British, and the whining backing vocals courtesy of Glen Matlock only reinforce this feeling. It's also one of the nastiest songs Iggy has ever recorded. Whoever inspired such ire in Iggy?

It could just be any drug-addled groupie, but there's also the feeling that the song may not actually be about any one person at all. The lyrics could be read as an attack on the drugs themselves rather than a supplier. Iggy was gradually cleaning up, replacing many of the hard drugs with drink, so this sort of reading may not be too far fetched. Whatever the truth, 'I Snub You' is still one of the most unpleasant tracks with which to end an album. It's one that was performed rarely, and didn't feature at all after 1980, until 2002, when it was one of the most surprising songs to be resurrected by Iggy for some of the summer shows. The Trolls rose to the challenge and turned in splendidly harsh performances to match Iggy's angry delivery.

Low Life

One of the two unreleased songs on the CD reissue allegedly from the *Soldier* sessions. It seems much more likely that this actually dates from later, probably from the many demos than Iggy and Ivan Kral made in 1980 for the *Party* album. There's none of the usual sounds of *Soldier* and although Thom Panunzio mixed *Soldier* in New York, which led to his assuming the producer's chair for *Party*, here he's actually credited with production. In any case, it's a rather good song, unusually understated for this period, gentle acoustic guitar and Iggy in reflective mood. He's lamenting his low life, no one calls him, he's alone, and all he's got is his bikini underwear... It's a shame that 'Low Life' was left undiscovered until 2000, as it demonstrates an entirely different side to the Iggy Pop usually presented to the public at the start of the 1980s.

Drop A Hook

With no vocals, this tune of unknown composition is all very well, but what really was the point of including it on the reissue of *Soldier*? For a start there's a number of excellent out-takes from 1979–1981 that could have been included instead. 'Brakes On' is one that springs to mind that would have fitted perfectly. 'Drop A Hook' isn't bad, in fact to me it's strangely reminiscent of some of Phil Manzanera's solo work. 'Drop A Hook' could easily have fitted onto the Roxy Music guitarist's 1978 album *K-Scope*, with its angular new wave guitar jabbing.

Down On The Street – 1979
New Values North American Tour

Iggy Pop – vocals
Brian James – guitar
Ivan Kral – keyboards, guitar
Klaus Kruger – drums
Glen Matlock – bass

With a new front line and another album in the can, the second tour of 1979 was very different from the first. Both Scott Thurston and Jackie Clark had left. Ivan Kral filled Scott's position on both guitar and keyboards and on this tour Ivan's love of synths was indulged as a number of tunes were drenched in bubbling spacey noises – 'Funtime' ended with a few minutes of burbling sci-fi whooshing, and even the straightforward rock of the opening 'Real Cool Time' contained more synth that one would have thought

possible. After guitarist Steve New dropped out at the last minute, Iggy hastily recruited Brian James, who had recently left the Damned. Iggy received much valuable publicity arising from the inclusion of both a Sex Pistol and a member of the Damned in the band. It seemed to indicate that the new punks were genuflecting in front of Iggy. It gave him a kind of seal of approval from the new wave.

A warm-up show at the small Showplace in Dover on 27 October preceded the first proper gig at Philadelphia's Hot Club two days later. From there, the band travelled back and forth along the East Coast before moving into Canada and then through the northern states to California. A final show at Hurrahs back in New York on 9 December was tacked on at the end of the tour.

Amongst the songs played, 'Your Pretty Face Is Going To Hell' received its first live performances. Despite the fact that Iggy was ostensibly promoting *New Values*, most of that album's tunes had been jettisoned in favour of a bunch of new songs from the recently recorded *Soldier*, an album that wouldn't be released until the middle of the following year... 'You Really Got Me', the Kinks garage classic, was a great choice for a cover, and one that could have been written for Iggy. The shows were pretty wild, with Iggy thoroughly enjoying his status as an elder of the punk generation. Though he would publicly decry the pigeonholing of the music business there's no doubt that he benefited from the punk label, as more and more people, enticed by the newer punks, sought out his back catalogue. Perhaps surprisingly, however, he was playing fewer and fewer Stooges songs. Iggy concentrated on new material and only a handful of early 1970s tracks were included. The show at Los Angeles' Stardust Ballroom 30 November was broadcast on KROQ Radio. Subsequently bootlegged and then released on the dubiously semi official OPM label as *Heroin Hates You*, it's a great example of this tour. Iggy is on form, dominating the band and controlling the show. Interestingly the opening music for many of these concerts was a tape of Robert Fripp's hypnotic experiments with loops of tape and beautiful shimmering sustained guitar. Fripp had been giving performances of these 'Frippertronics' throughout 1979 but none were actually released until *God Save The Queen* in March 1980, which raises a question: from where did Iggy get these tapes?

The usual set list was:

'Real Cool Time', 'Knocking 'Em Down', 'Loose', 'Take Care Of Me', 'Dog Food', 'You Really Got Me', 'New Values', 'TV Eye', 'Sixteen', 'Your Pretty Face Is Going To Hell', 'Play It Safe', 'Funtime', 'I Wanna Be Your Dog', 'China Girl', 'One For My Baby', 'Five Foot One', 'No Fun'

With the tour complete, Iggy returned to Berlin for Christmas. With his relationship with Esther now over, however, there was nothing to keep him there. During 1980, he let the lease on his apartment lapse and moved back to the USA to be near his son. Over the next couple of years, Iggy and Eric would spend a lot of time together, which resulted in Iggy kicking many of his drug habits in an effort to be a good father.

In the meantime, another UK tour had been booked, which would begin the most intensive year of gigging that Iggy had ever undertaken.

Freedom and Respect

1980

Down On The Street – 1980 *Soldier* UK Tour

Iggy Pop – vocals
Rob Duprey – guitar
Ivan Kral – keyboards, guitar
Klaus Kruger – drums
Billy Rath – bass

Despite the short gap between tours, Iggy had written many new songs that he was keen to showcase on the road. He took the brave step of opening each show with two brand new tracks, and then slamming the audience over the head with the lengthy experimental piece 'The Winter Of My Discontent', which sometimes segued into parts of the Doors' 'The End'. To further baffle his long-term fans this was also the first tour that didn't feature Stooges songs (at least at first – 'I Wanna Be Your Dog' crept in towards the end of the European leg). Most of the still unreleased *Soldier* was played, so the audiences were confronted with a show containing at least ten unfamiliar songs. The short tour opened at Friars in Aylesbury on 2 February and ran for just two weeks around the UK ending up at the Electric Ballroom in Camden on Valentine's Night. Billy Rath, fresh from a stint with Johnny Thunders, took over the bass from Glen Matlock, and Rob Duprey, joined as Iggy's guitarist, a position he retained for the next three years.

The sets were fairly fluid. The same songs were usually played each night but the running order would vary quite considerably. The opening gig at Aylesbury ran like this:

'Hassles', 'Sacred Cow', 'Loco Mosquito', 'The Winter Of My Discontent', 'Sister Midnight', 'Play It Safe', 'Five Foot One', 'Joe And Billy', 'Dog Food', 'I'm A Conservative', 'One For My Baby', 'China Girl', 'I Snub You', 'Take Care Of Me', 'Knocking 'Em Down'

Down On The Street – 1980 *Soldier* North American Tour

When the tour switched to the USA, it begin with three gigs at Old Man Rivers in New Orleans. After the third show on 18 February, Billy Rath was fired. His playing had been somewhat erratic during the UK dates, and his heroin problem was considered to be too severe for him to continue on the tour. Faced with finding a new bass player in a matter of days, Iggy's problems

were then compounded when Klaus Kruger decided to quit as well. He had been growing gradually more disillusioned with the rock 'n' roll lifestyle led by Iggy and the band for some time, and in particular Klaus' naturally courteous nature placed him in direct conflict with Iggy's less than charitable stance towards women on the road. A new rhythm section needed to be found and broken in – and Iggy had just over a week. Ivan Kral and Iggy started auditioning but before long they encountered Douglas Bowne, who had just left his drumming job with John Cale and was up for a lengthy tour. Mike Page, one-time bassist with the New York Dolls, and a friend of Rob Duprey, also came to Iggy's rescue. Along with Duprey, Page would remain with Iggy until 1983, and would prove to be a stabilizing influence on the band.

> **Iggy Pop** – vocals
> **Douglas Bowne** – drums
> **Rob Duprey** – guitar
> **Ivan Kral** – keyboards, guitar
> **Michael Page** – bass

With only a few days rehearsal behind them the new band set off on nearly a full year of touring. The USA dates featured much the same set list, plus the addition of 'Lust For Life' (Mike Page loved playing this one) and the Animals' 'I'm Crying'.

Down On The Street – 1980 *Soldier* European Tour

In mid April, they headed back to Europe and added 'Funtime', 'I Wanna Be Your Dog' and the Rolling Stones' 'I'm Alright' to the regular set list, with the inevitable 'Louie Louie' as a special guest at a couple of gigs. The tour ended back in London at the Music Machine on 31 May. This tour was receiving some mixed reviews with some comments over whether Iggy was overdoing it. He appeared tired and/or drunk at some concerts and although the band was a solid homogenous unit, poor sound and ineffective equipment, especially in some the more out of the way venues, frequently let them down. The touring gradually took its toll on Iggy's health. Determined to keep off hard drugs, he was turning more and more to alcohol as a method of sustaining him. In turn this led to sleeplessness and increasing fatigue. But as the records weren't selling that well, touring was the only sure way of making any money. Both Iggy and Arista records were determined that the next album would be successful.

PARTY

Arista SPART 1158 (UK). Released – June 1981.
Arista 4278 (US). Released – September 1981.
Produced by **Thom Panunzio** and **Tommy Boyce**

When the European tour finished at the end of May 1980, Iggy and Ivan Kral spent the summer refining the songs they'd been writing together. Kral claims that nearly fifty songs had been written and demoed in his room at the Warbeck Hotel in Manhattan. Iggy had taken a room two floors above Ivan and they spent all their time off the road working on the new songs.

The demos, recorded on Kral's new four-track tape deck were mainly just Ivan on acoustic guitar, accompanied by a simple drum machine and sometimes his new Prophet 5 synthesiser (one such demo can be heard on the 2000 reissue of *Party* – 'Speak to Me').

From the fifty or so songs about twenty were selected to take into the Record Plant in New York. In August, Iggy once again led his touring band into the studio. This time there would be no repeat of the troubles that had beset the *Soldier* album. The band was now a tight-knit, cohesive unit and only three weeks were needed to nail *Party*. The trouble started after the band had done their work.

Kral and Pop had worked hard to create what they considered to be some of the most commercial material that Iggy had ever made. They were trying hard to please Arista, because Iggy had promised to deliver a commercial album. In *I Need More*, Iggy recalls the day when Arista MD Charles Levinson flew in to check on the album's progress. Levinson reportedly said, 'Jim, you've now spent over $100,000 on this album, and we don't hear a single. What can we do?' To which Iggy replied that if they wanted a number one hit album then they should get Phil Spector in. Or if not Spector, then Blondie producer Mike Chapman would be great. Somehow between then they ended up with Tommy Boyce, the production genius behind the Monkees and, in Arista's eyes, a dead cert for achieving 'hits'. Of course what they ended up with was nothing like hit single music...

Returning to the Record Plant in October 1980, Iggy found that Boyce was of the opinion that none of the original material was commercial enough for Arista and so he had already earmarked a couple of covers for Iggy to try. The only original song that Boyce felt had merit was 'Bang Bang', a track written by Kral and Pop during the summer. Tommy Boyce remixed 'Bang Bang' extensively, to the disgust of Kral who couldn't bring himself to listen to the finished track.

Iggy spent the rest of 1980 touring to promote *Soldier* and then took some much deserved time off. This rest ended up as a six-month sabbatical as Arista prevaricated over the release of *Party* until June 1981 in Europe, and August in the States, a year after it had been recorded. Iggy and Ivan Kral were disappointed with the finished album, feeling that their original vision had been watered down.

Party received the usual mixed reviews, but it failed to recoup the money lavished upon it by Arista. Many of the reviews seemed to feel that it represented a decline in quality and there are obvious faults with the record. Whilst the Uptown Horns certainly enliven some of the weaker songs, they still seem hopelessly out of place. A jolly horn section is simply not what an Iggy Pop record really needs. And the final song selection is rather weak; there were plenty of stronger songs that had been demoed or nearly finished that would have improved the album no end. The tremendous rocker 'Brakes On', the wistful and delightful 'Speak To Me' and the slightly cracked and loopy but charmingly gauche 'I'm The Original One' have all cropped on bootlegs and all are arguably superior to many of the songs on *Party*. Certainly they would have given the album more diversity, as one of the other major criticisms, first levelled by Charles Levinson, is that most of the songs sound rather samey. There's not enough shade or colour, and it ends

up sounding rather one-dimensional. Iggy himself, looking back on his career in 2001, decided that *Party* was the worst album he'd made.

Having said all that, *Party* still has a lot to recommend it. The stronger songs, such as 'Pleasure', 'Houston Is Hot Tonight' and 'Pumpin' For Jill' are superb. The much-maligned 'Bang Bang' is actually an excellent pop song, and with Tommy Boyce's slick production did manage to become a minor new wave hit. It was even playlisted on BBC Radio 1 for a while, though it failed to reach the UK Top Forty. Even the two covers aren't as bad as is generally claimed. Iggy's voice is quite suited to big ballads and so 'Sea Of Love' is actually successful, if slightly cheesy. And the less well known 'Time Won't Let Me' ends the album on a terrific note, full of clever string effects and a sterling performance from Iggy. But Iggy trying to be an all round singer was not what the public were used to and *Party* ends up being a confused record, unsure of its market and lacking strong direction or focus. And anyone who came to his gigs expecting the sort of semi-chart-friendly sounds to be found on *Party* would have been in for a shock.

Pleasure
Party starts as it means to go on, with riffs and horns and shouty gang vocals. Odd snippets of what seem to be truths and even regrets ('It's my life', 'I got no wife') punctuate the rather throwaway lyrics addressed to an unknown 'baby' whom Iggy is demanding gives him pleasure. There's little more to the song than that, but it accomplishes its job as the opening track admirably. The horns sympathetically augment the up and down guitars and apart from the very start of the start of the song aren't at all obvious. In fact they are all but inaudible by the end.

Rock And Roll Party
A lurching drum beat and some heavy bass introduce what is effectively the title track. Kral's guitars and some desultory handclaps usher in Iggy's excellent vocals. It's a wry reflection on Iggy's rock 'n' roll lifestyle and is sung with no small measure of humour and a refreshing element of self-mocking. 'Where is the wine?' crops up a lot, as do beautiful girls and the usual bums that surround Iggy. At the three-minute mark Iggy sings the title of the song in a blast of off key notes – a device that he would use more effectively on his next album. As with 'Pleasure', it's an extremely catchy and commercial song.

Eggs On Plate
A highly autobiographical song, which explicitly outlines Iggy's relationship with Arista boss Clive Davis, who is referred to in dismissive (and insulting) terms. It's a jumpy nervous tune, which Kral had first offered to Patti Smith. The almost stream-of-consciousness rap powers above bongos and new wave jittery guitars. Amongst the gang backing vocals Iggy addresses a lot of his gripes – if he's a success and everybody knows his name then who does his name belong to then? He's 'looking for love in the wine' which follows on from the previous song. But instead of that big $100,000 house what has he got? Just four walls and an orange carpet. But this isn't really a complaint. Iggy loves his life; he's not impressed with the promises of the record company. He's got his band and his four walls and that's sufficient.

Surprisingly, for what appears to be a one-take track, this song received a lot of live performances.

Sincerity

Another boys in the band song about cameraderie on the road. Although it boasts some neat saxophone and a ramshackle boozy charm, nothing can disguise the fact that it's the weakest song so far. The horns are intrusive and too simplistic to warrant interest and the 'we're going to get a beer' chorus is simply cheesy and crass. He may well be sincere, and Iggy's vocals are certainly strong, but it's a throwaway song.

Houston Is Hot Tonight

Making up for the simplicity of the previous song, 'Houston Is Hot Tonight' pulls one of the most effective tunes on *Party* out of the bag. Here the horns are used well as punctuation on the choruses. Kral's music is both eerie and memorable and the production is a few steps up from everything we've heard so far. Frankly, it makes the listener wonder if we're still on the same album as the overall dense sound and atmosphere of this song is so far removed from the rest of *Party*. Kral and Duprey trade licks like Ronnie and Keith in the Stones, there are superb percussion touches flashing between the speakers, the vocals are double-tracked to create a multitude of Iggy's and the unshowy, solid drumming is assisted by some judicious handclaps. The band sounds simply huge in the instrumental break around the minute mark.

Lyrically it's the most oblique song so far, which again emphasises the differences with the rest of the album. After praising Chicago in 'Sincerity', Iggy here claims that the winters there just do him in, but other than that there's little that makes much sense. But the vocals give off an air of impending doom and menace, which perfectly complements the intensity of the music.

Pumpin' For Jill

With its straight-ahead beat and whining guitars, the backing for this song sounds remarkably close to many by the Cars, then riding the crest of their success. It's something of surprise to find an Iggy Pop song played in such an unashamedly commercial Top Forty style, but it's such a good song that it works beautifully. The main body of the song, concerning Iggy's lowly plight as a gas station attendant who nobody notices and treats like dirt is a delight. Although 'Pumpin' For Jill' sounds like it could have sexual connotations it's clear that it only relates to the fact that he holds down his gas station job purely because he doesn't want to lose Jill. The third verse about the Mardi Gras is great – Iggy's delivery sounds true and heartfelt. Iggy sings/speaks the verses in his relatively new, deep baritone gravelly voice, before the second half of the song dissolves into the lengthy la-la-la coda. Sadly this section doesn't develop over its two-minute duration – some sort of climax would have been preferable to the repetitive la-la-la ing. However this is a minor gripe.

Happy Man

From the sublime to the ridiculous. This is simply one of the most embarrassingly trite songs Iggy has ever recorded. Quite what possessed him to include this nonsense on *Party* ahead of some of the songs that were left behind ('Speak To Me', 'Brakes On', and more) is utterly baffling. Over an impossibly upbeat and ludicrously cheery backing, Iggy sings his daft song about being a happy man. The horns emphasise the stupid chirpiness of it all. And the most bizarre thing about the song is the fact that the opening bars sound *exactly* like the theme tune to one of the BBC's most successful sitcoms – *Only Fools And Horses*. It must be a complete coincidence but compare the two and you'll hear remarkable similarities.

Bang Bang

This is light years away from the inanity of 'Happy Man'. Remixed and overdubbed under the supervision of Tommy Boyce, 'Bang Bang' features stirring organ, choppy strings, busy percussion and a multitude of production effects to create one of the most convincing Iggy Pop songs of this period. Despite Ivan Kral's misgivings, it's clear that 'Bang Bang' is a huge improvement on the overall production of the rest of the album. There's also an urgency and intensity about the musicianship that is missing from too many other *Party* songs. Iggy sings with conviction and passion and the result is a near faultless new wave hit. Except, for some baffling reason, it wasn't a hit. 'Bang Bang' received some airplay in both the USA and the UK – it was played repeatedly on Peter Powell's important early evening drive-time show on BBC Radio One, but the single didn't bother the charts at all.

In terms of sound, 'Bang Bang' sounds like it's copped a few ideas from Blondie (and why not?). Iggy's vocals have been given an effective echo which enlarge the musical picture successfully. Lyrically, there are a few more autobiographical giveaways – 'I want no intimacy' is somewhat significant. Although it's not so explicit on the recording, Iggy would later explain the song as being about throwaway sex with young groupies. Iggy's ambivalent feelings about this are made explicit at the start of the song. The lyrics effectively sum up the conveyor belt strings of girls on the road. It's not pretty, but the lyrics make no apology for this lifestyle. The song was subsequently covered by Bowie on 1987's *Never Let Me Down* and live throughout the *Glass Spider* tour the same year.

Sea Of Love

Another change of direction. Drenched in strings and with a great guitar solo slapped in the middle, 'Sea Of Love' sees Iggy in full-on crooner mode. Ivan Kral always encouraged Iggy's love of big band music (and Sinatra in particular) and reckoned that Iggy should do more in that vein. But it's debatable whether Kral quite reckoned on this syrupy cloying cover. Included on the album to give *Party* a more commercial sheen, it's really not one of Iggy's finest three and a half minutes. Undoubtedly he performs it well enough, silencing any who may question his vocal ability, but it's simply too saccharine a song for Iggy. And it really doesn't work on this album, coming after trite nonsense and sarcastic reflections on groupies.

Time Won't Let Me

With its zappy Wurlitzer-type keyboard effects and some splendid horn plus an impassioned vocal from Iggy, this song ends the album on a high note.

It's upbeat and fun, but thankfully avoids the silliness of songs such as 'Happy Man'. It's a cover of the Outsiders' number five hit of 1966. The Outsiders were a Cleveland bar band who hit upon the then fairly novel idea of adding a brass and horn section. Interestingly, Detroit influenced Australian band Radio Birdman often played it along with 'TV Eye' in the mid 1970s.

Speak To Me

An extra on the CD reissue, this is one of a bunch of demos recorded before *Party*. It's a lovely song. Understated and solemn with its acoustic guitar and warbly synth, and Iggy treats the vocal with care. It's sung in a half whisper, which achieves a welcome air of intimacy. The almost hallucinogenic synth interlude is delightful, mainly because it's so unexpected. Lyrically it's the opposite of 'Rock and Roll Party', portraying Iggy alone at a party, not surrounded by his band, and worrying about how he can dance with the girl of his dreams.

There are a number of other equally good demos from this period, which have only been issued on bootlegs. 'Brakes On' is especially good, which some terrific downward bass runs from Page and a jagged guitar line from Kral. The song begins with the tune already at full pelt and Iggy straining at the leash.

One For My Baby

Iggy had been performing this Sinatra tune in concert since 1979, but this was the only time he would record it in the studio. A mournful after-hours song, 'One For My Baby' suits Iggy perfectly. Here some gentle bass, brushes on the drums and a honking sax far off in the distance, back him. Singing in a surprisingly high register on the verses before coming right down on the title, Iggy once again displays a total mastery of the song.

Down On The Street – 1980 'Nightclubbing' Tour

A small tour of small clubs took place in September 1980. Tired of the lengthy travelling that needed to be undertaken around the USA, Iggy picked a few cities where he had a strong following and booked a week of shows in each town (Club 688 in Atlanta, Waves in Chicago, Bookies in Detroit and so on). In contrast to the extensive tour of earlier in the year, Stooges tunes were back in with a vengeance. Also back was, appropriately, 'Nightclubbing', alongside a number of *Soldier* tunes and one of the new songs worked on by Pop and Kral over the summer. 'Puppet World' wouldn't be included on the finished *Party* and this tour saw its only live performances.

The 26 September gig at Bookies in Detroit was bootlegged extensively from a live radio broadcast. It provides a fascinating glimpse into this rarely documented tour. The audience is rowdy, and Iggy sounds fed up and irritated at times, pleading with the crowd to be quiet so he can sing 'One For My Baby'. The rest of the gig finds the band ploughing though the songs with real venom. After nearly six months of solid gigging they had the set nailed, and this allowed Iggy room to roam, safe in the knowledge that his band could follow whatever he did. The summer 1980 concerts may not have been Iggy's best, but the band was certainly one of the most versatile and quick witted that he had ever worked with. The set list ran:

'Raw Power', 'I Wanna Be Your Dog', 'Dog Food', 'TV Eye', 'Shake Appeal', 'Puppet World', 'Knocking 'em Down', 'Lust For Life', 'One For My Baby', 'Search And Destroy', 'Take Care Of Me', 'Funtime', 'Nightclubbing', 'I'm Alright'

Down On The Street – 1980 North American Tour

After a break in October, during which Iggy finished off *Party*, the touring continued. Beginning on Halloween in Oakland and ending six weeks later at the Shaboo Inn in Willimantic, this intensive tour (there were few days off) contained much the same set as the *Nightclubbing* tour but with the added attraction of a number of new tunes from the recently completed *Party*, including 'Brakes On' which in the final event wouldn't make the album on its release the following summer.

The constant touring netted Iggy a steady income throughout the year. But with *Party* not set for release until the following summer, these funds were stretched. Iggy's record sales during the 1970s had never been enough to bring comfort. He had to work hard to live. Back in New York for the winter, Iggy resolved to take some time off and gather his strength.

1981

Down On The Street – 1981 *Party* European Tour

Iggy Pop – vocals
Douglas Bowne – drums
Rob Duprey – guitar
Ivan Kral – guitar
Michael Page – bass
Richard Sohl – keyboards

The six-month break before this tour kicked off in Copenhagen on 11 June 1981 was the first time Iggy had taken off since recording *New Values* two years before. In that period, he spent some time with Anne Wehrer working on the reminiscences that would become the book *I Need More*.

The tour was set up to promote *Party*, which Iggy did with a vengeance, as more than half the album was regularly played each night. 'Flesh and Blood' was a new track destined never to make any album, and very odd it is too. Over a robotic beat it sounds like a sort of *Idiot* leftover. The rest of the set comprised a smattering of other Arista tunes, 'Gloria', a couple of Stooges classics, and a couple from the Iggy/Bowie albums. Plus, of course, 'Louie Louie'. The sets were pretty fluid – if you saw one of these shows you'd probably have experienced at least some of the following:

'Search And Destroy', 'Eggs On Plate', 'Bang Bang', 'Funtime', 'Rock 'n' Roll Party', 'Lust For Life', 'Pumpin' For Jill', 'Knocking 'em Down', 'Dog Food', 'I'm Bored', 'New Values', 'Sincerity', 'Five Foot One', 'Louie Louie', 'Flesh And Blood', 'Gloria'

'The Passenger' was sometimes added during the UK leg in July, but otherwise the set remained fairly constant. The band was the same line-up of musicians as the previous year but with the addition of Richard Sohl on keyboards, which allowed Ivan Kral to concentrate solely on the guitar. Like Kral, Sohl had previously been a member of the Patti Smith Group, founding the band with Patti and Lenny Kaye in 1974. Sohl, sensitive and delicate, found it hard to fit in with the sometimes brutal, macho world of an Iggy Pop tour.

Down On The Street – 1981 *Party* North American Tour

On 31 July, the US leg of the tour opened at the Ritz in New York. But already cracks were beginning to appear. The long lay-off prior to the tour had taken its toll on Iggy and Ivan's working relationship. Apparently Kral had phoned Ron Asheton for advice on how to deal with Iggy. Ron told Ivan that sometimes it's just impossible to deal with Iggy and the simplest thing to do would be to leave. During the June–July European tour, it became clear that Iggy and Ivan had badly fallen out and, after just three shows at the Ritz in New York, Ivan Kral abruptly quit the band on 2 August 1981. Iggy usually fired people, rather than have them quit, so this caused a major upset. Iggy, frustrated, spent some time bad-mouthing his ex-colleague, calling him 'a dumb-ass-fuckin'-guitar-player-twit who just wants to make money and make it in America'; he was though big enough to recognise Kral's genuine talent: 'He's selling himself short because there's this wonderful, beautiful European music in his heart.' Frank Zappa always claimed that touring can drive you crazy and this is precisely what Kral wanted to avoid. He felt trapped, and unable to grow creatively, and the touring and constant parties left him tired of the whole rock scene. Kral felt bad about leaving and claims that a while later he bumped into David Bowie who told him, 'You owe Jim one,' which made Ivan feel even worse. Kral went on to work with John Waite who was to have considerable success in the 1980s.

Gary Valentine was the last-minute replacement. A veteran of Blondie tours, Valentine was no-nonsense player whose aggressive style was perfect for Iggy's band. After just a couple of days break to allow Valentine to get up to speed, the touring continued around North America ending up in New York again on 3 September.

The set was much the same as that toured around Europe, though 'Houston Is Hot Tonight' and 'Raw Power' were added on the US tour. 'Dog Food' and 'China Girl' would also crop up occasionally.

Down On The Street – 1981 'Follow The Sun' Tour

Iggy Pop – vocals
Carlos Alomar – guitar
Clem Burke – drums
Rob Duprey – guitar
Michael Page – bass
Gary Valentine – guitar

Iggy fired the sensitive Richard Sohl after the summer tour because he wasn't 'upfront' enough, and replaced him with Bowie's regular guitarist, Carlos Alomar, which meant that this October–December tour featured three guitarists. Blondie's Clem Burke took over the drum stool as Douglas Bowne moved on to jazzier pastures (he's recently been working with Marc Ribot). Starting on 26 October, the tour slowly worked its way across the USA from east to west – hence the name. Mostly they played small clubs but a couple of prestigious support slots for the Rolling Stones at the Silverdome in Pontiac on 30 November and 1 December provided some contrast. The basic set only changed slightly from the main *Party* tour, although a few early Stooges numbers were now back in, and 'I Need More' and 'I'm A Conservative' cropped up again. Carlos would play lead on the first live performances of 'Dum Dum Boys'. Even 'The Winter Of My Discontent' was dusted down on a few occasions, and this tour provided the first performances of Johnny Kidd's 'Shakin' All Over', another tune so perfect for Iggy it's a wonder he'd never tried it before. For no obvious reason, Iggy took to wearing fishnet stockings, suspenders and skirts on this tour. He claimed it was more comfortable than his usual distressed jeans, but this rather odd appropriation of female clothing resulted mainly in more than the usual number of bottles being thrown at the stage. For the first Stones show, Iggy sensibly wore his regular clothes, but reverted to the stockings for the second night. Predictably the Stones crowd were not impressed with this cross-dressing and Iggy was on the receiving end of a hail of missiles throughout his set. Charmingly he claims to have kept a lot of the debris. The tour ended two nights later in Toronto on 3 December.

The Old Waldorf gig in San Francisco was videoed and was eventually issued by Revenge in 1990. It's a poor quality, very homemade-seeming document of a very odd gig. Iggy seems distracted for much of the show and, although the musicians do their best, the whole thing seems oddly lacklustre. Iggy appears to be tired, or drunk, and a far cry from the compulsive performer of just a few years previously. The show was also made available as a bonus on the DVD of the Paris 1991 concert although, bafflingly, it appears only in black and white on this issue.

A typical set list was roughly as follows:

'Some Weird Sin', 'Houston Is Hot Tonight', 'TV Eye', 'Rock 'n' Roll Party', '1969', 'Bang Bang', 'Dum Dum Boys', 'Eggs On Plate', 'I'm A Conservative', 'I Need More', 'Lust For Life', 'Pumpin' For Jill', 'Nightclubbing'

The year ended with Iggy back in New York. After the commercial failure of *Party*, Arista had not renewed his contract. Anne Wehrer estimates that Iggy had made upwards of $400,000 on his recent tours but most of this money had been squandered and Iggy still had no permanent home or savings. Once again, despite all his hard work, Iggy was virtually penniless and now, for the first time in some years, without a record deal.

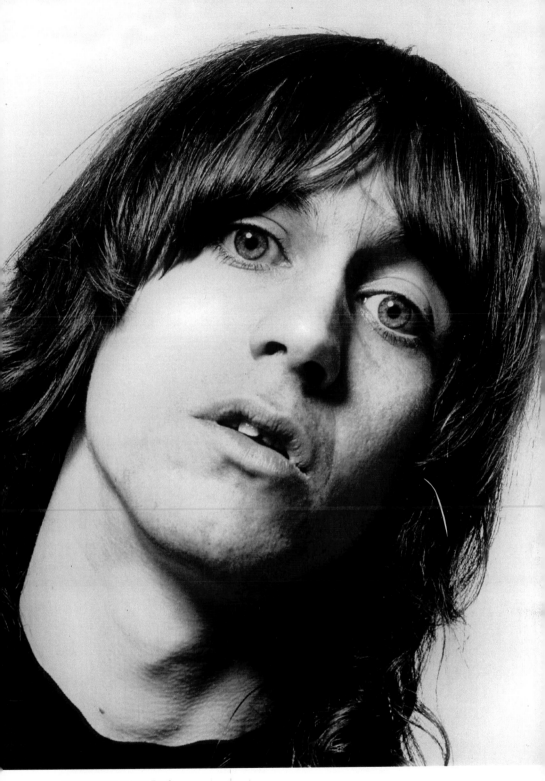

Jim Osterberg or Iggy Pop?

Stage diving, 1970

Iggy and the Stooges in late 1973.
Clockwise from top left: Scott Thurston, Ron Asheton, James Williamson, Scott Asheton, Iggy Pop.

Iggy on tour, Paris, 1977

Above: On stage with David Bowie, New York, 1985

Right: Iggy in concert, 1980

From the original agency caption: 'See-through plastic trousers
pubic hair bare chest: *White Room* TV show, UK, 1996'

Opposite top: 1986. Iggy is back with a new recording contract

Opposite below: Performing at the South Side Festival, Neuhausen, Germany, 23 June 2001

With Nina Alu at the *Kerrang!* Awards, London, 28 August 2001

1982

ZOMBIE BIRDHOUSE

Animal CHR 1399 (UK). Released – September 1982.
Animal APE 6000 (US). Released – September 1982.
Produced by **Chris Stein**

This is a real oddity in Iggy's catalogue. It was recorded solely as a one-off album for Chris Stein's newly formed, but short-lived, Animal Records in the spring of 1982 with only Rob Duprey from the old band on board. Duprey worked closely with Iggy writing the new songs. Many came from instrumental experiments that Rob had been working on for some time. Iggy had taken a cheap apartment in an Italian area of Manhattan. With little money, he lived on pasta or Chinese food. The work with Duprey kept him going.

The Blondie guitarist Stein had set up Animal Records to release low-key New York albums. As soon as the company was formed, people were telling him to sign Iggy. Chris was keen and approached Iggy at the end of the 1981 tour saying, 'I'd like to record you. It's a rumour now anyway, we might as well go ahead.' Keen to record Duprey's quirky songs, but desperate to avoid the major label hassles he had had with Arista, Iggy was delighted to sign with Animal. Iggy spent the spring working up the new material with Duprey. Iggy wanted the new songs to show him in the best possible light. 'I felt that, particularly on my last two albums, I was losing the articulation of what I wanted to be saying.' With Stein producing, Pop and Duprey entered Blank Tapes studio in New York in June 1982. Clem Burke played drums and Stein contributed some occasional bass but otherwise it was just Rob Duprey on 'all else', which kept the costs down to under $30,000.

The unusual cover, showing Iggy seated at a café table with a Coke and a 7-Up, was photographed by old flame Esther Friedmann in Haiti. Iggy travelled there with Anne Wehrer during the summer, ostensibly to continue working on the book of reminiscences *I Need More*. But he spent much of the time drunk and, after years of drink and drug abuse, was having trouble sleeping. His health suffered because of this and the booking of an autumn tour to promote *Zombie Birdhouse* was seen as something of a last chance for Iggy.

Zombie Birdhouse was issued in September 1982 and was ignored pretty much everywhere. Reviews were scarce, but those that were written were generally rather baffled by the record. It was nothing like Iggy's live show and was unlike most other records released in 1982. Strange songs about trappers and bulldozers failed to inspire the record-buying public and *Zombie Birdhouse* sold poorly. Nonetheless those who did bother with it found that *Zombie Birdhouse* contained not only some of Iggy's most imaginative songs, but also some his most impassioned and impressive singing. It's an album that takes time to get used to and, by being so resolutely out of step with 1980s trends, it's stood the test of time surprisingly well.

Run Like A Villain

The album opens in fine style with this up-tempo angular track. Elements of the backing track had originated in the 1981 live song 'The Winter Of My Discontent'. With its lop-sided semi-tribal beat and layers of growling guitars it's immediately apparent that this track is far more committed than most of the songs on the previous two albums. Iggy's vocals are recorded up close and every nuance of his guttural delivery is clear – the quality of the recording is so good, it's as if he's standing right behind you. Although lyrically this song seems to address some of the big issues of the time (notably nuclear war), Iggy chooses to end the song with absurd nursery-rhyme lines. In many live renditions, these became even sillier. So, despite the sideways swipes at nuclear devastation, it appears that Iggy wasn't getting too heavy after all. Issued as a single to promote the album it failed to hit the charts.

The Villagers

With a strange stop-start beat, which seems to wrong-foot the listener every time, 'The Villagers' fades in with a whine of guitars. Iggy sings at the edge of his usual register and sometimes beyond, hitting some slightly cracked notes at times. But somehow it works. The song addresses the gang mentality of man and has some darkly eerie imagery. The semi-spoken sections serve to reinforce the picture. The killer line, which Iggy clearly felt summed up 1982 America, is 'In the space age the village idiot rules, on TV for all to see.' Iggy had received some flack for his public support of Reagan two years earlier, so it's tempting to read this a sort of political retraction. There's also a despairing and chilling cry of 'the villagers', which is horridly drawn out and sounds like the dying moan of some wounded animal. An impressive piece of mood writing.

Angry Hills

This is one of the most conventional songs on this album, but also one of the best. Keeping to a strict verse-chorus structure it has a simple rhythm and some impressive vocals. Iggy's opening line winds its way from an almost subterranean depth to the top end of his register in one breath. It's a great beginning, really capturing the listener, and a trick that is then repeated throughout the song. There's some calming backing vocals from Duprey, which add another dimension to the song.

Life Of Work

The sleeve of *Zombie Birdhouse* announces that 'There are no synthesizers on this record' but clearly some kind of electronic device was used to generate the ominous drone that introduces 'Life Of Work'. Coming on like an updated 'Mass Production', it sounds like some sort of mutant factory machinery and the dragging groaning noise continues right through the song as Iggy almost chants the lyrics. Commenting obliquely on the daily grind of work is something that at first seems odd for someone who's never done a regular day's work in his life, yet with this album Iggy seems to be taking further the persona of a blue collar everyman, a process begun on *Party*.

The Ballad Of Cookie McBride

This song appears cheerful and goofy, with its pseudo country and western images and twangy guitar. Yet by the end Iggy has twisted expectations around – no longer a simple tale of a trapper up on a ridge, he's now headed for an 'unmarked grave' and later still a 'rain filled grave'. Yet the music retains its upbeat and faintly daft air.

Ordinary Bummer

Written solely by Iggy, this is a terrific ballad. Gently performed, deftly sung, 'Ordinary Bummer' is short and sweet. Of course being Iggy, the girl of his affections swears like a sailor, but that was when he knew he had to love her... Live renditions spoil the relative sweetness of the song by substituting 'fuck' for 'love', which rather takes the romance out.

Eat Or Be Eaten

Led by a squealing keyboard and some frantically sharp drumming, this is one of the catchiest tracks on *Zombie Birdhouse*; the ants-in-your-pants rhythm lodges itself in your brain after just one listen. Once again there are allusions to tribes and hunters, giving the album an air of uniformity. The crisp recording boosts the track too, as Chris Stein's mastery of the studio graces even the slightest of tunes with a sharp new wave sheen. As with many of the *Zombie Birdhouse* songs, the impression is that they had a lot of fun recording this one.

Bulldozer

One of the funniest songs Iggy has ever recorded. Set to a pounding riff, which genuinely does conjure up images of big machinery, Iggy seems to be making the lyrics up as he goes along. The opening 'Bulldozer' is simply fabulous – a huge deep roar that is just topped for drama by an even longer and more absurdly drawn out 'Bullllldozzzeerrrrr' toward the end. Iggy sings with far more passion than the simple lyrics really demand, but it all adds to the absurdist feel. There's even a bit in the middle where Iggy breaks off to giggle infectiously at the ridiculousness of it all. One of the highlights of the album.

Platonic

A wonderful song that doesn't appear to be directly about a platonic relationship, but more inspired by the Platonic ideals of Ancient Greece. His singing is a revelation – tender and passionate, but sung in a commandingly deep croon. With its straightforward arrangement and conventional instrumentation (including some lovely guitar work and shimmering synthetic strings from Duprey), it is the most radio-friendly song on the album. So, of course, it was not chosen as a single.

The Horse Song

Complete with Rob Duprey's constantly neighing guitar, this song finds Iggy tongue tied and embarrassed, staring at his shoes. It's not about anything else but, as a study of nervousness, it is exemplary. The verses buzz with multi-tracked guitars over Clem Burke's clip-clop drumming. The most revealing line of possibly the whole album comes with a burst of passion, as

Iggy declares that he's through with being the 'bad guy'. But he's still not sure why he feels like a horse.

Watching The News

A truly bizarre, seemingly improvised piece of paranoid nonsense. Over a backing of sound effects, random dialogue and chattering percussion, Iggy spits out his off-key, chanted monologue, obliquely addressing crime, and climaxing with a weird line about the President pushing all the buttons 'in a giggling fit'. Interestingly, Iggy mutters, 'Who are these people?' in exactly the same manner as on 'Caesar' ten years later... There are a number of glaring edits implying that the track is culled from a much longer attempt. The 'song' fades out as Iggy tunelessly chants the opening lines to the hymn 'Oh Come All Ye Faithful' which alerts the listener to the fact that Iggy appropriated the old melody for 'Angry Hills'.

Street Crazies

Iggy aligns himself once again with the street people, those who've been pushed out of society. The gruff chant, based around a loosely African rhythm, is the whole song. The bongos and the whistling, whining keyboards add to the simple home-made nature of the track, as if it was made up on the spur of the moment. Instruments fade up and down, in and out, seemingly at random as if the sound mixer has had some sort of fit. Yet somehow it all works. Iggy had great fun with this song in concert, dragging it out to at least twice the original length.

Pain And Suffering

Added to all the CD issues of *Zombie Birdhouse* is this oddity from the 1983 Canadian animated film *Rock and Rule*. Directed by Clive Smith, this rather bizarre film, (with music from Iggy, Debbie Harry, Lou Reed, Cheap Trick and even Earth Wind and Fire), tells the story of Angel, a member of a punk band in the apocalyptic future. Mok, who wants to use her voice to summon up a demon, kidnaps her, which is where Iggy's song comes in... Musically, the tune isn't far removed from 'Five Foot One' but, instead of singing, Iggy narrates in a hugely echoed monster voice, before singing the title in his exaggerated bulldozer manner.

*   *   *

Soon after the release of *Zombie Birdhouse*, Karz-Cohl publishing issued *I Need More*. With its wealth of pictures, Andy Warhol's introduction, song lyrics and previously unseen poems, *I Need More* was much more than just a book of stories about the Stooges and other guys. But it's those stories, written down just as Iggy dictated them, that make the book so entertaining. You can really hear Iggy speaking throughout. The stories themselves are so outrageous at times that it is hard to believe it all. In fact, Iggy has all but disowned the book in recent years, blaming too much drink for some of the wilder tales that have been recounted. Even so it is well worth tracking down. If you can find the original, with all the pictures, then do so. The more recent reprinting by Henry Rollins' 2.13.61 Publications omits the photos.

Down On The Street – 1982 *Zombie Birdhouse* Tour

Iggy Pop – vocals
Rob Duprey – guitar
Frank Infante – guitar
Larry Mysliewicz – drums
Michael Page – bass

Iggy took nine months off the touring circuit, his longest break for five years, before embarking on the *Zombie Birdhouse* tour in October 1982, but this tour would continue with few breaks until July 1983, becoming one of his longest ever. The band was a mixture of old and new with Mike Page and Rob Duprey (on both guitar and keyboards) joined by yet another ex-Blondie member, guitarist Frank Infante. Drummer Larry Mysliewicz signed up after being recommended by Clem Burke. The tour opened in Trenton, New Jersey on 13 October before hitting New York the next day. After travelling all over the States, the tour ended up back in New York two months later, before jumping the Atlantic to play Paris and London. Whilst in the UK, Iggy made a memorable appearance on a new TV music show called *The Tube*. His performance, on 17 December, saw Iggy playing 'Run Like A Villain', 'Eat Or Be Eaten' and a superbly sleazy 'Sixteen'.

Iggy initially seemed re-energised after completing *Zombie Birdhouse*, an album he was justly proud of. In fact, during the tour every song from the album would be played – even the weird 'Watching The News'. Most nights would see at least ten songs from the album performed – a strong show of support from Iggy. Significantly, none of the Arista albums had received quite such a push. Even by the end of the tour, most of *Zombie Birdhouse* was still being played live, although strangely none of the songs have been given an outing since.

The rest of the set was made up of what were gradually becoming the regular Iggy live tunes – 'Loose' and 'I Wanna Be Your Dog' from the early days, 'Your Pretty Face...', 'Search and Destroy' and 'Raw Power' from the Williamson era, 'Kill City', a few from the Berlin albums and a few from the Arista albums. It was a good mixture and the band played them all with a muscular energy that had occasionally been missing from some of the recent line-ups. Yet, despite a strong start, Iggy clearly wasn't in the best of shape as the tour progressed. While his drug intake was gradually falling, his drinking was increasing accordingly and Iggy would dub the 1983 leg of the tour 'The Breaking Point', as he seemed to see this tour as something of a last-ditch attempt to make a success of his career. Anne Wehrer felt that 'The Breaking Point' referred to the fact that Iggy was at real low, and that he wasn't sure whether he'd be able to continue for much longer. 'I'd be sitting in some roadside motel, getting ready to play for 300 people in a fucking suburb of Albany that didn't give a fuck, and I'd be sitting there chugging double bourbons and thinking, "Am I drunk enough yet? Am I up for the gig yet?" But I always wanted to go out. I was always going for it.' As ever, touring seemed to rejuvenate Iggy and during 1983 he was attacking his first Australasian and far East concerts with a vigour and commitment that the *Party* tour had seemed to lacking.

New track 'Little Boxes' opened many of the early shows before being dropped in favour of 'Raw Power'. Some audiences were treated to renditions of the rarely performed 'Hassles', others got 'Louie Louie' (which sometimes segued into 'Hang On Sloopy'), 'One Two Brown Eyes', 'Shakin' All Over' and even 'Little Red Rooster'.

A typical set is therefore hard to pin down but here's one from the Ritz in New York on 9 December:

'Little Boxes', 'Raw Power', 'Run Like A Villain', 'Eat Or Be Eaten', 'Sixteen', 'Street Crazies', 'Platonic', 'Search And Destroy', 'Angry Hills', 'Life Of Work', 'The Villagers', 'Loose', 'Ordinary Bummer', 'Louie Louie', 'Bang Bang', 'Horse Song', 'Cookie McBride', 'Bulldozer', 'Fall In Love With Me', 'Kill City', 'Your Pretty Face Is Going To Hell'

Towards the end of 1982 Iggy's son Eric was told to leave the private school he'd been attending. Pretty much dropping out of school at the age of twelve, Eric shared a New York apartment with his dad. Christmas 1982 was spent with father and son learning to live with each other. They didn't have long as Iggy was back out on tour early in the New Year. Eric became streetwise very quickly, learning how to sober his father up, how to get him home when he was stoned, how to clear up the mess left behind. It was a very different sort of education, but one that seemed to benefit both parties.

1983

Down On The Street – 1983 'Breaking Point' Tour

Iggy Pop – vocals
Rob Duprey – guitar
Frank Infante – guitar
Larry Mysliewicz – drums
Michael Page – bass

The US tour resumed on 11 February in Berkeley and continued until the end of March. Further changes were made to the set: 'Mass Production' was dug up for its first (and last) tour and, to accompany it, further Bowie tunes such as 'Dum Dum Boys', 'Some Weird Sin' and 'Neighborhood Threat' were revived. A few more Arista songs including 'I Need More', 'I'm A Conservative' and, surprisingly, 'The Endless Sea' were brought back too. Some more interesting covers were attempted, sometimes including 'House of the Rising Sun' and, going right back to Iggy's first record, 'Mona'. It was an eclectic mix of songs; with just a few exceptions, most of these tunes would never be played live again after the 1983 tour.

An early show at Berkeley in February 1983 ran as follows:

'Mass Production', 'Nightclubbing', 'Eat Or Be Eaten', 'The Endless Sea', 'I'm A Conservative', 'Ordinary Bummer', 'Street Crazies', 'The Villagers',

'Life Of Work', 'Sixteen', 'Run Like A Villain', 'Some Weird Sin', 'Loose',
'I Need More', 'I'm Bored', 'Bang Bang', 'Louie Louie'/'Hang On Sloopy',
'Hassles'

In April 1983, Iggy took his band into the Synchro Sound Studios in Boston.
With Ric Ocasek, guitarist with the Cars, in the producer's chair, three new
songs were recorded. The semi-official compilation *Nuggets* contains these
tracks and they can also be found on numerous bootlegs, but the songs have
never received an officially sanctioned release. This is a shame, as 'Fire
Engine' is a muscular blast of a song with powerhouse drumming pounding
throughout the song. The guitars are loud and buzzing and Iggy is on top
form vocally. 'Warrior Tribe' and 'Old Mule Skinner' continue themes from
Zombie Birdhouse. In fact, 'Old Mule Skinner' is very similar to 'Cookie
McBride'. 'Warrior Tribe' contains some excellent lead guitar over the
extended coda and, as with 'Fire Engine', the overall sound is expansive and
echoing. A full album of songs like these would have been most welcome.

Beginning in mid June in Osaka, the band then embarked upon their first
Japanese and Australian tour. The powerful new song 'Fire Engine' would kick
off most of these shows. 'Fortune Teller' was revived again, as was 'Real Cool
Time'. 'No Fun' was played, often in an inspired and lengthy medley with
Lou Reed's 'Waiting For The Man' (though on some occasions it would segue
into 'You Really Got Me' instead). '96 Tears', 'One For My Baby' and Bo
Diddley's 'Who Do You Love?' upped the number of covers, which might
have implied Iggy was getting complacent had the performances not been so
energetic. The Australian dates featured the New Christs performing their
first-ever live shows in support of one of their heroes. Iggy pulled out of his
gig at the Tivoli in Sydney at the very last minute – halfway through the New
Christs' support slot. To partially compensate the disappointed crowd the
support band played 'TV Eye' and 'Search And Destroy' at the end of their
set. The excellent Melbourne gig at the Seaview Ballroom on 3 July has been
bootlegged many times and, while the song order may have been mucked
around with, it's still a great show. This is the approximate song order:

'Fire Engine', 'Loose', 'Penetration', 'Fortune Teller', 'Five Foot One',
'No Fun'/'Waiting For The Man', 'I'm Bored', 'One For My Baby', 'Run Like
A Villain', 'Louie Louie', '96 Tears', 'I'm A Conservative', 'The Villagers',
'The Passenger', 'Mass Production', 'Dum Dum Boys'

The Australasian tour marked the end of an intensive period of life on the
road. Iggy was tired of this nomadic life, and disappointed with the way the
music business was going. The current trend of New Romantics didn't
impress him: 'I was competing with people like A Flock Of fucking Seagulls.
I've spanned so many musical movements now... I see 'em come and I see
'em go, you know?'

The most lasting legacy of the Japanese tour was Suchi Asano. At the
second Tokyo gig, Iggy noticed a beautiful girl in the audience. As the show
ended, Iggy asked a roadie to find her. This was not an unusual occurrence
and roadies were well used to asking girls to come backstage for Iggy, but
this was different. Iggy though had simply referred to the girl in the glasses.

There were numerous girls in glasses and so the roadie chose the one he *thought* Iggy had meant. Iggy was quite short-sighted anyway and the spotlights had handicapped his view of the crowd somewhat, so to this day no one has ever been quite sure if the right girl came backstage. Fortunately, Suchi and Jim hit it off straight away and phone numbers and addresses were swapped when the time came to leave Japan. Iggy spent a fortune on the phone to Suchi whilst in Australia – no one had ever seen him like this before. Iggy was clearly entranced by her. When he returned to the States, Iggy resolved to bring Suchi to America. This meant dealing with immigration and the best way to avoid any long-term problems would be marriage.

Repo Man

With the tour over, Iggy returned to Los Angeles for a time. In an attempt to clean up, once and for all, Iggy entered a detox clinic. Iggy worked with Steve Jones, who attended the same clinic, on a song for Alex Cox's surreal pseudo-sci-fi film *Repo Man*. It follows a similar pattern to that established on 'Fire Engine' earlier in the year – booming drums thrusting the song along while a fiercely repetitive hard rock riff grinds remorselessly throughout the song. It's one of Iggy's neglected gems and deserves wider exposure. Produced by Danny Sugerman and featuring Clem Burke and Nigel Harrison from Blondie as well as Jones, the song pointed one way forward for Iggy. It would have been an interesting direction, had Iggy followed it up. But this was the only song completed in Los Angeles before Iggy decided to leave Kill City in favour of the far more cosmopolitan environment of New York. Los Angeles offered too many distractions and Iggy found it a struggle not to fall prey to all the temptation.

China Girl [Bowie version]

In 1983, after years of huge critical success, but surprisingly modest worldwide sales, David Bowie released *Let's Dance*, a calculated attempt to score a multi-million-selling hit album. *Let's Dance* was deservedly a massive seller, utterly contemporary, coolly danceable, produced by one of the hottest producers around – Chic's Nile Rogers – and, in the title track, the album contained one of Bowie's all-time classic songs. On the downside, there was none of the experimentation, none of the risk taking usually associated with a David Bowie album, which left many long-term fans feeling short-changed. Intriguingly, for such a commercial and upbeat album, track two was an Iggy Pop song – the remake of 'China Girl'. It was a fine cover, although it lost the darkness and menacing tone of the *Idiot* version – incredibly Bowie said that he felt the original 'didn't have enough balls' but it's doubtful that anyone would say his version was stronger. Bowie added a new Nile Rogers guitar intro (the catchy but faintly irritating 'Oh oh oh' refrain) and a storming bluesy guitar solo from a young Stevie Ray Vaughan.

Bowie's version of 'China Girl' became one of his biggest hits when it was issued as the second single from *Let's Dance* in June 1983. So successful was the cover and so huge were the sales of *Let's Dance* that the royalties effectively enabled Iggy to retire and entirely live off the proceeds for the next couple of years. This enabled him to, in no particular order, pay his taxes, take some holidays, buy an apartment, learn to compose songs properly on his guitar, spend some time in detox, and 'drive the car, but with a license, go to the bank, but with a bank account', as Iggy put it in 1986 – all without having to worry about where the next cent was coming from. Finally, in 1984, Jim got married.

Suchi and Jim moved into a New York apartment. This was Jim's first permanent residence since he'd abandoned his Berlin apartment several years previously, and his first proper home in the USA since the heady days of the Fun House. Jim delighted in taking out the trash, doing the laundry and, best of all, vacuuming the apartment. For the first time in years he seemed truly happy and contented.

Once the 'Breaking Point' tour had finished in mid July 1983, Iggy would not perform live for more than three years, and when he did it was a new, healthy, fit, totally focused and in control Iggy that took to the stage. The 'China Girl' pension was vital in ensuring that Iggy would be able to continue. The restructuring of his life that occurred between 1983 and 1986 brought stability and sanity for the first time in nearly twenty years. Without the break, it's doubtful whether Iggy Pop would still be making records and playing concerts today.

1984

During the winter of 1983, Iggy and Suchi enjoyed a long holiday in Bali and Borneo, accompanying David Bowie, his son Joe and Bowie's close companion Coco Schwab. Thankfully, despite the fact that *Let's Dance* had propelled Bowie into unheard of heights of mega-stardom, David and Iggy had no trouble picking up their friendship from where they had left off in Berlin six years before. David and Iggy enjoyed each other's company so much that they began talking of making a new album together. In the short term, this led to a number of new songs written by the duo, which ended up on Bowie's 1984 album *Tonight*.

Jim and Suchi then travelled to Canada where they holidayed with the Bowie entourage while David made *Tonight* at Le Studio in Morin Heights. In addition to the new songs 'Tumble And Twirl' and 'Dancing With The Big Boys', David recorded three further Iggy Pop songs for *Tonight*. 'Neighborhood Threat' was at least played with conviction and intensity, but both 'Tonight' and 'Don't Look Down' were severely hampered by Bowie's peculiar decision to rework the songs into gently lilting reggae. Although the decision to record 'Tonight' as a duet with Tina Turner was potentially impressive, the limp reggae backing is dreadfully weak. Even the mighty Tina couldn't rescue 'Tonight' from sounding weak and thin.

The new songs were far better. 'Tumble And Twirl' was a giddy impressionistic look back at their Borneo holiday, and although Iggy doesn't appear on the song his lyrics are quite obvious. 'Dancing With The Big Boys' features Iggy's voice dominating David's, as the duo declaim the faintly silly vocals with all the melodrama they can muster. The powerful horn led track,

according to Bowie at the time, represented the sort of sound he had been searching for all through the sessions, but only successfully achieved on this, the final song. 'Big Boys' achieved a wider audience when it was chosen as the b-side to Bowie's worldwide hit 'Blue Jean' – the twelve-inch single featured two remixes of 'Big Boys' of which the extended mix by Arthur Baker is actually very impressive, and is arguably better than the basic song. The dub mix, by removing many of the vocals, is by contrast rather dull.

Tonight was produced by Hugh Padgham. He later confessed to being somewhat worried when he heard that the legendary Iggy Pop was going to attend the sessions. Padgham was totally unprepared for the bespectacled intellectual who sat reading quietly in the corner of the control room for most of the time...

During the summer of 1984, Iggy began seeking new challenges. He enlisted the help of a good acting agent and took drama lessons with a bunch of new young actors who were mainly unaware of who he was. He let it be known that he wanted to work and that he was happy to play anyone – 'from teachers to psychopaths' – on stage or in front of the cameras. Initially at least, Iggy attended lots of auditions, and failed them all. This in itself was a humbling experience, but the new positive Iggy Pop was not in the least downhearted and simply persevered. His first on-screen acting appearance came in 1985's *Sid and Nancy*, Alex Cox's depiction of the doomed romance between Sid Vicious and Nancy Spungen. Iggy's character was a surprised hotel guest, and all he was required to do was walk down some stairs, looking, you guessed it, surprised. Later in 1985, he scored the minor role of a pool player in a roadhouse in the Tom Cruise and Paul Newman smash *The Color Of Money*. It was another extremely small part but Iggy was delighted to meet director Martin Scorcese.

The rest of year was spent writing. He would lug his typewriter into the park, watch the world go by and bash away. He spent a long time improving his guitar playing until he was able to compose successfully on his own. Ironically it was at this point that he hooked up with Steve Jones again, who provided Iggy with a whole bunch of new tunes into which Iggy's new and positively upbeat lyrics could be fitted. The next year would see Iggy's fortunes improve enormously as he gained a new manager and a new record deal.

1985

Having forged a successful working relationship with Steve Jones on 'Repo Man', Iggy continued into 1985 by writing a series of new songs with Steve. Spending a few months in Los Angeles, the pair worked with a drum machine loaned by Iggy's friend Olivier Ferrand, and they constructed an impressive set of demos, which would be crucial in revitalising Iggy's career. Jones was a huge Stooges fan; many of the Sex Pistols' best tunes were directly influenced by the sound and style of *Raw Power*. Yet the new songs they wrote together were quite a departure for both musicians. With the emphasis on melody rather than power riffing, the new tunes were actually surprisingly commercial. As well as original songs, the duo worked on some rearrangements of classics. Sly and the Family Stone's 'Family Affair' was played relatively straight with the addition of some sweet female harmonies, although 'Purple Haze' was dramatically reworked into a doomily impressive slice of gothic rock. Iggy even added some of his own lyrics alluding to *The Texas Chain Saw Massacre*.

There were a number of equally good ballads, of which 'Beside You' would be reworked eight years later for *American Caesar*. The Billy Idol-esque 'Woman Dream' was wisely left on the shelf, but the fact that 'When Dreaming Fails' was left behind after these sessions is a shame, as it's a powerfully emotive song.

The demo tapes also included early versions of 'Cry For Love' and 'Winners and Losers', a pounding drum machine-powered chunk of rock. These would be the only tracks from the demo sessions that actually made it onto *Blah-Blah-Blah* the following year.

Iggy then had the good fortune to meet Art Collins. Art had begun his career in Atlantic Records' promotion department, handling the Rolling Stones. He then joined Rolling Stones Records, where he eventually became president. In 1982, he turned to management; first with Joe Jackson and then, over the years, for Marianne Faithfull and Marshall Crenshaw amongst others. In 1985, he signed on as Iggy's manager, remaining so until his untimely death in 2005. The two men got on incredibly well, their brotherly relationship based on mutual trust and respect, unlike many manager-artist set-ups. There wasn't a more hands-on manager in the business. Over the next twenty years, Art would frequently be found on tour with Iggy. Like a trainer giving ringside encouragement to his boxer, Art would towel Iggy down during gigs, give him pep talks, and then usher him away from the hangers-on and backstage frenzy after the gig, to allow Iggy time and space to wind down. Art also knew the business inside out, and was well liked. He opened doors for Iggy, and it was Art, pushing the undeniable quality of the new songs, who landed the record deal with A&M. The massive boost in Iggy's popularity following the release of *Blah-Blah-Blah* was also carefully planned and orchestrated by Art.

The most crucial year in Iggy's career since his rebirth as a solo artist almost ten years before would turn out to be 1986. And, once again, David Bowie would be vitally involved.

BLAH-BLAH-BLAH

A&M AMA 5145 (UK). Released – October 1986.
A&M SP 5145 (US). Released – October 1986.
Produced by **David Bowie** and **David Richards**

In the autumn of 1985, David Bowie was halfway through filming *Labyrinth*, a children's film co-written by Monty Python's Terry Jones and directed by the Muppets' Jim Henson. In addition to starring as the Goblin King, David was recording a number of songs for the film. These were co-produced with legendary producer Arif Mardin in New York and, during his stay, David met up with Iggy, who played him the demo tapes he'd made with Steve Jones. Iggy was justifiably very proud of his new songs and was keen to prove to David that he'd not been wasting the funds generated by 'China Girl'. Bowie loved the recordings, so much so that he offered to produce the proposed album. Along with the undeniable commercial aspects of the new songs, it was Bowie's involvement that finally sealed the deal with A&M. There was a delay while *Labyrinth* was completed and by the time Bowie was available Steve Jones wasn't. So, unfortunately, Iggy's new partner wasn't involved in the making of the album.

Such was Bowie's enthusiasm for the new project that he offered to help write some more songs. Iggy and David ended up with so many new songs that most of the original tracks on the Pop-Jones demo tape were dropped in favour of the new Pop-Bowie tunes.

Recording got under way at Mountain Studios, near Montreux in Switzerland in the winter of 1985–1986. This was near to Bowie's home, and he had mixed *"Heroes"* and recorded much of *Lodger* here. Bowie would continue to use Mountain Studios on and off for the next decade. The main studio engineer, David Richards, was enlisted as co-producer. In the absence of a band, Bowie called upon the multi-instrumental services of Erdal Kizilcay. This extremely talented Turkish musician had first assisted Bowie on demos for *Let's Dance* in 1982, and would continue to be Bowie's right-hand man for many years. Kizilcay and Richards programmed the drum sounds and built up the rhythm tracks for the new album. Kizilcay also played bass, guitar and keyboards. Another Bowie session man, Kevin Armstrong, was drafted in to replace Steve Jones. Armstrong had played with David at Live Aid in 1985 and had previously been a member of Thomas Dolby's band.

Sessions ran smoothly, and were totally unlike any recording process Iggy had ever been involved with before. For the first time, the music tracks were digitally constructed. Chips and samples were borrowed from Queen's Roger Taylor to create some of the Linn drum sounds, and quite some time was spent listening to state-of-the-art sounds on records by Prince and Bruce Springsteen, amongst others, in order to come up with something even better. Bowie was determined that the resulting record would be an Iggy Pop record and worked hard to keep off the finished product. Consequently, David is credited with production only, although there are a number of extremely Bowie-esque backing vocals, and the rogue saxophonist isn't named either. The vocals are officially credited to just Pop, Armstrong and Kizilcay. Listening to the 'no, no, no' parts on 'Baby It Can't Fall' or most of the backing vocals on 'Real Wild Child', however, quickly reveals Bowie's presence.

Blah-Blah-Blah was released in September 1986 to almost unanimous approval. Suddenly Iggy was everywhere promoting the new record, and this was the new family-friendly Iggy, short hair neatly parted, smart, not ripped, jeans, cool leather jacket. Iggy encapsulated his new image with the pithy phrase 'same guy, just sober'.

He was tanned, lean and fit, and responded to interviewers with keen interest, sharp wit and that infectious foghorn laugh. It was so easy to like

Iggy that many forgot that just a few years before he'd been totally obnoxious and wasted most of the time. Iggy stressed time and again how this was the first record he'd promoted when he wasn't strung out on something. 'I grew increasingly curious as to what it would be like to be very sober... it became almost an obsession... I also found myself suspecting that my promiscuity, sexually, was getting in the way of my music, because it didn't allow me a home life... and I thought that with a home life, perhaps I'd have a better foundation for harder and better work.' Iggy repeatedly said how he was now able to do better work. He took great delight in pointing out to French TV that his forthcoming concerts would represent the first time he'd ever done a sober gig in France. He often referred to the changes in his life over the previous few years ('my quest was to make order out of chaos'), how he liked cleaning the house, reconciling his bank statements, shopping for food. Iggy was at great pains to prove to the world that he was just a regular guy. His new clean image put his wild excessive behaviour firmly into the box marked 'History'. He would talk about his self-destructive past in a slightly shocked and amazed tone. Nothing was denied, but Iggy seemed to be implying that he'd grown out of the drugs and booze and girls and the trashy lifestyle that he'd once lived. 'The memories do come up... but it's more kind of like looking back at a strange television show... I can still remember why I did those things, *very clearly*, and in a real funny and silly way I'm proud of it too...'

To be a success in the 1980s, pop stars needed to be seen to be clean. Sting, Springsteen, Dire Straits – these were the biggest stars of the day. Even Bowie had been utterly sanitised and made totally safe, to the extent that his 1987 album *Never Let Me Down* represented, ironically, the biggest let-down of his career. To succeed in this climate, Iggy needed to present a much safer image than ever before. The charm offensive that accompanied *Blah-Blah-Blah* even saw Iggy appear with his cheerful beaming smile on the cover of British style bible *The Face*. Iggy had somehow, bafflingly, become a style icon. The photos from *The Face* shoot were so good that they would be used on the covers of most of the *Blah-Blah-Blah* singles.

The album was released to excellent reviews, most of which commented with some surprise on the fact that Iggy was a) still alive and b) still capable of producing meaningful music. As with *The Idiot*, the Bowie connection was seized upon, with many remarking that *Blah-Blah-Blah* showed Bowie as a far more potent musical force than did his own recent records.

The cover too was a far cry from previous records. Iggy glares angrily out of the picture, his arms defiantly folded. He looks as though he means business.

Real Wild Child (Wild One)

Opening the album with a statement of intent the like of which had never been heard before. 'Real Wild Child' was an extraordinarily appropriate song for Iggy. Originally a simple rockabilly hit for, amongst others, the clean-cut Crickets, 'Real Wild Child' seemed to sum up the public image of Iggy perfectly. Never mind that he was approaching forty, and was years away from being 'just outa school', Iggy was certainly a wild one, and it was a brilliant choice of opening song. The beginning, with Iggy's deep echoed

'I'm a real wild one, wild one, wild one...' set the scene before the listener was whizzed off into a world of synth drums, zappy keyboards and the sort of production Billy Idol would have pawned his last bottle of hair bleach for. The excellent guitars are mixed low; as the song is dominated by the thumping drum machines and tinny synths. It's fast, furious, totally 1986, horribly dated today (but what the hell), and such an infectiously danceable song that's it's quite impossible not to like it. It's also light years away from the desperation of *Party* and the whole drink-and-drugs image of just a few years before. The song's clean and utterly radio-friendly sound is something never previously associated with Iggy and led, predictably, to accusations of selling out, of becoming a Bowie clone, and of losing sight of his audience. But 'Real Wild Child' would prove to be Iggy's most successful UK single and was simply the most crucial lead-off song on any of his albums in presenting Iggy to both a new, young audience and to his older fans. To criticise it seems both churlish and petty. It's not the best Iggy song ever, but it accomplishes its aim of reintroducing Iggy to the world admirably.

The twelve-inch remix features a massively extended backing track, which rather outstays it's welcome. The song is simply not strong enough to warrant nine minutes. However, it's interesting if you want to hear David Bowie's backing vocals which are separated out here, and there is at least some amusement to be had from all the vari-speeded and backwards vocals – at least it sounds like the remixers had a lot of fun doing it.

Baby It Can't Fall

This one song sums up all that is great and all that is cheesy about *Blah-Blah-Blah* in that it is characterised by a pounding drum machine, ersatz horns, whizzing keyboards, spangly guitars and much studio trickery (listen to the faintly silly effects on the word 'fall' all through the choruses). It's a great tune, however, with a splendid vocal performance from Iggy and a memorable Bowie melody. Iggy's lyrics are resolutely positive and sung in a throaty chant. Clearly directed at his new wife and achingly romantic, it's purely and simply a refreshing love song. Towards the end, the 'horns' kick up a storm before a rather incongruous Hammond organ effect takes centre stage.

The twelve-inch version featured on the b-side of the 'Fire Girl' single is a triumph of mid-1980s remixing, suffering as it does from an over-reliance on badly dated jittery scratching effects, annoying stuttering and a horrid trebly mix. It's so far removed from Iggy's usual sound that it's hard to see how he approved this one.

Shades

One the best Bowie tunes of the decade, reminiscent of the stirring 'Absolute Beginners' also written during the summer of 1985, is married to one of Iggy's most obviously romantic lyrics. Another song inspired by Suchi, Iggy describes how he gains pleasure from the simple things in life, such as a 'really fine pair of shades'. In other circumstances, the song could easily sound trite and silly, but it's delivered with such conviction, and performed with such power and genuine feeling that it becomes one of the undoubted highlights of the album. The music is huge, pounding drum machines and soaring guitars punctuated by some stirring 'Whoo Whoo's. This massive echoing production style would be reprised on Bowie's own 'When The Wind Blows' the following year. The keyboards are warm and inviting and Iggy's vocals are equally embracing and rich, approximating the trademark 1980s Bowie croon at times. The lyrics are soppy, but it works and it's a truly awe-inspiring piece of 1980s pop, unquestionably one of the best Iggy Pop ballads ever recorded.

As the song runs to six minutes the single featured an edit – but, oddly, instead of cutting 'Shades' to a more radio-friendly three or four minutes, just twenty seconds were pointlessly trimmed as it fades just before the ending. A 'clean' radio version was also prepared. Ever since the fiasco over Frankie Goes To Hollywood's club smash 'Relax' two years earlier, UK radio had been wary of potentially 'rude' words. To prevent any problems the word 'come' was replaced with 'swim' from the next line. The resulting 'swim in the night/swim with delight' couplet ends up sounding rather daft. A&M needn't have worried anyway as radio play for 'Shades' was minimal compared with that of 'Real Wild Child' and the single failed to match its predecessor's success.

The 1986 concerts saw the band contributing backing vocals to the song. By 1987, the 'Whoo Whoo's had been dropped and Iggy performed the song without any extra vocals. It's not been played live since 1987.

Fire Girl

One of the few songs on the album left over from the Steve Jones demo sessions. Surprisingly it's one of the least rocky songs, although this may be down to the unremittingly chirpy backing track, which is horribly trebly and dominated by obviously programmed and uninteresting percussion. Sadly, the song, which contains a lovely melody and a great singalong chorus, is badly let down by the frighteningly cheap-sounding production. This is not hindsight – even in 1986, 'Fire Girl' was tinny and thin and stood out amongst most of the other songs as being something of a disappointment. Even Iggy's vocal sounds uncharacteristically half hearted. There are elements of the demo song 'When Dreaming Fails' which were incorporated into 'Fire Girl' – pity the original version wasn't used instead of being reworked into this programmed mess of a song.

The twelve-inch mix takes the irritating production still further as, along with 'Baby It Can't Fall', it features some of the worst excesses of the burgeoning 1980s remix technology. On the plus side, you get to hear a lot of the instrumental elements that were buried in the album mix, including some neat guitar.

A guitar-led early version, featuring an obvious Bowie on backing vocals has recently appeared on bootleg – being far less fussy and fiddly it's frankly far more successful than the finished song.

Isolation

As with 'Shades', this is another strong Bowie melody, all grandeur and pomp and magnificence. Iggy rises to the occasion with one of the most triumphant lyrics on the album. He revels in being an iconoclast, a survivor, proud to stand in isolation. The lyrics sum up what Iggy was feeling in the mid 1980s – the need for acceptance, balanced by the knowledge that he'll never fit in. He's got a life to live but in isolation. It's a powerful song and is all the more impressive when one realises that it was pretty much a one-shot deal. Bowie came up with the tune towards the end of the sessions and Iggy stayed up late one night to record his vocal in one attempt. Iggy describes the song's creation as simply 'Let's go down to the basement and play some music.' There's some uncredited saxophone under the choruses – almost certainly Bowie – and the backing vocals are terribly similar to 'Absolute Beginners', but it all works wonderfully. There's an element of desperation in Iggy's slightly histrionic singing, and the performance is certainly one of Iggy's most impressive recorded vocals.

Cry For Love

The first track to be lifted from *Blah-Blah-Blah* was arguably Iggy's strongest solo single to date. Steve Jones's stirring tune is delivered with verve and commitment and Iggy's vocals are strong and confidently sung in his deep rich baritone. There are some snide asides against insultingly bad TV and an unusually personal line about Iggy's issues with self respect, but otherwise it's a generally upbeat lyric. The music relies a little too heavily on the string effects but Jones's propulsive solo makes up for this. In fact, this is the only recorded Steve Jones contribution on the album and was taken directly from the original demo when Kevin Armstrong couldn't beat Jones' power. The chorus is catchy and unusual, and the production top notch. From the downward slide of the opening guitar to the final fade it's a truly marvellous song.

The twelve-inch mix (the 'Manic' mix found on some singles is the same as the regular twelve-inch mix) is great fun. It somehow rises above the over-reliance on 1980s remix tricks and happily pounds away for seven minutes. Even the synthetic strings sound better on the remix.

The seven-inch single features the removal of the third line of each chorus, 'on every sammy morning'. This shortens the song by just a few seconds and only succeeds in unbalancing the chorus. A very odd piece of editing.

For the initial 1986 concerts, 'Cry For Love' was used as the final encore, although later gigs added 'Search And Destroy' to close the show on more familiar ground.

Blah-Blah-Blah

Frantic synthetic percussion and vocal samples dominate this diatribe against US imperialism and commercialism in general. Intriguingly, the percussion track is strongly reminiscent of that on 'Lust For Life' (and Johnny (Yen?) crops up again), though the tone of the song is far more frenetic. The vocal is a patchwork of political and personal imagery with Shimon Peres and Rambo and Iggy himself ('little ol' me, glamorous me') giddily name-checked throughout the song. There are digs at 'we are the world' and Americans as 'spoiled brats' and the real meaning of the song is summed up in Iggy's explanation of the title. *Blah-Blah-Blah* is a 'polite way of saying, "Fuck you"; but really polite.'

An excellent live version, recorded in Zurich on 12 December 1986, crops up on the b-side of 'Fire Girl'.

Hideaway

Another hugely romantic Bowie tune, plus some more uncredited Bowie backing vocals, underpinned by massive drum machines and pounding sequencers. For those worried that Iggy was drifting too far from his origins, some of the synth bass on the choruses is oddly reminiscent of that on '1969'. It's an impressive song, but doesn't quite have the memorable hooks of 'Isolation' or 'Shades' and seems somehow more lightweight. The lyrics continue the politicising of the title song – 'my country got raped by big industry' but drift back to the personal by the end: 'You are one thing I will not waste' is again directed firmly and positively at Suchi.

Winners and Losers

Another Steve Jones-penned tune and it's the hardest, most unrelenting song on the album. Characterised by grinding guitars and fiercely thumping drums that match Iggy's harsh vocals all the way. Although reviewers would remark that this was a return to the hard rock of the Stooges, it clearly isn't. The production and tone of the song, not to mention the effective string samples, are as far removed from the sound of *Raw Power* or *Fun House* as the rest of *Blah-Blah-Blah*. However the overwhelming metallic grind of the Kevin Armstrong's guitars marks it out as much tougher than the other new tunes. Sneakily stealing a verse from 'Scene Of The Crime' to great effect, 'Winners And Losers' treads a fine line between realism and parody. It's almost trying too hard to achieve a big modern Iggy rock sound and nearly falls flat on its face. But somehow it succeeds – the unchanging beat and repeated power riffing borrowing elements from both Billy Idol and Goth rockers the Sisters Of Mercy (and in turn influencing much of their 1987 album *Floodland*, especially 'Dominion', 'Lucretia' and the ten-minute magnum opus 'This Corrosion'). The only slightly disappointing part is the ridiculously quick fade – as if they'd run out of time and just turned the sound off. There's no sense of resolution. For such a powerful six-minute song to end on an anti-climax like this is a real shame.

Strange but true – 'Winners And Losers' features on the b-side of the 'Cry For Love' twelve-inch single but the version here has lost the opening drum beats, which take up all of a second, crashing straight into the body of the song.

Little Miss Emperor

Those who bought the album on cassette or in the new compact disc format were rewarded with an extra track not available on vinyl. It is a strong synth-led track with loads of shuffling programmed percussion (which is highly reminiscent of 'Highwire Days', the final song on the Psychedelic Furs' 1984 album *Mirror Moves*). There are also some fun stereo effects with fake handclaps and skittish synthetic strings. Once again, we get a brilliantly sung track (arguably Iggy's most accomplished performance on this album) and the vocals are augmented with the synth effects, some throbbing bass, and delightful piano.

The lyrics reference Ginsberg and Iggy once again castigates stifling sameness, but at its heart, like most of *Blah-Blah-Blah*, lies another love song for Suchi. The machine gun-like synthetic strings at the song's long fade are

thrilling and make for a far better conclusion to the album than the absurdly fast fade to 'Winners And Losers'.

*   *   *

As the first single from *Blah-Blah-Blah*, 'Cry For Love' was promoted with a competent video, but failed to chart. A&M then issued 'Real Wild Child' as a follow-up to coincide with Iggy's UK tour dates. The song was picked up by daytime radio and propelled Iggy into the UK Top Ten. He even made his first appearance on the top-rated chart show *Top of the Pops*, where his performance drew angry complaints. His crime – not bothering to mime properly and dancing on top of a keyboard! Buoyed with their unexpected success, A&M proceeded to issue three further singles – 'Shades', 'Fire Girl' and 'Isolation' none of which bothered the Top Forty. Apart from 'Isolation', each single featured a dramatic remix on the twelve-inch version. The 'Manic' mix of 'Cry For Love' was probably the most successful, as it restated the themes and passion of the original in a new mix dominated by the synth strings. 'Real Wild Child' boasted some amusing and entertaining nonsense with the vocals sped up, slowed down and run backwards which succeeded in stretching the song to nearly nine minutes. The remixes of 'Fire Girl' and 'Baby It Can't Fall', the b-side of 'Shades', are less successful, being uninspired and largely irritating. Allowing for the live version of 'Blah-Blah-Blah' on the b-side of 'Fire Girl', every track from the album was actually issued on a single.

Down On The Street – 1986 *Blah-Blah-Blah* Tour

Iggy Pop – vocals
Kevin Armstrong – guitar
Seamus Beaghen – keyboards, guitar
Phil Butcher – bass
Gavin Harrison – drums

The *Blah-Blah-Blah* tour saw a rejuvenated and re-energised Iggy Pop on stage. The power and the passion were back; the negative elements were largely gone. As he was fond of telling almost every interviewer along the way, this was the first tour he'd undertaken sober, the first tour that hadn't involved copious quantities of drugs, the first tour on which groupies were barred. Iggy was a married man, with a home and a bank account. This was a rock tour that fitted right into the 1980s: clean and efficient, giving the audiences a professional performance in return for their hard-earned cash. Probably the most surprising aspect of this tour is that Iggy was able to combine all these attributes with his usual animalistic stage antics. Sure, at first he was rather more restrained than in the past; mindful of his new, slightly younger audience, Iggy rarely swore or taunted the audience; and his stage clothes (tight jeans, black T-shirts and a smart leather jacket) seemed rather more 'designed' than ever before. But the fire and energy he put into his gigs left no one in any doubt that Iggy hadn't sold out. There was no excess, no embarrassment, just straight-up Iggy rock. He could get on with delivering his songs and performing his act safe in the knowledge that the songs would be performed expertly.

The band, tightly drilled and highly competent, consisted, for the first time ever, of entirely British musicians. Kevin Armstrong had been a Bowie sideman for a while before helping out on *Blah-Blah-Blah*. On keyboards, and occasional second guitar was Seamus Beaghen who had recently been touring with Madness. Up-and-coming British drummer Gavin Harrison was hired after touring with Zerra One, and bassist Phil Butcher had recently worked with Shriekback. The tour opened on 29 October in Santa Barbara and weaved across the States for three weeks before jumping to Europe in late November. The resurrected Iggy Pop's tour ended up in London's Brixton Academy for two shows on 17 and 18 December.

What was arguably missing was an element of danger. The *Blah-Blah-Blah* concerts demonstrated that, while the band were certainly no slouches, their playing was too clean, too polite, possibly too reserved for many of the older songs. The *Blah-Blah-Blah* songs sounded great, with Beaghen's keyboards sometimes incorporating new sampling technology, but the Stooges numbers clearly suffered from a lack of dirt. Kevin Armstrong was an expert guitarist, switching from a delightful sound on 'Gimme Danger' to an overdriven blast of noise on songs such as 'Search And Destroy' with admirable ease. But whilst he had variety and ability in spades he couldn't quite reach the dirty messed-up crunch that songs such as 'I Got A Right' or 'Raw Power' really required. As a result there was a slight feeling from some fans and reviewers that the new mature Iggy had lost some of his bite. But this was a minor quibble. On the whole, the 1986 concerts were an outright success. Iggy received mainly rave reviews everywhere he went, with most concentrating on the stark contrast between the new series of concerts and the Stooges days of broken glass and peanut butter, with most coming down firmly on the side of the new shows. Iggy was, not for the first time, or the last, portrayed as a survivor, a legend of excess, a showman of extraordinary abilities.

The set list for the 1986 shows was pretty fixed. The intention was to introduce Iggy to a new audience, and reintroduce him to those he'd lost over the previous few years. As such, you can't complain too much about playing safe with such a conservative set list – it was very much the new album plus Iggy's Greatest Hits – the other Bowie-Pop collaborations, and a smattering of acknowledged Stooges classics. Early concerts concentrated firmly on *Blah-Blah-Blah*, with all ten songs being played during most of the shows. Interestingly, apart from 'Five Foot One' there was nothing from the period 1978–1982.

The Ritz show in New York on 14 November was filmed by MTV and an hour's worth of the set was broadcast. Subsequently, Revenge used the tapes as the basis for their live album extracted from this show. It's a fine example of the 1986 tour and, although it's not the whole show, Revenge has unexpectedly kept in all the new songs, rather than the obvious classics.

The Zurich Volkshaus concert on 12 December was recorded by A&M and has since leaked out as an excellent quality bootleg. 'Blah-Blah-Blah' from this show was issued a b-side the following year.

'I Got A Right', 'Gimme Danger', 'Some Weird Sin', 'Real Wild Child',
'Sister Midnight', 'Blah-Blah-Blah', 'Baby, It Can't Fall', 'Nightclubbing',

'Fire Girl', 'Five Foot One', 'Shades', 'TV Eye', 'Little Miss Emperor', 'China Girl', 'Hideaway', 'Winners And Losers', 'Isolation', 'Lust For Life', 'Raw Power', 'Cry For Love'

As the tour progressed, first 'Little Miss Emperor' was dropped, then 'Isolation' and 'Hideaway' were played less and less. Instead 'Down On The Street' and 'Loose' were added creating, with 'TV Eye', a great little *Fun House* section in the middle of the gig. Crowd-pleaser 'The Passenger' also crept into the set before the European shows and, as 'Cry For Love' wasn't quite doing the business as the final number, 'Search And Destroy' was tacked onto the end of the show to really go out with a bang.

At the end of 1986, Harrison left the band. Since then his skills have kept him in huge demand as a drummer for hire with artists as varied as Lisa Stansfield, Eros Ramazzotti and Kevin Ayres. In recent years he has been a member of the excellent British progressive-experimental band Porcupine Tree.

Iggy returned to the States to spend Christmas with his parents and Eric for the first time in many years.

1987

Down On The Street – 1987 Pretenders Tour

Iggy Pop – vocals
Andy Anderson – drums
Kevin Armstrong – guitar
Seamus Beaghen – keyboards, guitar
Phil Butcher – bass

Having very successfully re-established himself as a live performer of power and passion, Iggy spent Christmas with his folks at their new home in Myrtle Beach, South Carolina. After just a month off the road, he blasted back in mid-January with a series of high-profile support slots on the Pretenders' North American tour. These gigs won Iggy further new fans. His one-hour sets for these concerts were basically a cut-down version of the previous autumn's shows, mixing new songs with acknowledged classics to devastating effect. 'I Wanna Be Your Dog' was the only notable new addition. Chrissie Hynde can't have relished trying to follow Iggy's mesmerising performances. During the tour, Iggy played a number of regular solo shows in major cities (including Wolfgang's in San Francisco on 2 March and New York's 1018 Club on 5 April), for which the band played the full set as performed the previous year.

The band remained the same except that Andy Anderson joined on drums. Although he had formerly played in Steve Hillage's band, it was his recent work with the Cure that secured him the gig.

After the lengthy North American tour, Iggy took the band over to Japan for a week of dates in mid-April, further reinforcing his burgeoning popularity there.

Down On The Street – 1987 European Tour

Iggy Pop – vocals
Barry Adamson – bass
Andy Anderson – drums
Kevin Armstrong – guitar
Seamus Beaghen – keyboards, guitar

After another month off and with Phil Butcher replaced by the muscular bass powerhouse Barry Adamson (ex Magazine) who had just left Nick Cave's Bad Seeds, Iggy set off on a European summer tour. He would play some of the first major outdoor shows of his career, and began his long and continuing relationship with many of Europe's most prestigious music festivals. The set list remained broadly the same as before, with the addition of a number of early Stooges tunes – 'Real Cool Time', '1970' (which didn't really fire up as much as it should) and a superb 'Dirt', in which Adamson's brilliant bass seemed to restore the song to its original 1970 glory. These, plus a great rendition of 'Sixteen', led to a corresponding reduction in the number of *Blah-Blah-Blah* songs. Other occasional performances included a few rare outings for 'I'm Sick Of You' – the song's first live appearance since the 1972 Kings Cross gig, and 'Lust For Life' which, perhaps surprisingly, was not often played on the 1987 tours.

With 'No Fun' and a blistering 'TV Eye' as the final numbers, these Iggy summer shows were a huge success and paved the way for his continued success in Europe. The opening gig at the Provinssirock Festival on 6 June was broadcast live across Scandinavia, showing Iggy thoroughly enjoying himself, playing both to the huge crowd and to the cameras. In Gothenburg on 27 June, he supported David Bowie, then halfway through the controversial *Glass Spider* tour. Back in 1977, Iggy had been asked what he was planning for his first tour after the break-up of the Stooges. He replied that he had no plans to change his act at all – 'as if I would have a big spider come down from the ceiling!' Weirdly, ten years later, David began his *Glass Spider* concerts by descending from the belly of a huge glowing spider...

In between all the outdoor shows, Iggy found the time for a quick trip around the UK, pleasing those fans who had been unable to get to the Brixton gigs the previous December. The tour put Iggy firmly back in the spotlight – this time for all the right reasons. The concerts were professional, but never dull. Iggy had tons more energy than ever before and put on a terrific performance, and he appeared to be having a wonderful time. The regular set list was:

'I Got A Right', 'Real Cool Time', '1970', 'Gimme Danger', 'Some Weird Sin', 'Winners And Losers', 'Shades', 'Five Foot One', 'Real Wild Child', 'Dirt', 'Down On The Street', 'The Passenger', 'Blah-Blah-Blah', 'Search and Destroy', 'Sister Midnight', 'Raw Power', 'Sixteen', 'I Wanna Be Your Dog', 'No Fun', 'TV Eye'

*   *   *

Risky – Ryuichi Sakamoto featuring Iggy Pop
CBS 6510177/6510176 (12" single)

As the tour ended, this marvellously moody single slipped out almost unnoticed. Ryuichi Sakamoto had begun his pop career as a member of the Yellow Magic Orchestra, Japan's answer to Kraftwerk. The YMO married a powerful western pop sensibility with Sakamoto's orchestral leanings and a strong sense of playful humour. Their records have stood the test of time well. YMO split in the early 1980s and all three members forged solo careers. Sakamoto has had a loose partnership with David Sylvian for many years, and achieved perhaps his biggest success in 1983 with 'Forbidden Colours' – Sylvian's brilliant vocal over Sakamoto's evocative theme from the film *Merry Christmas Mr Lawrence*. By 1987, Sakamoto was attempting to create a rock album called *Neo Geo* with ex-Material bassist Bill Laswell as producer. The initial idea was to get Peter Gabriel to sing on the tune that became 'Risky'. But Laswell could not schedule a session with Gabriel and called on Iggy instead. The vocal was added to the song at George Benson's studio in Hawaii in the summer of 1986. The ensuing ballad falls into a similar category as songs such as 'Shades' in that it's a long, slow, synth-led track. But Sakamoto's classical training and mastery of technology raise the song above much of *Blah-Blah-Blah* in terms of lightness of approach and gentleness of production. Iggy matches the song's slightly jumpy feel by contributing one of the best vocals of his career. Ironically, in view of the lyrics referring to 'corporate dungeons', the song was later used in a huge Japanese motorcycle ad campaign.

In contrast to the leaden twelve-inch mixes from *Blah-Blah-Blah*, Julian Mendlesohn's remix of 'Risky' is delightful – a subtle rejigging of the standard verse-chorus approach of the original and a clever use of the potentially tiresome scratching beloved by 1980s remixers.

*   *   *

When the protracted bout of touring finally ended in Hamburg on 12 July, nine months of virtually non-stop work were brought to a close. This period saw Iggy's highest worldwide profile ever, his most successful singles ever, and the re-establishment of Iggy Pop as a truly great performer. No longer a joke, no longer an unreliable junkie, no longer a waster, Iggy Pop was by 1987 touted as a rock 'n' roll survivor, an inspirational figurehead to outsiders and punks everywhere, yet relatively safe and almost wholesome. It was an astonishing transformation, and one that Iggy appeared to want to disprove almost immediately.

He dropped out of sight after the summer tour and took stock of his situation. His new-found popularity had brought about two major changes. In the first place, he was fully solvent for perhaps the first time in his life. The tour and album had actually made money; money which hadn't immediately been drunk or snorted or smoked. Jim and Suchi were now comfortably off, not mega rich like so many other 1980s rock stars, but able to buy a second home in Mexico, and not have to worry about taxes. The second major change was that the name Iggy Pop had been resurrected as a genuine force to be reckoned with in the business. From now on, Iggy would have some clout when it came to negotiating contracts and record deals. Most of the improvements were a direct result of Iggy's partnership with Art Collins.

But Iggy clearly felt uneasy in the middle-of-the-road arena into which the business was pushing him. Now he was back and, with Art's assistance, was fully in control of his life and work. Iggy decided to return to his hard rock roots. His career, for finally that's what his music had become, could take it.

1988

With the summer 1987 tour out of the way, Iggy took some well-earned time off. Back home with Suchi, he pondered his future. The *Blah-Blah-Blah* revival of his career was extremely valuable, but it needed to be followed up swiftly in order to build on the resurgence of interest in his work. What was apparent, however, was that Iggy's new higher profile and commercial stock had also caused a renewal of interest in the Stooges. In late 1987, a selection of 1973 rehearsal material was issued in France as *Rubber Legs*. It was widely exported around the world and attracted an excellent response. Soon after, the French label Revenge began issuing more and more archival Stooges material to further favourable reviews and sales. Skydog then dug up all the tapes they possessed from the two Michigan Palace shows of 1973 and 1974. Issued in March 1988, this new expanded edition of *Metallic KO* was very successful in winning new supporters to the Stooges sound.

With this in mind, Iggy decided that his new album should restate the Stooges manifesto of hard and dirty rock. He wanted a powerful, dark, but natural sound, light years away from the synth pop-rock of *Blah-Blah-Blah*. To help achieve the updated Stooges rock sound that he wanted, Iggy resumed his partnership with Steve Jones, who encouraged Iggy's songwriting and co-wrote four tunes. After working with Bill Laswell on the Sakamoto song 'Risky' the year before, Iggy asked if he'd like to produce the new album. Laswell was, on the face of it, a rather unlikely choice of producer. He had begun his career as part of the funk experimentalists Material but his more recent production of Motörhead's *Orgasmatron* and *Rock 'n 'Roll* and PiL's *Album* was what had attracted Iggy's attention. Seeking a modern heavy sound, Iggy was impressed with the depth on the PiL record and Laswell's ability to record heavy metal legends Motörhead with clarity. Iggy had spent the second half of 1987 demoing his new songs. His guitar playing improved dramatically during this period. Without a band, Iggy had to pick a new set of musicians to work on the album. With Steve Jones' assistance, they first called upon drummer Paul Garisto, who had recently left the Psychedelic Furs after three years. Garisto was a big hitter, renowned for his solid reliable style, and was perfect for the new sound. Leigh Foxx, who had previously toured with Patti Smith and Tom Rush in the 1970s and had recently been working with Yoko Ono, joined on bass. After the sessions, Foxx would tour with Debbie Harry and is now a regular member of Blondie. The only survivor of the *Blah-Blah-Blah* tour band, Seamus Beaghen, completed the line-up, and travelled from London to New York to sit at the keyboards.

Sessions got under way in April 1988 at Sorcerer Sound in New York. Recording was completed with a minimum of fuss in just three weeks, before Iggy and Bill Laswell relocated to BC Studio in Brooklyn to complete the vocals. This is, in fact, one of the most impressive aspects of *Instinct* – although the songs themselves can seem rather plodding and repetitive, saddled with surprisingly muddy sound at times, Iggy's singing is uniformly excellent, and is beautifully recorded.

INSTINCT

A&M AMA 5198 (UK). Released – June 1988.
A&M SP 5198 (US). Released – June 1988.
Produced by **Bill Laswell**

Speedily released in June 1988, *Instinct* gathered generally positive reviews, especially from those who had been waiting for a harder Stooge-like sound for years. UK music paper *Sounds* lead the way by calling *Instinct* a 'resonant, dignified album'. On the downside, however, the album contains ten songs of pretty similar tempo and instrumentation, leading to some, quite justified, accusations that many of the tracks were rather samey.

Cold Metal

Start as you mean to go on. Steve Jones cranks out the riff like his life depends on it, Paul Garisto beats the living crap out of his drums and Iggy crashes into the song snarling and spitting out the words – a far cry from the controlled singing of *Blah-Blah-Blah*. 'Cold Metal' is, on first hearing, an exhilarating track. It Rocks, with a capital R. But a somewhat basic tune lies behind all the swaggering bluster, and it is one that doesn't really sustain the listener's interest over repeated plays. The sound is also surprisingly thick. Not layered or dense with instrumentation, but simply clogged and swampy. All the instruments seem to mush together – there's little clarity. This is a criticism of all the songs on *Instinct*, though the fact that this overall sound dominates the album implies that it is intentional.

Nevertheless 'Cold Metal' is a fun piece of music, and Iggy's lyrics show a great sense of confidence, placing Iggy in American history, as a 'product of America' in fact. The first verse is almost a potted history of Iggy's youth – complete with his first squeeze of a breast by the railroad tracks. The phrase about building the interstate highway refers to the demolishing of Fun House and the break-up of the original Stooges. These autobiographical references give the song a much-needed grounding in realism.

Released as a single ahead of the album 'Cold Metal' failed to chart despite an impressive video directed by Sam Raimi, more famous for cult horror film *The Evil Dead*. An excellent extended version of 'Cold Metal', remixed by Andy Wallace, featured very effective added horns but was only ever released on a single given away free with the 11 March 1989 edition of *Sounds*.

High On You

Taken at quite a pace this song is probably the most impressive piece on *Instinct*. It contains some abstract but introspective lyrics, delivered with some considerable passion, and the references to the 'terrorist in my heart' imply that there's still a fire burning inside. Musically, there are some cool touches which are mostly buried in the general buzz of the guitars and the overwhelmingly bassy mix – the clanging piano on the chorus and the groaning backing vocals on the verses are intriguing effects which deserved to be better heard. On the plus side, Iggy's vocals are quite excellent, the tune itself is memorably fierce and catchy and Steve Jones takes one his best solos.

It was also one of the highlights of the following tour, often prefaced by an explanation as to why Iggy didn't take anything else any more. All he needed now was the audience – 'I'm getting high on you.'

Strong Girl

With a huge drum beat throbbing throughout, this track lurches along for more than five minutes without ever getting anywhere. Once again, Seamus's keyboards are all but lost in the mix, which is a shame as they would have added some much needed colour to the song. The bump and grind of the monstrous rhythm actually gets rather tedious after Steve's solo and umpteen 'na-na-na-na-naaaah's. This Steve Jones tune is simply not as strong as the production that holds it together.

Tom Tom

As 'Tom Tom' blasts into being, it begins to confirm the listener's worst fears about this album – that it's all going to sound the same. It is another mid-paced rocker with neither sufficient musical nor lyrical interest to grab your attention. 'I'll take my Tom Tom and go' is not the most inspiring of lyrics... In fact, it's an alarmingly pedestrian song. The drumming, though resolutely solid, is very simple and frankly dull. There's no brightness, nothing to lighten the leaden thumping rhythm, nothing to relieve the continuous growl of Steve Jones' guitar. The best bit is the double-tracking of Iggy's voice right at the end, as a thoaty extra Iggy sings 'absolute you' in his deepest tones.

Easy Rider

Some contrast at last, as 'Easy Rider' begins with some delicate guitar work. But it only lasts a few seconds before 'Jones the Riff' cranks into one of the better tracks on the album. At least the pace has picked up after the plodding of the previous two songs and 'Easy Rider' contains one of the best tunes (written by Jones) on *Instinct*. Iggy responds to the frantically chugging guitars with some imaginative imagery in the lyrics and an excitingly raucous vocal, especially when he sings the title. 'Easy Rider' sounds more alive than most of the other songs on *Instinct*, boasting a much more natural sound (the drums are crisp, rather than boomily muffled) and an excellent mix, in which Seamus's stirring Hammond organ effects can be clearly heard.

'Easy Rider' also translated well to the stage and was easily one of the strongest new tunes in concert.

Power And Freedom

Back to the dense, murky mix that bedevils most of the album. The drums are way down, the bass drowning everything that isn't Jones's guitar. Mind you, the lead guitar, bursting out of both speakers is hugely impressive. Iggy delivers a soaring vocal too. All his singing on this album is exemplary – having worked hard on his voice over the previous couple of years his range was better than it had ever been, full of depth and resonance.

The title obviously harks back to *Raw Power*, but now it's married to freedom – a state where 'no one cool will save ya.' It kicks off side two excitingly but it is a pity that the song itself is so similar to 'Cold Metal.'

Lowdown

Although it still has that thick deep mix, 'Lowdown' actually works well as a vehicle for one of Iggy's most appropriately subterranean vocals ever. The lyrics remind the listener of various tracks on *Blah-Blah-Blah,* and echo similar sentiments expressed in 'Isolation' or 'Hideaway'. But it's a hole in his heart, which is causing him to feel low down. No more than that. A year or so before, Boy George famously remarked that he'd rather have a cup of tea than sex. Maybe Iggy's similar desire expressed here for a nice cuppa indicates that he too is slowing down and growing up.

Instinct

Kicking off at a furious pace, the title track is one of the highlights of the album. Plus you get to hear some slimy keyboards from Seamus, which aren't buried under the rest of the band. Iggy's voice, with added echo, sounds menacing and committed. The lyric returns to the poisoned rivers and dark places of 'Cold Metal', as he describes how instinct keeps him running 'like a deer'. The excellent dead-stop ending adds enormously to the sense of drama exhibited here.

Iggy was clearly impressed with this song, choosing it as the opening number for the duration of the following world tour.

Tuff Baby

Then we're back to a 'Tom Tom'-esque grind, another thudding tune saddled with some lame lyrics and a rather surprisingly half-assed vocal. It plods for way too long while Jones lays down a squiggly solo. Only the last verse rescues the song – 'chaos in the old suburbs' sings Iggy sounding at last like he means it. A surprising choice for the *Instinct* tour, 'Tuff Baby' at least sounded more exciting in concert.

Squarehead

At first it seems too similar to 'Power and Freedom' but, once you get used to that, 'Squarehead' turns into one of the best songs on *Instinct*. Iggy describes all the things you can do him – even stuff hamburgers in his hair apparently – but he 'ain't gonna be no Squarehead'. And boy does he mean it. Obviously written as a riposte to those who had accused him of selling out with his neat image and polite *Blah-Blah-Blah* album, 'Squarehead' delivers its message with a wry smile. It's only by the time you get to this song that you realise that the other songs have been so very po-faced. Most Iggy Pop albums (even the slick *Blah-Blah-Blah*) contain a lot of humour, but it's only 'Squarehead' that manages to inject some much-needed levity into the album. Even the chanting of the title underneath the guitar solo is pretty funny.

'Squarehead' also features another strong mix, especially towards the end as multiple guitars battle Iggy for supremacy.

*   *   *

Following the strong performance of *Blah-Blah-Blah* in the charts, *Instinct* disappointed by not scoring as highly. The dreadful cover can't have helped. It did, however, gradually become one of his bigger-selling albums, thanks in part to the lengthy tour which followed, taking Iggy all around the world for the first time.

Down On The Street – 1988–1989 *Instinct* World Tour

Iggy Pop – vocals
Seamus Beaghen – keyboards, guitar
Paul Garisto – drums
Alvin Gibbs – bass, vocals
Andy McCoy – guitar, vocals

To do justice to the tough metal sound of *Instinct*, Iggy put together what was arguably his hardest-rocking band ever. Paul Garisto and Beaghen stayed on board, but Steve Jones was unwilling to commit to such a lengthy schedule, so Iggy sought the services of ex-Hanoi Rocks guitarist Andy McCoy. McCoy in turn recommended his friend Alvin Gibbs, once the bass player in noted punk band UK Subs, as the final member of the line-up.

The new band's first job was to mime in the video for the forthcoming single 'Cold Metal'. Iggy fan and *Evil Dead* director Sam Raimi shot the promo at the Triangle Studios in Los Angeles where Laurel and Hardy and, appropriately, the Three Stooges had made many of their films. With a set made from seemingly randomly placed bits of twisted metal, the band completed their work in one day. Although he wasn't in the regular tour band Steve Jones popped up in the video. He would make occasional appearances on stage during the early parts of the tour, usually joining the group for encores at a few venues.

Rehearsals began in mid June with a list of thirty-five songs. The band started with the *Instinct* material and worked backwards, running through three or four songs a day. Some tracks like 'Cry For Love' never made the final set, others such as 'Some Weird Sin' only appeared occasionally. Once the basic set list had taken shape, it varied little over the course of the tour. All the musicians were told that this was to be a clean tour, with no drinking or drug usage, which raises the question of why Andy McCoy was chosen – his chemical and alcohol excesses were legendary. Alvin Gibbs's excellent tour memoir, *Neighbourhood Threat – On Tour With Iggy Pop*, describes the moment when Iggy nearly threw McCoy out of the band after he turned up late for rehearsals smelling of liquor. Iggy exploded, threw a mike stand through the drum kit and told McCoy to 'get your shit together or you're out'. Wisely, McCoy was never late for rehearsals again.

The band breathed new life into the older tunes, including a number of songs from *Kill City*, as well as some more obscure Stooges tunes not played live for many years such as 'Penetration' and 'Your Pretty Face Is Going To Hell'. Most significantly, only two songs from *Blah-Blah-Blah* were played – 'Real Wild Child', which would remain in Iggy's live set for ever more, and the Steve Jones power rock song 'Winners And Losers'. In a tacit acknowledgement that 'Winners And Losers' had derived from the Stooges anyway, it was reworked into a brilliant medley with its predecessor 'Scene Of The Crime'.

Minor differences in the set list included the gradual replacement of 'Your Pretty Face...' with 'Beyond The Law', the early disappearance of 'Shake Appeal' and 'Easy Rider', which were played at the initial concerts but only rarely after that, and the inclusion of 'TV Eye' halfway the through the autumn. One of the highlights of the shows was '1970', with a new conclusion worked up by Andy McCoy. McCoy expressed a desire to write some new songs with Iggy, but Andy's reputation for unreliability preceded him. None other than Alice Cooper warned Iggy that McCoy would probably not be the best new partner, so McCoy remained purely as a gun for hire throughout the tour. Like the other band members, he never worked with Iggy again. Other highlights of the *Instinct* shows included the brilliant 'Winners And Losers'/'Scene of the Crime' medley and the *Kill City* songs. With a good half dozen cuts from the new album mixed into the running order, this was one loud and tough tour:

> 'Instinct', 'Kill City', '1969', 'Penetration', 'Power And Freedom', 'Beyond The Law', 'High On You', 'The Passenger', 'Sixteen', 'Five Foot One', 'Johanna', 'Shake Appeal', 'Tuff Baby', 'Real Wild Child', 'Winners And Losers'/'Scene of The Crime', 'Search And Destroy', 'TV Eye', 'Cold Metal', 'Squarehead', 'No Fun', 'I Wanna Be Your Dog', '1970', 'I Got A Right'

Iggy roughened up the clean-cut image he had cultivated over the past few years. With his hair grown longer, he dyed it a greasy shade of orange and allowed it to stick up at vaguely comical angles. If the image he was seeking was Rock Star Dragged Through A Hedge Backwards then he achieved it admirably. The neat T-shirts and smart leather jackets of the *Blah-Blah-Blah* tour were also ditched in favour of leather vests, ripped jeans and skull rings. The dishevelled appearance looked great on stage, but rather comically studied in the various interviews and promotional work. The 1988 tour also saw Iggy resuming his stage-diving habits. After seeing some flamenco dancers, Iggy also began incorporating a few flamenco moves into his stage routine.

The tour opened at the Whisky-A-Go-Go in Los Angeles on 8 July, supported by Social Distortion. (Later gigs saw rising stars Jane's Addiction as the main support act. Later still, the feedback-drenched British band the Jesus And Mary Chain supported Iggy, but no one in the tour party liked their sullen attitude.) After an intro tape of African drumming to whip the crowd into even more of a frenzy, Iggy cheerfully called, 'Hello, you motherfuckers,' as the band launched into 'Instinct'.

Seamus played some cool keyboards, usually a swirling Hammond sound, but effortlessly switched to second guitar when needed. Alvin Gibbs and Paul Garisto made a brutal rhythm section, with Garisto anchoring the whole thing to his mighty snare. Coming from glam-metallers Hanoi Rocks might have left Andy McCoy open to flashy excess, but his playing on this tour was economically precise. He had just the right balance of technique and feeling, and above all his playing entirely suited the songs. The Stooges songs were recognisably Stooge-like yet updated enough to fit right in with Iggy's current style. For the first time in many years, the whole set sounded like it was all one – the fact that the show opened with 'Instinct' followed by '1969' proved that the twenty-year gap between the songs really didn't matter. They fitted together perfectly. Steve Jones joined them onstage for the encores, but McCoy was really the man of the night. Backstage after the first night, members of the Cult mixed with various Ramones and Iggy's son Eric, now eighteen.

The band and crew travelled the States in a bus that slept twelve. Iggy and Suchi would generally follow, flying whenever possible. Alvin Gibbs's *Neighbourhood Threat* refers to the drug use of the rest of the band but it appears that, with only one lapse, Iggy remained clean throughout the tour. To complete a ninety-minute show each night, performing with as much energy as Iggy expended, required a lot of concentration and an extremely high level of fitness. To achieve this, Iggy took lots of rest, had regular work-outs, ate a high-protein diet, and barely touched alcohol. This is a regime that Iggy has followed ever since.

The Boston show on 19 July was broadcast on the King Biscuit Flower Hour, a well-known purveyor of quality radio rock concerts. This of course led to numerous high-quality bootlegs. Thankfully, Revenge Records also issued the gig in 1989 for general consumption. The mix could have been better. It sounds rather thin, with Garisto's drums to the fore at the expense of the guitars. Fortunately the KBFH version was later released, with a much better mix. Oddly, virtually every version of this show has a slightly different track list, but this doesn't detract from the fact that it's a vintage Iggy show. Alvin Gibbs bemoaned the fact that he screwed up the intro to 'Search and Destroy', but it's not really noticeable. Iggy's vocals are strong, the energy levels are high and the songs are excellently played. Especially good are the fast segues between 'Kill City', '1969' and 'Penetration'. There's no room to breath between these songs. The long intro to 'High On You' allows Iggy to deliver a rant about drugs, although he claims he would never take back all those times he got drunk and took off his clothes. Now he just gets high 'on you!' In an interview with Q magazine he said much the same thing – 'I don't regret the drugs, because you can't. You can't start blaming things on certain chemicals.'

The Boston gig is an excellent reminder of an excellent tour.

On 26 August, Iggy performed at the prestigious Reading Festival. This UK Festival had long been one of the highlights of the summer. After playing some of the European outdoor summer gigs in 1987, this was the first of many appearances at UK festivals. Iggy did not disappoint the English crowd. The high-powered band was ideal for the bigger stages and the solid mix of old and new satisfied hardcore fans and casual festival-goers alike. Iggy would learn from Reading, and from the other festival gigs he played in 1988. Many of his subsequent stage performances would borrow heavily from the same mix.

After trips to South and Central America the tour returned to Europe, concluding the year with an extensive jaunt around the UK finishing up once again at the Brixton Academy in London on 20 December.

On the whole, the tour ran smoothly, apart from the odd hitch such as in Brazil (where Iggy raving at a poor hotel concierge when the accommodation wasn't up to scratch embarrassingly made a full-page spread in the Brazilian paper *Ilustrada*). The gigs continued into 1989 with further European concerts before moving to the Far East at the end of January. A handful of Japanese concerts were followed by a clutch of Australasian dates, which brought the tour to an end in mid February.

The most dramatic incident occurred towards the end of the tour in New Zealand on 1 February. At the festival in Wellington headlined by Antipodean rocker Jimmy Barnes, the stage was draped in Pepsi advertising, which claimed the drink was the 'Voice Of A New Generation'. For some reason, this so enraged Iggy that, after 'TV Eye', he screamed, 'I'd rather drink my own piss than touch that vile shit!' The rest of the gig saw Iggy rant at Pepsi even more, ending up with such comments as 'Pepsi want to rot your guts and brains with their poisonous shit. Fuck them!' Comments such as this didn't go down terribly well with the corporate sponsors, who threatened to sue the arse off Iggy if such defamatory remarks were repeated the next night. Consequently the second show saw Iggy hardly saying a word, though his anger was plain to see when, after staring at one of the banners, he let out a scream of pure disgust.

With the tour over, the musicians went their separate ways. None would ever work with Iggy again. Significantly, with the exception of 'Cold Metal', none of the *Instinct* songs were ever performed again.

1989

Once the *Instinct* tour had finished in February, the rest of 1989 saw Iggy lying low, with no new record or tour to promote. He spent much of the year working on a series of new songs, which, for the first time in ages, were composed mainly on his own, on an acoustic guitar.

The new demos included some surprisingly tender ballads. Many of the songs which appeared as full electric recordings on *Brick By Brick* started off as simple acoustic demos – that they worked well in either format demonstrates the quality of the new songs. A selection of the demos would be used as b-sides over the following year, but a number of songs were never officially released. 'LA Blues' (not the *Fun House* track) is a genuine blues, which features some quietly confident singing from Iggy over a simple tune. 'Think Alone' is more urgent, with its faster strumming and descending riff. The tune would be speeded up and electrified in 1991, and was given an entirely new lyric. As 'Love Bone', it was played during the summer 1991 tour but very rarely after that. The other unreleased songs are pleasant enough, but unremarkable, apart from the fact that it's rare to hear Iggy this quiet. His guitar playing is competent but simple, though his vocals are characteristically full and resonant.

Apart from writing new songs, Iggy spent some time making his first major film: John Waters' *Cry-Baby*. Set in the 1950s, it comes across as a skewed version of *Grease*. With his co-stars Amy Locane and a young up-and-coming actor named Johnny Depp, Iggy had a wonderful time. Playing the chattering loony Belvedere didn't really stretch Iggy, but his role adds another dimension to the movie.

Then it was back to the music business.

He first recorded a song for Wes Craven's film *Shocker*. 'Love Transfusion' is a generic heavy rock song, co-written by Alice Cooper. With its booming drums and squealing guitar solo, there's precious little to differentiate the song form most other West Coast metal of the time. Iggy even sounds rather like Alice.

Next, as his contract with A&M had expired with the release of *Instinct*, Iggy spent some time looking for a new deal. Impressed by the quality of the demos, and with the acquisition of some of Iggy's back catalogue, Virgin signed a worldwide deal with Iggy. Since 1990, Virgin has issued all new Iggy Pop records. Around the same time as the release of *Brick By Brick*, Virgin issued both *The Idiot* and *Lust For Life* on CD. They were promoted by the inclusion of tracks as b-sides to the new single, 'Home'.

Brick By Brick

1990

Towards the end of 1989, Iggy began hunting down musicians and possible producers. The whole thing suddenly came together when Don Was contacted Iggy to make a cameo appearance on the Was (Not Was) album *Are You Okay?* (Iggy and Eric are part of the team of backing vocalists on the Leonard Cohen-led 'Elvis' Rolls-Royce'.) Iggy and Don Was got on so well that Was agreed to produce Iggy's new record, a move that delighted Virgin as Was could rustle up some crack session players.

Robert 'Waddy' Watchel was one of the most respected guitar players on the West Coast. He first came to be noticed playing with Stevie Nicks and Lindsay Buckingham in the early 1970s, and later worked with Warren Zevon, the Everly Brothers, Joe Walsh and Bryan Ferry, amongst many others. Before joining the *Brick By Brick* sessions, Waddy had been recording and touring as part of Keith Richards' X-Pensive Winos, a role which seriously impressed Iggy.

Kenny Aronoff had spent most of the 1980s as part of John Cougar Mellencamp's band. By 1989–1990, he was beginning to branch out and had recently demonstrated his versatility on a slew of records by artists from Elton John to Bob Seger to Belinda Carlisle. Since 1990, he's drummed for a multitude of players as diverse as the Smashing Pumpkins and Melissa Etheridge.

David Lindley's pedigree deserves a book all of its own. A world-renowned multi-instrumentalist who, with his own band El Rayo-X, combines American folk, bluegrass and blues with African, Arabic, Celtic and Turkish sources. Lindley remains one of America's most in-demand session players. During the 1970s, he was Jackson Browne's main collaborator and worked extensively in the folk-country sphere playing with David Crosby and Graham Nash, Ry Cooder, and Linda Ronstadt amongst many others. Since 1990, he's developed his eclectic mix of world music alongside his session commitments with artists such as Warren Zevon and Rod Stewart. Lindley would provide *Brick By Brick* with some stunning slide guitar and, on occasion, a bouzouki.

Keyboard player Jamie Muhoberac's father had played with the likes of Barbra Streisand, Neil Diamond and even Elvis. Jamie's keyboards have assisted a huge number of artists over the years – from the Stones, Clapton, and Tina Turner to newer artists such as Bush, Seal and Alanis Morissette.

Concurrent with the Iggy album, Muhoberac, Aronoff, and Lindley were recording Bob Dylan's *Under The Red Sky*, which was also being produced by Don Was. Another *Brick By Brick* contributor, Slash, also guests on the Dylan album.

BRICK BY BRICK

CD VUS 19 (UK) Released – Jul 1990
Produced by **Don Was**

Recording took place at Oceanway Studios and Hollywood Sound Studios between 15 February and 23 March. Don Was and his engineer, Ed Cherney, ran a tight studio – the musicians were mainly veterans of the West Coast session scene and were well rehearsed. As well as the seasoned session guys, Slash and Duff McKagan, respectively lead guitarist and bass player for the huge LA metal band Guns 'n' Roses, contributed to a number of songs. Slash even got to co-write the excellent 'My Baby Wants To Rock And Roll'. All the other original tracks are credited, for the first time, to Iggy alone. Two covers were added to the album – John Hiatt's 'Something Wild', which features Hiatt on guest vocals, and 'Livin' On The Edge Of The Night' written by Jay Rifkin and Eric Rackin for the Michael Douglas movie *Black Rain*. The song was recorded prior to the main *Brick By Brick* sessions and was originally intended only for the film. But Virgin added the song to the album as a bonus track, where it sits awkwardly after the very effective conclusion of the title track. Its non-appearance in the album booklet betrays its last-minute addition.

Don Was's production results in a truly great-sounding Iggy Pop album – contemporary, but not in the way that *Instinct* was utterly rooted in the rock sound of 1988. In the same manner that his later Rolling Stones productions simply nail that unique Stones formula and stick to it, Don Was gives *Brick By Brick* a kind of timeless Iggy Pop sound. This is what you'd hope all Iggy Pop albums should sound like; not only pounding, rocking, snarling and nasty, but also beautiful, crooning, delicate and sensitive too. Only on this album would you find such a vitriolic piece of music as 'Butt Town' and such a tender love song as 'Moonlight Lady'. The dynamics are perfect.

Rolling Stone was not alone in calling Iggy 'an elder statesman', but its review awarded four stars and decided that the record was 'excellent'.

Charles Burns contributed the grotesque cartoon cover. Burns is the Harvey Award-winning cartoonist and illustrator whose work first came to public notice in *Raw* magazine in the early 1980s. Iggy may have been attracted by one of Burns's most popular characters, Dog Boy, a red-blooded all-American boy with the transplanted heart of a dog. It's a baffling album cover, seemingly with little to connect it to the music. Iggy doesn't appear, though there are (unintentional?) echoes of Kate Pierson's beehive hairstyle in the girl on the right.

Home

Kicking off the album with one of Iggy's best rockers ever, 'Home' grabs the listener by the balls and doesn't let go. Its stop-start drumming, Kenny Aronoff pounding away, sounds utterly natural – a straightforward drum kit, played perfectly. And none of the echo or boomy effects that dated *Instinct*.

'Everybody needs a home' is the simple message of the song, and Iggy disarmingly sings about his home and family, which is a lovely admission of happiness.

Slash's lead wriggles and squeals like it's trying to escape but Don Was's production just nails it, and drives it on home. Iggy, for the first time on

record, is credited with guitar too. His thrashy acoustic strum is a welcome addition to much of the album.

'Home' is full of intensity from the start, and crashes along for three minutes, building to what seems to be a great climax. Then at 3.22, just when you expect a terrific ending, the whole song ratchets up another gear altogether and proceeds to scream even more powerfully than before. Iggy starts singing defiantly about those who would presume to stand in his way, and you absolutely believe him. It's a truly thrilling and exhilarating track and should have been a hit. But, of course, being an Iggy Pop single, it wasn't.

Main Street Eyes

A fascinating rumination on the conflict between gaining mainstream acceptance and sticking firmly to personal ideals of integrity and honesty – the crime of 'phony rock and roll' is at the crux of the song. Iggy wants only self-respect; he's not a huge mainstream star but he's real, he's decent and he'll fight for that. The song is brilliantly constructed, the relative harshness of the verses (Iggy's voice backed only by sparse guitar and drums) contrasting with the lovely melodic singalong choruses. Lindley adds some delicate violin and a touch of mandolin, the first recorded use of that instrument on an Iggy Pop album. The imagery is constantly striking and disturbing, and Iggy's vocals, especially on these talkie sections, are beautifully recorded, up front and crystal clear. Although it's a great contrast to 'Home', it's just as successful.

I Won't Crap Out

'Main Street Eyes' segues directly into this tune, a more urgent piece of music dominated by Iggy's declamatory vocals and some powerful drumming from Aronoff. Ostensibly a declaration of intent, of how everything will get better, as long as Iggy doesn't crap out, there's also time for a few well-placed digs against phonies and trendies. Iggy sings like a man possessed, almost spitting out the words in his passionate delivery. The song builds to a superbly powerful climax as Iggy begins improvising about how he's gonna live – 'not like some fuckin' dead fucker'.

To promote the album, Iggy appeared on Nicky Campbell's BBC Radio One show on 17 September 1990. During the fascinating and lengthy interview, Iggy played a number of songs on his electric guitar. The performance of 'I Won't Crap Out', on live national radio, concluded with 'I'm tryin' to live – not like some small dead cocksuckin' mother piece of shit fucker' which, unsurprisingly, left the usually garrulous Campbell somewhat lost for words.

Candy

Possibly the most commercial song ever recorded by Iggy Pop, 'Candy' became a sizeable hit in the USA and a minor one in the UK. 'Candy' was always envisaged as a duet, but first choice Chrissie Hynde couldn't make it. Prior to working on *Brick By Brick*, Don Was had been producing much of the B-52s' *Cosmic Thing*. Was suggested Kate Pierson from the B-52s. Pierson's raucous yet vulnerable vocals elevate the song enormously. Backed by a stirring performance from the band, including lots of tambourines, some subtle restrained piano and a virtuoso performance from Aronoff, Iggy and Kate deliver a captivating vocal.

Interestingly, the song is actually about Betsy, Iggy's thirteen-year-old girlfriend from 1970 – 'Geez, it's been twenty years.' 'Candy' implies that Iggy still holds a torch for her after all this time, a sentiment that can't have impressed Suchi. It may be that Iggy was just using Betsy as a starting point and the song is a fiction, but as nearly all the other songs on *Brick By Brick* seem to come very much from the heart, you can't help wondering. In true Motown style, the second verse is sung from Candy's point of view and she's as cut up about the break-up as Iggy is.

Butt Town

Butt Town is where we all live, according to the sleeve notes of *Brick By Brick* – it's a place where superficiality rules, where the cops are more interested in their own physiques, and if you stay too long you'll turn into your own worst nightmare. Although 'Butt Town' is ostensibly a diatribe against Los Angeles, more vicious than 'Kill City' fifteen years earlier, Iggy often commented that there are elements of 'Butt Town' in most major cities. The song rocks harder than anything else so far on the album. Slash detonates the main riff over Duff's muscular bass and Kenny Aronoff's solid beat. Interestingly this song had been demoed as an acoustic number and it's a measure of the quality of the songwriting that the stripped-down demo works equally well.

The Undefeated

After the metal of 'Butt Town', 'The Undefeated' is ushered in on a gentle acoustic guitar, courtesy of Iggy himself. A cheery 'Here we go' gets the song up and running, and it's a thoroughly entertaining mid-tempo singalong. The chorus is sung by the Leeching Delinquents who included his son Eric (weirdly credited as Ewreck Benson) with loads of his friends, various record company guys, accountants – basically everyone Iggy could round up and drag into the studio that day. The massed chorus seems to swell in numbers throughout the song until it genuinely sounds like hundreds of people. Iggy pokes gentle fun at the leeching delinquents that his son hung around with. Iggy points out the need to be challenged, that you should do more than just sit around watching TV (has he forgotten he did just that in the early days of the Stooges?). There's almost a father-son advice feel to some of the song, but then Iggy seems to be good-naturedly aligning himself with the emerging stoner generation. A slightly confused song, but terrific fun.

Moonlight Lady

Originally demoed with different lyrics and called 'I Am', this song is one of the gentlest tracks Iggy has ever recorded. Unashamedly romantic, with a lush acoustic backing that even features a bouzouki, 'Moonlight Lady' is almost soppy in its cataloguing of the lovey-dovey things Iggy does for his lady. There are some lovely touches – the keyboard rumbles underneath the 'I'm on fire' middle eight are great, but you have to listen hard. The lyrics are genuinely affecting – it's a love song, nothing more nothing less. And you'd have to be made of stern stuff not to appreciate the sentiments.

Something Wild

John Hiatt guests on this cover of his own song (he would eventually record

it himself on his 1993 album *Perfectly Good Guitar*). Although it's one of the weaker songs on *Brick By Brick,* the band and Iggy especially put in a sterling performance. The song pumps away, the drums keeping a martial beat going, Waddy contributing some of his best guitar work, and engineer Ed Cherney getting in on the act with his 'Annoying Vocal Whine'. Lyrically it's an odd one for Iggy, being generally too wordy for his usual style, but somehow he manages to carry it off.

Neon Forest

It starts with the tape winding up into the band already hitting that relentless groove, one that they continue to mine for the duration of the song. The overall vibe is strongly reminiscent of songs by Neil Young and Crazy Horse. Interestingly *Ragged Glory*, the Young album recorded later in 1990 featured a song called 'Love To Burn', on which the Horse plough their ramshackle furrow of muscular rock and which is remarkably similar to 'Neon Forest'.

With both Iggy and Waddy on guitar, the song just drips Rock. Iggy's vocals give the impression of being a one-take recording, there's lots of little asides and Iggy counting the band in. If it is a first take, it's a truly remarkable job – a brilliant performance, assured, dominant, and full of character. Iggy's backed by the impossibly chipper chorus of Sweet Pea Atkinson, Sir Harry Bowens and Donald Ray Mitchell – all singers with Was (Not Was) and whose harmonious voices chant the title at regular intervals. Iggy seems to be painting a picture of himself as someone who inhabits a twilight world of neon, roaming the city at night 'like a cartoon cat'. This doesn't quite square with Iggy's genuinely settled home life, but is nevertheless portrayed very convincingly. The crucial line highlighting the psychic reasons behind American drug use was often altered in concert to refer to whichever country or city he was performing in. Writer Irvine Welsh heard the song in Glasgow in 1991 and was inspired to write the harsh and unrelenting novel *Trainspotting*, the film of which was to play an important part in resurrecting Iggy once again in the mid 1990s.

Starry Night

This song highlights Don Was's influence over the arrangements – the demo is played very straight and is frankly rather dull. Under Was's guidance, the whole feel of the song is dramatically altered – Iggy now sings in a cheerful manner, perfectly matching the optimistic, almost comical backing vocals, the cod-reggae beat, tinny keyboards and genuinely funny lyrics. The woozy slide guitar at the end sounds like something Talking Heads might have done and the song is now intentionally jaunty. Iggy is simply saying that it doesn't matter about your job, your magazines, your money, we're all the same under the stars. Wise words, but delivered in a light-hearted style that makes for a very satisfying interlude between the pounding 'Neon Forest' and the G 'n' R style 'Pussy Power'.

Pussy Power

With both Slash and Iggy powering their way through the song, 'Pussy Power' is nothing but a monster riff overlaid with some of Iggy's deepest ever vocals. The title is chanted by a chorus of multi-tracked sepulchral Iggys and works brilliantly. In many ways, this song sets the template for loads of Iggy tracks in the forthcoming decade, the stuttering rock attack, the relatively simplistic tune, the bass-heavy vocals. While the formula would gradually become stale over time, here it's fresh and exciting and enlivened by young guns Slash and Duff who bring their swaggering confidence and cocksure arrogance to a track which aligns Iggy with the younger generation once again. Iggy is eyeing up girls, and from the evidence of this song is behaving like the unreconstructed old reprobate that the previous five years seemed to have swept away. Amongst all the grown-up songs and middle-aged attitudes on the rest of the album it seems anachronistic and slightly juvenile. As later albums would show, Iggy would slide further back into the twilight world of girls and dope as the decade wore on. 'Pussy Power' was not the blast from the past it seemed at the time, but rather the shape of things to come.

My Baby Wants To Rock And Roll

A stunning tune, courtesy of Slash, fiery lyrics and a bravura performance from all the musicians combines to make this song everything that *Instinct* promised to be, but signally failed to deliver. The lyric is caustic and striking, once again there's some stunningly evocative imagery on display, and the last verse contains shocking references to a drug overdose. The old dispassionate observer Iggy is back. There's none of the confessional style of earlier on the album. This tells it like it is, no judgement, no mercy. Iggy does more old-fashioned hollering on this song than on any other track and Slash's descending guitar gives us the most metal song on the album – it's a fitting climax.

Brick By Brick

The intended final track, the title song, is performed just by Iggy on his acoustic guitar, with slight embellishments from Waddy. Jamie adds some keyboard swells towards the conclusion. Suddenly we're back with the confessional Iggy, the balladeer, the mature adult singer-songwriter. It is a beautiful little song, successful mainly due to the understated nature of the performance. Iggy is very closely miked, the guitars are crystal clear. Returning to the theme of 'Home', Iggy takes the metaphor further to describe, clearly and without ambiguity, the house that he's building for his life, 'brick by brick'. It's a house with balance and dignity, and it's being built with what he believes in. Never has there been a more heartfelt lyric. Leave the guy alone, give him some peace, let him live his life with his wife, let him be true to his simple heart. After all, it's not too much to ask, is it?

Livin' On The Edge Of The Night

Sadly, the beautiful ending was ruined by Virgin, who insisted on adding this semi-hit to the album. The sub-Billy Idol tune, swathed in girly choruses and rinky-tink piano is not one of Iggy's better moments. It's undeniably catchy, but is way too simplistic and obvious. The chorus vocal sounds so like Billy Idol that you wonder why the song wasn't given to him in the first place. At least Idol would probably have had a hit with it.

The single came in multiple formats, backed with various cuts from *The Idiot* and *Lust For Life*, or in some cases by the acoustic demos for *Brick By Brick*. There are two, ever so slightly different, mixes.

*   *   *

Brick By Brick was a moderate success in Europe and the USA. Reviews were generally kind and encouraging, singling out Iggy's courting of the new wave of rock stars with Slash and Duff as proving that he still had his finger on the pulse of modern music. 'Home' was a strong radio hit, slightly edited to remove the swearing, but 'Candy', issued in a myriad of single formats (7" single, cassette, 10" coloured vinyl, 12" single and CD) was a very popular song on college radio throughout 1990. Its success didn't really translate into the national charts but Iggy's profile was considerably raised by this duet.

Well, Did You Evah?

Perhaps encouraged by the popularity of 'Candy', Iggy contributed a duet with Deborah Harry to the *Red Hot And Blue* album. This was a collection of Cole Porter songs recorded by contemporary artists with all the proceeds going to an AIDS charity.

Among songs by artists as varied as U2, David Byrne and the Thompson Twins was this little gem. Originally featured in the film *High Society* which starred Bing Crosby, Frank Sinatra and, in her last major film, Grace Kelly, 'Well, Did You Evah?' was given a chunky makeover by Chris Stein, Simple Minds' drummer Mel Gaynor and session bassist Guy Pratt. The track was recorded at Red Night Studios in New York with Stein and Steve Lillywhite producing. Iggy and Debbie sound, quite frankly, drunk. They giggle like schoolkids and try to outdo one another with silly phrasing and irrelevant chat about Pia Zadora. And the song ends in sniggering after Debbie says 'Now fuck off' to Iggy's obvious delight. It's so engaging that the listener can't fail to become caught up in the clearly great time they are having recording the song. Of course it's not essential, which makes the song's inclusion on the 2005 anthology *A Million In Prizes* somewhat surprising. It was released as a single (backed by a Thompson Twins track) in time for Christmas 1990. To promote the single, Alex Cox directed a very funny video featuring Iggy in a tux and Debbie glammed up to the max.

Down On The Street – 1990 *Brick By Brick* Tour

Iggy Pop – vocals, guitar
Whitey Kirst – guitar
Larry Mullins – drums
Craig Pike – bass

As *Brick By Brick* had been recorded with session musicians, a whole new band needed to be recruited for the planned world tour. Instead of 'name' musicians, Iggy opted for a gang of unknown young players chosen primarily from amongst Eric's friends. Michael Charles Whitehorn Kirst had appeared as one of the Leeching Delinquents chanting the chorus on 'The Undefeated'. Whitey originally learnt the drums, but switched to guitar because two of his elder brothers (he's the youngest of eight siblings) also played drums and, as he put it, he didn't want 'to become redundant. And it's a lot easier to carry a guitar.' At only twenty-three he proved to be formidable guitarist; he had the speed and the precision required for the Stooges tunes Iggy wanted to perform on the forthcoming tour, yet could also turn his hand to the more melodic recent material. Having grown up on the drums he also had the required sense of rhythm that all great Iggy guitarists need.

Larry Mullins (not the U2 drummer, Larry Mullen Jnr, despite what some sources claim) thrashed his drum kit wildly from behind a mane of long hair and possessed the power and strength required for the endurance test of some of the longest concerts Iggy would ever perform. Completing the band was Craig Pike, from Los Angeles. He had been working as the promotions director at the Hollywood Palace during 1989 before Whitey recommended him for the job of Iggy's bassist.

None of the musicians had ever played in a major group before. This had the effect of separating Iggy from his band more than ever. As if to make up for this, however, Iggy joined his band by playing guitar onstage for the first time.

Early autumn was spent in intensive rehearsal. The younger band members, who introduced elements of speed metal and thrash into the tunes, revitalised many of the older tunes. Iggy loved the new harder sound.

From October through to the end of the year, Iggy and his band toured North America. Compensating for the lack of European shows in 1990, Iggy promoted the release of *Brick By Brick* with a series of radio appearances in the UK and mainland Europe. He would often play a number of songs solo, accompanied only by his electric guitar.

The new shows were some of the longest gigs he would ever play. Although the main set remained pretty static for most of the tour, the encores would vary in length considerably depending on the audience reaction.

An early set list ran as follows:

'Raw Power', 'Five Foot One', 'Dirt', 'Loose', 'I Won't Crap Out', 'Lust For Life', 'China Girl', 'I Got A Right', 'Butt Town', 'Something Wild', 'Search And Destroy', 'Dum Dum Boys', 'My Baby Wants To Rock'n'Roll', 'Neon Forest', 'Home', 'Brick By Brick', '1969', 'Candy', 'I Wanna Be Your Dog', 'Main Street Eyes', 'No Fun', 'Foxy Lady', 'Pussy Power'

As usual with any Iggy Pop tour, a few songs were dropped as the tour progressed. Early casualties included 'Dum Dum Boys' and 'I Won't Crap Out' (the loss of which meant that nothing from the new album was played until at least eight songs in). 'Main Street Eyes' gradually dropped out of sight and 'Something Wild' was replaced with the more reliable 'Real Wild Child'. Jimi Hendrix's 'Foxy Lady' was a surprise choice for an encore, but one which suited Iggy well.

The new band coped with the material extremely well. Larry's drumming was especially fierce, pushing a splendid rendition of 'Dirt' along at almost twice the speed of the *Fun House* version. Songs such as 'I Got A Right' and 'Lust For Life' were also played much faster, becoming sharper and more metallic than ever in the process. As if to prove that the band had versatility, 'China Girl' was played with surprising tenderness, and the complexities of the newer material caused no problem. The main set usually ended with an enlarged 'Brick By Brick'. This would begin with Iggy solo, before the band crashed in after the first verse. '1969' would grind into life with Larry pounding out the tribal beat for some time, before Whitey slashed into the chords.

The most notable aspect of this tour is that Iggy, despite a relatively neat appearance (short hair and jeans being the stage outfit) began to get more and more wild as the tour progressed. For the first time in many years, he started to disrobe mid-concert. He would frequently be found with his jeans round his ankles with only a guitar to cover his crotch. Sometimes he didn't even bother with the guitar, letting it all hang out. These displays of public nudity were nothing new, he had been dropping his pants onstage since the early Stooges concerts, but on this tour it became a regular occurrence, leading people to wonder if it wasn't getting a little too contrived and rehearsed. Iggy countered by claiming that his new band had rejuvenated him and that he was simply attacking his new live shows with more energy than ever before, and that if his trousers came down, well, that was entirely out of his control. The music was taking him over...

With plenty more dates booked for 1991 the new decade had started well.

1991

Down On The Street
– 1991 *Brick By Brick* Tour continued

Iggy Pop – vocals, guitar
Whitey Kirst – guitar
Larry Mullins – drums
Craig Pike – bass

Early in 1991, the tour moved to Europe. Between mid January and the end of March, Iggy travelled all over the continent, beginning with a UK jaunt and in February a series of club gigs in Athens which delighted his perhaps surprisingly large Greek fan base. Subtle changes to the set list included the introduction of 'The Passenger', 'Down On The Street' and hardy perennial 'Louie Louie' to many of the encores, and the occasional substitution of 'I Won't Crap Out' for 'Brick By Brick', though on the whole the high-octane set remained stable.

Iggy had begun pulling people from the audience to dance with him on songs such as 'Lust For Life' – this crowd-pleasing move would be expanded over the years until by the end of the decade performances of 'The Passenger' would see the whole stage swamped with madly dancing members of the audience.

A month after the first Paris concert at Le Zenith, a second show was added to the schedule, this time at the larger Olympia on 15 March. The reason for this addition was that renowned video director Tim Pope (probably most famous for his left-field surreal promos for the Cure) was to film the gig for the home video market. Fortunately, Pope recorded a blinding gig. For the filming, Iggy played one of the longest sets of the tour. At one point, he caught his arm on a guitar string, resulting in a nasty cut. This gave rise to the title of the film when he danced in front of the baying audience and instructed them to 'Kiss my blood!' Issued later that year, *Kiss My Blood* was the first official Iggy video product. It received an '18' certificate in the UK, earned by Iggy's full-frontal display. It's inexplicable, but somehow Iggy Pop remained indefinably cool – even with his jeans and his underpants round his ankles, tripping over as he hopped manically about the stage. No one else could get away with this sort of behaviour. No one else would even try.

Down On The Street
– 1991 European Summer Festivals

Iggy Pop – vocals, guitar
Whitey Kirst – guitar
Larry Mullins – drums
Craig Pike – bass

Iggy's full-throttle live set was ideal for the massive outdoor stages of the lucrative European festival circuit. He had played a few of these shows in 1987 and 1988, but 1991 saw the first full assault on what would become a valuable regular in Iggy's diary. As well as the exposure to a whole new audience, many of whom might never have seen an Iggy Pop concert otherwise, the festivals also provided Iggy with a massive new following in radio- and TV-land as many of the big gigs were broadcast across Europe. Mostly, the summer sets played between the end of June and the end of August would be short and furious, often little more than an hour in length as Iggy cherry-picked a handful of new songs and mixed them with the obvious crowd-pleasers. He rarely headlined these sorts of shows – that honour would usually go to the latest young chart-topping bands, which meant that Iggy would often be found playing during the late afternoon to a crowd restless to hear the headline act. That he was able to frequently win the audience over is a testament to his years of experience of hostile crowds and his incredible energy.

The 1991 summer gigs generally featured a slightly shorter set than that played on the tour earlier in the year. The song order was also reworked so the sets would now begin with the tribal stomp of 'Down On The Street' before being propelled into 'My Baby Wants To Rock And Roll'. By this stage, nearly half the set was comprised of Stooges songs.

This typical set from the Leysin festival on 12 July featured in a radio broadcast and has therefore been widely bootlegged:

'Down On The Street', 'My Baby Wants To Rock'n'Roll', 'Raw Power', 'Gimme Danger', 'TV Eye', 'Dirt', 'Lovebone', 'Five Foot One', 'China Girl', 'Lust For Life', 'Candy', 'Real Wild Child', 'The Passenger', 'No Fun', 'I Wanna Be Your Dog', 'Home'

The show at Juan Les Pins a couple of days previously had featured the same set, with a lengthy encore during which 'Search and Destroy', '1969' and 'Foxy Lady' were performed, amongst others.

A new song, 'Lovebone' was regularly played during the summer, but very rarely after that. Based on the 1989 demo 'Think Alone' but severely rocked up and with new lyrics (no prizes for guessing what 'Lovebone' is all about),

it's a fun live track, but ultimately disposable, which probably accounts for its non-appearance on any studio album.

After the summer festivals, Iggy returned home. He'd spent the best part of a year on the road, travelling more widely than ever before and playing to some of the biggest crowds he'd ever faced. He spent the next year and half mostly out of sight, off the touring circuit and with no records to promote. The live video *Kiss My Blood* filled the gap, as did various pseudo-official archive releases. Iggy was happy to drop out for a while – it allowed him time and space to recharge and refocus.

Why Was I Born?

In the meantime the only new product, in late 1991, was this grinding piece of horror-film music that Iggy contributed to the soundtrack of *Freddy's Dead – The Final Nightmare*, one of the weakest instalments in the *Nightmare On Elm Street* series. It's actually rather a good song, with Iggy scarily intoning the defiant lyrics over some of Whitey's finest guitar squeals. After two minutes, the songs suddenly picks up speed as Iggy whines out the title.

Amusingly, 'Why Was I Born?' was nominated in the Worst Song category at the 1992 Golden Raspberry Awards. Presented on 29 March 1992, these awards – the antithesis of the Oscars – honour the worst performances in the same categories as its more prestigious counterparts. 'Why Was I Born?' lost out to the truly dreadful 'Addams Groove', MC Hammer's ludicrous attempt to update the theme from *The Addams Family*.

1992

Down On The Street – 1992 South American Concerts

Iggy Pop – vocals, guitar
Hal Cragin – bass
Larry Mullins – drums
Eric Schermerhorn – guitar

South America, and especially Brazil, has a massive audience with an appetite for rock. The annual *Rock In Rio* festival attracts world record crowds every year. Unsurprisingly, Iggy Pop has a strong following in South America and, with a hefty fee waved in front of him, the chance to play at the enormous Estadio Obras Sanitarias in Buenos Aires on 14 August was just too good to miss. Larry remained from the 1990–1991 band, but Iggy needed a new lead guitarist, as Whitey was unable to make the trip. Eric Schermerhorn had recently been playing with David Bowie's Tin Machine, alongside the Sales brothers, and was a versatile and inventive guitarist. He had also been a member of the quirky They Might Be Giants along with bass player Hal Cragin. As Craig Pike had moved to London, Eric recommended Hal for the vacant bassist role. Sadly, Craig died, aged just thirty, as a result of injuries suffered in a car accident in London on 23 May 1993.

Iggy and Eric put together one of the most unusual set lists of recent years for the handful of South American dates. Strongly weighted in favour of the Stooges, including an unprecedented five from *Raw* Power (plus 'I Got A Right' and a welcome return for 'I'm Sick Of You' from the same era). 'Winners and Losers' was resurrected for one last time and 'Search And Destroy' made such a powerful opening it's amazing that it is usually lost in the middle of the set.

'Search And Destroy', 'The Passenger', 'Penetration', 'Raw Power', 'I Need Somebody', 'Shake Appeal', 'Home', 'My Baby Wants To Rock'n'Roll', 'Loose', 'Winners And Losers', 'China Girl', 'Real Wild Child', 'TV Eye', 'Candy', 'I'm Sick Of You', 'I Got A Right', 'No Fun', 'I Wanna Be Your Dog', 'Lust For Life', 'Louie Louie'

After the gigs, Eric and Iggy began writing a number of songs together. Iggy had been working on short stories and verses about old girlfriends with a view to turning some of them into his next album. In the event, this plan fell by the wayside although 'Girls Of NY' contains some of the original ideas. Meeting producer Malcolm Burn changed his mind. Burn suggested writing about life as an American in the 1990s, a direction that Iggy eagerly embraced.

Arizona Dream

The autumn of 1992 was spent working on songs for Emir Kustarica's film. Kusturica had made a number of films including *Time of The Gypsies*, which had attracted widespread critical acclaim. *Arizona Dream*, starring Johnny Depp, Jerry Lewis and Faye Dunaway, was his first American film, but Kusturica brought a number of people with him from his native Sarajevo. Among them was composer Goran Bregovic, who sent Iggy three tunes that required lyrics. Iggy approached this project with enthusiasm. The songs were as far removed from his usual style as could be, but Iggy had long held a strong interest in European folk music, and so Bregovic's gypsy inspired tunes delighted him.

In The Deathcar

Bregovic's shuffling gypsy tune complete with massed mandolins, is graced with a moody low key sung-spoken vocal from Iggy. The incongruous angelic female chorus and the gentle horn punctuation add further dimensions and the result is an extremely atmospheric and surprisingly memorable track. Iggy's lyrics once again hint at the corruption of young women, which at his age was getting more and more uncomfortable to hear about. For such an unusual song, it was surprising that it was issued as a single in some European countries, and Iggy demonstrated his love of the track by playing 'In The Deathcar' on some of his 1993–1994 dates.

TV Screen

Over a keyboard introduction and the gentle chunk of the percussion, Iggy sings in his deepest voice. It's another vaguely obscure attack on the power and influence of television: 'TV Screen makes you feel small, no life at all.' Again the choral backing vocals create an unusual, but successful, framework for Iggy's lyrics.

Get The Money

Like a cracked cheerleader, Iggy chants the lyrics over a jolly horn and chorus-led ('Money, money, money...') song. There are some strange autobiographical references to school days and Iggy gets increasingly hysterical. Topical nods to the recently departed newspaper magnate and pension-fund embezzler Robert Maxwell tie in loosely with the title, but this has to be one of the oddest songs Iggy's ever done – rather like 'Watching The News' in both tone and content.

This Is A Film

The soundtrack concludes with a reworking of 'In The Deathcar', over which Iggy explains what the film is about. It's a very effective final track, with Bregovic's music augmented by a mournful sax.

*　　*　　*

The *Arizona Dream* soundtrack was issued around the same time as *American Caesar* in 1993, providing a stark contrast and showcasing an interestingly perverse side to Iggy.

1993

ggy's second Virgin album was a darker, moodier affair than the relatively commercial *Brick By Brick*. It was produced by Malcolm Burn and engineered by Mark Howard, both long-time associates of Daniel Lanois, perhaps known best for his production work for U2 and Bob Dylan, among many others. He was an inspired choice of producer for Iggy – like Lanois, Burn had learnt to record his artists cleanly, with minimum studio trickery, but coaxing maximum vibe and atmosphere from the performances.

Always a voracious reader, Iggy would get through hundreds of books on the road. He delighted in showing people his library at home. In the early 1980s, Iggy had ploughed through Gibbon's *Decline And Fall Of The Roman Empire* and retained a fascination with all things Roman. The title of the album came first – *American Caesar* – with Iggy envisaging himself as a sort of modern-day Caesar. He wanted to explore various human emotions on the new record – loneliness, hatred, jealousy, paranoia and love – and how they fitted into life in the USA in the 1990s. The resulting series of vignettes were quite different from the sort of songs he'd written before. Iggy also wanted the album to sound more of a piece, and so he kept the same tight band that he'd used in South America during the summer of 1992 rather than hiring a raft of session players.

Iggy and the band warmed up with a date at the Continental in New York on 13 January 1993 (where they debuted 'Wild America' and 'Sickness') before a short tour of Australasia as part of the travelling *Big Day Out* Festival in late January. Another new song, 'Hate', was unveiled in Australia. The set was again Stooges-heavy, with the whole of side one of *Fun House* now being played. On 1 February, Iggy guested on Nick Cave's version of 'Little Doll' at Adelaide University. The *Big Day Out* set list was:

'Down On The Street', 'Loose', 'Raw Power', 'Dirt', 'TV Eye', 'Hate', 'Real Wild Child', 'Search And Destroy', 'I Wanna Be Your Dog', 'No Fun', 'The Passenger', 'Lust For Life'

Suitably broken in, the band reconvened in New Orleans at Daniel Lanois' Kingsway Studios during the spring of 1993. Kingsway was a rambling and ramshackle old mansion, which had been converted to a warm and inviting studio where musicians could live comfortably and record in the high-ceilinged rooms. The casual ambience of the building permeates most of the records made there and *American Caesar* is no exception.

AMERICAN CAESAR

Virgin CDVUS64. Released – September 1993
Produced by **Malcolm Burn**

Various extra musicians, called in as and when needed, augmented the regular band. Malcolm Burn added moody guitar, keyboards and harmonica, 'Mixin' The Colours' was boosted by Katell Keinig's backing vocals, plus percussion from Daryl Johnson and atmospheric guitar from Bill Dillon, both members of Daniel Lanois' band. Elsewhere, Lisa Germano contributed some delicate backing vocals to 'Beside You' and Henry Rollins delivered a little monologue in the middle of 'Wild America'.

Rollins was delighted to assist one of his heroes. His original band, Black Flag, had been strongly influenced by the Stooges, and their brand of muscular punk owed a huge debt to Iggy. Since the band's demise, Rollins had built up his image as a fast-talking, wise cracking, rock and roll marine commando. His testosterone-fuelled persona as a sort of militaristic über-punk was extraordinarily successful. Rollins began recording a number of spoken-word albums, full of extremely funny raps and monologues, almost poetically delivered with a superb sense of rhythm. (One hilarious tale recounts his increasingly desperate attempts to outperform Iggy whenever their paths crossed at festivals. Often Rollins would play before Iggy and his performances would become more and more extreme in an effort to beat the master. But even though Rollins would give it everything he'd got, eyes bulging, scarcely able to breathe, Iggy always effortlessly topped whatever Henry had done.) Rollins also put himself forward to remix *Raw Power* in 1995, before Iggy himself took the job.

A number of songs were recorded virtually live in the studio, with only minimal overdubs. Others were more complex, with multiple backing vocals and all manner of effects from Burn.

The resulting album met with a lukewarm response from Virgin. It was suggested that Iggy might record a few more commercial tracks. Iggy responded positively to this, with the result that *American Caesar* became the longest studio record he'd ever made. The late additions, recorded at Bearsville Studio in New York a month or so later, included a new version of the 1985 track 'Beside You', which follows the Steve Jones demo faithfully, the short and sharp 'Sickness' and a storming take on 'Louie Louie' – the first proper studio recording of this perennial live favourite. In keeping with the album's themes, Iggy also updated and politicised the lyrics.

Now satisfied that they'd got a varied and impressive collection of tunes, Virgin issued *American Caesar* in September 1993 to a raft of strong reviews. *Rolling Stone* awarded the album four stars and stated that Iggy had reclaimed 'the slashing, psychedelic-tinged grunge rock he helped pioneer as a Stooge' and *Melody Maker* praised the thinly veiled attacks on the underbelly of America and called the record 'a broad, bold masterpiece'.

The cover was remarkable. A starkly lit picture of Iggy showing his age, his hair hanging lankly below his shoulders for the first time since the Stooges, his face craggier and more sunken than ever. But there's a steely intensity in his gaze. Amusingly a fake parental warning sticker appeared in the bottom left corner: 'Warning – This is an Iggy Pop record'.

Character

Traffic noises give way to a delicately atmospheric piece of guitar noodling from Eric, over which Iggy delivers a distorted and barely intelligible monologue about how the screwed-up guys he used to play with had character. They played guitar 'like they meant it'. 'Character' is a weird little opening, wistfully reminiscing about the old days for just over a minute. It's the calm before the storm.

Wild America

Without warning, Eric launches into the jagged lurching riff of 'Wild America'. Iggy sings the see-sawing tune in an exaggerated but slightly rusty whine, his voice leaping impressively on the song's title. Schermerhorn follows him every step of the way until it suddenly grinds to a shocking halt. And as if that weren't enough, Henry Rollins has a chat with Iggy at about the three minute mark.

The band plays this terrific track at full throttle, Eric rides that double-tracked riff throughout and Larry plays some kick-ass drums. Iggy delivers his vocal in a kind of amused amazement as he recounts various scenes from his life. It's almost as if he's caricaturing himself but, after the serious intent of 'Character', this seems unlikely. Iggy seems slightly incredulous, as if unable to believe that all this can actually happen to him. As with some of the songs on *Brick By Brick*, the story unfolding is at odds with his securely and sedately married life. But it's so in keeping with the Iggy persona that the twilight world appears totally real. The song opens with a night-time trip during which Iggy meets a Mexican girl and her 'butchy girlfriend'. The resulting little vignettes are related with no judgement, no side to them. It's just the usual shit that happens to Iggy. Over an increasingly violent build-up towards the climax (where keyboards attempt to jostle the guitars for prominence) the lyrics become a sort of updated 'I Need More', as Iggy lists all the stuff that people want. It's a telling, and largely impossible, list.

Mixin' The Colors

A very different musical palette is utilised on 'Mixin' The Colors'. Atmospheric ambient guitar from Bill Dillon, the drums deftly mixed into an echoing gunshot, and some seriously over-amped harmonica create a totally different mood from 'Wild America' and, with Iggy singing quietly, closely miked, this is a strong contender for Iggy's moodiest song. Lyrically it may be a tad obvious – Iggy is simply stating that races are mixing, and

Iggy's quite happy about it. The message, gently but firmly delivered, is of toleration and peace, to live and let live. Although the notion that music can help achieve racial harmony is nothing new ('Ebony and Ivory', anyone?) here the idea is presented calmly and rationally. It's happening, it's good, the kids know what to do, just look at MTV.

Musically, the swampy rhythm and bouncing bass complement the crisp drumming (although the step-by-step bass descent at the end of each chorus makes you think that Iggy will be doing the 'Stray Cat Strut' before too long) and the inclusion of harmonious female backing vocals, doubling Iggy's lead, is effective and satisfying.

Jealousy

A slow, brooding, dark piece of music, this begins gently enough with Eric's delicate figures, some faraway drums and floaty keyboards. But then it starts to build. Traces of burning electric guitar creep into the mix, on the verge of escaping but restrained and expertly held in check. Iggy's growling throaty vocal is the same, gradually swelling with the music into a multi-tracked chorus by the conclusion. Lyrically, it's an interesting take on how rock 'n' roll can circumvent class and money differences. The first verse disparagingly describes a rich ass with a model girlfriend and a limousine. The second outlines her background. Iggy's jealous, he feels his blood boiling. But how to compete? Rock 'n' roll is how...

Hate

After the dark atmospheres of the previous songs, 'Hate' lurches dangerously into life, its brutal pounding rhythm matched by the anger in Iggy's voice. Abstract images of what feeds Iggy's hate – evil looks, the stupidity of those in power – are thrown into the mêlée, but Iggy sways sideways at the end – 'Why am I afraid?' he calls over Eric's thrashing guitar. Again though, the mix seems to hold the song back, restraining the pent-up rage and never allowing it to boil over. The guitars have clearly been recorded very loud but are mixed low creating an angry electrical buzzing which mushes with the bass, over which Larry's drums are clear and sharp.

The song is all but over by the four-minute mark, but the band remorselessly continue for another three as Iggy wails 'Afraid' and Eric coaxes all sorts of fearsome sounds from his guitar which is then layered to create a wall of noise.

It's Our Love

This is a total contrast, a brilliant mood lightener, and a genuinely beautiful piece of music. 'It's Our Love' even has a stirring synthetic orchestral accompaniment which threatens to tip the song into syrupy parody but just about stays on the right side of sincerity. To add to the old-fashioned feel, Larry's drums sound like they were recorded from the next room and there's a tremendously huge Spectoresque feel to the strings. Ten years on from their first meeting, Iggy openly and touchingly celebrates his marriage to Suchi (who is credited as 'spiritual advisor to Mr Pop' in the sleeve notes). There are some fine lines about alienation and loneliness, which pretty much sum up Iggy's situation back in 1983. The vocals find Iggy straining slightly with some of the higher notes, but you can't fault him for trying.

Plastic And Concrete

The first dumb-ass rock song so far on the album. It whizzes along with a
Ramones-style riff, up and down, with little variation. Iggy even sings in an
intentionally dumb manner. But it sounds like filler, despite the obvious care
taken over the mix – listen out for the odd tinkling bell sounds in the
background – and Eric's marvellous solo which sounds like it's from another,
rather better, song altogether.

Fuckin' Alone

Over Eric's lilting tune, gently powered by bongos, acoustic guitar, and a
whirring keyboard effect that sounds weirdly like a didgeridoo, Iggy delivers
what can only be described as a rap. His excellent sense of rhythm just about
keeps the words in line as he reflects what he sees in the world – drifters,
presidents and super freaks, coffee beans, the evening breeze and Jeeps with
huge speakers playing a mix of metal, rap and salsa (much like this song). But
amongst this bewildering catalogue of modern life, Iggy remains alone. Proud
to stand in isolation on *Blah-Blah-Blah*, now he's simply alone. And not just
any kind of alone, he's *fuckin'* alone. 'This is me,' he sings. 'OK OK.' But it's
the same for everyone – we've all got to figure life out for ourselves.

It is a surprising song to find on an Iggy Pop album. But the combination
of spoken-sung rap and the acoustic backing works very effectively (the
multi-tracking effect of the guitar on the choruses is beautifully done) and
creates one of the highpoints of the record.

Highway Song

Continuing the acoustic vibe, 'Highway Song' is dominated by Iggy's
cheery strumming, with Eric adding some keening electric guitar over the
choruses (which echoes the electric overdubs on the Velvet Underground's
'Rock 'n' Roll'). The brisk pace and rockabilly approach mirror the travelling
homeless images in the lyrics and, although it's not an original subject for a
rock song, Iggy pulls it off, mainly because it's not something he would
normally do. In concert in 1993, Iggy explained the background a little:
'Once you start running, you can't stop, or lie down anywhere. I always
wanted to be in a circus, 'cause you'd feel like a freak. I like being a freak.'
The always-on-the-road, travelling-man persona is one that fits Iggy very
well, though the chorus claiming that nothing is 'gonna take the road outta
my heart' verges on the parodic and is undeniably cheesy. But the song is so
positive and infectiously catchy that the corny aspects quickly fade.

Beside You

One of the extra tracks recorded to give Virgin something more commercial,
this sees Iggy return to a Steve Jones tune from 1985. Hardly varying from
the demo track, 'Beside You' is an effective and very catchy love song
directed once again at Suchi, which neatly encapsulated his feeling then and
in 1993. As with many of Jones's melodies it can be criticised for being a
touch plodding, but 'Beside You' achieves its simple aim of being a cool pop
song admirably. Hal Cragin's bass work is excellent, Malcolm Burn's angelic
keyboards during the last couple of choruses are very apt and Lisa
Germano's backing vocals are delightful.

It was issued as the second single from *American Caesar* in May 1994. Following an uncharacteristically lacklustre appearance on *Top of the Pops*, it just scraped into the UK charts, and this was despite the varying b-sides and myriad of formats, that were available to tempt the customers.

Sickness

Another contrast – this short and powerful punkish track continues the human condition themes of the album – jealousy, hate, love and now sickness. But this is love sickness, the insidious sort of love that can cause a man to lose everything. The ceaselessly rising guitars are dramatic and thrilling but ultimately it's a slighter song than most others on *American Caesar*, and one that makes the listener begin to question the wisdom of including all these tracks. Is the album perhaps too long?

Boogie Boy

Another rather throwaway song, and one that continues the doubts over quality control that began with 'Sickness'. It's a one-take, live-in-the-studio recording containing an immediacy missing from some of the other more distanced songs. The lyrics are dumb, intentionally so of course, but dumb nonetheless, and coming after the adult brooding quality of songs such as 'Jealousy' is something a disappointment. So Iggy likes to eat spaghetti then go out and make some noise? Fine, but this is probably the weakest track on the album. And it lasts far too long.

Perforation Problems

'Perforation Problems' addresses another aspect of the human condition – drug addiction. Graphic images of needles and horrendous memories are frightening, but with such strong lyrics it is something of pity that the melody is rather weak. The generic thrash generated by the band seems sadly inferior to the lyrics. But the harshly miked harmonica is excellent and Iggy's vocals are some of the strongest on the album.

Social Life

This is another track recorded live in the studio. Accompanied by some beautiful acoustic guitar, gentle bass and faint keyboards Iggy outlines the problems inherent in a difficult social life. This may be Iggy's peculiar experience of parties, where he constantly suffers people coming on to him, with no one to talk to properly. But it's one that is so accurately described that everyone can identify with Iggy and imagine that the song relates to their own personal experiences of dreadful social situations.

Louie Louie

With no break, Iggy mutters 'and now... the news' and it's 'Louie Louie' time! Amazingly, apart from a rough jam in the studio in 1972 this is the only studio recording of 'Louie Louie' that Iggy has ever made. Thankfully it's a monster. Eric amps his guitars to the max, Malcolm adds a one finger piano stolen from 'Raw Power' and Iggy double-tracks his sneering vocals on the choruses. Strangely, Iggy doesn't sing the X-rated lyrics he'd spent years performing in concerts from 1973 onwards, but changes all the verses to reflect the world in

1993. Iggy would later laughingly refer to this as 'the geo-political twist' and it's tempting to read political messages into the new lyrics, but I get the impression that Iggy is actually avoiding making any genuine political points. He touches on health insurance, AIDS, the homeless but this is 'Louie Louie' folks. OK, so the news looks like a movie, but all he wants to do is sing his dumb songs, no bullshit, and get the hell outta there. He's a rock star – sure, there are all these problems in the world but at the end of the day what can he do? Iggy is not absolving himself of personal responsibility – after name-checking a number of social issues he mutters 'I'm tryin' to right, but... hey' but it's the apparent responsibility for world problems that rock stars such as Bono or Sting appear to take on board that Iggy is saying is not for him. All he can do is sing...

Caesar

Casting himself as Julius Caesar, Iggy indulges his love of Rome and acts out the role with gusto. Historically it's nonsense, but there's a tremendous amount of fun to be had from Iggy's manic 'Throw them to the lions... ha ha ha...' Later, he acts out the snivelling soothsayer warning Caesar to beware the Ides of March amongst other characters. The echoing monologue is recounted over a circular atonal guitar motif, plus occasional bass and percussion effects. Perhaps the most surprising track Iggy had recorded since 'Watching the News' over ten years previously, it appears that this song was invented on the spot. Inspired by the faded magnificence of the studio, Iggy found himself spouting his Roman tale over one of Eric's most unusual improvisations. The result surprised even Iggy. Memories of Gibbon's *Decline and Fall of the Roman Empire* mixed with images of modern-day generals and superhuman figures in Iggy's mind and 'out of me poured information that I had no idea I ever knew, let alone retained, in an extemporaneous soliloquy I called "Caesar".'

It was even more surprising when Iggy often performed this marvellously absurd track on the following tour.

The track ends when the guitar suddenly stops. Then we hear Iggy asking Malcolm, 'We got that, right? ... You see I could go more for numbers like that on the record...'

Girls Of NY

'Caesar' was obviously intended to be the final track of the album but, as with *Brick By Brick*, Virgin clearly disagreed and at their insistence again a final number was added. Evidence of the late addition can again be found on the inner sleeve as the font used for the track's title is different and there is no space to add the lyrics.

Anyway, it's a corking track with which to close the album. Larry keeps up a solid kick-drum beat as Eric picks out a cool acoustic riff and Hal walks his bass all around. Iggy narrates his descriptions of the girls of New York in a sardonic yet sympathetically wistful voice. Larry picks up his sticks and builds up a gradually more complex drum pattern as Iggy catalogues the cosmopolitan peoples of New York. Then he carefully and affectionately describes a particular girl, she's got character, she's got soul – which brings us neatly back to the opening track of *American Caesar* – and that's the kind of girl Iggy wants to know. He continues with one of my favourite lines of all – wearing combat boots, she's trouble, and the way Iggy says 'trouble' leaves me in no doubt that it's exactly the sort of trouble that he's after… He wants that girl, with the 'hint of dirt in her eye'; she's trouble, she's sexy. It's a brilliant conclusion to the song. Simple, direct and heartfelt, as all great Iggy Pop songs should be. The only downside is yet another extremely rapid fade out (see also 'Death Trip', 'Fall In Love With Me' and 'Winners And Losers'), which once again ends the album all too quickly.

*　　*　　*

The album contained a message from Iggy written on the CD itself, which contains the following telling admission – 'You tell how you really feel, you get burned. I'm ready to go down in flames…' – which implies that Iggy has genuinely bared his soul on this album. The message continues, 'I tried to make this album as good as I could, with no imitations of other people and no formula shit. This is individual expression.' It certainly is.

Wild America

Just before *American Caesar* hit the shops, the 'Wild America' EP was issued. On 7" and 12" single and CD, 'Wild America' only slightly bothered the bottom end of the UK charts, due mainly to the fact that the EP contained three tracks unavailable anywhere else. On some European versions, a fourth bonus track, 'Sodom', was added. All the songs hailed from the productive *American Caesar* sessions and the personnel were as on the album.

Credit Card

Probably omitted from the album due to its similarity to 'Plastic and Concrete', both musically and lyrically (it deals, not surprisingly with the modern need for plastic money). 'Everything is really hard, if you ain't got that credit card' is a somewhat obvious comment. The frantic backing isn't too interesting either. Perfect b-side material however.

Come Back Tomorrow

An excellent song, with snappy drums and a cool circular guitar pattern interspersed with some buzzing stabs from Eric. Iggy's vocals are recorded bare, no effects or echo. He sings the main part of the song fine but seems to struggle slightly towards the end, hitting the edge of his range. Again the lyrics echo one of the album tracks – this time it's 'Jealousy'. But the message is to pick yourself up and start again – think of the waves, they always come back.

My Angel

Iggy sings in the same gentle but extremely low voice as on 'Jealousy', but here it's peppered with tenderness and love as befitting a song named 'My Angel'. The band rise to the occasion and, boosted by Malcolm Burn's shimmering keyboards, assist with a calm piece of music. A genuinely delightful song, and probably more successful than the more bombastic 'It's Our Love'. The wobbly whistling at the fade is a pretty touch.

Sodom

Another quiet reflective track, sung in Iggy's deepest voice (although he seems to struggle slightly with the key). Sodom is of course the Biblical town of debauchery, and Iggy claims to live there. Later in the song it becomes a war zone, though Iggy is used to people getting hurt. The plodding beat drags the song rather, but it deserves to be better known, only appearing on just a few European versions of the 'Wild America' EP.

The main musicians remained on board for the following tour. But before he took to the road to promote *American Caesar*, Iggy made a number of further, rather intriguing recordings.

Evil California

Iggy contributed new vocals to a song called 'These Blues' which ended up on the soundtrack to Robert Altman's brilliant Hollywood movie *Short Cuts*. Left-field musician Terry Adams, a founder member of experimental band NRBQ, had recorded the original music. Played by Adams and Annie Ross and the Low Note Quintet, 'Evil California' is simply one of the oddest tracks Iggy has ever been involved with. Sounding like something from a New Orleans jazz band complete with slide trombone, the song features Iggy's sombre yet amusing narration about how evil California is. The song also cropped up as a b-side on some formats of the 'Beside You' single.

Les Amants

Performed by Les Rita Mitsouko, a kitsch French duo of Fred Chichin and Catherine Ringer, 'Les Amants' was originally written for Leos Carax's 1991 film *Les Amants Du Pont Neuf*. Carax's film actually featured Iggy's song 'Strong Girl' in a crucial scene where the lovers Michele and Alex dance on the bridge of the title. 'Les Amants' was given a new vocal from Iggy when he teamed up with Les Rita Mitsouko in Paris. The lascivious mutterings make Iggy sound like a dirty old man, and the swaying tune with Ringer's wailing vocals doesn't really fit the bizarre monologue that Iggy adds. 'Les Amants' was also added to some formats of 'Beside You'.

My Love Is Bad/Easy Lover

More successful is this swinging guitar- and horn-led track, a proper collaboration between Les Rita Mitsouko and Iggy, recorded for their 1993 album *Système D*. The chorus, with Iggy and Catherine snarling at one another, is especially memorable. Iggy's French isn't bad either.

Together with the *Arizona Dream* soundtrack, these songs threw light on another side to Iggy's music. One that was far removed from the usual rough and raw hard rock usually associated with him.

Down On The Street – 1993 *American Caesar* Tour

Iggy Pop – vocals, guitar
Hal Cragin – bass
Larry Mullins – drums
Eric Schermerhorn – guitar

Another world tour, this time promoting *American Caesar*, kicked off in July, taking in festivals and indoor venues throughout Europe. With few breaks, the tour continued for the rest of the year through North America in the autumn then back to Europe for the winter and into 1994.

Iggy refined, if that's the right word, his crowd-pleasing, hard-rocking, no-bullshit persona. Apart from the new songs, the rest of the set comprised the expected old favourites, with only one or two surprises. 'I'm Sick Of You' was regularly played live for the first time (it had only made a few appearances on the summer 1987 tour) and 'Johanna' received another welcome resurrection.

The relatively fixed basic set would be augmented throughout the year with a variety of *American Caesar* songs such as 'Social Life' or 'Perforation Problems' which would crop up depending on Iggy's mood. Towards the end of 1993, 'Cold Metal' was brought in for the final encore and, somewhat surprisingly, some of the European shows featured 'In The Deathcar' as an incongruous mid-set song, often following the rage of 'No Fun'. The absurd monologue 'Caesar' would usually close the main set, provoking sheer bafflement amongst those in the crowd unfamiliar with the new material. Iggy seemed to thoroughly enjoy this little bit of play-acting. The new songs, such as 'Hate' or 'Wild America' really came alive in concert, and 'Fuckin' Alone' grew from the gentle rap of the album version to a real live tour de force, as Eric replaced the delicate acoustic backing with a swaying electric guitar riff. Somewhat surprisingly, only 'Home' remained from *Brick By Brick*.

It was a lengthy tour, but the medium-sized venues continually sold out, proving that Iggy's appeal showed no signs of waning.

The usual set list ran:

'Down On The Street', 'Raw Power', 'TV Eye', 'Hate', 'Real Wild Child', 'Loose', 'I Wanna Be Your Dog', 'No Fun', 'The Passenger', 'Search And Destroy', 'Fuckin' Alone', 'Lust For Life', 'I'm Sick Of You', 'Wild America', 'Home', 'Social Life', 'Beside You', 'Sickness', 'Louie Louie', 'Caesar', 'China Girl', 'Johanna'

1994

Down On The Street
– 1994 *American Caesar* Tour continued

Iggy Pop – vocals, guitar
Hal Cragin – bass
Larry Mullins – drums
Eric Schermerhorn – guitar

The *American Caesar* tour continued into 1994 with much the same set list as before. After a brief set of dates in Japan, Iggy returned to Europe between February and April and, after another short break, hit the festivals in July. In some Mediterranean countries, 'In The Deathcar' replaced 'Social Life' (especially in April in Greece and the Balkans, where Iggy was phenomenally popular). The summer gigs usually featured a slightly shortened set concentrating on the acknowledged classics at the expense of newer material. Added to the summer gigs was the old Elvis number 'Rip It Up' which proved, if nothing else, that Iggy and his band could rock 'n' roll as well as anyone. A live recording of 'Rip It Up' was taped at an Elvis tribute show in October.

The usual set list was:

'Down On The Street', 'Raw Power', 'TV Eye', 'Hate', 'Real Wild Child', 'Loose', 'I Wanna Be Your Dog', 'No Fun', 'The Passenger', 'Search And Destroy', 'Fuckin' Alone', 'Lust For Life', 'Wild America', 'Home', 'Social Life', 'Beside You', 'Sickness', 'Louie Louie', 'Caesar', 'China Girl', 'Cold Metal'

A large chunk of the Phoenix Festival gig on 17 July was broadcast on Channel 4 in the UK, which showed Iggy playing in the early evening sun to a largely indifferent crowd. This was the curse of the festivals. Many in the actual crowd had no great interest in Iggy Pop and, despite his best attempts, Iggy often received a lukewarm reaction. But it was worth it for the media exposure which resulted.

Iggy was still helping out on some songs by thrashing his guitar. His onstage playing rarely consisted of much more than a few power chords, but it at least allowed Eric the space to blast a few solos. Otherwise the power trio coped admirably with the range of material that was required. The encores alone demonstrated their versatility – from the atonal noise of 'Caesar' via the melodic strum of 'China Girl' to the harsh grind of 'Cold Metal.'

1995

Much of 1995 was spent making films and working as an artist. Iggy painted a poster ad for Absolut Vodka. The final picture, depicting one of Iggy's cats seemingly blissed out on vodka, was arrived at only after a previous attempt containing words like 'tits' and 'ass' was rejected. He contributed to a charity auction in June, organised by Brian Eno on behalf of the War Child organisation. Musicians and artists donated their own creations of 'Pagan Fun Wear' for a London auction, which raised money for orphans in Bosnia. Iggy's contribution was a three-foot-long 'Basis Penis Party Sheath' which was delivered by cycle courier to Eno's house. In his diary, Eno wonders what on earth his neighbours thought…

Iggy took a number of film roles. The first was Rat-Face in *Tank Girl*, Rachel Talalay's largely unsuccessful film based on the cartoon character. He also filmed the rather more impressive sequel to *The Crow*. Called *City Of Angels*, Tim Pope's film artfully tapped into the Goth metal scene and, as well as playing the spooky character Curve, Iggy donated a live recording of

'I Wanna Be Your Dog' to the soundtrack. Possibly the most successful acting role was in Jim Jarmusch's *Dead Man* as Salvatore 'Sally' Jenko. This moody reworking of the Western genre starring Johnny Depp, with appearances from Robert Mitchum and John Hurt, became a deserved underground cult hit. The final film made in 1995 was *Atolladero*. A bizarre sci-fi Spaghetti Western directed by Oscar Aido, *Atolladero* is set in the twenty-first century and is basically about a good cop being hunted by the bad guys. Iggy, in his biggest role to date, plays Madden, the 150-year-old Judge's evil henchman. But he's dubbed into Spanish.

NAUGHTY LITTLE DOGGIE

Virgin CDVUS102 Released – Feb 1996
Produced by **Thom Wilson** and **Iggy Pop**

Late autumn 1995 found Iggy and his band, now calling themselves the Fuck-Ups, at Track Records in North Hollywood. With producer Thom Wilson at the board, assisted by Iggy himself, the plan was to record and release the new album quickly. Many of the tracks would be caught pretty much live in the studio in an attempt to harness the explosive live sound of the band. It was also a reaction to the overblown length of his previous record. Referring to the extra tracks Virgin required before they would release *American Caesar*, Iggy laughed, 'Last time they asked for some candy and I gave it to them. I kept the same musicians for this album but made it more "fast food". I avoided making it too arty-farty. I wanted it to make me smile and make my butt move…' Reflecting life on the road, the musicians were credited with their nicknames – Larry Contrary, Eric Mesmerize and Hal Wonderful. Whitey Kirst crops up on the driving opening track, 'I Wanna Live' (where he's listed as the Mighty Whitey).

A solid satisfying guitar sound and some very crisp, unshowy drumming characterises the album. Iggy's vocals are invariably excellent and all the songs crackle with a fresh nervous energy thanks to Thom Wilson's great production. The relatively short length of the album is enhanced by the lack of spaces between songs – as soon as one finishes the next thuds in. However many of the songs themselves are rather tired and uninspired, relying heavily on clichéd riffs and the undoubted ability of the band to pep them up. Great production and --some tremendous individual performances aside, much of *Naughty Little Doggie* doesn't engage the listener as much as other Iggy albums. But, and with Iggy's records there is always a but, whenever I listen to *Naughty Little Doggie* I always come away feeling refreshed by the simple pleasure of hearing a great band play some catchy simple no-frills rock 'n' roll.

The cover photo showed an old, lined Iggy wearing an army helmet. It's a dumb photo that does Iggy no favours at all. At least the harshly lit *American Caesar* cover was impressive, and the dour, moody picture on the front of *Avenue B* hinted at the introspective material within. *Naughty Little Doggie*'s picture was just ugly and deeply off-putting.

The album was released in February 1996 to generally favourable reviews and, with the emphasis once again on Iggy's longevity in the business, any failings of the record were usually overlooked just because Iggy was still with us. *Musician* reckoned that the album celebrated 'his own survival and career longevity with warmth and confidence'. *Entertainment Weekly* partly criticised the scrawny garage-band rock of most of the tunes but conceded, 'What prevents all of it from sounding embarrassing is Iggy's voice – which still has the yearning soul of the eternal adolescent.'

'I Wanna Live' preceded the album as a promo-only single. Quite why it wasn't issued as a commercial release is baffling, as it would have been Iggy's best chance of a hit since 'Candy'.

I Wanna Live

The opening of the song is terrific, with one guitar grinding out the riff on the right for a few bars before Larry kick-starts his drums and a second guitar doubles up the riff in the left speaker. What a dynamite way to begin an album. This classic Iggy rocker, sung in a kind of self-mocking gurgle over a patented Whitey groove sets a standard that the rest of the album never quite reaches again. The lyrics are intriguing, with Iggy becoming more aware of the ageing process, but determined to live 'just a little bit longer'.

'I Wanna Live' was adopted as the life-affirming opening song for the next three years' concerts, but has not been played since.

Pussy Walk

Eric came up with this bouncy circular tune, which lurches happily along for nearly four minutes. Over the bump and grind of the music, Iggy cheerily tells of his latest problem, a problem that he believes afflicts most men of a certain age – whatever he does, wherever he goes, he can't stop thinking about pussies. The narration gets progressively more unhinged as Iggy's voice becomes more and more incredulous – this is becoming a nightmare for him. What is he going to do? The verses are actually pretty funny in a defiantly unreconstructed, totally non-PC way. The manner in which Iggy recounts his tale contributes to the amusement. He's almost affronted that so many beautiful girls should come up him, that he couldn't go anywhere without bumping into pretty women, and this causes him, without warning, to bizarrely wonder... 'Can your pussy walk?' Unfortunately the joke doesn't last. After the first few listens, the amusement to be gained from a forty-eight-year-old behaving like a sniggering teenager soon palls. On the plus side, probably thanks to Thom Wilson's recent production of *Smash* by the Offspring, the overall sound of 'Pussy Walk' is crisp and commercial, while still retaining sufficient metal crunch. In fact, the whole album shines with this excellent, bright and up-beat vibe and the sound is easily the equal of that on records by newer punk acts such as Green Day or the Offspring.

Innocent World

Far more impressive is this cool remembrance of younger days, 'always having lots of fun, smoking dope and just being young'. There's a slightly sad wistful air to Iggy's vocals, as if he still wishes that he were back in those innocent times. The music may be rather unoriginal but Iggy's impressive vocal and the singalong chorus lift the song, as do Eric's layers of guitars.

Which proves that there's far more going on than is immediately apparent. Great solo too.

Knucklehead

Sort of a companion to *Instinct*'s 'Squarehead', but this time Iggy is railing against the knuckleheads he keeps meeting. Wherever he goes, DJs, priests, telephones – they all want something from him. But what can he do? 'Knucklehead' is a genuinely humorous track, unlike the teenage tittering of 'Pussy Walk', with some neat little touches such as Iggy's waspishly aggrieved 'Ouch!' after telling us that he's being poked 'where it hurts'. Again, Eric's multitude of guitars are very important to the success of the song and the flickering from speaker to speaker of the various vocals on the line 'I, I, I...' is a another clever touch.

To Belong

Some reviewers described 'To Belong' as Iggy's attempt to ape the Nirvana sound (due only, one suspects, to the clanging, chiming guitar on the slower verses and the rush of the heavier choruses). In fact, Iggy had been recording songs like this for years, but 'To Belong' is very strong. The gentleness of the verses (the first tenderly describing a bird with a broken wing) contrasts smartly with the raucous bark of the choruses. The song's theme is one that Iggy has touched on before (notably 'Main Street Eyes') – that of how to belong without surrendering your soul. Iggy's solution is 'to defy'. Although Iggy seems to be singing at the edge of his register, Wilson has captured his committed vocals brilliantly.

Keep On Believing

A rush of guitars from Schermerhorn sees multiple overdubs piling up on this thrillingly jumpy Eric tune. At first, the vocal line seems disconnected from the backing, but it somehow all hangs together. Recounting a midnight walk in the park where Iggy happened to meet the 'cutest chicest chocolate queen', 'Keep On Believing' is the first obvious sign that Iggy's marriage was failing. Despite apparent encounters with girls on previous records, the listener was often left with the impression that earlier songs were fictionalised. 'Keep On Believing', with its attention to domestic details ('fed the cat'), seems sadly real as it revels in the genuine hope that there's something better out there. And even the title, 'Keep On Believing', implies that Iggy is wishing for more, hoping, believing that matters will improve. Sadly, mainly due to Iggy's inability to keep his fly buttoned, his marriage was falling apart. Lengthy tours, and recent film shoots, had kept Iggy away from his New York home for long periods. Iggy and Suchi simply grew apart. The following song also offers a weary look at this sad state of affairs.

Outta My Head

The thudding drums and droning trebly guitars evoke memories of the Velvet Underground. After a promising beginning, however, the song degenerates into a rather plodding track, with an uninteresting melody and vocal – the choruses are especially poor. And apart from the satisfyingly crunchy guitars, 'Outta My Head' really drags. Even some unusual eastern-inflected guitars in the left speaker during the final choruses can't save it. By pushing the song's length to well over five minutes, the simple tune is ground into the dirt.

Shoeshine Girl

A gentle acoustic tale of meeting a Goth girl on the way to the Lollapalooza festival. Beautifully played by Eric and Hal, with Larry on brushes, Iggy's story is cool and fascinating and acts as a sort of prelude to the acoustic numbers on *Avenue B*. Hal's keyboards are also worthy of a mention and add a lovely atmosphere.

Heart Is Saved

This tumbling rush of guitars and drums breaks the spellbound mood. Three minutes of excellent punk pop, 'Heart Is Saved' was also issued as a single, but didn't hit the charts despite the undoubted commercial bent to the tune. Further live tracks from the 1993 Feile Festival bulked out the b-sides. Some interesting lyrical asides hint that Iggy was tiring of the rock world somewhat. His next move, creating the personal *Avenue B*, was a reaction to precisely this sort of music, the music that he felt he was expected to make.

Look Away

Aside from the amateur psychology on show here – Johnny didn't make it, but Iggy did – this song is basically a straight retelling of the life of Johnny Thunders, the junkie guitar player for the New York Dolls and later his own band the Heartbreakers. Johnny's undeniable talent was wasted through junk and he died penniless and alone. Iggy, of course, had been through similar experiences but had somehow come through and survived. This 'but for the grace of God' type song is a real oddity in Iggy's catalogue. He rarely bared his feelings quite so openly and unambiguously. The repetitive strum-along melody is however rather dull, and despite the obvious strength of the lyrics, was a surprising choice for the 2005 anthology. It makes for a strangely unsatisfying conclusion to this uneven album.

(Get Up I Feel Like Being A) Sex Machine

Omitted from the album but used as a b-side to both the 'Heart Is Saved' single and the reissue of 'Lust For Life', was this faithful attempt at James Brown's 'Sex Machine'. The band can actually funk it up surprisingly well, and there's some neat piano thrown in too. Iggy even replicates many of Brown's asides, which raises the question – why bother? It sounds and feels like a superior, but still throwaway, jam that should have been quietly dropped at the end of the session and, despite Iggy's acknowledged love of the Godfather of Soul, the Godfather of Punk does himself few favours with this somewhat lacklustre cover.

*   *   *

As his marriage fell apart Iggy lined up promotional work and further touring for 1996.

1996

Down On The Street – 1996 *Naughty Little Doggie* tour

Iggy Pop – vocals
Hal Cragin – bass
Whitey Kirst – guitar
Pete Marshall – guitar
Larry Mullins – drums

To promote *Naughty Little Doggie*, Iggy embarked upon another lengthy tour. Eric Schermerhorn was now working with Matt Johnson on the next The The album (and more recently he's been spotted in Seal's band), so Whitey Kirst returned to the lead guitar spot. As Iggy had decided to stop playing guitar during gigs, long-time guitar tech Pete Marshall was promoted to an onstage role as an aggressive rhythm guitarist. Hal and Larry remained on bass and drums, fast becoming Iggy's most durable rhythm section. Iggy himself retained the long peroxide white-blond hair he had sported in the *Crow* film and took to wearing almost transparent PVC trousers, often without underwear. These trousers provoked minor outrage when he wore them in February 1996 on *The White Room*, a new music show on Channel 4.

Not surprisingly, the tour contained a number of *Naughty Little Doggie* songs, and a total absence of *American Caesar* tracks. This continued the trend whereby the current album would be promoted alongside a generous scattering of classic Iggy tunes. Then the next tour would keep much the same bunch of oldies, and include only songs from the new album and so on. There were a few welcome returns to the set list including 'Sister Midnight' and 'Death Trip', but otherwise the old tunes were pretty much the same as had been played throughout the 1990s. As usual, the new songs became casualties as the gigs progressed – 'To Belong' was only played occasionally and 'Look Away' was dropped from the summer festival shows. But 'I Wanna Live' followed by 'Down On The Street' made for a terrific opening to the show. Often included in the encores was Bo Diddley's classic 'Who Do You Love?' and, depending on the gig, 'Louie Louie' would sometimes crop up as an extra.

The usual set list ran:

'I Wanna Live', 'Down On The Street', 'Heart Is Saved', 'Raw Power', 'Pussy Walk', 'Search And Destroy', 'Five Foot One', 'Sixteen', 'Sister Midnight', 'I Wanna Be Your Dog', 'Look Away', 'The Passenger', 'Lust For Life', 'Home', 'I'm Sick of You', 'No Fun', 'Death Trip', 'Knucklehead', '1969', 'Who Do You Love?'

The tour began with a couple of months in North America in April and May before transferring to Europe for the summer. Kieran Grant, writing in the *Toronto Sun* about the Warehouse gig on 12 April, had nothing but praise for the show, especially the repeated stage dives. Even though he was nearing fifty, Iggy would continue to leap from the stage during most concerts, a move that Iggy reckons he actually invented. He first hurled himself from the stage during the Stooges second-ever gig, back in 1968. 'Ever seen little boys when they want attention, they'll make themselves perfectly still and then they'll just fall flat faced on the floor? I did that, except off a five-foot stage.' The *Toronto Sun* also commented on Iggy's still-impressive physique – 'His sinewy torso made him look like he'd just leapt from the pages of a Marvel comic book.' Iggy worked hard at keeping his fitness but it paid off. 'Do I like my body?' he was asked in 2000. 'Man, I love it!'

Summer 1996 saw the release of Danny Boyle's film *Trainspotting*. Based on Irvine Welsh's harrowing book about Scottish junkies, the film was an equally uncompromising prospect. But the performances from Ewan McGregor and especially Robert Carlyle were astonishing and the film became a surprise runaway success. Part of its appeal was the defiantly cool soundtrack. As well as modern dance anthems such as Underworld's hedonistic 'Born Slippy', the soundtrack featured Lou Reed's 'Perfect Day' plus Iggy's 'Nightclubbing' and 'Lust For Life'. *Trainspotting* had a huge impact and effectively reintroduced Iggy to a new generation. The fact that he was added to the line-ups of many European festivals, sandwiched between bands half his age, is largely due to the success of 'Lust For Life' in *Trainspotting* which opened up a whole new audience. Reissued as a single with a video showing a gurning, dancing Iggy intercut with clips from the film, 'Lust For Life' promoted both Iggy and the film at the same time.

The Loreley Festival on 22 June saw Iggy supporting headliner David Bowie. As a result of the exposure given to the song in *Trainspotting*, Bowie had started performing 'Lust For Life' too. His version was a strangely lumpen, stripped-down techno take, far removed from Iggy's visceral performance earlier in the day.

At the Rock Of Gods Festival in Athens on 14 July, Iggy was hit on the head by a bottle. According to Whitey, 'he went ape, started bleeding and climbed the lighting rig on the side of the stage like King Kong waving his arms about like little airplanes were attacking him, then started screaming, "You can't kill me, I'm Iggy fuckin' Pop".' For some reason, Iggy then decided to push the show's length and threw in a number of covers at the end – 'Wild Thing', 'Johnny B Goode' and 'My Funny Valentine' – although these would all be played at other gigs it was rare to get them all together.

The rest of the summer gigs passed without major incident. Iggy was now peddling a high-voltage show that appealed to a wide audience. The fact that so many of the songs were so old and so familiar was primarily due to the nature of large outdoor festivals. Most of the crowds were not hardcore Iggy fans and so a general set with broad appeal was necessary. What was to become disappointing to the faithful was Iggy's insistence on sticking with this repetitive set of tunes even at smaller venues, where a more varied show could easily have been performed.

This was almost the year that the Stooges reformed. Producer Rick Rubin contacted Ron and Scott Asheton who both expressed an interest in working with Iggy again. The idea was put to Iggy, who responded favourably, resulting in a number of friendly phone calls between Pop and the Ashetons. But then Iggy took off to Europe for the summer gigs and Ron heard nothing more from him. However, the fact that all the parties were not opposed to a reformation was encouraging. But it took another seven years for anything concrete to happen.

1997

Down On The Street – 1997 Summer Gigs

Iggy Pop – vocals
Hal Cragin – bass
Whitey Kirst – guitar
Pete Marshall – guitar
Larry Mullins – drums

Iggy joined the travelling festival called ROAR (Revelations Of Alternate Rhythms) for the summer of 1997. The tour courted controversy from the start, as it was sponsored by Skoal Smokeless Tobacco. The organisers were accused of promoting tobacco to teens and the North American tour sold badly. Iggy found himself playing for largely indifferent crowds who refused to enter into the intended carnival spirit.

The festival set list was:

'I Wanna Live', 'Down On The Street', 'Heart Is Saved', 'Raw Power', 'Search And Destroy', 'Sister Midnight', 'Five Foot One', 'I Wanna Be Your Dog', 'The Passenger', 'Lust For Life', 'Home', 'I'm Sick Of You', 'TV Eye', 'No Fun', 'Sixteen'

In Columbus on 6 June, Iggy attempted a stage dive, but the predominantly young crowd, which had been pushed back by the police after rushing the stage during the Bloodhound Gang's set, was too thin to support such a dive. He hit the concrete hard. Roadie Jos Grain pulled him back onstage, but it was clear that he was badly injured. Typically, Iggy tried to go on with the show, but with one arm hanging horribly limp and blood pouring from his head it didn't look good. According to Whitey, 'He started saying all this weird cool shit on his knees, singing and talking at the same time, really cool stuff, then he started fading...' At that point, Jos hoisted him off stage to a waiting ambulance while the band played on for a while. Iggy had amazingly not broken anything, but his shoulder was dislocated. He continued with the tour, with Jos gaffer-taping the bad arm to his side so he didn't damage his shoulder any further. But the injury wouldn't heal and, following medical advice, Iggy finally dropped out of the tour, allowing Sponge to take over his headline slot. Critics accused Iggy of bailing out of a sinking ship, as the tour was playing to half-empty arenas most of the time, but Iggy was keen to stress that it was only the shoulder that was forcing him off the road.

The rest of 1997 found Iggy at home, alone. After years of struggling with their marriage, Jim and Suchi had parted. Iggy threw himself into his work. Determined to prove that he could be a great artist as well as make money, Iggy spent his time on a huge variety of projects.

Monster Men

The first was purely to generate cash. He wrote 'Monster Men', the theme song for the cartoon series *Space Goofs*. It's cheery, catchy and goofy, with barely a whiff of noise, plenty of cheesy la-la-la backing vocals, and certainly no angst or anger. Only the sudden burst of guitars during the middle eight reminds you that this is Iggy.

With a tremendous cartoon of Iggy on the cover, 'Monster Men' was possibly the most bizarre single ever issued in Iggy's name. Incidentally the more interesting remix version opens with a cheeky sample of 'Real Wild Child' – this mix is also slightly heavier and less reliant on the bouncy keyboards. As with most of his singles, it bombed.

We Have All The Time In The World

In 1997, composer David Arnold set about updating a number of James Bond film themes. Among the many guests on the album *Shaken and Stirred* were Chrissie Hynde (taking on 'Live and Let Die') and David McAlmont, whose angelic voice came close to out diva-ing Shirley Bassey on 'Diamonds Are Forever'. But Arnold wanted to close the record with the emotional closing song from *On Her Majesty's Secret Service*. The original, sung by the glorious voice of Louis Armstrong, was a hard act to follow, but in choosing Iggy Pop for 'We Have All The Time In The World', Arnold hit the jackpot. Iggy's rich baritone is ideally suited to the stirring tune. Backed by Arnold's beautiful string arrangements, Iggy delivers a bravura performance, prompting *The Times* to call it 'improbably emotive'.

I'll Be Seeing You

This delightful duet with Françoise Hardy appeared on the French album *Jazz a Saint Germain*. It was billed as a tribute to the free spirit of Paris in the 1950s and this song encapsulates the light jazz swing of the period. Iggy's voice blends surprisingly well with Ms Hardy's and this song, as with the Bond theme, demonstrates clearly that Iggy really should make that Sinatra-style crooner album that plenty of people want to hear.

In between all this he continued to work on his first film soundtrack, for Johnny Depp's film *The Brave*, of which there will be more in the next chapter.

Iggy also contributed the theme to the TV series *Home To Rent*, narrated Edgar Allan Poe's 'The Tell Tale Heart' for an album of Poe short stories, and contributed to Bill Laswell's latest project – *Hashisheen*. This combined recitals and atmospheric effects and music to tell the story of Hassan Ibn Sabbah, the legendary chief of the nomadic assassins in the ancient Middle East. Iggy featured as the narrator on two stories – 'The Western Lands' and 'A Quick Trip To Alamut'. He even cropped up in a choir of various artists on a song in the *Rugrats Movie*.

This variety of work was augmented by the gradual licensing of his music for use in adverts and films. Over the next few years, many Iggy or Stooges songs would be picked up by advertisers all over the world and used in commercials for cereals, Reebok, cruise liners, Toyota, various phones and many more. It was this, more than record sales that finally turned Iggy into a wealthy man.

1998

Probably the most mature and truly adult piece of work attempted by Iggy Pop, *Avenue B*, named after the street where he had lived with Suchi in New York, is a melancholy and sombre reflection on ageing, divorce and being alone. It's not a depressing album, however, as it contains a surprising amount of wry sardonic humour and there's more musical invention on display than at any time since *Brick By Brick*. Significantly, this may be attributed to Don Was, who had returned to the producer's chair. There was also Iggy's new-found confidence as a confessional singer-song-writer and, on the surprisingly poetic interludes, he reveals himself to be a witty and self-deprecating writer of some power.

Although Iggy repeatedly stressed that the songs were not necessarily about his recent divorce from Suchi, it's a conclusion that is inescapable, especially on the spoken pieces. The opening 'No Shit', for example, cannot possibly be about anyone else, and while 'She Called Me Daddy' may fictionalise actual events, the general story and overall mood reeks so much of Iggy's real life. Some of the songs, too, such as 'Motorcycle' and the title song are archly autobiographical. Fortunately, despite the emotional subject matter, the songs never get mawkish or dissolve into self-pity. The lyrics are matter-of-factly delivered, there's no introspection or navel-gazing.

Iggy began work on the album in the winter of his fiftieth year, 1997–1998. He was, as he describes it, really alone. Iggy's lifestyle and the amount of time he spent on the road had meant that Jim and Suchi had simply drifted apart. Separated by 1997, they would be divorced in 1999. Suchi published her first novel, *In Broken Wigwag*, in 2000.

During the winter, Iggy first turned to writing a series of monologues, almost short stories. He never intended anyone to see them but later looked back at his journal and realised, 'This shit is punchier than a lot of songs you've written.' At the same time, he was working on the mournful, sombre soundtrack for Johnny Depp's film *The Brave*. It was Depp's debut as director and took an uncomfortable look at the plight of a poor Native American who decided that the only way out of his family's abject poverty was to offer himself to the makers of a snuff movie for $50,000. Despite the potentially depressing subject matter, the film offered new insights into family love and many sequences are deeply emotional and touching. Iggy had begun work on the soundtrack as far back as 1995, when Depp first discussed the project with him. Sadly, Iggy's quietly impressive soundtrack was never issued on its own, and the only surviving music, outside of the film, exists on *Avenue B*, when Iggy realised that the vignettes he had written would provide useful

linking passages between songs when spoken over the moody strings he'd
created for *The Brave*.

Iggy also worked on a series of new songs. Alone, without his band, Iggy
used only an acoustic guitar. He spoke of the warmth he received from
holding the guitar and the pleasure he gained from creating gentle melodic
songs. Since Suchi had left, there had been a number of short-lived liaisons
and some of these were incorporated into the new songs. These were, for the
most part, bittersweet looks at the plight of a man faced with finding love
and affection in middle age. Iggy was at pains to point out that not all the
songs were strictly true, but the overall impression was that Iggy's life had
become a series of failed relationships.

Don Was produced the initial sessions in the spring of 1998, during
which most of the acoustic numbers were taped. Bassist Hal Cragin had
spent some with Iggy recording the spoken interludes at Studio 12A (in
reality, Hal's apartment), but the bulk of the album was taped at a loft on
Mott Street, New York, and at the Teatro in Oxnard, California. The Teatro
was a converted cinema owned by Daniel Lanois; it was chosen as a venue
by engineer Mark Howard, a long-time associate of Lanois. Howard had also
been the engineer on *American Caesar*.

With the album virtually complete, Iggy spent the summer back in
Europe with Whitey, Hal, Larry and Pete.

Down On The Street – 1998 European gigs

Iggy Pop – vocals
Hal Cragin – bass
Whitey Kirst – guitar
Pete Marshall – guitar
Larry Mullins – drums

A sporadic series of festival gigs (including the massive Roskilde festival in
Denmark and the prestigious Bizarre gathering in Cologne), saw Iggy and
the band playing pretty much the same set that had been hauled out over
the previous few years. No real surprises, apart from the occasional 'Johanna'
or 'Who Do You Love?' – a solid, competent set. The slightly more obscure
numbers were often dropped for the shorter festival slots, and fewer *Naughty
Little Doggie* songs were played in 1998:

'I Wanna Live', 'Down On The Street', 'Heart Is Saved', 'Raw Power',
'Search And Destroy', 'I Wanna Be Your Dog', 'The Passenger', 'Lust For
Life', 'Home', 'I'm Sick Of You', 'TV Eye', 'Sixteen', 'Pussy Walk', 'No Fun',
'Johanna', 'Louie Louie', '1969', 'Who Do You Love?'

After the summer gigs, Iggy called up Don Was. He'd got a couple more
songs that he wanted to record. One was another spoken-word track, a
disturbing monologue called 'I Felt The Luxury'. Iggy wasn't sure how the
backing should be played, but Don had the perfect solution. He'd recently
worked with the notable Blue Note jazz trio Medeski, Martin and Wood, and
thought that their rhythmic approach would suit '...Luxury'. Iggy need

some persuading – a jazz trio? On an Iggy Pop record? But Iggy respected their work, and agreed to try Don Was's idea. It was an unqualified success. 'I Felt The Luxury' was transformed by Medeski, Martin and Wood into a woozy lounge jazz track, with Iggy's foghorn narration of a severely soured relationship ambivalently laid over the top. Delighted with the results, Iggy arranged for the trio to record some more music at the Theatre in New York. They first reworked one of the acoustic songs. 'Avenue B' was named after the street where Iggy lived, and was 'originally three times more depressing', according to Pop. With Billy Martin's drums now pushing the song along, 'Avenue B' became something else entirely. No longer depressing, it gained a hopeful air, the much-needed miracle of the lyrics seemed like it might actually happen. Then 'Español' was rerecorded. The original had been a straightforward rock track written by Whitey; the jazzified version was a bouncy blast of Hispanic nonsense.

AVENUE B

Virgin CDVUS163 Released – September 1999
Produced by **Don Was**

The album was completed and mixed that autumn, but Virgin held back release for nearly a year. In the meantime, Iggy moved on. Tired of New York and wanting a fresh start he rented a friend's apartment ('a cheap and nasty condo', according to Iggy) in a poor area of Miami. New York had been bothering Iggy for some time – for a start it was so expensive ('Sure I can afford to [live in New York], but I don't want to be around a bunch of fucking millionaires!'), and he hated the self-congratulatory aspect of the music business there. Especially the endless round of awards for over-the-hill rock stars, celebrated for simply remaining alive – 'I ain't bald, I ain't fat and I ain't ready for that. So I took another direction.'

He had long owned a holiday home in Mexico and had mastered Spanish some years before, so the Hispanic flavour of Miami appealed to him. After a few months Iggy decided to move to Miami permanently. He found a small one-storey house in Little Haiti. It was unremarkable, with a decent-sized yard, a stream running through the plot and a porch on which to sit and relax. Only the Cadillac (and later a Rolls-Royce) indicated that the house was occupied by anyone out of the ordinary. The anonymity of Miami was a huge contrast to the celebrity-obsessed world of New York and Iggy found enormous pleasure in his simplified peaceful Florida life. Best of all in Iggy's eyes, Miami was not cool.

With a new direction in his music, and a new home, Iggy felt refreshed after the sessions. *Avenue B* would be one of the most impressive records he had ever made.

No Shit

This is an astonishing piece with which to open an album. Over a dourly morbid backing of strings (courtesy of David Mansfield, Iggy's collaborator on *The Brave* soundtrack), Iggy intones his new manifesto. Stars, whether rock stars or film stars, rarely acknowledge the ageing process, so it's quite a shock to hear Iggy solemnly declare that he's considering 'the circumstances of my death'. The listener is aware that this voice is true; it seems as though sober, sombre Jim has temporarily replaced Iggy, possibly for the first time on record. But it's a transient thought as it's so clearly Iggy who says that he's not going to 'take any more shit'. The beauty of this track lies in the crystal-clear recording. Iggy's voice is direct and upfront, on headphones it's as if he's standing right next to you. The clarity is apparent when you realize that Iggy is actually speaking rather quietly. The dark subject matter is matched by the downbeat dignity of the music from *The Brave*.

Nazi Girlfriend

This follows without a break and continues the quiet introspective mood. It's the first of a number of songs on *Avenue B* relating to failed relationships. Iggy sings in a close-up, unemotional voice, intoning this somewhat unsavoury tale about his Nazi girlfriend. It's about a real person, and he feels compelled to make a 'full report', but in doing so he places the listener in an awkward position. We feel like eavesdroppers, as if Iggy is making us privy to secrets, to details, that maybe we shouldn't be told. The backing is determinedly downbeat; gentle vibes and moody bass undercut Iggy's simple acoustic guitar. There's some casual whistling and humming after the second verse, which only emphasises the confessional tone even more.

Mojo magazine asked if it was hard writing about such personal stuff. Iggy robustly denied that it was, claiming that it was actually harder dealing with people's reaction to the record. 'I thought, dude, you're a songwriter, you're looking at the end of your active life, you should be able to write detailed specific songs with a good melody that you can sit and play alone in a room, that should provoke emotion without depending on noise. That requires personal subjects. I had a fuck of a subject.'

Avenue B

Reworked by Medeski Martin and Wood from Iggy's original depressing acoustic number into a bittersweet reflection on his New York home, the general mood here recalls Lou Reed's more positive 'NYC Man' from 1996's *Set The Twilight Reeling*. Iggy's song is far more realistic than Lou's celebration of the Big Apple: 'I am gonna need a miracle,' sings Iggy in the chorus. He knows about fame and death and money 'and what they do to you', but the most surprising verse is the last. He watches the students out of his window, 'walking in their student clothes', which recalls the similar line in 'Pussy Walk', but just three years later Iggy has grown up. He's looking at them with regret, with the realisation that they are no longer for him. He feels empty, having 'given every part of me'. It's a shocking admission of age, almost one of defeat. Clearly the miracle didn't occur. Iggy moved out of New York soon after.

Musically, the punchy Hammond organ pushes the song along. It works brilliantly, and is the sort of instrument that would benefit many other Iggy songs, if only he'd experiment a bit more often. Billy Martin's shuffling drums are pretty impressive too.

Miss Argentina

Another remembrance of a lost love. Iggy's lyrics idolise the girl, she's described in glowing terms, literally – 'her skin is copper' and 'her vibe is golden'. But once Iggy has praised the girl in every detail, he admits that he felt smothered by her, she buried him, and concludes sadly that 'Venus is a dangerous game.' As with all the songs so far on *Avenue B*, it's the little touches that lift each track – here Larry Mullins' gentle tabla playing adds a slightly exotic dimension to the simple acoustic tune.

Afraid To Get Close

Over a very similar segment of *The Brave* soundtrack as on 'No Shit', this minute-long interlude features one of Iggy's many cats asleep on his pillow. He realises that all creatures need togetherness, warmth and love. He regrets how his writing is isolating him from others, and how he continually seems to hurt people. But the concluding lines are ambiguous – is Iggy holding another vulnerable girl in his arms, or his cat? Either way he's trying to shy from the responsibility for another's life.

Shakin' All Over

The mood is abruptly shattered by Whitey's piercing guitar introducing this muscular blast through Johnny Kidd's 1965 hit. Oddly the song is taken at a somewhat sedate pace, but Don Was's widescreen production more than makes up for this. Larry's drums are looped by engineer Andrew Scheps to give the track a modern sheen, and although it's not the best cover Iggy has ever made it's certainly an excellent attempt to update a real garage classic. Whitey's guitars growl and burn most effectively over the last minute of the track.

Long Distance

Then just as suddenly we're back with the close-miked confessional writer. This time, Iggy is backed by an electronic heartbeat of a rhythm track while shimmering keyboards and some gentle slide from Don Was floats dreamily above. It's a very unusual musical setting for an Iggy Pop song but married to the equally dreamy vocals it works surprisingly well.

Iggy is once again cast as the disreputable fifty-year-old falling for a French girl half his age in order to wipe out the pain of a previous rejection. Although Iggy is sick of being alone, the romance seems doomed to long-distance calls.

Corruption

Under another producer, 'Corruption' could have been a rather unremarkable rock track. But Don Was invests it with a dark resonance as Iggy declaims his highly imperious lyrics over a swampy swirling backing track. The drums are drenched in echoing effects and the guitars are boosted beyond belief, distorting and melting everything in sight. Iggy rises to the occasion by delivering his most impassioned vocal so far. It's a far cry from the rather staid, reserved attempt at 'Shakin' All Over'. Hal Cragin keeps the bass pumping out the same riff throughout the song. His co-writer Whitey returns again and again to same bruising riff but then flies off on the choruses leaving Hal to continue the pounding.

Iggy's lyrics rail against the fact that 'corruption rules my soul.' He's still sick of all the dips, sick of all the stiffs, sick of the lies of the righteous, sick of the way he feels lost, but although he's screaming about it he's well aware that 'everything leads to corruption'.

As the most immediately powerful song, musically at any rate, 'Corruption' was chosen as a single. It sold next to nothing despite the inclusion of two non-album tracks.

She Called Me Daddy

The final spoken word interlude is also the most unusual in that the uneasy mood is somewhat broken by Iggy's laughter. The filmic strings from *The Brave* are especially affecting. However the words are a devastatingly brutal report of the end of a relationship. Unwilling to end it himself, Iggy froze her out, but she still didn't leave. Now she's finally gone, Iggy is left wondering why he did it. But his question is answered in the last line – 'she called me daddy...'

I Felt The Luxury

The uneasy mood continues on what is surely one of Iggy's most impressive songs ever. Over Medeski Martin and Wood's queasy take on cocktail-lounge jazz, Iggy narrates this disturbing tale. Iggy's voice is slightly distorted, the music too seems to have been recorded at too high a level, which only increases the claustrophobic feeling. Iggy begins by describing a girl who padded around the house and curled up affectionately on the couch. Then, one day, 'She wouldn't shut up.' Iggy's delivery of the next line, relating that the girl is now in hospital (and 'may die'), is astonishingly detached and is utterly chilling because of it. The seeming lack of concern over what he's apparently done is truly frightening and puts the listener in a very awkward position. Is this a true story, like so much of the rest of the album appears to be, or is it a fiction? Could it be just a fictional tale about someone so callous he put his girlfriend in hospital simply because she became too much trouble? Or is there more to it? The song offers no clues and instead the scary vibe simply remains with the listener for a long time.

In most of the interviews promoting *Avenue B*, Iggy was at great pains to stress that most of the stories and songs were not strictly based on him, but rather offered a general view of the failure of relationships in middle age. However, taken at face value, 'I Felt The Luxury' is certainly one of the most uncomfortable tracks Iggy has ever made. Surprisingly, this tune was regularly performed on the autumn 1999 tour, with Whitey and the usual band mining an angular groove while Iggy recounted his sorry story.

Español

Dispelling the miserable vibe of '...Luxury' is this superb track, sung in Spanish. Originally written by Whitey, this tune was reworked by Medeski, Martin and Wood into a bouncy, organ-led, Latin-infused corker. With additional percussion from Lenny Castro, 'Español' is pure fun. According to the sleeve notes, Iggy plays the excellent electric guitar, though it's possible that Whitey's original lines were retained. The lyrics simply celebrate the fact that Iggy, an American gringo, can speak Spanish. He'd picked it up over many years – a holiday house in Mexico and friends in Miami helped – and was now fluent.

Motorcycle

Just Iggy and his warm guitar, for this gentle story of yet another girl admired from afar. This time the girl/motorbike analogy is somewhat clumsy, but is delivered with such conviction that one can't help being carried along. Iggy's voice is full of expression and truth. He claims not to believe anything any more, including love. After the parade of failed relationships throughout *Avenue B* it's little wonder. A lovely song however.

Façade

With a cry of 'Play', we're back to the full band sound of 'Shakin' All Over' but performed with solid dignity and resonance. The delivery of the vocals and the measured pace of the tune conjures up comparisons with Lou Reed's work of the same period. Iggy concedes that he feels tired at one point, as he eloquently describes how he's no longer inclined to maintain a façade. He's tough and he'll keep going but he's not going to put on a front any more. He's alone and his life may not be quite what he had in mind but, bringing the album full circle, he's got his books, and a sweater and slippers too, and he'll get by. It's a quietly impressive admission that he's old, he's made mistakes but so what? A tremendous, though slightly understated, conclusion to a hugely impressive album.

Rock Star Grave

This grungy rocker was also taped at the *Avenue B* sessions, but the heavier sound didn't fit on the album so it was used as the b-side to the 'Corruption' single. Iggy seems to have trouble fitting all the words in, but otherwise it's a fairly standard Iggy rock track. Whitey contributes some terrific guitar and the multi-tracked, ultra-deep vocals are impressive. Just when you think it's all over, Whitey picks up the pace and Larry beats out a gallop to take the track to its conclusion.

Hollywood Affair

More interesting is this Johnny Depp tune, over which Iggy contributes some mellow vocals. The song itself is not especially remarkable, but creates a beautiful late-night mood for Iggy's tale of another 'silly escapade'. One again, love is Iggy's problem.

*   *   *

Once the sessions were completed, Iggy took himself off to Miami and set about creating a new life for himself. He spent the winter of 1998–1999 alone in his new home.

1999

Down On The Street – 1999 spring and summer gigs

Iggy Pop – vocals
Hal Cragin – bass
Alex Kirst – drums
Whitey Kirst – guitar
Pete Marshall – guitar

The first sight of Iggy in 1999 was on VH1's *Behind The Music*, which first aired in March. As was often the way with this series, the focus was on the human aspect, specifically the relationship between Iggy and his son Eric. But amongst the mawkish drama was some glorious early footage of the Stooges and interviews with both Ron and Scott and, surprisingly, James Williamson. Looking every inch the successful corporate honcho, Williamson spoke candidly and enthusiastically about the old days. VH1 deserve praise for persuading the notoriously interview-shy Williamson to appear.

A number of low-key gigs in Florida and the south in April and May found Iggy still dragging round much the same set that he'd spent the last three years performing. The difference this time was that, after eight years on the drum stool, Larry Mullins had moved on. His place was taken by Whitey's older brother Alex, who seemed to rejuvenate the band. And with Alex on board they adopted a name – the Trolls.

As usual, Iggy returned to Europe for the lucrative festivals during July and played virtually the same set yet again:

'I Wanna Live', 'Down On The Street', 'Heart Is Saved', 'Raw Power',
'Search And Destroy', 'Real Wild Child', 'I Wanna Be Your Dog', 'Sixteen',
'TV Eye', 'The Passenger', 'Lust For Life', 'Home', 'I'm Sick of You',
'No Fun', 'Cold Metal', 'Louie Louie', 'Johnny B Goode', 'Shakin' All Over',
'1969'/'Who Do You Love?', 'I Got A Right'

Despite all the new material waiting for release, Iggy was content to hit the festivals with the usual crowd-pleasing tunes. The number of covers frequently utilised as encores hinted at the boredom Iggy might have been feeling playing the same songs over and over. But fortunately this didn't translate to the performances Iggy was giving, which were as fiery and energetic as ever.

Virgin waited until after the festivals before finally releasing *Avenue B*. The album seemed to catch many people by surprise, and few reviewers could refrain from commenting on how mature and adult the album was, especially in comparison with *Naughty Little Doggie* and the regular festival gigs. To seasoned Iggy watchers, the album was not so surprising. He'd been threatening to make a record like this for years. In 1996, promoting *Naughty Little Doggie*, Iggy had said, 'I seriously plan to put out some albums which aren't rock 'n' roll, that's for motherfucking sure. One way or another I'll do it.'

Most reviewers were, however, left slightly baffled by the album. *Entertainment Weekly* gave it a B- and guardedly commented, 'Once you get over the shock of hearing these bruised lullabies, you may warm to the tasteful, thought-provoking songcraft.' *Mojo* praised *Avenue B* for being an 'audacious, moving record', referring to Iggy as a poet-crooner, 'cerebral, but fiercely physical; pensive, older, a lot more worn at the edges, but fucking and fighting like a champ'. *The Wire* thought it represented 'Iggy's painfully delayed rites of passage', whereas Q magazine praised the 'artful musings of a horny old man'.

NME's Stuart Bailie perceptively commented that Iggy's previous self-mocking manner had allowed him to appear harmless. Now *Avenue B* appeared to portray the real Iggy, and it wasn't a pretty sight.

But Iggy believed strongly in his new album and was determined to promote it fully. With this in mind a series of relatively small venues were booked to showcase *Avenue B*.

Down On The Street – 1999 *Avenue B* tour

Iggy Pop – vocals
Hal Cragin – bass
Alex Kirst – drums
Whitey Kirst – guitar
Pete Marshall – guitar

Playing smaller intimate venues, more suited to the confessional tone of *Avenue B*, proved to be a wise move. A one-off date at the Astoria in London on 30 September was followed a month later by a short trip around selected American cities. On 8 November, he returned to Paris and spent the next month performing in theatres in most European capitals.

The regular set list was:

'No Shit', 'Nazi Girlfriend', 'Español', 'Raw Power', 'Search And Destroy', 'Shakin' All Over', 'Corruption', 'Real Wild Child', 'I Wanna Be Your Dog', 'I Felt The Luxury', 'Home', 'Lust For Life', 'The Passenger', 'Cold Metal', 'Avenue B', 'TV Eye', 'I Got A Right', 'No Fun', 'Death Trip', 'Sixteen', 'Louie Louie'

The concerts would begin with Iggy on his knees, clutching his guitar and intoning the sombre 'No Shit' before accompanying himself on 'Nazi Girlfriend'. This was the most low-key beginning to an Iggy Pop concert ever and many audiences would heckle and shout during this introduction. Iggy was not deterred, however, and resolutely stuck with it for the whole tour. He would begin the encores in the same way, by playing 'Avenue B' or sometimes the even quieter 'Miss Argentina'. A surprising, though very effective, take on 'I Felt The Luxury' may have tested the patience of those wanting only Stooges retreads, but Iggy was determined that the more challenging material should be played. As if to compensate, 'Johnny B Goode' and 'Who Do You Love?' were frequently resurrected for further encores as and when necessary.

A film crew was on hand at the Ancienne Belgique in Brussels on 2 December, though the resulting DVD was bafflingly not issued until 2005. It showed a solid, if unspectacular concert, with the band on fine form and Iggy full of energy and fire. His vocals are mainly very good though he veers alarmingly off key during 'Shakin' All Over.'

The short tour ended up with two shows at the Shepherd's Bush Empire in London on 7 and 8 December. Then Iggy went back to Paris for a TV show on Canal+. After the filming, a private show at the same venue went on into the night. Also recorded by Canal+, this gig has been extensively bootlegged and featured Medeski, Martin and Wood instead of the Trolls. Special guests Chrissie Hynde and French chanteuse Vanessa Paradis, at the time the girlfriend of Johnny Depp (who played guitar on 'Hollywood Affair'), helped Iggy out. For Depp, the chance to appear on the same stage as his hero was a dream come true. Back in 1981, Depp's band the Kids had opened for Iggy in Gainsville, Florida. But the teenage Johnny and his friends, boozed up and full of youthful bravado had attempted to heckle Iggy and received withering scorn in return. Iggy had of course recently scored the soundtrack for Depp's film *The Brave*, as well as acting with him in *Cry Baby* and *Dead Man*. The private show saw Iggy performing a number of the slower, jazzier *Avenue B* songs, most of which didn't feature on the main tour, plus a selection of jazz standards and torch songs with his guests. It was a superbly entertaining hour, made all the more fun because it was so wholly unexpected. Since 1972, when Iggy had surprised Clive Davis with a note-perfect 'The Shadow Of Your Smile' there had been constant attempts to get him to play these sorts of songs. His gruff baritone really suited the new version of 'One For My Baby' and Iggy really pulls out the stops on 'You Go To My Head' with Vanessa Paradis. The late-night show ended appropriately with 'Nightclubbing', a song not played live since 1987.

Aisha

Coinciding with the autumn dates was this single by industrial dance duo Death In Vegas. The track featured a sterling Iggy vocal telling a harrowing tale of a murderer with a portrait of a serial killer on his wall. Iggy should record more of this sort of heavy dance music as his throaty growl of a vocal suits the mood of the piece so well. The song is characterised by a circular buzzsaw guitar and some throbbing bass. Iggy's old band mate Seamus Beaghen plays the keyboards. The single came in a variety of mixes, but it's the original, also featured on the album *The Contino Sessions*, that is the most effectively scary.

Remembered Boy

Down On The Street – 2000 European festivals tour

Iggy Pop – vocals
Alex Kirst – drums
Whitey Kirst – guitar
Pete Marshall – guitar
Mooseman – bass

The band, now christened the Trolls, still comprised Whitey on guitar, his brother Alex on drums and Pete Marshall on second guitar, but Hal Cragin had moved on. He was replaced by Lloyd 'Mooseman' Roberts, previously the bassist in Ice T's controversial rap/metal band Body Count, who provided a huge bass sound for the others to play off.

Before the band returned to Europe, the spectre of Jim Morrison was raised once again. This time it was none other than Ray Manzarek suggesting that the remaining Doors may well reform and they would love Iggy to replace Morrison. 'Wouldn't he be great, man? The three surviving Doors with Iggy Pop... I'd really dig that.' Iggy's response is unrecorded, but it's unlikely to have been favourable. The remaining Doors did eventually get back together (though drummer John Densmore soon dropped out), with the Cult's Ian Astbury providing a creditable Morrison impersonation.

After a gig in Warsaw on 23 May, Pete Marshall and manager Art Collins were involved in a frightening air incident on their way back to New York. Halfway across the Atlantic, Pete spotted a passenger ranting and singing. Although the flight attendants appeared not to be bothered, Pete was convinced she was high and told Art Collins it was a 'bad acid trip'. When she grabbed a bottle of vodka and started flailing it around dangerously, Marshall and Collins overpowered her and tied her up with the demonstration seat belts. She was arrested upon arrival in the USA. Art Collins was quoted in *Rolling Stone* as saying that in future he would 'never travel without duct tape'.

The T In The Park festival on 9 July saw Iggy in the middle of a frankly bizarre bill, which included tribute band the Bootleg Beatles and Scottish 1960s darling Lulu. A rather out-of-place Iggy hit the stage at 5 pm before Supergrass, Macy Gray and Travis closed the day.

Like the 1999 shows, the Warsaw gig opened with 'No Shit'/'Nazi Girlfriend' but later shows dropped the low-key beginning and jumped straight in with the fast and fun 'Español'. Otherwise there were few surprises (except for an unconfirmed reappearance of 'Lovebone' at Zeebrugge on 14 July).

Early September saw a week of dates in Germany. Dubbed the 'Millennium Tour Of Germany' these shows were notable for the debut of a number of new songs including 'L.O.S.T.' and 'Sterility'.

A typical German set list went:

'Español', 'Raw Power', 'Search And Destroy', 'Shakin' All Over', 'Corruption', 'Real Wild Child', 'I Wanna Be Your Dog', 'Down On The Street' (usually segued with 'Gloria'), 'Home', 'Sterility', 'The Passenger', 'Cold Metal', 'I'm Sick Of You', 'TV Eye', 'I Got A Right', 'No Fun', 'Death Trip', 'Sixteen', 'Lust For Life' (sometimes played as a medley with 'Johnny B Goode'), 'L.O.S.T.', 'Louie Louie'

During 2000, Iggy contributed his distinctive vocals to a track by noisy grungesters At The Drive-In. 'Rolodex Propaganda' appears on their album *Relationship of Command* and is a thrillingly complex slab of modern prog punk.

In late 2000, Iggy called his band to Miami to record what would arguably be the most extreme album he'd ever made.

BEAT 'EM UP

Virgin CDVUS200 Released – June 2001.
Produced by **Iggy Pop**

'What you've got here is this guy in a fifty-four-year-old body who still unreasonably believes in this infantile rock 'n' roll myth of "I wanna do my music my way, I don't want a fucking producer…" and everybody'll like it… maybe.' Iggy was clearly over his midlife crisis. He had decided that the mature direction hinted at on *Avenue B* was a dead end. So, like many middle-aged men, he embarked on a second childhood. And, being Iggy, he really went for it. The back-to-basics rock of *Beat 'em Up* was serious business, a return to the balls-out anger of the early Stooges or, as one reviewer described it, 'the rawest, raunchiest, heaviest, snottiest, loudest, grittiest, angriest disc he's made in decades'.

In a press release issued on 16 February, Iggy's manager, Art Collins, was memorably quoted: 'I'm not saying this is another *Raw Power*, but if *Raw Power* is a true Iggy album, then this is another true Iggy album.' He went on to say that there would be some 'ranting on the album, some humour, some rock on it'.

Beat 'em Up was recorded during the winter of 2000–2001 at the Hit Factory Criteria Studios in Iggy's new home of Miami Beach. For the first time since *Raw Power*, Iggy produced the record himself and the result turned out to be the complete antithesis of *Avenue B*. The moody jazz and orchestral poems were gone, brutally replaced by the Trolls in full bludgeoning, aggressive, fuck-you mode. No strings, no delicacy, just guitars, bass and drums recorded simply and powerfully. All the tracks were written by Iggy and Whitey, except 'Mask', 'Go For The Throat' and 'V.I.P.', for which Mooseman and Alex Kirst received a credit too. Iggy was assisted at the board by engineer Danny Kadar. He had helped Iggy with the new mix of *Raw Power* and the same everything-in-the-red, approach was followed with *Beat 'em Up*. Many of the songs place the drums dead centre with Iggy howling over the top. Guitars and bass widen the sound with Whitey frequently double-tracked so that the buzz of his guitar attacks the listener from both sides. 'L.O.S.T.' demonstrates this set-up well. Iggy was generally recorded flat, no echo, no effects, and his voice is often partially buried in the swirling morass of noise, screaming to be heard above the volume.

Some of the songs (such as 'L.O.S.T.' and 'Sterility') had been debuted during the summer 2000 concerts. The band remained the same powerful line-up that had toured Europe during 2000 – Whitey, Alex, and Mooseman, with Pete Marshall on occasional guitar – and they were looking forward to a full year of concerts in 2001. Then Mooseman was shot dead, soon after completing work on the album. The drive-by attack took place in Compton, Los Angeles, on 2 February 2001, and Mooseman was killed outright. The killers were never caught. *Beat 'em Up* was dedicated to his memory.

The ensuing tour saw Pete Marshall switch to bass, reducing the Trolls to an immensely strong power trio. They embarked upon a North American tour before the album was issued, hammering audiences with the new material, which, for the first time in ages, received an excellent response from the crowds. The main reason was the ultra-heavy super-fast approach adopted by the Trolls.

Upon its release in June, *Beat 'em Up* received great reviews. Mary Lynn McEwen, writing for the online weekly *FFWD* in July 2001, gave the album four out of five and commented: 'Whitey Kirst's punchy guitar slashes out like a surgeon wielding a Swiss army knife – it's choppy and dangerous, and you want to look away before something really frightening happens... You get it all here – Iggy the crooner, Iggy the growler, Iggy the philosopher and Iggy the rager, raging against the dying of the night where the street fight that is rock mocks the slippery stranglehold of the recording industry.'

Other reviews were more restrained but still positive – Q praised the 'return to blitzkrieg riffing... closer to nu-metal than old Stooges. No fool, Iggy knows his appeal is as much iconic as musical these days, and milks it – mockingly – to the max on "VIP".' *Rolling Stone* awarded three stars in deference to Iggy's 'loudest, most adolescent and downright unwholesome album since the Stooges imploded.'

In trying to compete with newer bands, the Trolls occasionally fall into the trap of sounding derivative. Bands such as Creed are touchstones for some of the heavy sound achieved on *Beat 'em Up*. Iggy listened to a lot of punk and metal bands of the day to check out what sort of market he was working in. None of what he heard unduly worried him, but clearly some of the vibe rubbed off. The lyrics are generally rages against pretty much everything, condemning society's ills and offering social commentary, but many of the songs contradict each other leaving the listener unsure of exactly what Iggy is reacting against. The venomous attacks on the music business contain more bite, however, as this is clearly something that Iggy has experience of.

What is often overlooked is that *Beat 'em Up* was not as one-dimensional as many reviews imply. While there is undeniably a lot of 'blitzkrieg riffing', some of the songs are contemplative and calmer, and in tracks such as 'V.I.P.' there is bags of humour too. However, at fifteen tracks (plus a hidden bonus) the album could be accused of being overlong, and the insistence on no keyboards or other instruments tends to create a rather homogenous sound over the whole album, that of suffocating guitars and claustrophobic anger. A little lightness may have lessened the ferocious impact of *Beat 'em Up*, but would have made it less intense, if possibly more enjoyable.

Mask

The listener gets literally beaten up by the savage attack of the Trolls coupled with Iggy's insane vocals. The battering-ram beat from Alex Kirst is matched in power by Whitey's itchy and scratchy guitar sound. Mooseman's bass is just monstrously huge. Then there's Iggy, his voice distorted and compressed into the mix, yet he's hollering at full pelt. The furious, hysterical rant in the middle of the song, directed at everyone and anyone who has ever pissed him off begins at full strength before unbelievably rising in intensity, as Iggy screams out 'Where is the soul, where is the love?' Man, does this guy mean it. Iggy has never produced a more manic opening song.

Even Iggy seems to have thought that 'Mask' was extreme. Aware that the record company would want to hear how the album was going, he deliberately recorded the slightly more melodic songs that make up the middle of the album first. Virgin therefore heard 'Talking Snake' and 'Savior' and the like and went off happy. Only then did Iggy and the Trolls set to work on 'Drink New Blood' and 'Mask' and the other really out-there songs. As Iggy has explained on numerous occasions, the inspiration for 'Mask' came from seeing the nu-metal band Slipknot. They wear matching boiler suits and frightening masks onstage, so that no one knows what they actually look like. After their gig, people were coming up to the band members, now wearing their regular clothes, and asking, 'Which mask are you?' Iggy found this to be a fascinating concept – that a mask defines people; that your appearance, no matter how grotesque, kind of defines who you are, but 'you look better that way.' Iggy takes this one stage further – how can you tell who is beneath a mask? The sudden ending, after three minutes of fearsome rage, is a real shock.

'Mask' was utilised as the opener for all the 2001–2002 concerts.

L.O.S.T.

One of the oldest songs on the album, 'L.O.S.T.' had been debuted the previous summer on the German tour. It stomps along menacingly as the lyrics ominously talk of a 'garden of evil' and seem to have given up all hope. The oppressive double guitar crunch is massive, scraping and grinding for the duration. Iggy's rough-hewn croak adds a further threatening dimension.

Howl

Once again, Iggy sounds insane – howling like a rabid wolf over the noise of the band. It takes thirty seconds of guitar noise and Iggy howling to get to the bassy grind of the riff. The anger in the lyrics (which begin with 'Fuck it,

I feel like howling, got nowhere to turn') is offset by some pleasingly odd effects, which bubble spookily after each line. The choruses also feature various vocal lines which collide with each other. Alex keeps the solid beat, though the bass is so huge he's barely audible at times. The song is possibly a touch too long for the repetitive tune to carry.

Football

Not a song about sports, but one in which Iggy compares himself to a football. He's been kicked around in the dirt, passed back and forth, trying to score. The analogy is rather clumsy but the meaning is clear. This is the first slow track on the album, and one that bears a passing resemblance to 'I'm Sick Of You' in its loping verses. Iggy's vocals on the choruses sound like they were recorded from the next town – he's screaming but sounds so very distant, buried under a ton of amped-up guitars. Closer inspection reveals some clever doubling of the vocals at this point. Unfortunately though the song is rather too pedestrian and ends up being one of the least memorable on the album.

Savior

A more mellow verse, led by Whitey's carefully picked guitar, followed by a severely over-amped chorus. An interesting lyric addressing the problem of what a modern-day saviour would make of us, and what would we make of him in modern dress. He might be a rapper, or own a pitbull. The unearthly wounded cry of 'Get me out of here' is like a frightening voice from beyond the grave. Eschewing noise and fury for atmosphere, 'Savior' is possibly the most impressive track on the album. Great ending, too.

Beat 'em Up

The title song is also one of the best of the album. With a tremendous kick from the Trolls, plus some excellent backing vocals too, Iggy outlines his manifesto – what do you do about those who rip you off and exploit the poor, the downtrodden and the naïve? The answer is in the title. The song carries some similarities to the Rolling Stones' 'Pretty Beat Up' from the *Undercover* album. Alex and Mooseman lock tight with a monstrous thudding rhythm. It's a slightly weird call to arms from Iggy, especially in the light of the final track 'V.I.P.', where he casts himself as a snobbish snooty celebrity, lording it over the plebs, and therefore implies that neither 'V.I.P.' nor 'Beat 'em Up' is to be taken too seriously.

Talking Snake

Possibly the most commercial track here finds Iggy expertly crooning the mellow verses over stuttering guitars, before the power chords of the chorus crash in. The lyrics continue the main themes of the album, namely that people are out to get you, screw you over, and you've got to fight for your rights, fight for truth and justice. Here the talking snake (who could be anyone – but my money is on a politician, or maybe a slimy TV pundit) is simply saying that everyone should be happy.

The Jerk

Could this be one of the suckers from the previous song? We all know people like this, with fake smiles and corny pick-up lines. Iggy's just laughing at him, and rightly so. The music follows the lyrics, with appropriately jerky stop-start runs. Inexplicably included in the live set ahead of many superior songs, this is one of the weaker tracks. The shouty choruses are derivative and frankly dull.

Death Is Certain

Death is certain and, as Iggy outlines in the second verse, is it really any worse than listening to jerky music, whilst wearing a suit, and eating crappy food? The downward guitar runs are suitably doomy. Obvious influences on this song include the Doors – Iggy sings 'a lively cry' exactly like Morrison's 'alive she cried' – and Iggy's own 'My Baby Wants To Rock And Roll', from where the verses seem to have been nicked. Whitey takes a scorching solo on what is one of the best-produced and most melodic tracks. Interestingly, after *Avenue B*, Iggy seems to have put his fear about ageing behind him. Death is certain, but he's clearly not afraid.

Go For The Throat

An astonishingly hyper song, full of maniacal screaming and a truly frightening first verse about being in a coma, nearing death, but fighting back with everything he possesses. Not content with railing against hypocrisy and snakes, now Iggy is fighting Death! Later verses see him flailing about how he's so fucked up because 'they took away my innocence and gave me shitty fame' which is a telling comment from someone who'd been in the business for over thirty years. The band rides a fearsome groove, which relentlessly pounds, and the vocals start off with Iggy sounding like a serial killer, and somehow end up even more totally insane. It's a deeply unpleasant, but horribly compelling song; scary to listen to, but clearly scared inside too.

Weasels

Another broadside, this time against the weasels of the music business. By now, Iggy's intense anger is getting a little wearing. But contained within the lyrics is a new and fascinating angle – it appears that at least some of these particular enemies might be his old band members, now carving out their own path in the industry. But despite some impressive singing on the choruses it ends up as arguably the weakest track on the album.

Drink New Blood

How much more rage can we take? Iggy's getting progressively more violent and unhinged as the songs hammer by. Whitey gets to play some blinding guitar and Mooseman's bass rumbles menacingly while Alex thrashes his drums to death. Iggy concludes with a violent outburst of screaming. The breathless chanting of the song's title leaves the listener physically winded and drained.

It's All Shit

From the careful, measured fade-in via the slower decisive beat, 'It's All Shit' thankfully lowers the intensity somewhat. Iggy muses logically on the best way to identify the substance referred to in the song's title. Then, without warning, it turns into a more regular song, before Whitey gets all atonal over the 'nobody cares' ending. A surprisingly satisfying track.

Ugliness

A car drives up at the start, before Iggy screams, 'Ugly!' A favourite of Pete Marshall's, 'Ugliness' seems to collect most the of *Beat 'em Up*'s themes into one song. Ugly guys, songs with no soul, people with money but no talent ('You see the cocksuckers on MTV, and they ain't even got a good CD') – they are all rounded up, lined against the wall and shot by Iggy's venomous diatribe. The music is one big mush of sound although you can still hear Iggy's handclaps and car horns thrown into the mix. The clarity apparent on many other songs is eschewed in favour of this live in the studio bash.

V.I.P.

Finally, some light relief. Over a repetitive bass and lurching drumbeat, Iggy mercilessly parodies those who relish their celebrity status. It's a scabrously funny track, complete with amusing impersonations of flunkies and smarmy flight attendants offering drinks. For once, Iggy has squarely hit the nail on the head – what would happen if a VIP woke up one day to find he'd lost his status? No more good tables, attractive women, or entourages saying 'Right boss'... In the end, what is the point of being a VIP if not to gain all those things – and the chance to use the VIP toilet! The end of the song switches from the abstract to the specific, as Iggy talks about the 'VIP reflection effect' whereby family, girlfriends, guitar players, accountants of the VIP can all revel in his glory and become pseudo VIPs themselves. Then there's the 'difficult' VIP (and this aspect seems to come from the heart), that garners the 'wrong kind of attention'.

It's a terrific and underrated track; somewhat out of place at the end of *Beat 'em Up*, but nonetheless an extremely welcome piece of acerbic social commentary.

After just over a minute of silence a hidden track appears...

Sterility

Iggy asks if the band is ready, as the guitars crank up on this one-take burst of energy. Iggy's vocals go into meltdown, the band have turned everything to eleven at least and they play with every ounce of strength. 'Sterility' continues the themes of the album; 'sick, sick, sick of your lies,' sings Iggy. As with 'Ugliness', this is the closest you'll get on an album to the power and noise and energy and guitars and screaming and outright fun of Iggy's live show. Iggy ad libs wildly, then goads Whitey to crank it up still further as the guitarist hits another blazing solo, over which Iggy improvises another 'Mask'-like rant, which cleverly brings the album full circle.

*   *   *

The cover, a cartoon of a well-endowed lady in a lockable bikini, is crass and ugly, and the bright yellow background is lurid and inappropriate. But at best it makes a welcome change from the endless series of pictures of Iggy looking older and more haggard with each passing year. Much better is the hugely cool photo on the CD booklet of Iggy and new beau Nina cruising the streets in his convertible. It would have made a great cover picture. With his goatee and a cowboy hat perched on his straggly hair, Iggy looks happy but dangerous.

Also recorded at the sessions was a short snappy cover – 'Fix Me', an old Black Flag number, was taped for an album coordinated by Henry Rollins. All the tracks on *Rise Above* were Black Flag covers and the proceeds from the album went to benefit the West Memphis Three – teenagers jailed for the 1993 murder of three eight-year-olds purely because their long hair, a love of heavy metal and the fact that they read Stephen King novels made them, in the eyes of the prosecution, obvious Satanists. There was no actual evidence, no motive and no link whatsoever to the unquestionably awful murders. One of the accused was mentally handicapped and his 'confession' has long been discredited; yet they remain in prison. One of the three is on death row.

Iggy and the Trolls take on 'Fix Me' was fast and sharp and all over within a minute. A tremendous track however.

Down On The Street – 2001 *Beat 'em Up* tour

Iggy Pop – vocals
Alex Kirst – drums
Whitey Kirst – guitar
Pete Marshall – bass

A month of low-key dates prior to the release of the album featured a number of new songs, unfamiliar to most of the crowds. Playing mostly small theatres and clubs in April and May, Iggy and the Trolls also performed at the Coachella festival at Indio, California on 28 April where they unveiled the new songs before a massive unsuspecting crowd.

The early shows often featured 'Talking Snake' and 'The Jerk' but, by the summer gigs, these were rarely played. During the summer 'Death Is Certain' tended to replace 'Go For The Throat'. 'Ugliness' and other *Beat 'em Up* tunes would occasionally be performed.

In addition to the festival gigs, Iggy was to be found on many TV and radio shows promoting the shows and the recent album. As always, Iggy came across well, personable, amusing, opinionated and full of outrageous stories. The days of the Stooges and the wild excesses were firmly behind him and Iggy was happy to look back over the past thirty years with fond amusement. Did you really drip candle wax on yourself and roll on broken glass onstage? asked *Kerrang!* magazine 'Yes,' replied Iggy, 'but not at the same show. That would have been foolish.'

Most of June and early July was spent promoting the new album in Europe with some strategic interviews and well-placed gigs. Then the festivals beckoned Iggy back, including a return to the Reading-Leeds Festival on 24 and 25 August. The set list remained pretty static all year:

'Mask', 'Español', 'Beat 'em Up', 'Drink New Blood', 'Search And Destroy', 'Howl', 'Corruption', 'Real Wild Child', 'I Wanna Be Your Dog', 'Go For The Throat', 'Sterility', 'Home', 'The Passenger', 'I Got A Right', 'Cold Metal', 'Death Trip', 'TV Eye', 'L.O.S.T', 'No Fun'

The Glasgow Gig On The Green show on 26 August attracted much publicity in the regular press thanks to the bizarre requests Iggy had apparently made – backstage he wanted broccoli, so he could throw it away because he hates it. The Scottish press lapped up the other demands too – a copy of the *New York Times* plus pizza and red wine proved no problem, but seven dwarves? A spokesman for Regular Music, the company staging the festival, was quoted as saying (with his tongue firmly in his cheek), 'Getting hold of seven dwarves isn't exactly a tall order...' The story had the desired effect of selling more tickets, so perhaps Iggy's demands weren't so ridiculous after all.

Down On The Street – 2001 North American Autumn tour

With September taken as a holiday the band were refreshed and ready for a month-long North American tour. The set list remained as before but in general the oppressive sound of *Beat 'em Up* seemed to work better in smaller venues. Starting in Athens on 18 October and winding up with two nights at Irving Plaza in New York on 12 and 13 November, this concluded the most intensive period of touring for some years. Iggy had to work hard to maintain his fitness, but still picked up a number of injuries. He had developed a limp after years of throwing himself off stages and he noticed that everyday bruises and scrapes were taking longer to heal. But what other fifty-four-year-old would subject himself to such a punishing regime? Iggy resolved to cut down on his live appearances. In future he wouldn't commit to such lengthy tours, only selected gigs with long enough breaks between shows to allow his muscular but ageing body to recover.

Down On The Street – 2002 European summer festivals

Iggy Pop – vocals
Alex Kirst – drums
Whitey Kirst – guitar
Pete Marshall – bass

The set list for the July and August shows was virtually identical to the *Beat 'em Up* gigs the previous year, the main differences being the regular use of 'Sixteen' in the encores and sometimes moving 'Raw Power' to the final encore:

'Mask', 'Español', 'Beat 'em Up', 'Drink New Blood', 'Search And Destroy', 'Howl', 'Corruption', 'Real Wild Child', 'I Wanna Be Your Dog', 'Death Is Certain', 'Sterility', 'Home', 'The Passenger', 'I Got A Right', 'Cold Metal', 'Death Trip', 'Sixteen', 'TV Eye', 'L.O.S.T', 'No Fun', 'Raw Power'

Having been playing this set for over a year, the Trolls excelled on this tour. Sandwiched between outdoor gigs were a selection of inside shows at medium-sized venues – the Esparrago Festival in Cadiz on 12 July was

followed by a show at the Brixton Academy the next night; Glasgow Barrowlands served as a warm-up for an appearance at the metal-orientated Download Festival on 19 and 20 July. The tour was notable for Iggy's first Moscow concert at the Krylya Festival on 7 July and appearances in Croatia and Budapest. As with many festival gigs, the shows were frequently broadcast live across Europe.

After the summer gigs, Iggy planned his next move. He was determined that the next album would avoid the criticisms of sameness that were sometimes thrown at *Beat 'em Up*. Iggy chose maximum variety and decided to work with as many people as possible. With that in mind, he had been in contact with power punks Green Day and Sum 41 with a view to them writing songs for him. Iggy had also been impressed with rap punk electro artist Peaches and arrangements were made to record with her. The Trolls entered the studio in late 2002 to record a number of new tracks as the backbone of the new album, around which the guest appearances would fall. But all this activity would be eclipsed by one piece of news. Iggy had decided to record four new songs with Ron and Scott Asheton. Without any fanfare, the Stooges were back.

2003

The press release that accompanied *Skull Ring* was a masterpiece of hyperbole: 'Slammin' backbeats to the midsection, punishing and relentless guitar riffs that fry the eardrums to a crisp, and lyrics that call for revolution of mind and soul even as they forever extol rock's eternal truths – summertime, cars, women, pain...' But in essence it was correct. *Skull Ring* is a distillation of Iggy's writing over the previous thirty-five years. The content of the songs really isn't all that different from those on *The Stooges*. And, fittingly, Iggy recorded four new songs with the Asheton brothers.

A Stooges reunion had been mooted many times and, in the mid 1990s, producer Rick Rubin had contacted Ron, Scott and Iggy with a view to reforming. All were apparently interested, but then Iggy took off on one of his many summer festival jaunts and dropped out of contact. In 1998, Ron joined up with Sonic Youth's Thurston Moore to record some songs for the soundtrack to Todd Haynes's film *Velvet Goldmine*. Starring Ewan McGregor as the Iggy-inspired Curt Wild and Jonathan Rhys Meyers as the Bowie-esque Brian Slade, *Velvet Goldmine* fictionalised the relationship between Bowie and Iggy and re-imagined the early 1970s glam scene as a gay heaven. Entertaining in its way, but denounced as a fictional travesty by both Iggy and David, the film contained a number of Stooges songs reworked by the Wylde Ratttz (Ron Asheton and Thurston Moore on guitar, Steve Shelley on drums, Mike Watt from the Minutemen and fIREHOSE on bass and Mudhoney's Mark Arm giving a passable Iggy impression). Although only one track, 'TV Eye', ended up on the accompanying soundtrack album, the band later spent a few days in the studio with John Lennon's son Sean assisting on keyboards. There was talk of a Wylde Ratttz tour to accompany the proposed album, though in the end nothing came of this. But the demand for Stooge material was obviously growing.

Ron had been playing Stooges songs with his occasional band Dark Carnival for years. Then Mike Watt began sneaking Stooges tracks into his live performances, with whichever band he was playing with. Bassist Watt was born in 1957 in San Pedro, California and with his friend D Boon, formed the highly influential Minutemen in 1979. The band took their name from the brevity of most of their songs. They recorded a number of adventurous, indie punk albums before Boon was killed in 1985 in a van accident following one of their shows. Watt and drummer George Hurley carried on, with fan Ed Crawford replacing Boon. They renamed themselves fIREHOSE and continued until early 1994.

Since 1995, Watt has played solo, though he frequently had the assistance of various members of Sonic Youth, Eddie Vedder and David Grohl. In 1998, he first worked with his hero Ron Asheton as part of the Wylde Ratttz and the two struck up an immediate friendship.

J Mascis, the leader of Dinosaur Jr, took Watt and Ron Asheton on tour and played a selection of Stooges tunes as the encore and, in 2001, with the addition of Scott Asheton on drums, they began playing a whole set of Stooges songs. Billed as Asheton-Asheton-Mascis-Watt they toured the USA and Europe and received a fantastic response. Iggy revealed that 'Everywhere I went I heard, "Hey, Ron's out on tour with Dinosaur Jr. doing Stooges songs and it's real good," or I was in Europe and I'd hear, "Ron and Scott are both out with Mike Watt doing Stooges songs at festivals." And I thought whoa, they're out there playing the material, so that kind of raised my eyebrow a little bit.' The audience was there, the musicians were getting sharper by the day, and the pressure on Iggy increased.

SKULL RING

Virgin 724359162027. Released September 2003.
Produced by **Iggy Pop**

Iggy was reluctant to record a whole album with the Ashetons. He was determined that the Trolls, his reliable and loyal band of many years standing, wouldn't be left out. In November 2002, Iggy and the Trolls recorded a batch of new material, very much in the vein of *Beat 'em Up* but with a slightly more melodic edge, at Miami's Hit Factory Criteria Studios. Iggy had decided that his next album would also feature a variety of artists. He'd struck up a working relationship with Green Day and had a number of songs that he wanted to record with them, and had lined up a duet with Peaches. 'I'm the kind of artist who works off other people best... trying to get all the pieces to fit like a jigsaw puzzle so I'd have a whole portrait but it would still have many facets. That's what I was hoping for.' The new album would therefore showcase all these different aspects of Iggy's writing. He even, and only half jokingly, suggested a duet with Justin Timberlake, which simply elicited shudders from Virgin. In recent years, Iggy had seen many bands encroaching onto his territory. Iggy Pop music was no longer quite as

unique as it had once been, and by joining forces with some of the Stooges' descendants, Iggy was in effect reclaiming what was rightly his.

At this point, Iggy decided that the time was right to regroup with Ron and Scott. By including new Stooges songs on a collaborative Iggy Pop album, the pressure would be off. The weight of expectation that would fall on a full Stooges album would be avoided. If the reunion didn't work out then it wouldn't matter – it was only a couple of songs... Iggy had low expectations at first: 'I didn't expect jack shit from it, I really underestimated my own group.' As the sessions progressed, however, it was clear to all three musicians that they still had something special. The songs were worked out in just three days; the recordings at the Hit Factory Criteria in January 2003 took just over a week. Ron played both bass and guitar. Iggy was seriously impressed with their dedication and focus, commenting that 'When the two of them lay down tracks in the studio just alone, guitar and drums together, they have the authority of old blues players, the kind of authority that I associate with Junior Kimbrough or R.L. Burnside. That's how it feels to me. Sometimes I just left them alone and they came up with whole tracks, and I came in and constructed vocals as we went along.'

The finished album was issued to some of the best reviews of Iggy's career. Inevitably, many concentrated on the reformation of the Stooges, though Iggy's other collaborations were also singled out for praise. The *Washington Post* came out with the brilliant line that, in Iggy's life, 'punk has never been just an attitude or affectation. It courses through his leathery veins and pops out of his eyeballs.'

The cover was also excellent – a series of photos of Iggy in a string vest, showcasing his leathery veins and darkly tanned skin. He looks his age, but incredibly healthy, which is something of a relief after the rather ill-looking appearances on previous album covers (*Naughty Little Doggie* especially).

Little Electric Chair

Kicking off the album with the first of four Stooges songs, 'Little Electric Chair' finds Ron doubling up on bass and guitar and Scott brutally pounding the skins. Iggy describes it as 'Ron being Stoogey, Stonesy, and me following suit.' And that's how it seems to be – Iggy starts the song off with very Jagger-esque 'Whooo's before embarking on his gruff whine of a vocal. The song is something of a throwaway, hanging onto Ron's, admittedly rock-solid, riff. The lyrics are somewhat goofy in the face of such relentless playing. But there's no doubt that this is clearly the sound of the Stooges. There's a palpable excitement associated with hearing Scott playing the drums and Ron furiously attacking the guitar. The song announces quite clearly that Stooges still have it, and it's great to have them back.

Perverts in the Sun

The difference between the Stooges and the Trolls (who feature on this track) is immediate – basically Whitey, Alex and Pete play much faster. Despite the appearance of speed, Ron and Scott don't actually play that quickly. But their power, yes their raw power, tramples everything in their path.

The Trolls seem to be enjoying this light-hearted depiction of Miami Beach. Iggy deftly describes the dirty parking lots where even the 'garbage can's got a tan' over the Trolls speedy sub-metal thrash. Iggy staunchly defended the Trolls against those that concentrated on the Stooges contributions to the album. 'For the last five years before this album was made, I've been out making a living, playing in the flesh, doing the real dirty deal with these guys. And if they're there when you piss and they're there when you sweat and they're there on the stinking bus, and next to you when you raise your arm in glory and everybody says, "Yea he's great," and you know the gig's doing great – then they need to be there on the record.'

Skull Ring

The Stooges run with this hypnotic mantra-like reincarnation of the 'Peter Gunn' theme. Iggy sings the verses in a chilly graveyard voice, with lots of spooky echo, before cheerily chanting the choruses, a succinct round up of the trappings of fame. Ron and Scott doggedly hang on to the same riff throughout and milk it for all its worth, until at the three minute mark Ron gets a brief but savage solo.

Superbabe

Back to the Trolls for this twisted look at guys being hypnotised by girls. 'It's about that trance-like power, the powers that can be exercised by the opposite sex,' explained Iggy. He wonders how he measured up after making love to a superbabe. The grinding music never really takes off though, despite the clever effects on the screamed title, and it seems too rooted in the basic grungy riff. Interestingly Iggy and the Trolls share the writing credits on all of their contributions to *Skull Ring*; a generous gesture.

Loser

Possibly the weakest of the new Stooges songs, mainly because it sounds least like a Stooges track. Maybe the Trolls would have suited this song rather better – although the Ashetons are credited with co-authorship, it's much more an Iggy song than the other Stooges tracks. In fact, Iggy was inspired to write 'Loser' after hearing the White Stripes. Massive Stooges fan Jack White was very nearly recruited into the band for the *Skull Ring* sessions, but he was keen to record a whole Stooges album and when schedules did not coincide, Ron handled the bass himself. 'Loser' was also the only new Stooges song not to be played live.

Private Hell

A change of mood and feel for this collaboration with latter-day US punks Green Day. California's Green Day (guitarist and singer Billie Joe Armstrong, bassist Mike Dirnt and drummer Tré Cool) were not only older, but considerably more intelligent than the dorky teens they appeared to be in their early songs. In 2004, Green Day would score their biggest worldwide success with the punk concept album *American Idiot*, a savage look at the alienation and disillusionment of ordinary Americans under Bush's post-War on Terror administration.

'Private Hell' started life when Iggy contacted Armstrong to write tunes for a bunch of poems that Iggy had written. Iggy had met the band a number of times at various festivals and recognised their keen songwriting talent. Armstrong called in his band mates and Iggy joined them at Berkeley's Studio 880.

'Private Hell' marries a bouncy Green Day tune to Iggy's description of his private life, a 'hell of excellent quality' apparently. It fits perfectly onto *Skull Ring*, however, thanks to their carefully studied Stooges thrash on the chorus (plus some inventive guitar on the verses) and one of Iggy's best vocals.

Little Know It All

For some baffling reason, despite a video and numerous TV appearances, the single 'Little Know It All' never made it to the shops. Promo copies float around the collectors' circuit but the actual single was never issued. Which is a shame as this excellent slice of teen power pop, a collaboration with Canada's Sum 41, could have been a big success.

Iggy felt that it was the most ambitious track on the album. Whilst this is debatable, it's certainly his most direct attempt in years to appeal to the youth of America. Iggy had in fact used one of Sum 41's albums as research before he recorded *Beat 'em Up*, but the collaboration came about when David Wolter, head of A&R at Virgin suggested to Sum 41's producer Greig Nori that he should write a song for Iggy. Nori and the band's main songwriter Deryck Whibley eagerly took up the suggestion. A lyricless demo was sent via Virgin to Iggy – he loved it and phoned Whibley to thank him. Whibley was astonished by Iggy's modesty when he said, 'I was in a band called the Stooges, I don't know if you've ever heard of them?'

Luckily the band were in LA at the end of April, coinciding with Iggy's session time, so they were booked to back him. The song was recorded at Cello Studios in Los Angeles, in just one day, 29 April, two days after the Stooges first performance in twenty-nine years at the Coachella Festival.

Sum 41 were amazed that the actual collaboration was so easy – Iggy finished off the lyrics immediately and recorded the vocal over a four-hour period. Iggy was impressed by the band's quietly efficient attitude. For Iggy it was simply a case of showing up and laying down his vocals. The way the lyrics hit back at those who target Iggy is especially revealing. After Iggy had left, the rest of the track, including backing vocals, was finished off the next day by the band and producer Greig Nori.

The finished song is extremely impressive, with Iggy's vocals blending effortlessly with the younger band.

Whatever

Apparently written and recorded in one night with the Trolls in 1960s garage-rock mode, 'Whatever' was inspired by Whitey. Iggy wanted a catchphrase that everybody would know – 'Whitey, my little stoner proletarian guitar player delinquent, went, "Uhhh whatever!" and so we worked from there...'

The song encompasses the 'notion of social drift', people drawing apart without a specific, clear goodbye. The lyrics hark back to the solitary Iggy of the late 1990s and portray a girl leaving him for no obvious reason. The song itself is unremarkable beyond the tricksy parts where the band cuts out at the end of each chorus leaving Alex on his own.

Dead Rock Star

The final song recorded with the Stooges is arguably the best. Opening with Ron's classic wah-wah sound before jumping into a 'Down On The Street' type riff, 'Dead Rock Star' also boasts a superior vocal and melody, allowing Iggy to demonstrate his range. Scott keeps the beat pounding as only he can, and it's clear that Scott still has that knack of holding the whole song together. Iggy described it as a 'step forward for the band, something stylistically we have never done – the sound of the Stooges in middle age'. The lyrics betray some of Iggy's fears and worries – 'I'm so afraid of failing, I hang on to the railing' and demonstrate that he's learnt an awful lot since the Stooges began, but not much of it is pleasant. This song could not have been written by a young band, only by one with years of hurt and disappointment and hard-earned experience. Not surprisingly, 'Dead Rock Star' became one of the new highlights of the Stooges concerts that followed.

Rock Show

From the sound of a band maturing with dignity to this electronic sample-led industrial duet with Peaches. Born Merrill Nisker, Peaches had hit the headlines in 2002 with her outrageous X-rated album *The Teaches Of Peaches*. She was angry, venomous and foul mouthed – all prerequisites of a male band, but deemed shocking and depraved from a woman. Peaches set out to challenge the perceived male supremacy inherent in punk. Her attitude impressed Iggy enormously. 'She's basically young and feisty, still takes drugs, gets drunk. And she's very witty, I think one of the more important writers and performers working right now.' Her song 'Rock Show', said Iggy, 'summed up a lot of what I wanted to say about the whole idea of "OK, what the hell is this whole thing about... this rock and roll thing?" I realised that if I covered one of her tracks with a rock band it wasn't gonna work. So I thought, what would Puff Daddy do? Let's just sample the whole thing and see if there's room for my voice, and it kind of worked.' 'Rock Show' was remastered and remixed at Hit Factory Criteria, with Iggy overdubbing his vocal as an 'answer' to Peaches. Their raucous voices blend well in two minutes of thumping electronically enhanced stripped-right-down rock.

Here Comes The Summer

Straight-ahead rock with the Trolls, containing three classic rock 'n' roll staples – the summer, cars and girls. The lyrics seem to apply to Iggy's love of playing the big summer festivals. The basic track is very Rolling Stones but, as this is a song that Iggy reckoned was 'meant to be played in the open air for a large group of people in a stadium or at least an arena', that was obviously the intention. Oddly, however, 'Here Comes The Summer' was apparently never played live.

Motor Inn

A second duet with Peaches, backed by her band Feedom. It's crude and funny, but repetitive and something of a closed circuit. Iggy gets progressively more dirty old man as the song bashes along. It's arguably the weakest on the album.

In addition to 'Motor Inn', Iggy worked on 'Kick It' with Peaches, which was issued on her album *Fatherfucker*. 'Kick It' is arguably the better track, with sly references to 'Search And Destroy' and a healthily irreverent take on Iggy's perceived persona. Peaches also issued 'Kick It' as a single and the accompanying video went into heavy rotation on some channels. Iggy cavorts and leers while Peaches struts and poses – just when you think they can't send themselves up any more, the zombies (well of course) come crashing in! Terrific fun.

Inferiority Complex

Iggy thought back to High School to come up with this track. Remembering how he was made to feel inferior and how he started to believe what people told him – 'I'm really not that good looking, I'm really not that smart, nobody really likes me. I've lived it and each member of the Trolls has lived it' – Iggy wrote the song for all the long-haired kids in school who feel similarly undervalued. The lyrics are occasionally overwrought and unnecessarily wordy for such a concept (standing on a ship waiting for the 'tugboat of respect'?), but on the whole it's a very effective piece of writing. Surprisingly dark and moody for this album, Whitey's guitar has a brooding, doomy quality and Alex creates a sombre beat.

Supermarket

This track ruins the unusual mood built up by 'Inferiority Complex' as Iggy describes himself as a commodity over another Green Day tune. He worries about his limited shelf life. But the song takes the idea further – 'talking about the whole idea of the commoditisation of life', commented Iggy. Ultimately however it sounds far more like Green Day than Iggy and although its powerful thrash is fun, 'Supermarket' comes across as (maybe appropriately) disposable.

Til Wrong Feels Right

With just his guitar for accompaniment, Iggy growls out this bluesy gripe about the entertainment industry that he's such an unwilling part of. The music was inspired by Mississippi Fred McDowell, the topical social commentary lyrics by Bob Dylan, and Iggy sounds like a venerable old blues man propped up on the veranda mumbling to anyone who'll listen. The business will 'make you like what you hate, make you eat what you don't want, live where you don't belong, and every other bloody thing', explained Iggy. It's a fascinating insight into Iggy's mind and makes one think that an Iggy unplugged solo album might be quite appealing. His lived-in voice suits this sort of naked recording.

Blood On Your Cool

After the moody introspection, the Trolls return to blast through this heavy track. Iggy wasn't sure whether to include it or not as he worried that the lyrics were too dark. It's a warning, that Iggy's kind of life isn't as good as it seems. Whilst this may seem rather hypocritical coming from a man who drives a Rolls-Royce and has homes in Miami and Mexico, it's not so much a warning about his current life, more about how hard it was to get there.

Thankfully, Iggy decided to put it on the album, as it's the best Trolls track. The chorus is fabulous, with Iggy doubling Whitey's downward guitar runs. Whitey gets a furiously metallic solo, and the rest of the band kick up a storm with so much conviction that you have to wonder who decided to fade this track out? And, my common complaint, why such a quick fade out? Just as you're getting into the song it disappears.

Nervous Exhaustion
An appropriate title for this rough bonus track – 'It's just me and the Trolls at our sloppiest,' remarked Iggy. Actually there's little that's sloppy about 'Nervous Exhaustion' as the Trolls are experts in creating such thrilling music. Hidden away at the end of the album after thirty seconds of silence, 'Nervous Exhaustion', like 'Sterility' on *Beat 'em Up*, sounds like a live-in-the-studio blast of noise. Iggy delivers his vocals down a tube, hitting against those who don't thank him (they make him angry), radio stations and Moby. It's a terrific way to end the album, a real return to basics, restating succinctly and powerfully what Iggy is all about.

*   *   *

Although 'Little Know It All' was advertised as a single on the cover of *Skull Ring*, and a large number of promos were sent to radio stations, a commercial release didn't happen. A second promo single containing 'Little Electric Chair' and 'Little Know It All' was more worthwhile as it also contained two extra tracks from the *Skull Ring* sessions.

Jose The Arab
The story of Jose who worked at Taco Bell (and who would be better off dead apparently) is a short straightforward bash. Over a frantic beat which conveys the impression of far more excitement than the song provides, Iggy sings with glee and Whitey plays some tasty guitar, but ultimately it's three minutes of filler.

Ready To Run
This is better – a stuttering riff and one of those Iggy vocals sung into a vacuum cleaner combine to produce a memorable track, equal to many on the album. In view of Iggy's love of heavy blues, it's fair to assume that 'Ready To Run' was at least partially inspired by Junior Kimbrough's 'You Better Run' (later covered by the Stooges in 2004).

*   *   *

Iggy also contributed a couple of jams to *Gimme Skelter*, an album that came with the Spring 2004 edition of *In Music We Trust* magazine. Amongst tracks by Mudhoney, Primal Scream, Weezer and others were Iggy's interludes – the first being a marvellously funny little rant which takes the line from 'Nervous Exhaustion' about being sick of Moby and runs with it. The second is a moan about how his bones keep clicking. Both monologues are sung/shouted over the Trolls' riffing. Inessential maybe, but rather good fun.

Rockicide – Millenia Nova featuring Iggy Pop
In spite of the corny title, this is a truly great song, and one that most Iggy

fans will have missed. Millenia Nova are a Munich-based duo – Matthias Neuhauser and Michael Meinl – and usually make pleasingly shimmery ambient pop. Iggy became aware of them when one of their tunes was used as a jingle on a New York radio station. Iggy liked it and when the duo contacted him to ask if he'd sing on their album he happily accepted. Iggy's almost self-parodic lyric actually fits the stirring mid-tempo synth-rock track remarkably well. Issued as a single (which also featured a variety of irritating mixes) in March 2003 ahead of the song's appearance on their album *Narcotic Wide Screen Vista*, 'Rockicide' was a minor hit in their native Germany but remains virtually unknown anywhere else.

Down On The Street – 2003 concerts

Iggy spent the year switching between regular Trolls concerts and a number of higher-profile Stooges gigs.

Iggy and the Trolls

Iggy Pop – vocals
Alex Kirst – drums
Whitey Kirst – guitar
Pete Marshall – bass

The Trolls concerts featured the usual mix of old and new. They spent most of June and July travelling around Europe, beginning at the prestigious Isle Of Wight Festival. On 26 July, they played at the Mt Fuji festival in Japan. The set was basically the same as the previous couple of years, but with the addition of a number of new *Skull Ring* tunes. 'TV Eye' was often preceded by a little 'Shadow Of Your Smile', the calm before the storm. The most surprising songs in the set came toward the end. Both 'I Snub You' and 'Knocking 'em Down' from *Soldier* were revived for the first time in over twenty years and would jostle each other for a place in the set:

'Loose', 'Down On The Street', 'Drink New Blood', 'Search And Destroy' 'Raw Power', 'Corruption', 'Real Wild Child', 'I Wanna Be Your Dog', 'Death Is Certain', 'Perverts in The Sun', 'Superbabe', 'Home', 'The Passenger', 'I Got A Right', 'Cold Metal', 'Shadow of Your Smile', 'TV Eye', 'Sixteen', 'Death Trip', 'I Snub You', 'No Fun', 'Louie Louie'

The Trolls then took a rest until Iggy rounded off the year with them on a handful of December dates. This was because Iggy and the Stooges were playing live for the first time in twenty-nine years.

Iggy and the Stooges

Iggy Pop – vocals
Ron Asheton – guitar
Scott Asheton – drums
Steven Mackay – saxophone
Mike Watt – bass

Originally the performance at the Coachella Festival at Indio, California on 27 April 2003 was to be a one-off event. Iggy, Ron and Scott called up Mike Watt, who knew all the songs from the J Mascis tour, to replace Dave

Alexander on bass. For Watt, a lifelong Stooges fan, this was an honour indeed. As one of the most respected bassists around, Watt took his duty very seriously. He felt that the responsibility was a heavy one and, aware that he was filling some much-loved shoes, wore a Dave Alexander T-shirt for the Coachella gig as a tribute. Watt was actually very sick and feverish on the day of the festival, but didn't let the others know in case they took him off the gig.

There was never a question of James Williamson being asked to rejoin the band. Williamson was now the Vice President of the Technology Standards Group at Sony Electronics Inc. and had not played guitar for many years. It was decided that they would only perform material from the first two albums – nothing from the *Raw Power* era.

Expectations ran extremely high, and the Stooges did not disappoint. Opening with a ferocious blast through 'Loose', straight into 'Down On The Street' followed by '1969' and 'I Wanna Be Your Dog' was a sure-fire way of getting attention. They played brilliantly, Ron hunched over his guitar blasting out harsh and fiery waves of noise, Scott kept it all anchored around his mighty drumming and Mike Watt proved his worth by locking in tight with Scott. Iggy raced about the stage as usual, thoroughly enjoying the experience of being backed by his oldest friends. Just when you thought it couldn't get any better, Steven Mackay popped up, halfway though '1970', just like on the album, to blow like a demon as if the previous thirty-three years hadn't happened. He remained onstage for the rest of the gig, which closed with a powerful and wild 'Fun House'. They played for just under an hour, by which time it was more than clear that the Stooges were once again a vital musical force, even with a set of songs that were more than thirty years old. Iggy and the Stooges determined to play some further gigs later in the year, after the already arranged festival dates Iggy would perform with the Trolls.

On 8 August, the Stooges hit Jones Beach Theatre in New York with the same set as performed at Coachella, but extended beyond 'Fun House' – this song, not played live since 1970, proved to be the real heart of the show. Sounding just like the original, the song was funky and furious, and just like it had been three decades before, it ended in total noise. Whereas 'LA Blues' had been separated from 'Fun House' on the album, in concert the two merged together as the song degenerated and collapsed into chaos. Apart from Coachella, the rest of the gigs would continue after 'LA Blues' with Scott counting in 'Skull Ring', which would literally explode out of the chaos. This was much more powerful than the album track with the addition of Mackay's sax.

The main Stooges set list would remain fixed for the remaining gigs. There were slight variations with the encores. Depending on Iggy's mood and stamina 'Not Right' and 'Little Doll' would sometimes be included, sometimes not. Most shows would also contain a reprise of 'Dog' with Steve blasting his sax all over the song. The usual set was:

'Loose', 'Down On The Street', '1969', 'I Wanna Be Your Dog', 'TV Eye', 'Dirt', 'Real Cool Time', 'No Fun', '1970', 'Funhouse'/'LA Blues Freakout', 'Skull Ring', 'Not Right', 'Little Doll', 'I Wanna Be Your Dog'

After the New York show, Iggy and the Stooges were booked to play Detroit on 14 August. This major homecoming gig was postponed at the very last minute as a massive power blackout hit much of the North East and Mid West. More than fifty million people lost power in a matter of minutes and it took nearly three days for a full service to be restored. Amid lots of jokes about raw power, the Stooges rescheduled the show at the appropriately named DTE Energy Music Theatre for 25 August. It was a thrilling return to Detroit for the band. Fortunately the show was filmed and issued on DVD the following year. After a return to New York, the band crossed the Atlantic to play their first-ever shows in Europe, including a massive gig at the Magny Cours racetrack on 13 September, which delighted the huge number of French fans.

October and November were spent promoting *Skull Ring*, including appearances at the MTV Latin Music Awards and on the David Letterman show – both with Sum 41. To warm up for the Stooges appearance at the *All Tomorrow's Parties* gig on 9 November in Long Beach, Iggy, Ron and Scott went on a mini tour of record and comic stores, answering questions and playing stripped-down songs to adoring crowds. With Scott back to drumming on boxes and only Ron's guitar covering all the music, these were fun and funny gigs. Iggy clearly enjoyed being so close to his fans and it was a generous gesture on the part of the Stooges to play so simply and directly. One such appearance is included as a bonus feature on the Detroit DVD.

Down On The Street
– 2004 Iggy and the Stooges concerts

Iggy Pop – vocals
Ron Asheton – guitar
Scott Asheton – drums
Steven Mackay – saxophone, percussion
Mike Watt – bass

A week of gigs in March took the Stooges to Japan for the first time. Fanatical audiences packed the halls ensuring a tremendous reaction. The Stooges responded by playing some of their finest gigs yet. They were getting more confident with every show and took to ending the main set with three songs from *Skull Ring*. In Tokyo on 22 March a brand new song, 'My Idea Of Fun', was slotted into the encore before 'Dog'. It wasn't played again, which is a pity as it's a great tune. Fortunately the Skydog semi official live album *Telluric Chaos* contains the whole show. It's a slightly muddy recording of a thrilling gig. Iggy screams for air at one point as the capacity Shibuya-Ax hall sweltered. 'Little Doll' was played in Japan but not during the summer shows.

The regular set list ran:

'Loose', 'Down On The Street', '1969', 'I Wanna Be Your Dog', 'TV Eye', 'Dirt', 'Real Cool Time', 'No Fun', '1970', 'Funhouse'/'LA Blues Freakout',

'Skull Ring', 'Dead Rock Star', 'Little Electric Chair', 'Not Right', 'I Wanna Be Your Dog'

Between June and August, Iggy once again played the European festivals including new stops in Istanbul and Novi Sad in Serbia. This was the Stooges first extensive European jaunt and was extremely successful.

They played the same fixed set, with slight variations at the end, depending on the length of their slot. Every gig was greeted with great reviews, positive crowds and a terrific reaction. Despite playing mainly old songs, Iggy and the Stooges thoroughly enjoyed the shows. Mike Watt was gaining in confidence too, no longer quite so worried that he wasn't worthy of a place in the Stooges. A show at Slane Castle in Ireland at the end of August found Iggy meeting Madonna, which indirectly led to his appearance in a Motorola TV commercial with her.

Iggy was the focus of the 5 December edition of the long-running ITV arts programme *The South Bank Show*. Melvyn Bragg interviewed Iggy, although little was revealed, but the show featured some great footage of the Berlin concert on 28 June. Other parts of the fascinating film showed Iggy driving around his old Berlin haunts. But the most revealing part came at the end – as Iggy came offstage, the camera followed the gradual transformation and winding down from wild Iggy Pop to an extremely tired and battered Jim Osterberg. Although plenty of people have commented on the sheer effort of will required to sustain Iggy's onstage antics I doubt that many had actually seen the transformation in quite this way.

2005

ggy and the Stooges issued their first new material since *Skull Ring* on the album *Sunday Nights*, a collection of covers of Junior Kimbrough songs. Amongst artists such as Spiritualized, Mark Lanegan, Jon Spencer's Blues Explosion and Whitey Kirst, Iggy and the Stooges recorded two versions of Kimbrough's 'You Better Run'. Kimbrough played a dark and disturbing take on the blues and was a big favourite of Iggy's. He didn't make a full album until 1991 when he was sixty-two. The first Stooges version of 'You Better Run' is fast and dirty rock but version two is more bluesy, with Mike Watt contributing some superb bass work. Ron's guitar is fabulous on version two as well. Iggy couldn't resist slightly adapting the lyrics to fit in with his persona. Both versions are terrific though. The whole album is well worth hunting down.

Summer 2005 proved to be something of a bumper time for Iggy Pop fans. Virgin issued *A Million In Prizes*, the first comprehensive collection covering Iggy's career, although the double CD was rather heavily weighted in favour of the early days. It sported a tremendously moody cover – Iggy bandaged and menacing – and some mainly accurate details of when and where the songs were recorded and it is a great primer for those just starting off with Iggy. To tempt the long-time fan were just two previously unreleased live

songs from the 1993 Feile Festival. Maybe one day we'll get a proper rarities compilation... At the same time, the Brussels 1999 concert was issued on a no-frills, no-extras DVD.

Also that summer, Easy Action issued the monster box set *Heavy Liquid*. Containing six discs stuffed with 1972–1974 Stooges material, *Heavy Liquid* managed to satisfy the diehards with the inclusion of previously unavailable rehearsals. The set also collected together nearly all the existing 1973 rehearsal recordings in one place for the first time. Live material, in mostly poor sound quality, bulked out the set, which also featured a thick booklet crammed full of pictures and fascinating information. *Heavy Liquid* was trailed by a double CD single called *Extended Play*, which contained a couple of tracks not included on the box set and four songs remixed into 5.1 surround sound for DVD-Audio.

Then, in August, Rhino Records issued the first two Stooges albums. Artfully cleaned up, and with a second disc of bonus material these were extremely welcome releases and served to promote the Stooges current activity as well as reminding everyone where they had started. Iggy hadn't received this much favourable publicity and promotion since *Blah-Blah-Blah* and his profile and regard in the music business had arguably never been higher. Ron and Scott were also finally accorded the respect they deserved and recognition for the Stooges achievements all those years before. Riding this wave of goodwill, the Stooges hit Europe's festivals again.

Down On The Street
– 2005 Iggy and the Stooges summer festivals

Iggy Pop – vocals
Ron Asheton – guitar
Scott Asheton – drums
Steven Mackay – saxophone, percussion
Mike Watt – bass

They played virtually the same set list as before, but with 'Little Doll' reinstated as the first encore number, its jungle rhythm being hammered out by Scott, assisted by Steve on shakers. 'Not Right' was moved to become a second encore number, if needed, after 'Dog'. 'Little Electric Chair' was dropped. '1970' ended with a long trippy guitar improvisation, over which Iggy added some words about 'taking a trip to the mindroom'. This then gave way to 'Fun House'. Ron Asheton was frequently introduced as the Heavyweight Champion of the World on this tour.

The regular set list was:

'Loose', 'Down On The Street', '1969', 'I Wanna Be Your Dog', 'TV Eye', 'Dirt', 'Real Cool Time', 'No Fun', '1970', 'Funhouse'/'LA Blues Freakout', 'Skull Ring', 'Dead Rock Star', 'Little Doll', 'I Wanna Be Your Dog', 'Not Right'

Despite most of the set comprising thirty-five-year-old songs, the Stooges received rapturous reaction wherever they went. These shows represented the first chance much of Europe had ever had to witness the Stooges live.

Mike Watt writes entertainingly in his online diary of the fun the band had at all these concerts, plus the heavy weight of responsibility that he still felt to get the bass parts absolutely right. He felt the strength of Iggy's angry glare if he deviated from the required pattern, which implies that the band were far more strongly rehearsed that many would have thought. Mike's diaries give a fascinating insight into the life of a working musician and can be found at www.hootpage.com.

The gig at the Blue Balls Festival in Switzerland fell foul of Lucerne laws. The usual maximum volume limit of 93 decibels had been raised to 100 for the festival, but a hearing in December 2005 found that the Stooges measured an ear-splitting 102.5 decibels and the organisers of the festival were fined.

The summer gigs were sadly interrupted by the sudden passing of Art Collins at the age of just fifty-two. Art's death, at his home in Pine Bush, New York on 27 July, was caused by cardiac arrhythmia. With no previous history of heart problems it was a terrible shock to his family and friends. He had been Iggy's manager since 1985 and Art's widow Nikki commented warmly on their 'brother-like relationship'.

Iggy was obviously devastated but he released a statement: 'Art was a big sweetheart. He was a marshmallow. This very down-to-earth guy was a kind of tonic for everyone he met, and he really loved rock and roll. He was immensely proud of his tenure with Atlantic Records, his work with the Rolling Stones, and I hope with me as well. He was my best friend.'

Although the Stooges weren't performing, Jim decided not to attend the 30 July funeral of his best friend, allowing Art's family to grieve in private.

The rest of the gigs continued with tour manager Henry McGroggan, another Iggy veteran, assuming managerial responsibility as well as running the tour. Concerts in Belgium, France and Spain during August culminated at the legendary Reading Festival in the UK on 28 August. The Stooges were in the middle of the list of acts – below Incubus, Marilyn Manson and headliners Iron Maiden, though many reviewers commented on Iggy and the Stooges' show-stopping performance and wondered why they weren't the headline act.

After just one day off, the *Fun House* show at Hammersmith on 30 August saw the Stooges opening the *Don't Look Back* season of gigs in which bands/artists would play a whole album from start to finish. For this gig only, the set comprised the complete *Fun House* album, kicking off with a throbbing 'Down On The Street' and rattling through the rest of the album, in order. 'Dirt' was a real highlight, with Ron's coruscating guitar work on this well worthy of a mention. 'Fun House' itself degenerated into the crazy improv noise of 'LA Blues', which then fell headlong into 'Skull Ring' and that was it. They played so intensely and so fast that the main set was over inside thirty minutes.

The sound in the Apollo was powerfully oppressive, with Ron's guitar occasionally overpowered by the punch of Mike Watt's bass, which hit you hard in the gut. Scott played a blinding gig, his drumming was demonstrably more than just simple beat keeping; he was almost leading the songs. And Iggy's vocals were terrifically strong. Despite the limp he's picked up over recent years, his dancing was ferociously wild, exhorting the band and the audience to get behind him and push him further.

After a very short break, Iggy came running back – 'You know we know some more songs, don't ya?' – and they hurtled through a bunch of stuff from the first album ('1969', 'Dog', 'Real Cool Time'), with Iggy calling loads of people out of the crowd onto the stage. It was absolute mayhem – fans commented on the heavy-handed bouncers and reported broken limbs amongst the more common cuts and bruises. The crowd stayed up there for 'No Fun' too, grabbing Iggy and trying to sing along. London's *Evening Standard* said, 'The crowd eagerly accepted Pop's invitation to invade the stage during the first encore. Yet for all the ensuing anarchy, there was order and the Stooges completed "No Fun" and "Real Cool Time" without missing a note or losing stage equipment.' The Stooges encored with 'Little Doll' and 'Not Right'. That ended the printed set list, so Ron had unhooked his guitar and was already leaving the stage when Iggy shouted for 'Dead Rock Star'. This became the final number.

Iggy brought the band back out to take the applause at the end, introduced them all (Ron was now the 'undisputed heavyweight champion of the world', apparently), then said in a threatening voice, 'I don't need to tell you who I am... but I know who you are...' Whatever that might mean...

With Don Gallucci watching fondly ('They nailed it,' he was heard to say) and the MC5's *Kick Out The Jams* blasting from the speakers as exit music, for a minute you could imagine it really was 1970.

One more show, headlining at Seattle's Bumbershoot Festival on 5 September ended a massively successful summer of gigging. After a well-earned rest, the Stooges returned to the stage for a couple of Brazilian gigs in November. In early 2006, they headed to Australasia to headline the *Big Day Out* travelling festival in the company of the White Stripes and Franz Ferdinand amongst others, which kicked off on 20 January in Auckland and crashed to a halt in Perth, Western Australia on 5 February. Iggy hadn't played Australasia for many years so this visit was especially pleasing for his massive following in the Antipodes. One middle-aged fan in Sydney was delighted to discover that the teenagers were shouting their support for the Stooges throughout the day, even during the sets from the other bands. The strength of feeling favouring the Stooges was enormous.

With a new album from the Stooges, and a biopic starring Elijah Wood planned for 2006, it is clear that the story is far from over.

Conclusion

Jim Osterberg lives quietly and sedately in Miami Beach. His only vice these days is a glass of red wine in the evenings. Iggy hasn't touched heroin since the early 1980s, and he finally stopped smoking dope and snorting coke when he moved out of New York in 1998; before that, his usage had been very intermittent. He even stopped smoking cigarettes around the same time. Since 1986, he has extensively worked out before each tour to maintain the incredible level of fitness that each gig requires. Iggy, like his contemporary Lou Reed, has taken up Tai Chi and practises for about forty minutes most days. To keep his energy up, he eats a lot of steak, likes his bacon and eggs for breakfast and drinks a lot of Cuban coffee – black and strong. In 2004, he joked that he was finally heeding his mother's advice: '"Eat three square meals and early to bed, early to rise, makes a man healthy, wealthy and wise." It works!'

His current companion is Nina Alu, half Nigerian and half Irish, buxom, voluptuous and half his age. She packed in her degree course in broadcast journalism at Howard University to live with Jim. She effectively looks after him, doing all the stuff that he doesn't seem capable of. Nina is happy to travel with Iggy on the road, and Iggy needs Nina to calm him down after a gig. In *Rolling Stone* in 2003, Nina said, 'I love Iggy Pop, and I respect him, but I don't think I could live with him. But Jim, Jim is sweet and peaceful and romantic… sometimes I'll catch him just looking at the trees and birds. It's endearing and almost childlike, just the way he looks at the world with those big eyes.' For his part, Jim says he absolutely loves Nina. He seems calm and happy.

In 2004, Iggy became a grandfather, although sadly his relationship with Eric seems to have worsened during recent years. At the end of the year, Iggy commented to *The Guardian*'s Miranda Sawyer that he still hadn't seen the baby.

The Stooges are recording their first new album in well over thirty years. Iggy has claimed that he wants to make one more great album before he's sixty, then he might retire. It's to be hoped that he's dissuaded from this plan. On the strength of recent records and concerts, one more great album could easily be followed by another and another. If he really does step down, what a ride it's been. Few musicians can claim to have changed the course of modern music so dramatically as Iggy Pop. Without him the last thirty-five years would have been so much duller.

As Iggy Pop approaches his sixtieth birthday, it appears that the Jekyll and Hyde relationship between Jim and Iggy is at last fully under control. The astonishing stage character and rock performer, Iggy Pop, shows little sign of slowing down. Off stage, Jim Osterberg is contented and totally in control. In 1998, Iggy reflected on the rocky relationship between Iggy and Jim and noted one vital difference. 'When I go to the bank, very definitely Osterberg, but the guy that makes the money, that's Iggy.' It's an important distinction: Jim now views Iggy as a job, Iggy is what Jim does to earn money. Just as other people might build cars or work in a shop, Jim works onstage, as Iggy Pop.

The last word belongs to Iggy. 'I'm flexible and available, basically, if the situation is right,' he said recently. 'I have one set with the Stooges... and I have another set that has different material with the Trolls.' Then he added, with that childlike grin and infectious foghorn laugh, 'And I can also do acoustic – maybe if you're having a birthday party?'

Discography

For clarity and simplicity, this listing details Iggy's major UK and US releases, plus notable other albums and singles which contain songs that are otherwise unavailable. I've tried to make sure that every officially released song is included somewhere.

If you need more information, the Internet is the best place for you. There are some invaluable resources there, which have succeeded in listing the minutiae of the huge variety of Iggy related releases. One of the very best is the exhaustive set of discographies to be found at http://home.online.no/~egon/iggy.htm Quite superb, with loads of information regarding everything including rare promo singles, imports and loads more. The sites www.iggypop.org and www.iggy-pop.com also contain valuable discographies that are well worth consulting.

Albums

THE STOOGES – The Stooges
Producer: John Cale
Remixed by: Iggy and Jac Holzman
Recorded: 19–21 June 1969, Hit Factory (later the Record Plant)
Released: August 1969 (US) Elektra EKS74051; September 1969 (UK) Elektra EKS74051
Musicians: Iggy Stooge, Dave Alexander, Ron Asheton, Scott Asheton
Tracks: 1969 / I Wanna Be Your Dog / We Will Fall / No Fun / Real Cool Time / Ann / Not Right / Little Doll

FUN HOUSE – The Stooges
Producer: Don Gallucci
Recorded: 10–24 May 1970, Elektra Sound Recorders, Los Angeles
Released: August 1970 (US) Elektra EKS74071; December 1970 (UK) Elektra EKS74071
Musicians: Iggy Pop, Dave Alexander, Ron Asheton, Scott Asheton, Steve Mackay
Tracks: Down On The Street / Loose / TV Eye / Dirt / 1970 / Fun House / L.A. Blues

RAW POWER – Iggy and the Stooges
Producer: Iggy Pop
Mixed by: David Bowie and Iggy Pop
Recorded: 10 September–6 October 1972, CBS Studios, London
Released: May 1973 (US) Columbia PC32111; June 1973 (UK) CBS-Embassy 65586
1996 remix: CBS CDCBS 32083 and Columbia COL485176–2
Musicians: Iggy Pop, Ron Asheton, Scott Asheton, James Williamson.
Tracks: Search And Destroy / Gimme Danger / Your Pretty Face Is Going To Hell (originally titled Hard To Beat) / Penetration / Raw Power / I Need Somebody / Shake Appeal / Death Trip

METALLIC KO – Iggy and the Stooges
Recorded live at the Michigan Palace: Side One 6 October 1973; Side Two 9 February 1974
Released: 1976 LP Skydog SGIS 008 (France)
Musicians: Iggy Pop, Ron Asheton, Scott Asheton, Scott Thurston, James Williamson
Tracks: Raw Power / Head On / Gimme Danger / Rich Bitch / Cock In My Pocket / Louie Louie
In 1988 *Metallic KO* received a welcome overhaul and was reissued as *Metallic 2xKO* (Skydog SKI 62232–1 (France) and Skydog SKI 622331 (UK))

Tracks: Raw Power / Gimme Danger / Search And Destroy / Heavy Liquid / I Wanna Be Your Dog (spoken) / Open Up And Bleed / I Got Nothing-I Got Shit / Rich Bitch / Cock In My Pocket / Louie Louie

In 1998 all the known tracks from these two gigs were compiled onto a double CD – the collection reverted to the original title – *Metallic KO* (Jungle/Freud CD 70)

Tracks (9 February 1974): Heavy Liquid / I Got Nothing / Rich Bitch plus a snippet of Baby, Where Did Our Love Go? / Gimme Danger / Cock In My Pocket / Louie Louie

Tracks (6 October 1973): Raw Power / Head On / Gimme Danger / Search And Destroy / Heavy Liquid / I Wanna Be Your Dog (spoken) / Open Up And Bleed

KILL CITY – Iggy Pop and James Williamson

Producer: James Williamson

Recorded: Spring 1975, Jimmy Webb's Home studio, Los Angeles (remixed and completed during Summer 1977)

Released: November 1977 (US) Bomp BLP 4001; February 1978 (UK) Radar RAD2

Reissued on 10" vinyl (Bomp BLP 4042/10) in February 1995 with the instrumental tracks missing

Musicians: Iggy Pop, 'Strait' James Williamson, with Brian Glascock, John Harden, Hunt Sales, Tony 'Fox' Sales, Scott 'Troy' Thurston, Steve Tranio, and Gayna (from the Count Dracula Society)

Tracks: Kill City / Sell Your Love / Beyond The Law / I Got Nothin' / Johanna / Night Theme / Night Theme (reprise) / Consolation Prizes / No Sense Of Crime / Lucky Monkeys / Master Charge

THE IDIOT – Iggy Pop

Producer: David Bowie

Recorded: Summer 1976, Chateau d'Herouville, France; Musicland, Munich and Hansa Tonstudio 2, Berlin

Released: March 1977 RCA APL1–2275 (US); RCA PL-12275 (UK)

Musicians: Iggy Pop, Carlos Alomar, David Bowie, Dennis Davis, Michel Marie, George Murray, Phil Palmer, Michel Santageli, Laurent Thibault

Tracks: Sister Midnight / Nightclubbing / Funtime / Baby / China Girl / Dum Dum Boys / Tiny Girls / Mass Production

LUST FOR LIFE – Iggy Pop

Producer: Bewlay Brothers

Recorded: June 1977, Hansa Tonstudio, Berlin

Released: September 1977 RCA APL1–2488 (US); RCA PL12488 (UK)

Musicians: Iggy Pop, Carlos Alomar, David Bowie, Ricky Gardiner, Hunt Sales, Tony Sales

Tracks: Lust For Life / Sixteen / Some Weird Sin / The Passenger / Tonight / Success / Turn Blue / Neighborhood Threat / Fall In Love With Me

TV EYE 1977 LIVE – Iggy Pop

Producers: Iggy Pop, David Bowie

Mixed: Hansa Tonstudio, Berlin

Recorded: 21–22 March 1977, Agora Ballroom, Cleveland; 28 March 1977, Aragon, Chicago; 26 October 1977, Uptown Theatre, Kansas City

Released: May 1978 RCA PL 12796 (UK); RCA APL1–2796 (US)

Musicians: Iggy Pop, David Bowie, Ricky Gardiner, Hunt Sales, Tony Sales (March 1977); Iggy Pop, Stacey Heydon, Hunt Sales, Tony Sales, Scott Thurston (October 1977)

Tracks: TV Eye / Funtime / Sixteen / I Got A Right / Lust For Life / Dirt / Nightclubbing / I Wanna Be Your Dog

NEW VALUES – Iggy Pop

Producer: James Williamson

Recorded: January 1979, Paramount Studios, Hollywood

Released: April 1979 (UK) Arista SPART 1092; October 1979 (US) Arista AB4237
Musicians: Iggy Pop, David Brock, Jackie Clarke, John Harden, Klaus Kruger, Earl Shackelford, Scott Thurston, James Williamson and the Alfono Sisters
Tracks: Tell Me A Story / New Values / Girls / I'm Bored / Don't Look Down / The Endless Sea / Five Foot One / How Do Ya Fix A Broken Part / Angel / Curiosity / African Man / Billy Is A Runaway
Bonus tracks on CD reissue: Chains / Pretty Flamingo

SOLDIER – Iggy Pop
Producer: Pat Moran
Recorded: August 1979, Rockfield Studios, Wales
Released: January 1980 (UK) Arista SPART 1117; February 1980 (US) Arista B4259
Musicians: Iggy Pop, Barry Andrews, Ivan Kral, Klaus Kruger, Glen Matlock, Steve New, plus Simple Minds and David Bowie
Tracks: Loco Mosquito / Ambition / Take Care Of Me / Get Up And Get Out / Play It Safe / I'm A Conservative / Dog Food / I Need More / Knocking 'em Down (In The City) / Mr. Dynamite / I Snub You
Bonus tracks on CD reissue: Low Life / Drop A Hook

PARTY – Iggy Pop
Producers: Thom Panunzio, Tommy Boyce
Recorded: August and October 1980, Record Plant, New York
Released: June 1981 (UK) Arista SPART1158; September 1981 (US) Arista 4278
Musicians: Iggy Pop, Douglas Bowne, Rob DuPrey, Ivan Kral, Michael Page
Tracks: Pleasure / Rock And Roll Party / Eggs On Plate / Sincerity / Houston Is Hot Tonight / Pumpin' For Jill / Happy Man / Bang Bang / Sea Of Love / Time Won't Let Me
Bonus tracks on CD reissue: Speak To Me / One For My Baby

ZOMBIE BIRDHOUSE – Iggy Pop
Producer: Chris Stein
Recorded: May 1982, Blank Tape Studios, New York
Released: September 1982, Animal CHR1399 (UK): Animal APE6000 (US)
Musicians: Iggy Pop, Clem Burke, Rob DuPrey, Chris Stein
Tracks: Run Like A Villain / The Villagers / Angry Hills / Life Of Work / The Ballad Of Cookie McBride / Ordinary Bummer / Eat Or Be Eaten / Bulldozer / Platonic / The Horse Song / Watching The News / Street Crazies
Bonus track on CD reissue: Pain And Suffering
Reissued in 2003 with a bonus disc of live recordings from 7 November 2002 gig in Minneapolis. This was taken from an unofficial recording called *A Zombie On Stage* and retains the dodgy bootleg quality. Good, frantic performances though.
Tracks: The Villagers / Fall In Love With Me / Ordinary Bummer / The Horse Song / Angry Hills / Bulldozer / The Ballad Of Cookie McBride / Platonic / Life Of Work / Kill City / Loose / Search And Destroy / Run Like A Villain / Bang Bang / Your Pretty Face... / Eat Or Be Eaten / Sixteen / Street Crazies

BLAH-BLAH-BLAH – Iggy Pop
Producers: David Bowie and David Richards
Recorded: Spring 1986, Mountain Studios, Montreux (some original tracks recorded at Olivier Ferrand's Studios, LA)
Released: October 1986, A&M AMA5145 (UK); SP5145 (US)
Musicians: Iggy Pop, Kevin Armstrong, David Bowie, Steve Jones, Erdal Kizilcay
Tracks: Real Wild Child (Wild One) / Baby, It Can't Fall / Shades / Fire Girl / Isolation / Cry For Love / Blah-Blah-Blah / Hideaway / Winners And Losers / Little Miss Emperor (CD/ cassette bonus track)

INSTINCT – Iggy Pop
Producer: Bill Laswell
Recorded: April 1988, Sorcerer Sound & BC Studio, New York
Released: June 1988, A&M AMA5198 (UK); SP5158 (US)
Musicians: Iggy Pop, Seamus Beaghen, Leigh Foxx, Paul Garisto, Steve Jones
Tracks: Cold Metal / High On You / Strong Girl / Tom Tom / Easy Rider / Power And
Freedom / Lowdown / Instinct / Tuff Baby / Squarehead

BRICK BY BRICK – Iggy Pop
Producer: Don Was
Recorded: 15 February–23 March 1990, Oceanway & Hollywood Sound, LA
Released: July 1990 Virgin CDVUS19
Musicians: Iggy Pop, Kenny Aronoff, Chuck Domanico, Charley Drayton, John Hiatt, David
Lindley, Duff McKagan, David McMurray, Jamie Muhoberac, Kate Pierson, Slash, Waddy
Watchel, with Sir Harry Bowens, Sweet Pea Atkinson, Donald Ray Mitchell, Alex Brown, Ed
Cherney, and the Leeching Delinquents
Tracks: Home / Main Street Eyes / I Won't Crap Out / Candy / Butt Town / The Undefeated /
Moonlight Lady / Something Wild / Neon Forest / Starry Night / Pussy Power / My Baby
Wants To Rock And Roll / Brick By Brick / Livin' On The Edge Of The Night

AMERICAN CAESAR – Iggy Pop
Producer: Malcolm Burn
Recorded: Spring 1993, Kingsway Studios, New Orleans
Released: September 1993 Virgin CDVUS64
Musicians: Iggy Pop, Hal Cragin, Larry Mullins, Eric Schermerhorn, plus Malcolm Burn, Bill
Dillon, Lisa Germano, Daryl Johnson, Jay Joyce, Katell Keinig and Henry Rollins
Tracks: Character / Wild America / Mixin' The Colors / Jealousy / Hate / It's Our Love / Plastic
And Concrete / Fuckin' Alone / Highway Song / Beside You / Sickness / Boogie Boy /
Perforation Problems / Social Life / Louie Louie / Caesar / Girls Of N.Y.

NAUGHTY LITTLE DOGGIE – Iggy Pop
Producers: Thom Wilson, Iggy Pop
Recorded: Autumn 1995, Track Records, LA
Released: February 1996, Virgin CDVUS102
Musicians: Iggy Pop and the Fuck Ups – Iggy Pop, Larry Contrary, Eric Mesmerize,
Hal Wonderful, The Mighty Whitey
Tracks: I Wanna Live / Pussy Walk / Innocent World / Knucklehead / To Belong / Keep On
Believing / Outta My Head / Shoeshine Girl / Heart Is Saved / Look Away

BEST OF... LIVE – Iggy Pop
Recorded live between 1977 and 1988 according to the sleeve, but it's clear that a number
of tracks actually date from 1991.
Released: July 1996 MCA MCD84021-2
Tracks: Raw Power / High On You / Nightclubbing / China Girl / Blah-Blah-Blah / No Fun /
1969 / TV Eye / Easy Rider / I Need Somebody / Five Foot One / I Wanna Be Your Dog / The
Passenger / I Got A Right / Some Weird Sin / Real Wild Child / Lust For life / Search And Destroy
Quite how MCA came to issue this collection is unclear. The songs are a mixture of tracks
from the various archive releases on Revenge (see below). Surprisingly those tracks listed as
being from the St Andrew Hall, Detroit in 1988 are actually from the bootleg recorded in
Berlin in 1991. The reason for the mislabelling of the source tape is probably down to the
fact that anything post-1990 should have been Virgin copyright, so by claiming to pre-date
the Virgin contract somehow copyright problems had been averted. No attempt had been
made to disguise the origin of the 1991 songs – Whitey even gets his name called in 'Raw
Power'! The mix of sources creates an uneasy balance of songs, from the slightly muddy

1977 Bowie tour tracks to the harshly percussive Boston Channel songs, but it's still a worthwhile release, collecting some powerful performances and good quality recordings.

AVENUE B – Iggy Pop

Producer: Don Was
Recorded: 1998–1999, 262 Mott Street NYC; Teatro Oxnard; the Theatre; Studio 12A Shacklyn Studios
Released: September 1999, Virgin CDVUS163
Musicians: Iggy Pop, Hal Cragin, Whitey Kirst, Pete Marshall, Larry Mullins, with Billy Martin, John Medeski, Chris Wood, and Lenny Castro, Michael Chaves, David Mansfield, Andrew Scheps, Don Was
Tracks: No Shit / Nazi Girlfriend / Avenue B / Miss Argentina / Afraid To Get Close / Shakin' All Over / Long Distance / Corruption / She Called Me Daddy / I Felt The Luxury / Espanol / Motorcycle / Facade

BEAT 'EM UP – Iggy Pop

Producer: Iggy Pop
Recorded: Winter 2000–2001, Hit Factory Criteria Studios, Miami Beach, Florida
Released: June 2001, Virgin CDVUS200
Musicians: Iggy Pop, Danny Kadar, Alex Kirst, Whitey Kirst, Pete Marshall, Lloyd 'Moose Man' Roberts
Tracks: Mask / L.O.S.T. / Howl / Football / Savior / Beat 'Em Up / Talking Snake / The Jerk / Death Is Certain / Go For The Throat / Weasels / Drink New Blood / It's All Shit / Ugliness / V.I.P. / Sterility (hidden track)

SKULL RING

Producer: Iggy Pop
Recorded: November 2002 and Spring 2003, Hit Factory Criteria Studios, Miami Beach, Florida
Released: September 2003, Virgin 724359162027
Musicians: Iggy and the Stooges / Iggy and the Trolls / Iggy and Green Day / Iggy and Sum 41 / Iggy and Peaches / Iggy Pop (solo)
Tracks: Little Electric Chair / Perverts In The Sun / Skull Ring / Superbabe / Loser / Private Hell / Little Know It All / Whatever / Dead Rock Star / Rock Show / Here Comes The Summer / Motor Inn / Inferiority Complex / Supermarket / Till Wrong Feels Right / Blood On Your Cool / Nervous Exhaustion (hidden track)

Archive Releases

Some of these albums are only semi-official. All have been available in the shops at some point, but many of these albums are sourced from bootlegs, and have been issued on an assortment of one-off labels, then transported all around the world. Most are now out of stock, but they contain so many good tracks that it is worth tracking down at least a selection of these albums. I have also included a number of singles and EPs, which complement the archival albums.
NB They have been listed in chronological order of *recording*, for ease of reference. This order therefore does not correspond with the date of release.

JUMPIN' WITH THE IGUANAS – The Iguanas

1995 – LP Fuller Blossom 36024036
The Iguanas' single plus assorted demos. Most of these tracks, plus others including 'Pipe Line' and 'If I Had A Hammer', are also available on the LP Norton Records ED251. Quite fun with bags of naive 1960s charm, but no obvious sign of Iggy as he's firmly behind the drums on all songs.
Tracks: Mona / I Don't Know Why / Again And Again / Twist And Shout / California Sun /

Slow Down / I Feel Fine / Blue Moon / Things We Said Today / Louie Louie / Wild Weekend / Tell Me / Summertime / Outer Limits / Johnny B. Goode / Perfidia / Travelin' Man / Louie Louie / Wild Weekend / Surfin' Bird / Walk Don't Run / Tequila

WHAT YOU GONNA DO – Iggy and the Stooges

1988 – 12' single Revenge CAX5 (limited edition of 3,000 copies on coloured vinyl)
Tracks: What You Gonna Do (live – claims to be from 22 September 1968, Union Ballroom, University of Michigan, Ann Arbor) / Gimme Danger (live 9 September 1973, Whisky A Go Go, Los Angeles)

NB A number of records were issued in the late 1980s claiming to contain the original mixes of the first two Stooges records. Usually called *Raw Mixes*, and often found on picture discs, these records contained nothing but poor quality transfers of the first two albums. There was nothing rare or different about these so-called *Raw Mixes*.

DECLARATION OF WAR: The Best Of The Fun House Sessions
– The Stooges
2000 – LP only Rhino Handmade RHM2 7707
Limited-edition vinyl collection of some of the tracks from the *Fun House* box.

LIVE 1971 AND EARLY RARITIES – The Stooges

1991 – CD Starfighter BM001
Compilation of early live tracks.
Tracks: I Got A Right / You Don't want My Name / I Need You / Who Do You Love / See Me Dancing / That's What I Like
These are tentative titles from bootleggers (e.g. – 'I Need You' should probably be called 'Fresh Rag'). The songs were recorded in May 1971 in St Louis. Possibly the worst quality live recording I've ever heard – if you can listen to this without getting a splitting headache I'd be amazed.
Bonus Tracks: TV Eye / 1970 (from Midsummer Pop TV transmission, Crosley Field Festival 13 June 1970).
Bonus Tracks: Ron's Jam (instr.) / What You Gonna Do
The origin of these tracks is unclear. They crop up on various reissues claiming to be from Wamplers Lake Festival 1968, or more likely 1969, or sometimes from the 22 September 1968 gig at the Union Ballroom at which the Stooges got signed. Whatever their origin, both tracks are of poor quality, and simply show the Stooges jamming and Iggy hollering.

I'M SICK OF YOU – Iggy and the Stooges

1978 – LP Line LLP 5126
The first appearance on album of the pre-*Raw Power* recordings, plus a couple of *Kill City* tunes to fill the album. Both *Kill City* songs claim to be alternative takes but they sound identical to me.
Tracks: I'm Sick Of You / Tight Pants / I Got A Right / Johanna / Consolation Prizes / The Scene Of The Crime / Gimme Some Skin / Jesus Loves The Stooges

ROUGH POWER – Iggy and the Stooges

1995 – CD Bomp BCD4049
A collection of the WABX broadcast of the early *Raw Power* mixes, plus other early mixes of the same songs. Quality is indeed rough at times.

RUBBER LEGS – The Stooges

1987 – LP Fan Club FC 037 / New Rose NR 330
First official appearance of the spring 1973 rehearsal often termed the CBS / New York session.
Tracks: Rubber Legs / Open Up And Bleed / Johanna / Cock In My Pocket / Head On / Cry For Me
The album contained a free single with two live tracks from the American Theatre in St Louis, 18 August 1973 – Gimme Danger / I Need Somebody

I GOT A RIGHT – Iggy and the Stooges
1987 – 7' coloured vinyl single Revenge SS1
Tracks: I Got A Right / No Sense Of Crime

JOHANNA – Iggy and the Stooges
1988 – 7' single Revenge SS6 (limited edition of 2,000 copies on green vinyl)
Tracks: Johanna / Purple Haze

DEATH TRIP – Iggy and the Stooges
1988 – LP Revenge MIG6
Different versions of the *Rubber Legs* tracks, plus Williamson / Pop rehearsals.
Tracks: Death Trip / Head On / Rubber Legs / Radio Ad. / Raw Power / I'm A Man / Ballad Of Hollis Brown
NB 'Death Trip' is simply a poor copy/mix of the *Raw Power* version. It crops up again and again on these albums.

PURE LUST – Iggy Pop and the Stooges
1988 – 12' single Revenge CAX1 (limited edition of 3,000 on coloured vinyl)
Tracks: I Got A Right / Johanna / Gimme Some Skin / I Got Nothing

RAW POWER – Iggy and the Stooges
1988 – 12' single Revenge CAX2 (limited edition of 3,000)
Duplicates some tracks from *Death Trip* but includes otherwise unavailable Williamson / Pop rehearsals.
Tracks: Raw Power / Head On / Purple Haze / Waiting For The Man / Radio Ad

OPEN UP AND BLEED – Iggy and the Stooges
1989 – CD Revenge HTM16
CD compilation of the Revenge vinyl only *Death Trip* and *Raw Power* EPs plus 'Open Up And Bleed' from the Whisky A Go Go in September 1973.

MY GIRL HATES MY HEROIN – The Stooges
1989 – CD Revenge MIG28
Further 1973 recordings issued for the first time.
Tracks: My Girl Hates My Heroin / Cock In My Pocket / Head On / Death Trip / Hey Baby / Search And Destroy / Raw Power / Gimme Danger / Open Up And Bleed / Jesus Loves The Stooges (instrumental) / How It Hurts
Apart from 'Death Trip', the other *Raw Power* songs are new recordings from rehearsals. 'Open Up…' is the same as on *Rubber Legs*, but 'Head On' and 'Cock In My Pocket' are different.

TILL THE END OF THE NIGHT – The Stooges
1991 – CD Revenge MIG42
Further 1973 recordings issued for the first time.
Tracks: Johanna / She Creatures Of The Hollywood Hills / Open Up And Bleed / Born In A Trailer / Till The End Of The Night / Wet My Bed (live)
'Johanna' and 'Open Up…' are different from those on *Rubber Legs*.

OPEN UP AND BLEED – Iggy and the Stooges
1995 – CD Bomp BCD4051
Collection of the 'CBS New York' session, plus live tracks from the Latin Casino in Baltimore.
Tracks: Rubber Legs / Open Up And Bleed / Johanna / Cock In My Pocket / Head On / Cry For Me / Rich Bitch / Wet My Bed / I Got Nothing / Heavy Liquid / She Creatures Of The Hollywood Hills / Rubber Legs.

YOUR PRETTY FACE IS GOING TO HELL
– Iggy and the Stooges
1995 – CD Golden Years GY008
Collection of 1972–1973 rehearsal tracks: Head On / Death Trip / I Got A Right / Hard To Beat / Cock In My Pocket / Rubber Legs / Johanna / Pin Point Eyes / Open Up And Bleed / Raw Power

Retitled *Studio Sessions* and issued with a new cover in 1996 on CD Pilot 008. 'Pin Point Eyes' is exactly the same recording as 'Cry For Me' and this retitling simply demonstrates how hard it is to pin down accurate information regarding these songs – not even the title is certain!

Reissued as *Your Pretty Face...* with a new cover, plus the 1973 radio advert, 'Tight Pants' and 'Scene Of The Crime' as bonus tracks, in 1998 on Snapper Music 156002.

Reissued again, minus the bonus tracks and confusingly retitled *Raw Power*, in 2000 on Neon NE34544.

HEAD ON – Iggy Pop and the Stooges
1997 – CD Pilot 142
Same tracks as on *Your Pretty Face...* plus a bonus disc of Iggy and the Stooges live at the Academy of Music, 31 December 1973. Which is the same live set as on *Double Danger*.

YEAR OF THE IGUANA – Iggy and the Stooges
1997 – CD Bomp BCD4063
Compiled from various Bomp releases, but includes the first appearance of 'Wild Love'.

HEAD ON – Iggy Pop and the Stooges
1997 – 2CD SMDCD142
Collection of 1972–1973 rehearsal tracks: Radio Ad / Head On / Death Trip / I Got A Right / Hard To Beat / Cock In My Pocket / Rubber Legs / Johanna / Pin Point Eyes / Open Up And Bleed / Raw Power / She Creatures Of Hollywood Hills / My Girl Hates My Heroin / Hey Baby / Jesus Loves The Stooges / How It Hurts / Born In A Trailer / Wet My Bed / Rich Bitch / I Got Nothing / Not Right
NB as with 'Death Trip', 'Not Right' is the original track from *The Stooges*, but a poor quality copy.

Until the *Heavy Liquid* box set this collection offered the best value and the most comprehensive set of rehearsal tracks.

SEARCH AND DESTROY – Iggy and the Stooges
1999 – CD Cleopatra CLP0556-2
Collection of 1972–1973 rehearsal tracks, plus Williamson / Pop rehearsals: Search And Destroy / Raw Power / Gimme Danger / Open Up And Bleed / How It Hurts / Death Trip / Rubber Legs / I'm A Man / Johanna / I'm So Glad / Cock In My Pocket / She Creatures Of The Hollywood Hills / Born In A Trailer / Till The End Of The Night

BACK TO THE NOISE – Iggy and the Stooges
2003 – CD Revenge 5931602
Collection of 1973 rehearsal tracks with a collection of rough-sounding, previously released live tracks on the second disc.

LIVE AT THE WHISKY A GOGO – Iggy and the Stooges
1988 – CD Revenge WM321
Recorded: 16 September 1973, Whisky A Go Go, Los Angeles
Tracks: Raw Power / Head On / Search And Destroy / I Need Somebody / Heavy Liquid / She Creatures Of The Hollywood Hills / Open Up And Bleed / Gimme Danger
One of the best live recordings of the Stooges. The complete show (although 'Gimme Danger', not available on the vinyl version, was added to the end of the set when it was

actually played third) from a very listenable audience tape.
Reissued in 1998 on Snapper Music SMMCD528 as *Live In LA*, with an alternative
version of 'Heavy Liquid' from another Whisky gig as a bonus.

CALIFORNIA BLEEDING – Iggy and the Stooges
1997 – CD Bomp BCD4069
Collection of live tracks from the Whisky gigs in September 1973 (none from the 16th) plus
rough-quality tracks from Bimbos club in 1974. Includes the only known Stooges live version
of 'Johanna'.
Tracks: Search And Destroy / Need Somebody / Open Up And Bleed / Johanna / Wet My
Bed / I Got Nothing / Head On / She Creatures Of The Hollywood Hills / Heavy Liquid

MICHIGAN PALACE – Iggy and the Stooges
2000 – CD Bomp BCD4079
Recorded at the Michigan Palace on 6 October 1973, this is the same as the second disc in
the current version of *Metallic KO*. Claims to have been remastered but it sounds the same to
me. If you have the double CD *Metallic KO* then this is superfluous.

DOUBLE DANGER – Iggy and the Stooges
2000 – Double CD Bomp BCD4076 (a vinyl version has fewer tracks)
Disc One recorded at the Latin Casino, Baltimore, November 1973.
Tracks: Raw Power / Head On / Gimme Danger / Rich Bitch / Wet My Bed / I Got Nothing /
Search And Destroy / Cock In My Pocket / I Need Somebody / Heavy Liquid / Open Up And
Bleed
Disc Two recorded at the Academy of Music, New York, 31 December 1973.
Tracks: Raw Power / Rich Bitch / Wet My Bed / I Got Nothing / Cock In My Pocket / Search
And Destroy / Gimme Danger / Heavy Liquid
Mastered from bootleg audience tapes, this is two discs of pretty poor quality. For hard-core
collectors only.

GIMME DANGER – Iggy and the Stooges
1988 – 12" single on coloured vinyl Revenge CAX 3
Tracks: Gimme Danger / Open Up And Bleed / Heavy Liquid/(I Got) Nothing / Dynamite Boogie
Basically a reissue of the long-deleted 1978 Skydog single *(I Got) Nothing* (SGIS 12), which
contained these three tracks from the final Stooges gig, plus the Williamson-Pop jam
'Dynamite Boogie'.

PENETRATION – Iggy Pop and the Stooges
2004 – CD Music Club MCCD565
A weird mixture of most of *Kill City* plus a number of 1972–1973 rehearsal tracks.

WILD ANIMAL / SUCK ON THIS! – Iggy Pop
1993 – Revenge MIG50 (both titles seem to carry the same catalogue number)
Recorded: 21 March 1977, Agora Ballroom, Cleveland.
Tracks: Raw Power / 1969 / Turn Blue / Sister Midnight / I Need Somebody / Search And
Destroy / TV Eye / Dirt / Funtime / Gimme Danger / No Fun / I Wanna Be Your Dog
Originally a high-quality bootleg, this Revenge release manages to jumble the regular set
order, but it's still an excellent reminder of the Bowie tour.
Reissued in 1999 as *Sister Midnight* (with a horribly garish cover) on Cleopatra CLP0581-2

PARIS HIPPODROME – Iggy Pop
1990 – CD Revenge MIG33/34
Recorded: 23 September 1977, L'Hippodrome, Paris.
Tracks: Sixteen / Lust For life / The Passenger / I Got A Right / Neighbourhood Threat /

Success / Fall In Love With Me / Raw Power / C C Rider-Jenny Take A Ride / That How Strong
My Love Is / I Wanna Be Your Dog
A 12" single (Revenge WMD CAX6) released at the same time contained 'The Passenger' and
'Nightclubbing' (which was taped at this gig but not included on the CD).

HEROIN HATES YOU – Iggy Pop
1997 – CD Other Peoples Music OPM2116
Recorded: 30 November 1979, Stardust Ballroom, Los Angeles
Tracks: Real Cool Time / Knocking 'em Down / Take Care Of Me / Dog Food / You Really
Got Me / New Values / TV Eye / Play It Safe / Funtime / I Wanna Be Your Dog / One For My
Baby / China Girl / Five Foot One / No Fun
Taken direct from the bootleg, maintaining that super lo-fi sound.

LIVE RITZ, N.Y.C. 86 – Iggy Pop
1992 – CD Revenge MIG44
Recorded: 14 November 1986 at the Ritz, New York.
Tracks: I Got A Right / Gimme Danger / Some Weird Sin / Real Wild Child / Sister Midnight /
Blah-Blah-Blah / Baby It Can't Fall / Nightclubbing / Fire Girl / Five Foot One / Shades /
Down On The Street / China Girl / Hideaway / Winners And Losers / Cry For Love
Taken from a radio broadcast this is an excellent quality disc.

At the same time, a CD single containing tracks from the Ritz show was issued on
Revenge CAX9CD and included 'Lust For Life' which was missing from the album. A reissue
of the album (confusingly with the same catalogue number) came with a bonus CD single
containing 'TV Eye' which was also excluded from the album.

Reissued again in 2000 by the King Biscuit Flower Hour as *Greatest Hits Live* (KBFR 40022)
with a slightly re-jigged song order and 'I Wanna Be Your Dog' from Boston 1988 added.

A 2003 reissue of most of the Ritz tracks, in a really odd order, was issued as *From The
Front Row* on Silverline 288173–9. This time however the songs were remixed into
DVD-Audio with Dolby 5.1 surround sound.

CHANNEL BOSTON – Iggy Pop
1990 – CD Revenge MIG40/41
Recorded: 19 July 1988 at the Channel, Boston
Tracks: Instinct / Kill City / 1969 / Penetration / Power And Freedom / Your Pretty Face… /
High On You / Five Foot One / Johanna / Easy Rider / Tuff Baby / 1970 / Search And Destroy
/ Squarehead / No Fun / I Wanna Be Your Dog
King Biscuit Flower Hour broadcast this superb gig, which was immediately heavily boot-
legged. Revenge got in with the first official release. As with their earlier live albums the CD
doesn't contain the whole show. A 7" single (Revenge SS19) adds 'Cold Metal' as the b-side
of 'Kill City' while the CD single (Revenge MIG CAX7) contains the 'Winners and
Losers'/'Scene of the Crime' medley.

This great show has been reissued a number of times, often with slightly different track
lists. 'Your Pretty Face…' is often dropped so that 'Cold Metal' and 'Winners and Losers' can
be reinstated. In 1997, KBFH issued their own version (King Biscuit/BMG 88033–2), which
boasted considerably improved sound compared with the Revenge disc and, apart from the
omission of 'Your Pretty Face…' contains the most complete version of the show on one disc.

2001 saw Disky release a shortened and reordered version called *Power And Freedom*
(SI640582)

BERLIN 91 – Iggy Pop
1992 – CD Narva 07
Recorded: 26 January 1991, Neue Welt, Berlin
Tracks: Raw Power / Five Foot One / Dirt / Loose / Lust For life / China Girl / I Got A Right /
Butt Town / Real Wild Child / My Baby Wants To Rock And Roll / Neon Forest / Home / Brick

By Brick / 1969 / Candy / Search And Destroy
A bootleg for sure, but one that was strangely stocked extensively in many UK shops includ-ing Tower Records, which is where I found it in 1992. A good-quality document of the *Brick By Brick* tour.

TELLURIC CHAOS – Iggy and the Stooges
2005 – CD Skydog B0009ESTAA
Recorded: 22 March 2004, Shibuya-Ax, Tokyo
Tracks: Loose / Down on the Street / 1969 / I Wanna Be Your Dog / TV Eye / Dirt / Real Cool Time / No Fun / 1970 / Fun House / Skull Rings / Dead Rock Star / Electric Chair / Little Doll / My Idea of Fun / I Wanna Be Your Dog / Not Right
Available as a bootleg for a while before Skydog picked up this set and sort-of-officially released it. A solid, manic Stooges set from a boiling Tokyo club ('Open the doors, give me some air!' screams Iggy at one point.) Notable for being the only place, at time of writing, where you can find the new song 'My Idea Of Fun' which is a more convincing example of Stooges songwriting than tracks such as 'Little Electric Chair' or 'Loser'. Plus it has Steve Mackay blowing the roof off.

Box Sets

1970: THE COMPLETE FUN HOUSE SESSIONS – The Stooges
1999 – 6 CD box set and bonus single
Rhinohandmade RHM2 7707 (Individually Numbered Limited Edition of 3000)
Every take from every *Fun House* session, in order, exactly as the Stooges recorded them, with 142 tracks, 109 of which are music and 33 are very short pieces of mainly uninteresting stu-dio dialogue. Includes the nine overdubbed and finished songs that make up the original *Fun House* album, and the single versions of 'Down On The Street' and '1970'.

The packaging contains extensive notes about the recording sessions, and the set is housed in a good-quality box decorated with a wraparound version of the *Fun House* cover. It's a fabulous set, probably the most impressive archival Iggy product there is, and well worth hunting down if you can still find it.

THE STOOGES – The Stooges
1991 – 5 EP box set
Revenge CAX1-5 limited edition 1000 copies.
All previously released material.
1 – PURE LUST EP
Tracks: I Got A Right / Johanna / Gimme Some Skin / I Got Nothin'
2 – RAW POWER EP
Tracks: Raw Power / Head On / Purple Haze / I'm Waiting For My Man / Radio Ad
3 – GIMME DANGER EP
Tracks: Gimme Danger / Open Up And Bleed / Heavy Liquid – I Got Nothin' / Dynamite Boogie
4 – SHE CREATURES OF HOLLYWOOD HILLS EP
Tracks: Open Up And Bleed / She Creatures Of Hollywood Hills
5 – WHAT YOU GONNA DO EP
Tracks: What You Gonna Do (live 1968?) / Gimme Danger (live at The Whisky A Go Go, 16 September 1973) / Ron Asheton interview

NIGHT OF DESTRUCTION – Iggy and the Stooges
1991 – 6 CD singles box set
Revenge BOX 01 Limited edition of 2000 copies.

All previously released material.
1 – **PURE LUST EP**
2 – **RAW POWER EP**
3 – **GIMME DANGER EP**
4 – **SHE CREATURES OF HOLLYWOOD HILLS EP**
5 – **WHAT YOU GONNA DO EP**
6 – **I GOT NOTHING EP**
Tracks: I Got Nothing / Search And Destroy / Cock In My Pocket
NB Tracks for discs 1 to 5 are the same as previous box set.

EXTENDED PLAY – The Stooges
2005 – Double CD single digipack Easy Action EAR006
Limited edition 5000 copies.
A taster for the *Heavy Liquid* box set.
Disc one (CD audio) contains tracks not included on *Heavy Liquid*.
Tracks: Hard To Beat (rough mix, London 1972) / Head On (Detroit 1973 with Bob Scheff on piano) / I Got A Right ('Incendiary' version intended for a US TV ad)
Disc two (5.1 DVD-Audio mixes) All recorded at Olympic Studios 1972.
Tracks: I Got A Right (version 1) / Louie Louie / Gimme Some Skin / I Got A Right (version 2)

HEAVY LIQUID – The Stooges
2005 – 6 CD box set plus booklet / photos / bags of information
Easy Action EARS003
1 – The Olympic Studio Tapes London 1972
Various attempts at 'I Got A Right', 'Gimme Some Skin', plus 'Money' and 'Louie Louie', taken from the recently discovered master tapes.
2 – Previously unreleased rehearsal from Morgan Sound Studios, Ypsilanti Michigan, March 1973.
3 – Los Angeles & Detroit rehearsals Spring 1973
Eleven tracks previously issued on various Revenge records and the myriad of following reissues.
4 – The Return To New York July 1973
'CBS Studios New York' – the same set as previously issued on *Rubber Legs* plus a bootleg quality recording of the first Max's gig on 30 July 1973.
5 – Previously unreleased audience recording of the complete first set at the Whisky A Go Go on 17 September 1973.
6 – Bimbos 1974
The most complete audience tape from Bimbos 365 Club San Francisco on 11 January 1974, run at the correct speed for the first time, plus a short interview segment.

NIGHTS OF THE IGUANA
1999 – 4 CD box set
Remedy REM99004-3
Boxed set containing four previously available live CDs.
1 – **WILD ANIMAL** live March 1977
2 – **PARIS HIPPODROME** live September 1977
3 – **RITZ, NEW YORK** live November 1986
4 – **CHANNEL, BOSTON** live July 1988

Compilation Albums

All contain previously released material except where shown.

NO FUN – The Stooges featuring Iggy Pop
1980 – LP only – Elektra EF 7095 (US) and Elektra ELK 52 234 (UK)
Compilation of tracks from *The Stooges* and *Fun House*.

CHOICE CUTS – Iggy Pop
1984 – LP only – RCA AFLI-4957
Compilation of tracks from *The Idiot* (side A) and *Lust For Life* (side B).

IGGY POP – Iggy Pop
1986 – 2 LP set – Arista ARPDL 2-1051-02
Double album compilation of tracks from *New Values*, *Soldier* and *Party*.

I GOT A RIGHT – Iggy Pop
1988 – LP Picture Disc only – Revenge MIG2W
Compilation of tracks from *Kill City* and *I'm Sick Of You*.
NB Another album called *I Got A Right* containing a different mixture of songs from *Kill City* and
I'm Sick Of You songs was issued in the USA around the same time on Invasion/Enigma E1019.

SONGS – Iggy Pop
1991 – CD Arista BMG 262178
Compilation of tracks from *New Values*, *Soldier* and *Party*.

THE STORY OF IGGY POP – Iggy Pop
1992 – double CD Arista/74321 11758 2
Another compilation of tracks from *New Values*, *Soldier* and *Party*.

NUDE AND RUDE: The Best Of Iggy Pop – Iggy Pop
1996 – CD Virgin CDVUS 115
The first compilation to span Iggy's career, though there is nothing from the Arista years and
as it is a single CD the collection is necessarily sketchy.

POP MUSIC – Iggy Pop
1996 – CD Camden BMG 74321415032
Another compilation of tracks from *New Values*, *Soldier* and *Party*.

THE MASTERS – Iggy Pop
1997 – Eagle EABCD011
Yet another compilation of tracks from *New Values*, *Soldier* and *Party*.

NUGGETS – Iggy Pop
1999 – double CD Jungle/Freud CD 074
Recorded: 1972–1991, all over the place
Tracks: Fire Engine / Warrior Tribe / Old Mule Skinner / Family Affair / Woman Dream / I Got
A Right / Gimme Some Skin / Rock Action / Modern Guy / Run Like A Villain / Eat Or Be
Eaten / Sixteen / Love Bone / The Winter Of My Discontent / Puppet World / One For My
Baby / Hassles / Flesh And Blood / I'm Crying / I'm Alright / You Really Got Me / Batman
Theme / Louie Louie / Hang On Sloopy / No Fun-Waiting For The Man / 96 Tears
A bewildering collection of live tracks, covers, TV appearances and demos. Most of these are
taken directly from bootlegs so goodness knows how Jungle licensed the tracks. Most are,

however, previously unavailable which makes this collection truly worthwhile. Highlights include the three Synchro Sound tracks from 1983, 'Rock Action' from 1977 'The Winter Of My Discontent' and the wonderful 'No Fun'/'Waiting For The Man' medley.

Nuggets effectively renders the earlier collections called *Wake Up Suckers!* (Skydog 62267) and *We Are Not Talking About Commercial Shit* (Skydog 62552) entirely superfluous as *Nuggets* absorbs all the vital tracks from these compilations.

THE HERITAGE COLLECTION – Iggy Pop
2000 – CD Arista 07822-14612-2
You guessed it – yet another compilation of tracks from *New Values*, *Soldier* and *Party*.

CLASSIC – Iggy Pop
2000 – CD A&M 490 690-2
Compilation of tracks from *Blah-Blah-Blah* and *Instinct* (includes the 12" mix of 'Cry For Love', on CD for the first time). The same compilation can also be found as *Millennium Edition*, *Master Series* and 2005's *Universal Masters*.

A MILLION IN PRIZES: The Anthology – Iggy Pop
2005 – double CD Virgin CDVUSD266
Disc 1 Tracks: 1969 / No Fun / I Wanna Be Your Dog / Down On The Street / I Got A Right! / Gimme Some Skin / I'm Sick Of You / Search And Destroy / Gimme Danger / Raw Power / Kill City / Nightclubbing / Funtime / China Girl / Sister Midnight / Tonight / Success / Lust For Life / The Passenger
Disc 2 Tracks: Some Weird Sin / I'm Bored / I Need More / Pleasure / Run Like A Villain / Cry For Love / Real Wild Child (Wild One) / Cold Metal / Home / Candy / Well, Did You Evah! / Wild America / T.V. Eye (previously unreleased live 1993) / Loose (previously unreleased, live 1993) / Look Away / Corruption / I Felt The Luxury / Mask / Skull Rings
The first career-spanning retrospective, which concentrates too much on the first few years, with disc two having to cover twenty-eight years. Iggy apparently chose the songs. But with only two previously unreleased tracks (live at the Feile Festival in 1993, and both inferior to the *Fun House* originals) there's little here for the seasoned Iggy fan. Some worldwide versions include the jazz duet 'I'll Be Seeing You', and the oddity 'In The Death Car' in place of 'I Felt The Luxury.' Early track lists included the Sum 41 collaboration 'Little Know It All', but the resurgence of the Stooges bumped this minor hit in favour of the new Stooges riffathon 'Skull Ring'. Nonetheless it's a solid compilation, with three terrific tracks in great sound from the pre-Raw Power sessions to really annoy the casual listener.

THE BEST OF IGGY POP – Iggy Pop
2005 – CD Camden 82876708402
Do we really need another compilation of tracks from *New Values*, *Soldier* and *Party*? Camden jump on the Iggy reissue bandwagon with this hopefully titled mix.

Singles

This is a listing of all the major singles containing Iggy Pop songs. I've concentrated on the UK and USA, although a few notable releases from other countries are included. It is not exhaustive – for that check the websites outlined at the beginning of the discography. Singles are in chronological release order.

MONA – The Iguanas
1964 – 7" vinyl Forte AR201
Tracks: Mona / I Don't Know Why

There were originally only 1,000 copies of 'Mona' which the Iguanas would sell or give away at gigs. It appears that a repressing was made in the 1980s. This was identical in almost every respect except that the catalogue number was scratched into the vinyl rather than stamped in.

1969 – The Stooges
1969 – 7" vinyl Elektra INT 80209 (France)
Tracks: 1969 / Real Cool Time

I WANNA BE YOUR DOG – The Stooges
October 1969 – 7" vinyl Elektra 45664 (US)
Tracks: I Wanna Be Your Dog / 1969

DOWN ON THE STREET – The Stooges
December 1970 – 7" vinyl Elektra 45695 (US)
Tracks: Down On The Street (edit with organ overdubs) / I Feel Alright (1970) (edit)
Also issued in a picture sleeve in France on Elektra INT 80252.

SEARCH AND DESTROY – Iggy and the Stooges
1973 – 7" vinyl Columbia 45877 (US)
Tracks: Search And Destroy / Shake Appeal
Some copies, with the same catalogue number, contain 'Penetration' on the b-side instead of 'Shake Appeal'.

SISTER MIDNIGHT – Iggy Pop
February 1977 – 7" vinyl RCA 10989 (US)
Tracks: Sister Midnight / Baby
A promo single (RCA JH-10989) featured 'Sister Midnight' in mono on one side and stereo on the other.

CHINA GIRL – Iggy Pop
May 1977 – 7" vinyl RCA PB 9093 (UK)
Tracks: China Girl / Baby

I GOT A RIGHT – Iggy Pop and the Stooges
1977 – 7" vinyl Siamese PM 001
Tracks: I Got A Right (mono) / Gimme Some Skin (stereo)
Production is credited to Philippe Mogane & James Williamson.

SUCCESS – Iggy Pop
October 1977 – 7" vinyl RCA PB 9160 (UK)
Tracks: Success / The Passenger

JESUS LOVES THE STOOGES – Iggy Pop and James Williamson
1977 ('in time for Christmas') – 7" single EP Bomp EP114
Tracks: Consolation Prizes / Johanna / Jesus Loves The Stooges

KILL CITY – Iggy Pop and James Williamson
April 1978 – 7" vinyl Radar ADA 4 (UK)
Tracks: Kill City / I Got Nothin'

SIXTEEN – Iggy Pop
April 1978 – 7" vinyl RCA PB9213
Tracks: Sixteen (live October 1977) / I Got A Right (live October 1977)
Both tracks taken from TV Eye 1977 Live.

I'M BORED – Iggy Pop
April 1979 – 7" vinyl ARIST 255 (UK)
May 1979 – 7" vinyl ARIST 0438 (US)
Tracks: I'm Bored / African Man

FIVE FOOT ONE – Iggy Pop
Jun 1979 – 7" vinyl Arista ARIST 274 (UK)
Tracks: Five Foot One (edit) / Pretty Flamingo
Also available as a 7" picture disc on ARIPD 274 (UK)

LOCO MOSQUITO – Iggy Pop
January 1980 – 7" vinyl Arista ARIST 327 (UK) (with picture sleeve)
Tracks: Loco Mosquito / Take Care Of Me

PUMPIN' FOR JILL – Iggy Pop
1981 – 7" vinyl Arista ARI 8112 (US)
Tracks: Pumpin' For Jill / Time Won't Let Me

BANG BANG – Iggy Pop
April 1981 – 7" vinyl Arista ARIST 407 (UK)
Tracks: Bang Bang / Sea Of Love

BANG BANG – Iggy Pop
1981 – 12" vinyl Arista SP-115. Four-track promo sampler.
Tracks: Bang Bang / Houston Is Hot Tonight / Pumpin' For Jill / Time Won't Let Me

ZOMBIE BIRDHOUSE
1982 – 7" Flexi-disc free with Melody Maker magazine.
Tracks: side A by Stiff Little Fingers; side B by Iggy Pop – The Horse Song / Bulldozer

RUN LIKE A VILLAIN – Iggy Pop
August 1982 – 7" vinyl Animal / Chrysalis CH FLY 2634 (UK) (with a picture sleeve)
Tracks: Run Like A Villain / Platonic

CRY FOR LOVE – Iggy Pop
October 1986 – 7" vinyl A&M AM 358 (UK)
Tracks: Cry For Love (single edit) / Winners And Losers
The 12" version (A&M AMY 358) contained the same as the 7" plus an extended remix of 'Cry For Love'.
The USA 12" single (A&M 392132-1) substituted 'Little Miss Emperor' in place of 'Winners And Losers'.
'Cry For Love' was one of Iggy's most widely issued singles – released in Australia and South Africa amongst others.

REAL WILD CHILD (WILD ONE) – Iggy Pop
November 1986 – 7" vinyl A&M AM 368 (UK) (some copies contained a poster)
Tracks: Real Wild Child (Wild One) / Little Miss Emperor
The 12" version (A&M AMY 368) contained the same as the 7" plus an extended remix of 'Real Wild Child (Wild One)'.
The USA 7" vinyl (A&M AM 2909) features 'Fire Girl' as the b-side.

SHADES – Iggy Pop
January 1987 – 7" vinyl A&M AM374 (UK)
Tracks: Shades (single edit) / Baby, It Can't Fall

12" vinyl A&M AMY374 (UK)
Tracks: Shades (single edit) / Cry For Love (extended remix) / Baby, It Can't Fall (extended remix)

FIRE GIRL – Iggy Pop
April 1987 – 7" vinyl A&M AM 392 (UK)
Tracks: Fire Girl / Blah-Blah-Blah (live in Zurich 12 December 1986)
The 12" version (A&M AMY 392) contained the same as the 7" plus an extended remix of 'Fire Girl'.

ISOLATION – Iggy Pop
June 1987 – 7" vinyl A&M AM 397 (UK) (with foldout poster cover)
Tracks: Isolation / Hideaway
The 12" version (A&M AMY 397) contained the same as the 7" plus an extended remix of 'Fire Girl'.

RISKY – Ryuichi Sakamoto featuring Iggy Pop
1987 – 7" vinyl CBS 651017 7
Tracks: Risky / Sakamoto track
The 12" version (CBS 651017 6) contained an extended remix of 'Risky' by Julian Mendlesohn backed with Sakamoto tracks.

COLD METAL – Iggy Pop
August 1988 – 7" vinyl A&M AM452 with poster cover
Tracks: Cold Metal / Instinct
The 12" version (AMP452 or AMY452) came as a limited edition picture disc and added 'Tuff Baby' as an extra track.
A Japanese 3" CD single (A&M S10Y3017) featured 'Cold Metal' and 'Tom Tom' and came in a special foldout sleeve.

HIGH ON YOU – Iggy Pop
November 1988 – 7" vinyl A&M AM475
Tracks: High On You / Squarehead
The 12" version (A&M AMY475) contained the same as the 7" plus a remix of 'Tuff Baby'.

COMPACT HITS – Iggy Pop
January 1989 – CD single compilation A&M AMCD909
Part of a series collecting various a-sides of a particular artist onto one handy CD single. All tracks previously released.
Tracks: Real Wild Child (Wild One) / Isolation / Cry For Love / Shades

SOUNDS – BLAST!
March 1989 – Four-track 7" vinyl EP free with *Sounds* magazine, 11 March 1989
Tracks: Cold Metal (exclusive remix by Andy Wallace) / tracks by Fishbone, Dan Reed Network and Blue Aeroplanes

SHE CREATURES OF HOLLYWOOD HILLS – Iggy and the Stooges
1989 – 7" single available only with Issue 5 of *Spiral Scratch* magazine.
Tracks: She Creatures Of Hollywood Hills / untitled jam

LIVIN' ON THE EDGE OF THE NIGHT – Iggy Pop
January 1990 – 7" vinyl Virgin VUS18
Tracks: Livin' On The Edge Of The Night (edit) / The Passenger (from *Lust For Life*)
The 12" version (Virgin VUSTG 18 which came in a gatefold sleeve plus discography) contained the same as the 7" plus 'Nightclubbing' and 'China Girl' from *The Idiot*.
The same four tracks are found on the 3" CD single (Virgin VUSCD 18).

LIVIN' ON THE EDGE OF THE NIGHT – Iggy Pop
January 1990 – 12" vinyl Virgin/VOZEP 02 CD single
Tracks: Livin' On The Edge Of The Night (remix) / Livin' On The Edge Of The Night / The Undefeated (acoustic demo) / Butt Town (acoustic demo) / My Baby Wants To Rock And Roll (acoustic demo)

HOME – Iggy Pop
June 1990 – 7" vinyl Virgin VUS 22
Tracks: Home / Lust For life
The 12" version (Virgin VUST 22) contained the same as the 7" plus 'Pussy Power' and 'Funtime'. The CD single (Virgin VUSCD 22) is the same as the 12" except that 'Sister Midnight' replaces 'Funtime'. A 'clean' version was issued on a promo CD single (PRCD3364).

CANDY – Iggy Pop featuring Kate Pierson
September 1990 – 7" vinyl Virgin VUS 29
Tracks: Candy / Pussy Power (acoustic demo)
The 10" limited edition coloured vinyl (Virgin VUSA 29) contains the same as the 7" plus the acoustic demo of 'My Baby Wants To Rock And Roll'.

CANDY – Iggy Pop featuring Kate Pierson
September 1990 – 12" vinyl Virgin VUST 29
Tracks: Candy / The Undefeated (acoustic demo) / Butt Town (acoustic demo)
The CD single (Virgin VUSCD 29) contained the same as the 12" vinyl.

CANDY – Iggy Pop featuring Kate Pierson
September 1990 – CD promo single Virgin PRCD IGGY
Tracks: Candy (single edit) / Candy (album version) / Candy (less guitar mix)

WELL, DID YOU EVAH! – Iggy Pop and Deborah Harry
December 1990 – CD single Chrysalis CHSCD 3646~3236462 3
Tracks: Well, Did You Evah! / (b-side by the Thompson Twins)
Also issued on 7", 12" and picture disc vinyl with same songs.

THE UNDEFEATED – Iggy Pop
1991 – CD single Virgin VUSCD37 (UK)
Tracks: The Undefeated / LA Blues (acoustic demo) / Brick By Brick (acoustic demo) / The Undefeated (acoustic demo)

GIVE PEACE A CHANCE by the Peace Choir featuring Iggy Pop (amongst many others)
1991 – CD single Virgin America GPACD 1
A reworking of the Lennon song by Sean Lennon and Lenny Kravitz featuring a cast of thousands.

WILD AMERICA – Iggy Pop
August 1993 – CD single Virgin V25H-38409 (US)
Tracks: Wild America / My Angel / Credit Card / Evil California

WILD AMERICA EP – Iggy Pop
August 1993 – CD single Virgin VUSCD 74 (UK)
Tracks: Wild America (LP Version) / Credit Card / Come Back Tomorrow / My Angel
A promo CD single (VILDT 93) contained a radio edit plus the regular album version. A promo 12" vinyl, confusingly with the same catalogue number, contains the four tracks from the CD single EP. The French edition includes an extra track 'Sodom'.

WILD AMERICA EP – Iggy Pop
August 1993 – 7" limited edition (10,000 copies) vinyl Virgin VUS 74
Tracks: Wild America (LP Version) / Credit Card / Come Back Tomorrow / My Angel

WILD AMERICA – Iggy Pop
August 1993 – CD single Virgin VJCP-20015 (Japan)
Tracks: Wild America / Louie Louie (live) / Credit Card / My Angel / Evil California / Home (live) / Hate (live)
Live tracks from the Feile Festival, 1993.

LOUIE LOUIE – Iggy Pop
August 1993 – CD single Virgin IGSWE (limited edition 2000 copies, sold only at the Hultsfred Festival, Sweden, 14 August 1993)
Tracks: Louie Louie / Hate

BESIDE YOU – Iggy Pop
May 1994 – 10" vinyl Virgin VUSA77 numbered limited edition of 10,000
Tracks: Beside You / Evil California (by Annie Ross and the Low Note Quintet, featuring Iggy Pop) / Home (live at the Feile Festival 1993) / F***in' Alone (sic)
The same tracks were also available on a cassette single VUSC77.

BESIDE YOU – Iggy Pop
May 1994 – CD single Virgin VUSCD77 (UK)
Tracks: Beside You / Les Amants (by Les Rita Mitsouko, featuring Iggy Pop) / Louie Louie (live at the Feile Festival 1993) / Beside You (acoustic version from Spanish TV)
A promo CD single DPRO14195 contained an edit and the regular LP version.

LOUIE LOUIE – Iggy Pop
1994 – CD single Virgin LLCD1
Tracks: Louie Louie / Evil California (by Annie Ross and the Low Note Quintet featuring Iggy Pop) / Home (live at the Feile Festival 1993) / Fuckin' Alone

LOUIE LOUIE – Iggy Pop
1994 – CD single Virgin IGFR 2 – PM 515 (France)
Tracks: Louie Louie / Les Amants (by Les Rita Mitsouko, featuring Iggy Pop) / Louie Louie (live at the Feile Festival 1993) / Beside You (acoustic version from Spanish TV)

I'M SICK OF YOU – Iggy and the Stooges
1994 – CD single Bomp BCD113
Tracks: I'm Sick Of You (1972) / Tight Pants (1972) / Scene Of The Crime (1972) / Shake Appeal (live 1978) / Scene Of The Crime (live 1988)/ I'm Sick Of You (live 1993) / Shake Appeal (live 1980) / I'm Sick Of You (live 1993)
Interesting collection of the 1972 London tracks, plus live versions of the same three songs over the next twenty years. The live tracks are all taken from bootlegs and vary in quality. The 1972 tracks were also available on 7" vinyl at the same time (Bomp EP113).

JESUS LOVES THE STOOGES – Iggy Pop and James Williamson
1995 – 10" vinyl Bomp BEP114/10 (US) (3D Sleeve showing a dead donkey, plus 3D glasses)
Tracks: Kill City / Johanna / Jesus Loves The Stooges / Consolation Prizes
Also available on CD single (Bomp BCD114) with the same 3D sleeve but different tracks – Consolation Prizes / Jesus Loves The Stooges (alternate take) / Johanna

I GOT A RIGHT: All The Versions And More... – Iggy and the Stooges
1995 – CD single Bomp BCD139

Tracks: various takes of 'I Got A Right' plus a live version from Paris Hippodrome 1977 and 'Gimme Some Skin' from 1972.
Also available on 12" green vinyl Bomp BMP12139 with fewer tracks.

I WANNA LIVE – Iggy Pop
January 1996 – CD promo single Virgin IPCDJ96 (UK) (Promo)
Tracks: I Wanna live (Edit) / Heart Is Saved / Pussy Walk
Oddly it appears that a full release for 'I Wanna Live' was pulled at the last minute, despite the song receiving some encouraging airplay.

HEART IS SAVED – Iggy Pop
1996 – CD Single Virgin VUSCD-102
Tracks: Heart Is Saved / (Get Up I Feel Like Being A) Sex Machine / Hate (live at the Feile Festival, 1993) / The Passenger (live at the Feile Festival, 1993)

PUSSY WALK – Iggy Pop
1996 – 7" vinyl Virgin 7PRO 11094 (Promo)
Tracks: Pussy Walk / I Wanna Be Your Dog (live at Rock For Choice, 1996)

TO BELONG – Iggy Pop
1996 – CD single Virgin IGPRO96 (One track promo)
Track: To Belong

LUST FOR LIFE – Iggy Pop
1996 – CD single Virgin VUSCD116
Tracks: Lust For Life / (Get Up I Feel Like Being A) Sex Machine / Lust For Life (live at the Feile Festival, 1993) / I Wanna Be Your Dog (live at Rock For Choice, 1996)

THE PASSENGER – Iggy Pop
February 1998 – CD single Virgin VSCDT1689
Tracks: The Passenger ('As featured in the Toyota Avensis TV Commercial') / Lust For Life / Nightclubbing

AISHA – Death In Vegas featuring Iggy Pop
1999 – CD single Deconstruction / Concrete HARD43CD
Tracks: Aisha / remixes / video

CORRUPTION – Iggy Pop
October 1999 – CD single Virgin 243 8 96243 2 8
Tracks: Corruption / Rock Star Grave / Hollywood Affair (featuring Johnny Depp)
A one-track promo CD single (VSCDJ 155) features a radio edit of 'Corruption'. Also available on limited edition 7" red vinyl (Virgin VUS155) containing just 'Corruption' and 'Hollywood Affair'.

MASK – Iggy Pop
2001 – CD single Virgin DPRO-16424 (Promo)
Tracks: Mask (single edit) / V.I.P. (album version)

ROCKICIDE – Millenia Nova featuring Iggy Pop
March 2003 – CD single Motor Music AH 46572 (Germany)
Tracks: Rockicide / various remixes

LITTLE KNOW IT ALL – Iggy Pop with Sum 41
2003 – CD single Virgin 7087 6 17871 2 2 (Promo)
Track: Little Know It All

LITTLE ELECTRIC CHAIR – Iggy Pop
2003 – CD single Virgin 7087 6 18043 2 4 (Promo)
Tracks: Little Electric Chair / Little Know It All / Jose The Arab / Ready To Run
Last two tracks are out-takes from the Skull Ring sessions and feature the Trolls.

MOTOR INN – Iggy Pop with Feedom, featuring Peaches
2003 – 12" vinyl Virgin 7087 6 18170 1 0 (Promo)
Tracks: Motor Inn (Felix Da Housecat's High Octane Mix – Engineering and additional production by Dave Hustler) / Motor Inn (Album Version)

KICK IT – Peaches featuring Iggy Pop
2004 – CD single Kitty-Yo XLS 176
Tracks: Kick It / Felix Partz Remake

Guest appearances and film soundtracks

I've only listed film soundtracks that include songs unavailable elsewhere. Many film soundtracks include Iggy songs that are easily found on the regular albums and these are not listed here. Please consult the websites detailed at the beginning of this discography if you need to know more.

Iggy sings on the all the following tracks unless otherwise indicated.

REPO MAN – Film Soundtrack
1984 CD MCA MCD39019
Repo Man

RYUICHI SAKAMOTO – NEO GEO
1987 CD CBS 460095 2
Risky
Also available on 7" and 12" singles.

SHOCKER – Film Soundtrack
1989 CD SBK Alive CDP93233
Love Transfusion

BLACK RAIN – Film Soundtrack
1989 CD Virgin CDV2607
Livin' On The Edge Of The Night (this was released some months before Brick By Brick, and the later multi-format singles)

VARIOUS – RED HOT AND BLUE: A TRIBUTE TO COLE PORTER
1990 CD MFSL UDCD542
Well, Did You Evah? – duet with Debbie Harry
Also available on various single formats.

THE CRAMPS – LOOK MOM NO HEAD!
1991 CD Restless 7725862
Miniskirt Blues

RAINDOGS – BORDER DRIVE-IN THEATRE
1991 CD ATCO 7567916802
Dance Of The Freaks (spoken part)

THE FINAL NIGHTMARE – Film Soundtrack
1991 CD Varese CV5333
Why Was I Born?

JOHN MORAN – THE MANSON FAMILY: AN OPERA
1992 CD Point 432 967-2
Iggy plays the Prosecutor, Jack Lord.

WHITE ZOMBIE – LA SEXORCISTO : DEVIL MUSIC VOL. 1
1992 CD Geffen GED24460
Black Sunshine

OFRA HAZA – KIRYA
1992 CD Warners 9031761272
Daw Da Hiya (narration)

VARIOUS – BACK TO THE STREETS (Celebrating the music Of Don Covay)
1993 CD Sanachie 9006
Sookie Sookie

SHORT CUTS – Film Soundtrack
1993 CD IMAGO 23013
Evil California (These Blues). (Performed by Annie Ross and the Low Note Quintet with
Iggy Pop)
Also available on the b-side of various 1993–1994 singles.

ARIZONA DREAM – Film Soundtrack
1993 CD Mercury 5121122
In The Deathcar / TV Screen / Get The Money / This Is A Film

VARIOUS – FAST TRACK TO NOWHERE
(Songs from "Rebel Highway")
1994 CD A&M 314540240 2
C'mon Everybody

VARIOUS – CONCERT FOR THE ROCK AND ROLL HALL OF FAME
1996 CD Columbia 4837932
Back Door Man (with Soul Asylum)

BILL LASWELL – MYTH: DREAMS OF THE WORLD
Stories Of The Greek And Roman Gods And Goddesses
1996 CD Dove Audio ISBN 0-7871-0734-4
HADES, The God Of The Underworld (narration)

THE CROW: CITY OF ANGELS – Film Soundtrack
1996 CD MH620472
I Wanna Be Your Dog (live)
Also available as a b-side on various 1996 singles.

TRAINSPOTTING – Film Soundtrack
1996 EMI CDEMC3739
Lust For Life / Nightclubbing
Although these are the 1977 original songs this soundtrack album sold extremely well and with 'Lust For Life' reissued as a single to promote the film, Iggy's profile was massively raised.
A second CD of music from the film called, unsurprisingly, *Trainspotting 2* (EMI 8212652) contained 'The Passenger' and the slightly odd but inessential Baby Doc remix of 'Nightclubbing').

VARIOUS – CLOSED ON ACCOUNT OF RABIES
A collection of stories and poems by Edgar Allan Poe
1997 CD Mercury 314 536 480-2
The Tell-Tale Heart (narrator)

VARIOUS – JAZZ A SAINT GERMAIN: Tribute to the free spirit of Paris in the 1950s
1997 CD CDVIR7072
I'll Be Seeing You (a delightful duet with Françoise Hardy)
Also available on a single – Virgin Visa 8449 (France)

DAVID ARNOLD / VARIOUS – SHAKEN AND STIRRED: New recordings of classic James Bond themes
1997 CD WB 3984 20738 2
We Have All The Time In The World

MONSTER MEN
1997 CD single Virgin LC3098
Theme song to the TV series *Space Goofs*.
Monster Men / Monster Men remix edit (Mr. Clean version by 2 Lazy) / other tracks not featuring Iggy Pop

HOME TO RENT
1997 Theme song to the TV series. Unavailable elsewhere.

THE BRAVE – film soundtrack
1997 Not released separately, though excerpts appear on the album *Avenue B*.

BILL LASWELL / VARIOUS – HASHISHEEN: The End Of Law
1998 CD Sub Rosa SR154
The Western Lands (narrator)
A Quick Trip To Alamut (narrator)

THE RUGRATS MOVIE – Film Soundtrack
1998 CD Interscope IND90181
This World Is Something New To Me (part of a choir of guest artists including Patti Smith and Lisa Loeb)

DEATH IN VEGAS – THE CONTINO SESSIONS
1999 CD Concrete 74321 661992
Aisha
Also available on multi format singles containing a variety of mixes of 'Aisha'.

AT THE DRIVE-IN – RELATIONSHIP OF COMMAND
2000 CD Virgin CDVUS184
Rolodex Propaganda

VARIOUS – RISE ABOVE
(24 Black Flag Songs To Benefit The West Memphis Three)
2002 CD Sanctuary SANCD125
Fix Me

PEACHES – FATHERFUCKER
2003 CD Ktty-Yo XLCD171
Kick It
Also available on multi-format singles containing various mixes.

MILLENIA NOVA – NARCOTIC WIDE SCREEN VISTA
2003 CD Stockholm Records
Rockicide
Also available on multi-format singles containing various mixes.

VARIOUS – SUNDAY NIGHTS
The Songs Of Junior Kimbrough
2005 CD Fat Possum FP1018-2
You Better Run (2 versions) by Iggy and the Stooges

Video/dvd

LIVE IN SAN FRANCISCO
1990 VHS Revenge ME109
Recorded: 25 November 1981, San Francisco
Tracks: Intro / Some Weird Sin / Houston Is Hot Tonight / TV Eye / 1969 / Rock And Roll
Party / Bang Bang / Dum Dum Boys / Eggs On Plate / I'm A Conservative / I Need More
(called 'Animals' on the cover) / Lust For Life / Pumpin For Jill

KISS MY BLOOD
1991 VHS Virgin VVD882
Director: Tim Pope
Recorded: 5 March 1991, Olympia, Paris
Tracks: Raw Power / Five Foot One / Dirt / Loose / Lust For life / China Girl / I Got A Right /
Butt Town / Real Wild Child / My Baby Wants To Rock And Roll / Neon Forest / Home / Brick
By Brick / 1969 / Candy / I Wanna Be Your Dog / No Fun / Search And Destroy / Down On
The Street / The Passenger / Louie Louie / Foxy Lady
One of the longest shows of the *Brick By Brick* tour with a bunch of extra encores. Iggy gets
naked, cuts himself and performs an excellent show. Strongly recommended.
Reissued on DVD as *Iggy In Paris* (Immortal IMM940039).
Reissued again on DVD in 2004 as *Kiss My Blood* (Silva Screen SSVE4001), which includes the
San Francisco 1981 show as a bonus (although for some reason the 1981 portion is here
presented in black and white).

JESUS? THIS IS IGGY
2002 DVD Quantum Leap QLDVD0341
DVD issue of a 1998 documentary – lots of archive clips including some 1969 footage of the
Stooges.

LIVE IN DETROIT – 2003
2004 DVD Creem DR-1485
Tracks: Loose / Down On The Street / 1969 / I Wanna Be Your Dog / TV Eye / Dirt / Real

Cool Time / No Fun / 1970 / Fun House / Not Right / Little Doll / Skull Ring
Excellent document of the Stooges' homecoming gig at the DTE Energy Theatre in Detroit
on 14 August 2003. Plus some bonus material – Ron, Scott and Iggy playing and talking at a
New York store.

KICK IT
2004 DVD Single Kitty-Yo XLS 176
The duet between Iggy and Peaches was available as a DVD single. The video directed by
Dawn Shadforth is hysterical, with Iggy hamming it up, Peaches posing and strutting and
that's before the zombies come storming in…
Tracks: Kick It (Video) / Kick It (Karaoke video) / Kick It (Freedom Remix – audio only)

LIVE AT THE AVENUE B
2005 DVD Virgin DVDVUS 267
Recorded: 2 December 1999, Ancienne Belgique, Brussels
Tracks: No Shit / Nazi Girlfriend / Espanol / Raw Power / Search And Destroy / Shakin' All
Over / Corruption / Real Wild Child / I Wanna Be Your Dog / I Felt The Luxury / Home / Lust
For Life / The Passenger / Cold Metal / Avenue B / TV Eye / I Got A Right / No Fun / Death
Trip / Sixteen / Louie Louie
Terrific concert from 1999. Why did it take so long to be released?

Films – acting roles

Rock And Rule (Ring Of Power)
1983 – voice of a monster
Sid And Nancy: Love Kills
1986 – hotel guest
The Color Of Money
1986 – pool player
Cry-Baby
1990 – Belvedere
Hardware (M.A.R.K. 13)
1990 – Angry Bob
Coffee And Cigarettes
1993 – as himself
Atolladero
1995 – Madden
Dead Man
1995 – Salvatore 'Sally' Jenko
Tank Girl
1995 – Rat Face
The Crow II: City Of Angels
1996 – Curve
Howard Stern's Private Parts
1997 – as himself
The Rugrats Movie
1998 – newborn baby
Snow Day
2000 – Mr. Zellweger

TV series – acting roles

Miami Vice – Smuggler's Blues
1985 – Tucker Smith
Miami Vice – Evan
1985 – Thumper
Tales from The Crypt – For Cryin' Out Loud
1990 – as himself, when an Iggy Pop concert is arranged
Star Trek: Deep Space Nine – The Magnificent Ferengi
1993 – The Vorta Yelgrun from The Dominion
The Adventures Of Pete And Pete
1993 series – Mr. Mecklenberg
Accidentally On Purpose

Cover versions

There are a multitude of covers of Iggy and Stooges songs to be found. Space does not permit a full list – the internet should provide full details if that's what you need, but for now here's a selection.
'I Wanna Be Your Dog' covered by dozens of artists from Richard Hell and Joan Jett to Uncle Tupelo, Chris Whitley, and even Snoop Dogg.
'No Fun' – famously covered faithfully by the Sex Pistols.
'1969' – memorably covered by the Sisters of Mercy in the 1980s.
'Down On the Street' – Rage Against the Machine.
'1970' – the Damned.
'T.V. Eye' – Wylde Rattz.
'Search and Destroy' – numerous covers include those by Red Hot Chili Peppers, the Go-Gos, Dictators, Everclear, EMF, and Beavis & Butthead!
'Gimme Danger' – Monster Magnet.
'Raw Power' – Guns 'n' Roses.
'Nightclubbing' – Grace Jones chose this as the title track for her 1980 album.
'China Girl' – David Bowie (of course), James and Pete Yorn are amongst the many.
'Fun Time' – R.E.M., Boy George, Peter Murphy.
'Lust For Life' must take the prize for the most used Iggy song – covers include those by the Replacements, the Smithereens, the Damned, Bruce Willis (on the *Rugrats Go Wild* movie soundtrack) and Tom Jones. Bowie even played the song live during 1996. It's also cropped up many times in commercials from Kellogg's cereal to Royal Caribbean Lines, and in umpteen films and TV programmes from *Trainspotting* to *Ally McBeal* and *Gilmore Girls*.
'The Passenger' – loads of covers include R.E.M., Siouxsie & the Banshees, Lunachicks.
In addition to all the covers, Iggy's songs have been licensed to innumerable television and movie soundtracks (either on screen or in the albums), radio and TV commercials, documentaries and rock histories, hundreds of compilation albums, video games, and even surf and skateboard videos.

Books

These books are either entirely concerned with Iggy Pop or contain substantial stories and information about him.

• **Mike West,** *The Lives and Crimes of Iggy Pop* (Babylon Books, 1982)
A long out of print scrapbook affair.
• **Iggy Pop With Anne Wehrer,** *I Need More: The Stooges & Other Stories*
(Karl-Cohl Publishing, Inc., 1982)
The first issue of this excellent book is the one to track down, primarily for the wealth of photos, most of which are not published elsewhere. A whole sequence of snaps shows the Midsummer Rock peanut butter incident, and there is a load of other great pictures. Some song lyrics are reproduced along with a couple of poems. And the stories that Iggy tells are fantastic. In recent years Iggy has partially disowned the book, but it's still a superb read. Republished in 1997 by Henry Rollins' company 2.13.61 Publications.
• **Per Nilsen (text) and Dorothy Sherman (interviews),** *The Wild One: The True Story Of Iggy Pop* (Omnibus Press, 1988)
A straightforward, no-nonsense account of Iggy's life and work from the very beginning. Per's excellent prose is augmented by Sherman's thorough interviews with most of the main players. There are masses of great photos and other memorabilia on display. The first edition takes the story up to the *Blah-Blah-Blah* tour. The book was updated the following year to cover the start of the *Instinct* tour, but a proposed third edition in 1991 never happened. Again, it's a hard book to find these days, but well worth searching for.
• **Alvin Gibbs,** *Neighbourhood Threat: On Tour With Iggy Pop* (Britannia Press Publishing, 1995)
Great tour diary from bass player Gibbs. Lots of fun 1988 road stories and some intriguing insight into Iggy's life. Recommended.
New edition published in 2001 by Codex Books.
• **Nick Kent,** *The Dark Stuff: Selected Writings On Rock Music, 1972–1995* (Da Capo Press, 1995)
Iggy contributes the Forward to this entertaining collection of rock writing.
• **Danny Sugerman,** *Wonderland Avenue* (Bulfinch Press, 1995)
Danny's autobiography which has an awful lot of dark stories about the Doors and Iggy and the dreadful things they got up to.
• **Legs McNeil & Gillian McCain,** *Please Kill Me: The Uncensored Oral History of Punk* (Penguin, 1996)
Excellent account of the US punk scene from the Velvets to the early 1980s. The Asheton brothers contribute some essential stories about the Stooges amongst masses of useful and illuminating information. Oddly for a book that seeks to celebrate the US punk movement, the overall impression is that of squalor and degradation – the drugs, the unsavoury sex, the deaths. Although many of the participants are undoubtedly talented, the reader if left with a strong feeling that much of the talent was squandered and lost. Ultimately it's a rather sad story.
• **Cliff Jones and Paul Trynka, 'Lust for Life'** (1997 – unpublished, despite extracts appearing in *Mojo* magazine)
• *35 Years of Noxious Sounds* (1998 (Italy) Sonic Book #16, November 1998)
Basic history and discography in English and Italian plus a CD containing four tracks by the Iguanas.
• **Mick Rock,** *Raw Power: Iggy and the Stooges, 1972* (Creation Books, 2000)
Sumptuous picture book containing hundreds of images from 1972, both on and offstage, plus an interesting 1972 interview with, and a foreword by Iggy. Redesigned and reprinted in 2005.
• **Joe Ambrose,** *Gimme Danger: The Story of Iggy Pop* (Omnibus Press, 2002)
The first attempt at a full biography of Iggy Pop. Contains some fascinating stories, many of which need to be taken with a pinch of salt, and it's generally a solid look at Iggy's life.

Song Index

NB – all songs written by Iggy Pop except where noted.
Each entry includes the first recorded appearance.